Socio-Medical Inquiries

Irving Kenneth Zola

Socio-Medical Inquiries

Recollections, Reflections, and Reconsiderations

Temple University Press
Philadelphia

Temple University Press, Philadelphia 19122
© 1983 by Temple University. All rights reserved
Published 1983
Printed in the United States of America

Library of Congress Cataloging in Publication Data
Zola, Irving Kenneth, 1935–
Socio-medical inquiries.
Includes index.
1. Social medicine. 2. Zola, Irving Kenneth
1935–   . 3. Medical sociologists—Massachusetts—
Biography. I. Title. [DNLM: 1. Sociology, Medical.
2. Physician-patient relations. 3. Delivery of health
care. W 62 Z86s]
RA418.Z64   1983   362.1   83-391
ISBN 0-87722-303-3
ISBN 0-87722-312-2 (pbk.)

To Michael Zola, my brother, who was and is always there when I need him

If **The Magus** *has any 'real significance,' it is no more than that of the Rorschach test in psychology. Its meaning is whatever reaction it provokes in the reader, and so far as I am concerned there is no 'given' right reaction.*

— John Fowles, Forward to *The Magus*

Contents

Preface

"If I had it to do over again" is a wonderful way of dealing with "might have beens." In recent years we have spent a lot of time doing just that. Some do it through the nostalgia of revivals, the recreation of times that were never as happy as we imagine them. Others invent history, as in Doctorow's *Ragtime*, or fictionalize it, as in TV docudramas. Some few get the chance to redo the past; several choice movies, for example, re-edited for television have added material to supposedly improve the original, and two of my favorite novelists, Gore Vidal and John Fowles, have rewritten earlier works. I recently discovered that an older favorite, Raymond Chandler, made this a modus operandi. All this gives me an excuse for something I've always wanted to do: to take another look at my own writings.

It has been over twenty years since I began formal research into the sociomedical area, and though there is a consistency and coherence to my work, I have continually refused to assemble it in a single book. Quite honestly, I have read many such books and am singularly unimpressed. Too often when authors try to incorporate their research into a broader conceptual frame, the chapters emerge filled with non sequiturs in data and in thinking. Such books, while promising much, often prove little more than expanded versions of previously published articles. Perhaps all the energy used in rewriting old material zaps the ability to extend it further. Besides, I am impressed that readers often grasp the implications of a work better than its author does.

I have been accused of many things, but never immodesty. And so I believe I can avoid the pitfall described above by being straight-forward about my intentions. First of all, I want to reconsider and occasionally reflect on my work without blotting out my mistakes or misperceptions. Since in the professional world we only publish our "significant results," fellow researchers and students are rarely able to learn from our missteps. I do not intend to drag the reader through all the blind alleys I have investigated, but a few seem worth sharing. Secondly, I want to sprinkle this book with recollections while I am still young enough to remember people and incidents vividly. I hope to describe the context of my writings and thus acknowledge not only my own intellectual roots but the spirit of the time that nurtured them. To those readers who find these aims boring or irrelevant I offer a third, more practical aim. I have never worried particularly about where I published my work, which has led to an unexpected problem. Sometimes, out of a sense of gratitude (I am grateful to any-one who lets me do what I want) I have published in the institution or country where I was working at the time. Thus many of my papers are found in foreign journals and very limited editions. Yet after nearly twenty years, requests for offprints continue, as do requests for reprinting permissions. So before my copyright runs out I wish to solve this problem by making the best of my sociomedical work more accessible, more coherent, and less expensive.

The format deserves some comment. I have organized the material more by theme than chronology. In any case, the exigencies of life as well as the whims of editors have determined when the papers saw the light of day. Also, I have done little rewriting and only some editing of the published pieces. Although it is impossible to omit all repetition—since without it certain articles would make no sense—I have tried to cut the detailed rendering of methods, findings, and ref-erences. I have also tried to avoid the temptation of updating any-thing, except for reference material. If I am aware that a previously unpublished reference is now in print, I have used the published reference. This occasionally leads to the anomaly of a cited reference being obviously later in time than the paper in which it appears.

This book, then, is both a collection and recollection. It contains much (but by no means all) of my writings about health care—its recipients and its providers. It is anchored in my association with the Massachusetts General Hospital as a consultant for over two decades, my twenty-year tenure as a professor in the Department of Sociology at Brandeis University, and my ten-years-plus experience as a counselor, first at Greenhouse, Inc. and then at the Boston Self Help Center. It is inspired by the words of my grandmother who told me never to throw anything away and my grandfather who never did. And lastly, it reflects the example (*Footholds* 1977) and observation of my close friend Phil Slater. He once noted that I spend a lot of time trying to integrate the various pieces of my life. This collection also has that function. Each time I look over my shoulder to understand where I have been, it helps to clarify where I am going. I hope this book does the same for the reader.

Acknowledgments

It is not easy to acknowledge all my indebtedness. My early work (1959-64) at Massachusetts General Hospital was underwritten by the then chiefs of the Department of Psychiatry (Dr. Erich Lindemann) and Medicine (Dr. Walter Bauer and Dr. Robert Ebert). Much of my research and later writing was supported by two federal grants, one from the National Institute of General Medical Sciences, Grant No. 11367, and one from the National Center for Chronic Diseases, Grant No. 86-67-261. Two yearlong consultantships were especially helpful in enabling me to reflect on my work. The first was for the academic year 1968-69 when I was a consultant-in-residence to the Behavioral Science Unit, Division of Research in Epidemiology and Communications Science, World Health Organization, Geneva, Switzerland. For this exceptional opportunity I will always be grateful to the chief of my unit, Dr. Al Wessen, and the director of the division, Dr. Kenneth Newell, as well as my colleagues Dr. Jerome Stromberg, Dr. Yuri Medvedkow, Dr. Guy Lavoepierre, Dr. Andy Arata and Mrs. Beatrix Rogowski. The year 1971-72 found me in a similar position at the Netherlands Institute of Preventive Medicine in Leiden where I benefited particularly from the help of Dr. Ewout Cassee, Dr. Willem Metz, and Drs. Peter Stroink. Many colleagues and friends have over the years read and criticized versions of these papers. They include: Ms.

Margot Adams-Webber, Dr. Bernard Bergen, Dr. Egon Bittner, Dr. Susan Dibner, Ms. Ann Goldberg, Ms. Marlene Hindley, Ms. Edith Lenneberg, Ms. Mara Sanadi, Dr. Philip E. Slater, Dr. Alwyn Smith, Dr. Mark Spivak, and Mr. Bruce Wheaton. For their sustained involvement in my early work I want especially to thank Dr. John D. Stoeckle and Dr. Leonora K. Zola.

Finally, I would like to thank my coauthors in chapters 3 and 4 of this volume: Dr. John D. Stoeckle, Chief of the Medical Clinics, Massachusetts General Hospital, and Professor of Medicine, Harvard Medical School; and Dr. Gerald E. Davidson, Medical Director of ELAN, Poland Springs, Maine, and Consultant in Psychiatry, Massachusetts General Hospital.

Part One

An Intellectual Autobiography

1 *The Continuing Odyssey of a Medical Sociologist*

Memoirs have usually been the province of people looking back on long and distinguished public careers. Recently social scientists have become more comfortable in this genre. They have written about what particular research experiences meant to them (Bowen 1964; Hammond 1964), and in later works mapped out the roots of their careers (Elling and Sokolowska 1978; Mead 1972). Although they have made the present book possible, I am trying in this and related works (Zola 1979a, 1982a) to extend the genre, to foster what I call socioautobiography.

Although what I have written here may first strike the reader as merely personal history, it is not. I am not trying to record my life or even its most significant events. (Some people may, of course, learn things about me that were previously unknown.) I *am* trying to delineate the role that personal and social events play in how one comes to understand the social world. I am also arguing that this information not only makes our biases clearer, but that we should consciously make our background work for us. In assembling this collection I have been continually struck by how much the events of my life have influenced what I do, see, and write about. It is not that I have been wholly unaware of this, but like most social scientists I have been loath to admit it. To do so, I feared, might open me and my work to the criticism of being tainted by personal involvement.

It was only years later, partly stimulated by the Women's Movement, that I realized that stifling my own voice was a political decision, not a personal one. It did not mean that *I* was being objective and nonideological, but rather that I was going along with someone else's notion of objectivity, someone else's ideology. This is evident in one of my first publications that gained any notoriety—"Observations of Gambling in a Lower-Class Setting" (Zola 1963a). This was a field study which took place in the Boston area where I had grown up, lived, and worked. When the article was published, much praise was heaped upon me for being a perceptive observer. I was appreciated for my techniques of gaining entry, my insight in picking informants, my ease in interviewing respondents, and my uncanny ability to adapt to so many different situations and roles. But consider the origin of these skills. I was neither trained in nor born to them, but rather socialized into them. I gained rapid entry to this community and its residents because I was, and am, a local resident (complete with Boston, really Dorchester, accent), because I was of the same social class and ethnic group and showed it in gesture, background, values, and vocabulary. I knew the right informants because I had spent so much time as a youth in bowling alleys, poolrooms, and bars that it was easy to recognize both the regulars and the "bookies." And I was able to adapt so well because my father, a former "bookie," now found that at last he could teach his college boy something. So he spent hours coaching me in how to play "the numbers," bet on the races and shoot pool.

By letting the world think that I was either a born field worker or well trained anthropologically, I both ignored and concealed the importance of my own social origins. I became another example of America's myth of individualism and individual achievement, an unwitting supporter of the melting-pot theory of immigration as well as the classless, mobile society.

When over a year later I began my work on "Sociocultural Factors in the Seeking of Medical Aid," I again exploited my background but made no mention of it (Zola 1962b). It was my experience from living in Boston, not anthropological field data or theorizing, which convinced me (but not my advisers) that ethnicity might be part of the everyday "medical" reality of an individual and should be the primary basis of sample selection. Here again I gained superb entry into the hospital, elicited nearly 100 percent patient cooperation and created a very viable and meaningful questionnaire. One respondent told a hospital staffer: "That doc asks the best questions of anyone here!" No one asked nor did I ever volunteer that my insight might be related to a long personal history (polio, accidents, etc.) of hospitalizations. Again, while accepting praise for my scientific skills, I unwittingly supported someone else's ideology. While I did give voice to the consumers' viewpoint in these studies, I did not make the major social and political statement I could have. For I could then, more than a decade before patients' self-help movement took flight, have given evidence about the importance of the consumers' perspective in the study, analysis, design, and change of the services they receive. After all, I was not merely a social analyst, I was a past, present, and future consumer! No one who read my articles ever knew this and few who did know me personally ever mentioned it. However, I only realized my mistake when I finally got around to studying and writing about disability (Zola 1979b, 1981a,b, 1982a,b, 1983a,b). Hopefully, it is also a mistake I can help others avoid by laying out in some detail the many personal and social influences on my writing. In so doing I want to legitimate the importance of biography in social observation and analysis. If I also convey something of the times in which this work was honed as well as tell an interesting story, so much the better.

THE EARLY DAYS

Both my parents immigrated to America as very young children. And although they remembered little of "The Old Country"—for my mother Poland, my father Russia—their naturalization papers were a constant reminder of their origins. In any case, our family name never let me stray far from my roots. Zola always provoked the remark, "Related to Emile?" Or for those less literary, "Sounds Italian!" Neither is true. My name is a fortuitous accident of Ellis Island, the first stop for immigrants to the United States. In fact, I do not know my true surname. All I know is that when my paternal grandfather and his brother came to this country, one took the name Zolloto and the other eventually became Zola. My father's naturalization papers only confuse the issue. On his photograph are three separate signatures: Bernard Zola, Barnett Zolloto, and Berko Zelesnick. With such a start in life it may not be surprising that much of my early research dealt with religious and ethnic identity.

My birth on January 24, 1935 was a welcome event to both sides of the family (the Zolas and the Weinbergs). To the former it was the sign that the youngest of their brood of eleven had finally settled down. To the latter I was the long-awaited, first-born male.

All in all my early life was very secure. I enjoyed love and praise from every direction. My mother's younger sister was barely sixteen years my senior, so she became my earliest babysitter and constant companion. My maternal grandparents doted on me and since my father's family was enormous and virtually all of them lived in Dorchester, I spent my weekends visiting relatives and playing with older cousins. Also, because there were eight years between myself and my younger brother, I reaped the benefits of being an only child for much of my life.

Even geographically I felt very stable and still do. Except for sabbaticals and leaves of absence I have lived all my life in the Greater Boston area. My first eight years were spent in a third-floor, three-room apartment in Dorchester, a poor inner-city suburb of Boston, and the next fourteen in slightly more affluent Mattapan. Family was never far away. At one point my parents, myself, my brother, my grandfather, my aunt, her husband and their two children all lived in the same three-storied house.

The only instability I recall was economic. But even this was something I heard about more than experienced, although my mother was always saying and worrying that we were on the brink of poverty. I knew that we did not own a car until I was a teenager, that we were the last people on the block to have a TV, that when we did go away for summer vacations it was in shared quarters with someone else, and that nearly all my clothes were made and remade by my grandfather, a tailor. And yet that special toy I wanted always seemed to appear before I felt deprived.

As my mother told the story, our economic problems were her fault for letting herself think she could waltz her way through life. She and my father were reportedly one of the best dancing duos in the South End. She was short, petite, and, in the eyes of her adoring son, had a stunning figure. So her stories of what might have been did not seem so far-fetched. And yet it was hard to believe that she really felt poor. She always seemed well-dressed, although she claimed it was only due to her extraordinary patience in shopping.

My father was a happy-go-lucky sort, only occasionally brought to ground by the criticisms of my mother, my grandmother, and later my grandfather. True to the cliché, he was a jack of all trades, master of none. He worked as a gas station attendant, tire salesman, electrician, shipyard worker, and then during the post–World War II years as a dress cutter in the garment industry. Yet his favorite job was one we were never allowed to discuss openly. For many years he was a "bookie," a man who illegally took bets on horses, dogs, or any other sporting event of interest. Though the money was good, my mother strongly disapproved and finally persuaded his brothers to get him a "decent job" in the garment industry. He went along, but I think he showed his resentment by never staying with one firm for more than a year or two. On the other hand, he was never out of work for long. He had what we called the Zola weakness—a love for gambling, and in retrospect handled it in a rather stable way. Though he rarely won and was always in debt to loan companies, he never brought us down with him. As far as I could make out, he gave my mother his basic earnings. She in turn gave him an allowance which he promptly wagered and lost. Since the money he brought home was always in cash, my mother suspected he skimmed some off the top. This meant we never had any savings, but we never fully sank. On those occasions when we came close, the Zolas and the Weinbergs were there to bail us out.

In short, love and security in my early years created a sense of community and embeddedness (and an understanding of what their loss might mean) that has become an inseparable part of me and my work.

POLIO

I used to think that my life till age sixteen was medically unremarkable and unrelated to my later career. Now I'm not so sure. At very least, several experiences provided an interesting backdrop. The first is one which few people know about. Even when friends and family look at old pictures, they never mention it. But a close look at those photos tell the story—I had ears which protruded almost perpendicularly from my head. I suppose Clark Gable could have provided a positive role model, but unfortunately Walt Disney provided an alternative—Dumbo, the flying elephant. And that's what some of the older boys dubbed me—Dumbo—and they had fun pulling my ears. When I tried to fight back all I got was a bloody nose. This unhappy time was intense but short-lived, because at the age of twelve I underwent corrective surgery to have my ears "pinned back." It was done during a vacation, and by the time I returned to school no bandages were visible. Even so, I was amazed that none of my friends said anything. A few remarked that I looked a little different and then supplied the explanation, "You've got a new haircut!" I never corrected them. But I also tucked away lessons about stigma, social acceptance, cognitive dissonance and "passing."

Certainly the medical world was no stranger to me, partly because of demographics. Given the number and proximity of my relatives, there seemed an almost monthly birth, death, illness, or disability. I suffered the usual childhood disorders, and though hardly frail, I made a number of trips to the hospital emergency room. Though I loved sports and managed to hold my own in most, I was, as they said in my neighborhood, a bit of a "klutz." Thus I recall such events as a line-drive resulting in a broken collarbone, an inept slide leading to a fractured ankle, a diving catch to a dislocated elbow, a wrong way turn to torn cartilage, and several falls in which I broke my nose.

These events were only preludes to two major traumas that I suffered between the ages of fifteen and twenty—first polio, and then four years later, an automobile accident. Each resulted in a year's confinement and each was severely debilitating. With polio, I lost all major bodily functions and for a time was paralyzed from the neck down. Over a two year period, sensation, motion, and strength gradually returned. I was left, however, with considerable weakness and nerve loss throughout my body, particularly in my right leg, stomach, and back. The car accident, which resulted in cuts, bruises, and a shattered right femur, was ironically more confining but less debilitating. For nine months I lay flat on my back in a body cast. And when the cast was finally removed I got up and walked almost as well as before the accident. A long thin scar and an implanted but fairly unobtrusive steel plate were the major physical reminders of this experience.

As a result of both of these "medical incidents," I wear a long leg brace on my right leg, a steel-reinforced back support, and use a cane. My children, when young, described me as walking funny. To the rest of the world, I limped. To me it was just something that got in the way, but for the next twenty years, until I was about thirty-seven, I devoted more psychological and physical energy to denying I had physical handicaps than I had realized. I detailed the events which changed my way of looking at myself in another book, *Missing Pieces* (Zola 1982b). At present I want to trace the manner in which these events affected how I came to see, appreciate, and understand the world.

It was a Friday in early December of 1950, and I had just returned from a convention of B'nai Brith Youth. I was working at the time as a messenger boy and "go-for" for a jewelry firm, James and Mitchell. As I walked across Washington Street in downtown Boston with a large electrical appliance in my hands, I suddenly felt weak. Despite all my efforts the package slipped gently to the ground. I was puzzled, but since the queasiness soon passed I dismissed it. Besides, I had a date that night. But much as I tried to be charming and attentative to my companion later that evening, it was no use. I had a stiff neck and a splitting headache, and on top of that felt periodically nauseated, dizzy, and chilled. The next day I felt worse, and in addition to everything else I had a fever. With my mother out of town, my father seemed doubly concerned. He called the doctor, who suspected a virus. On Tuesday I rose weakly from my bed. My legs, however, would not hold me and with a scream for help I collapsed. Within hours I was taken to the Haynes Memorial Hospital for contagious diseases, where my case was diagnosed as polio, the last such case till the following spring. I was never to walk normally again.

My early days in the hospital remain vivid. I thought I was going to die. I was isolated in a private room, visited only by my parents who were eerily dressed in long hospital gowns and face masks. The pain in my back seemed unrelieved by the drugs I was taking or the frequent hot packs. But what convinced me of impending death was the continuing loss of functions. Every time I was conscious enough to appreciate what was going on, another part of my body felt immobilized. When the process finally stopped, I knew I wouldn't die, but almost wished I had. I had little strength. I could only turn my head from side to side and raise my left arm.

But the end of the immobilizing process also signalled the end of my isolation, and I was soon transferred to the male polio ward where I spent the next six months. My spirits rose almost immediately upon my entry into the room. Not only was I warmly welcomed as the "new polio," but it felt good to see others in my situation. Even more important was seeing some patients actually move about; it made me hope that I too might recover.

Surprisingly, time did not drag. Every day—in fact, almost every minute—there was something to do. The structured part of the day was dominated by physiotherapists who maintained the stretching and the pain that went with it were for my own good. I remember awaiting their visits with dread. In their absence the nurses took over and prodded us to exercise. But despite the pain I needed little pushing. My recovery became a series of large and small goals—the first time I could wiggle a toe, keep my arm up for five seconds, stand unaided. Some advances, such as my first step and even my first spontaneous bowel movement (after three months of enemas), were semi-public; others, like my first erection (after months of impotence), were quite private.

But most important of all were people. I never felt deserted by friends or family. Every day was filled with a variety of visitors, and with them came endless books and forbidden goodies (the hospital canteen did not supply corned beef sandwiches, cheesecake, or liquor). Although I couldn't go out on dates, of course, I was still able to enjoy some of the fruits of adolescence. A local girl, who I still suspect had been assigned to me as a high school project, "adopted" me as her boy friend and visited me weekly. Even more important were the student nurses, often only a year or two older, who were a constant stimulation and encouragement for my budding sexuality. Thus by the end of my stay I was involved in a full-blown patient subculture, with myself and another young man the rowdy and randy leaders.

Of course there were setbacks. I remember trying to show off to my mother by taking two steps on my crutches. I proudly put my right foot forward and crashed to the floor. She fled the room in tears. But more indelible were two quite contrary medical experiences. Early in my stay, a physician patted me on the shoulder upon completing his examination and said, "Don't worry. In three months you'll be running around a ball field." But three months later I could barely sit up, let along run anywhere, and I was devastated. I felt cheated, lied to, so hurt that I refused to exercise. However, another orthopedist came by a week later. He didn't really comfort me, but he gave me the truth as he saw it. He said I would never run again or play contact sports and that it was unlikely that I'd ever walk unaided. Finally, he added that I would probably recover most functions, and what I didn't recover I could probably compensate for. I liked the idea of being able to make up for what I lacked, and so I went back to my goal-setting and game-playing.

Only the loss of a school year seemed beyond my control. During my hospitalization I was tutored three times a week by a retired Boston school teacher named Mrs. Nichols, and though I did well I could not delude myself that the material we covered was in any way equivalent to six months of my junior year at Boston Latin School. I was afraid I might not pass into the senior year; for me the words "being kept back," "repeating a year," "falling behind" were terms for personal failure. I finally expressed these fears to Mrs. Nichols, who told me not to worry.

Mrs. Nichols turned out to be my first miracle-worker. The officials at Boston Latin School had wanted me to take a series of tests equivalent to the junior year courses. Mrs. Nichols shrewdly argued that I was too weak both physically and psychologically to undergo the stress of the examinations. As an alternative, she recommended that I be put on probation for the first four months of my senior term. If I flunked, it proved I had insufficient preparation and should repeat my junior year. If I passed, on the other hand, I should receive credit for my absent time. The administration accepted her proposal, and I fulfilled her prediction. I returned to school, received honor grades and was soon removed from probation.

Perhaps Mrs. Nichols taught me more than she intended. First, I learned that you had to fight for what you wanted and be clever about it. Second, I learned that as long as people listened to your argument you had a chance of winning. Third, I realized that there are few things you can do entirely by yourself (so much for the American myth of rugged individualism). Finally, I realized that what I learned in my junior year had little relationship to what I achieved in my senior year. This meant that educational (later I included scientific) claims of knowledge being cumulative were more myth than reality. I retained and used all of these lessons in both my personal and academic life.

Although I devoted much of the next year to physical and academic recovery, three experiences distinctly influenced my subsequent intellectual growth. One dealt with the questioning of medical authority, the second with the opening of intellectual vistas, and the third with the importance of language.

Shortly after my discharge from the hospital we were faced with a dilemma. Anxious for me to have the best medical care, my parents consulted Dr. Green of Children's Hospital in Boston, the foremost local authority on polio. After a careful examination by him and his colleagues, they recommended full leg bracing. Almost matter-of-factly he asked where we lived. When my mother described a third-floor apartment, he flatly stated that since the braces were made of iron there was no way that I could navigate four flights of stairs. Instead, he recommended that I be removed from home and sent to the State Residential High School for Crippled Children. I remember that I asked about the consequences of not following his advice. He looked at me rather dubiously and mentioned the likelihood of arthritis and other complications by the age of thirty. Disappointed, my mother and I quickly conferred with each other. I'm sure she was reluctant to see me institutionalized once again. For my part, I prized my current adolescence over my later adulthood. I did not want to give up my friends or, more importantly, Boston Latin School. So with her support I said thanks but no thanks. It was a decision I never regretted. When for quite different reasons, I had myself braced some five years later (1956), changing technology had made much lighter equipment possible.

The lesson of this incident rooted deeply. I became very skeptical of any authority who made sweeping social judgments deemed in the best interests of someone else. Equally important was my realization that people must be allowed to take certain risks—few if any decisions were purely medical. I had the right even at sixteen to choose whether at thirty I might be seriously incapacitated. Without that choice, I would have been invalidated as a person. I think all my writings reflected this concern with validation. It seems no accident that I was concerned even in my earliest papers with how the world appeared to people who were "powerless" (McCord, McCord, and Zola 1959; Zola 1962a, 1963a)—a view that later led to my identification with the labelling school of "deviance" theory (Becker 1964).

My physiotherapist, Ms. Elizabeth Ernst, helped me question authority and opened my eyes in quite a different way. In retrospect, I think she was encouraging me to look beyond myself, to see the ways in which I was part of a larger world. One day she gave me two books to read. One was a textbook in psychology (the name of which I can no longer recall) and the other was Gunnar Myrdal's *American Dilemma* (1944). They were more than merely an introduction to the social sciences; they were a simultaneous opening of a dual approach to all human behavior. On the one hand, I learned about internal dynamics—about personality, intrapsychic phenomena and the uniqueness of the individual. On the other hand, I learned about the external world—the social, cultural, historical and political forces which conditioned the limits and potentiality of everyone's individuality.

The third important experience of that year dealt with how I expressed what I was learning. The staff at Children's Hospital had been right in certain respects. For several months the trip upstairs was totally exhausting; even without braces it often took three hours. So I spent the first hour after school sitting outside the apartment gathering my strength. But just before my ascent, the elementary school children streamed by on their way home. Soon they began to ask me endless questions about my disability. At first I was scared, but when I realized that they were only curious, I patiently tried to explain. And when they did not understand, they told me so. Gradually they taught me that if I really wanted to communicate with people, I had to do so in a language they could comprehend.

Ms. Ernst reinforced this insight in a quite casual but important way. It came out in a conversation with my mother, who had taken Ms. Ernst aside to express her concern about a course paper I had written. She was disappointed because she understood it so clearly.

"Shouldn't he be using more big words?" she asked. Ms. Ernst explained that it was more important to be understood than to be overpowering. My mother might not have been convinced, but I was.

THE CAR ACCIDENT

As difficult as polio had been, the car accident was worse. It occurred in early September of 1954 when I was about to enter my junior year at Harvard. I was quite pleased with myself. I was doing Dean's List work, lived in Adams House, was elected to the student council, had scholarships, a job and a steady girlfriend. Even physically I was doing well, although Harvard was far more spread out than Boston Latin School. The greater control I had over my schedule allowed me to make it from class to class without special permission to arrive late, as in high school. And with my growing strength I no longer needed anyone to carry my books. In style of dress I predated the hippie generation. I always wore a knapsack which contained all my books, paper and necessary equipment. In short, I felt extraordinarily independent. I was even able to drive. With my grandfather's help we had purchased a car and had made the necessary mechanical adaptations.

One of these adaptations deserves description. A long steel rod was attached to the gas pedal and bolted to the dashboard on a swivel hinge. Extending about another foot until it was several inches below the steering wheel, the rod ended in a round hook in which I could place two or three fingers. By pressing downward, I depressed the gas pedal and could thus accelerate.

My only problem late that summer stemmed from a minor car accident my family had been in. For two weeks it had deprived me of the means to visit my girlfriend, who lived miles away. So as soon as the car arrived from the repair shop, I borrowed it. Several times that evening I heard a strange clickety-clack, but every check revealed nothing. As customary when making a turn, I took my fingers off the gas lever and placed both hands on the wheel. But this time as we made a right turn there was a loud snapping sound. The rod came loose from the dashboard, and its protruding hook caught the wheel. Immediately the car locked in a turning position and accelerated to over sixty miles an hour. I yelled my companion's name and she fell under the dashboard. We hit a tree and stopped.

For the second time in less than four years I thought I was dead. I was covered in darkness. When I heard voices, I instinctively wiped my eyes, but still couldn't see. My temporary blindness was in fact the result of being soaked in blood. A hum told me that the motor was still going so I reached over and shut off the engine. The voice beside me said that she was all right; and for the moment I felt fine. Aside from the fact that I could not move because the steering wheel was bent against my chest I experienced no pain, and didn't until someone tried to move me.

It was only later that I could reconstruct what had happened. I was covered with cuts and bruises, of course, but these were relatively minor. The major damage was to my right leg, the one weakened by polio. It apparently hit the dashboard with enough force to shatter my entire femur. Though dazed, I was alert enough to refuse surgery by the staff at Boston City Hospital; I insisted instead on the orthopedist primarily responsible for treating my polio. Two operations later, I found myself in a body cast which extended from my right toe to just below my chest.

As soon as I emerged from postsurgical care (less than two weeks), my mother and I began to plan my recovery. This time we knew that keeping me mentally active was essential and we decided quite deliberately that I would not miss my junior year of college. Once more we activated our elaborate social network. I had numerous friends, and it proved quite easy to enlist the aid of at least one compulsive note-taker in every course in which I was interested. All agreed to either make a carbon copy of their notes or let me borrow them on a weekly basis. Several professors gave permission to take their classes in absentia so long as I fulfilled all other requirements. We obtained private proctors so that I might take exams under the same conditions as everyone else. The Harvard library set aside its overnight loan policy on required texts and the local public library arranged for me to borrow all other necessary books on a long-term basis. My younger brother, now eleven, became the book "picker-upper" and the "note-carrier." My aunt agreed to type all my papers. My uncle obtained a writing and reading board that I could use while flat on my back. And the rest of my family and friends stood by to deal with any other financial or physical contingencies. With this plan my mother approached Harvard's administration.

Her first stop was with a dean of students. He was impressed with our plan, he stated, but unfortunately Harvard did not allow such things. My mother listened patiently and then said, "Thank you. Now I'd like to see your boss." The result of the subsequent contest was never in doubt although Harvard insisted upon one compromise. They felt a full four course load would be too large a strain and only allowed me to take three. We acquiesced for the first semester. In fact, I took three courses for credit and audited two others. My grades were straight A's and in the second semester I was allowed a full four course load.

This experience reinforced several earlier lessons: that there is no need to give up, even against vast bureaucracies, as long as you can make people listen; that social networks can help overcome vast obstacles; and finally—an even more sobering intellectual fact—the relative unimportance of physical attendance at straight lectures. For aside from what one misses in seeing someone perform, or the shaded nuances of style, one can glean what's important from second-hand reports. I am sure that this is not a lesson appreciated in academic circles. I know that it had at least two influences on my own teaching. I have tried always to make the classroom a place where things happened, where people would want to be because of knowledge *they* created or shared, not where brilliant exegeses were handed down from the lectern. (I make no claim that I have always succeeded in this goal.) The second is that I thenceforth gained considerable respect for what one could learn and do independently.

As I said earlier, the car accident proved far more difficult psychologically than the polio. This time I was not surrounded by fellow patients in varying stages of a struggle, each cheering the others on. Instead I was imprisoned in a cast in my room with an unvarying view of the roof of the adjacent house. There was no endless stream of doctors, nurses, physiotherapists. There was no need for individual effort, no daily challenges to be met, no triumphs to report. Nothing! And that's what I experienced—a vast emptiness. Though I read day and night, watched TV, and had many visitors, the psychological experience was one of emptiness. In fact, with both parents working and my brother in school, I did spend much time alone. And when I was alone, I was really alone, with only the nearby telephone connecting me to the outside world.

Perhaps because of income or because of the time-limited nature of this experience, we made no financial investment in electronic gadgetry or outside help. In addition, there was no National Foundation for Infantile Paralysis (i.e., Polio) to pick up ancillary medical expenses or to send in "helping visitors." No one came by casually on their rounds to ask if I needed anything. If I had any wishes, I had to ask. And the people who had to respond were not salaried employees but my family. A sense of guilt plagued my almost every request. I felt completely dependent on someone else's largesse, and I hated it. As with my polio I was child-like once more, but this time there was no way to mask it. For my caretaker was no young nurse I could tease or fantasize about as she engaged in the most intimate of tasks, but my mother. We fought and yelled at each other continually. She screamed at me for cutting into her life again, just when she was getting free of the house and family. And I cursed her for being a whining, castrating wife and mother. Through it all, however, I knew that although I was hated because of the situation I'd helped create, I was loved because of who I was. Nevertheless, this knowledge did not prevent me from making a vow the day my cast was removed. I would never again be dependent on or vulnerable to her or anyone else. This experience also had intellectual consequences. I now identified with anyone who was an underdog—in today's vocabulary the stigmatized, the outsider, the oppressed. In fact, this identification was so strong that for years it was easier for me to understand and deal with the pain of others than with my own.

SCHOOLING

Schooling has been a major part of my life—a key both to psychological and social survival. Its roots go deep. As a Jew, education was part of my heritage, though in my family it existed more by word than by example. I was never really sure whether my parents graduated from high school, and though my mother's sister finished college and even took the law bar, it was something about which she rarely spoke. It was only in the third generation that anyone progressed much beyond high school.

I have never considered my early environment intellectually stimulating in itself. I have no recall of being surrounded by books, music, or other artifacts of culture. Yet two intellectual memories persist. One was a toy I played with till it fell apart—an enormous wheel which in one aperture spun out questions on history, geography, spelling, and in another supplied the answers. The second is a twelve volume set of books called *The Pocket University* (1934). My father purchased it when I was born, and though I don't think he read the volumes often, I knew he liked to see me poring over them. They are in my library to this day. On the other hand, I was rewarded enormously for doing well in both public and religious school. And although I revelled in all the praise from family and teachers, part of me could not understand what all the fuss was about. The grades always seemed more important than the content, and gradually I perceived that education was the means to something else.

Sometimes the means were so clear that subsequent events seemed preordained. I remember sitting on a back stairwell in 1942 playing cards with two older boys, one nine and the other eleven. I was seven years old. In between deals, the older said to the younger,

"Well, I guess I'll be going to Boston Latin School next year and after that maybe to Harvard." "Sounds like a good idea," I chimed in. "I guess I'll do that too." And I did. It is perhaps of historical interest that the elementary school I attended, the Christopher Gibson, was later immortalized in Jonathan Kozol's *Death at an Early Age* (1967). When I went there it was more fun.

The birth of my brother gradually pushed us out of our three-room apartment in Dorchester. At first I could not fathom the need for change. For years I had slept in the same room as my parents, and now I even had my own space—I slept on a sofa in the living room. But in June of 1944 we moved to a five-room apartment in Mattapan where we each had our own bedroom! It was a new world. Instead of rows of apartment houses, there were three-family houses everywhere, all with porches and many with yards. There was also more room to play. The streets were safer for stickball and I could run far and wide without having to be in view of my mother. A library as well as ball fields lay within walking distance. But most of all, family and Jewishness were now everywhere. My mother's parents lived across the street, all my father's relatives were within a fifteen minute walk, and synagogues seemed to be on every other corner.

After a few anxious weeks while beginning fifth grade, I felt quite at home. I found that achievement was even more rewarded in Mattapan than in Dorchester. Moreover, the idle boast made a year or two before during a poker game became a reality here. All my close male friends were busily prepping for admission to Boston Latin School. (You needed A's and B's in all major subjects.) The only issue that divided us was whether we would attend directly after sixth grade or take a detour through junior high.

The direct route was regarded as the more serious path, so that was the path I chose. And in 1946 I began a six-year daily trek on trolley, train and bus to Boston Latin.

In his recent autobiography Theodore White (1978) describes in detail his Latin School years. It amazes me that the school as well as the staff had changed so little by the time I began attending nearly two decades later. As in White's time, Boston Latin rewarded memorization, rigid thinking, rote learning. I could recite all the major characters, scenes, and even identify lines from William Shakespeare or *Lorna Doone*, but could explain little about the works they came from. I could translate, spout vocabulary lists and grammatical rules well enough to pass a college language requirement, but could neither speak nor understand a spoken word. I could declaim long Latin passages from Cicero's speeches, but knew nothing about the significance of the Roman Empire. I could rattle off important dates in history, the borders and capitals of any country, but could not say why we fought in any war or what these wars meant to the countries we fought in. I was prepared to do endless research and prepare long treatises on any subject, but I could not write a decent sentence.

My writing deficiencies were revealed to me when I first entered the office of my English composition section man at Harvard. "Well, well," he said without turning to face me, "so here we have yet another Boston Latin School product." "How could you know that?" I stammered in surprise. With my manuscript in his hand, he answered softly, "Who else could write English as if it were directly translated from the Latin?"

In subtle ways Boston Latin also encouraged us to cut corners. It was not so much the competition as the way we had to study. So much was required by rote that we learned how to prepare the answers to some exams far ahead of time. It was studying for College Boards, however, which proved most disillusioning. Each succeeding class (including my own) was instructed to bring back as many questions as possible to our teachers. We studied these before taking the exam as if they were only sample items, but in the language exams more than half the test questions were the same. I remember one classmate in particular who flunked French for the year, but received over 700 on his French achievement test.

I do not wish to imply that I was cynical during these years. Most of my teachers were task-masters who made us work hard and respect hard work. I in turn respected most of them for their erudition, their patience, their fairness. And although I admired their knowledge, I think I did so chiefly for the power and prestige it brought them. Some of these values must have slipped into my consciousness, because I remember writing on my admission application to Harvard College that I wanted to attend that venerable institution for its power, prestige and the economic opportunities it afforded. In short, Boston Latin School fulfilled its promise. It was a pathway out of the ghetto, and for that I will always be grateful. Boston Latin also taught me how to study, but studying, I was to find out later, was not the same as learning.

Six years is a long time to spend anywhere, and the memories of Boston Latin are still pleasant. Though I received my share of intellectual rewards, the permanent friendships I formed at that time are more important. For the first time in my life I numbered Gentiles among my closer acquaintances. And most important, these friends formed a nucleus of who became not only a source of reinforcement in all I was later to become (they were indeed on the same track), but also the network which helped me weather the crises of polio and my accident.

We were a tight, ambitious, and energetic group. My circle of friends consisted of about forty Jewish males, all from Dorchester-Mattapan and within three years of age, all of whom were members during our high school and early college years of Haym Salomon A.Z.A., a junior B'nai Brith organization. A friend and I recently studied a photo of this group taken in 1952. Of the forty-plus members at that time, all but one went to college; over twenty went to Harvard, the others attended such schools as Dartmouth, Yale, Williams. Of those we still knew about, at least three-fourths had graduate degrees, with a dozen M.D.'s and Ph.D.'s in the group. I am not sure how many of their own fathers had even graduated from high school.

My first year at Harvard (1952–53), unfortunately, proved little different than Boston Latin School. I did well by studying hard and memorizing. Though a few courses opened up interesting paths (an anthropology course by Clyde Kluckhohn, an introduction to Plato by Rafael Demos, a history of science by I. Bernard Cohen, and a broad survey of Western civilization by Samuel Beer) they might have accomplished little except for a confrontation with John U. Monro. At the time he was head of the financial aid office. He was later to become the Harvard dean and still later the president of Mills College. I went to complain about Harvard's allocation of funds to me for the coming year. In the course of my protest, he began to examine my previous as well as future plan of study. Ramrod stiff, graying, and crew-cut, he challenged my choice of courses. When I defended my choices, not on the basis of interest, but fear—the fear of losing my scholarships (I had about six different sources of support) if I didn't get grades of B or higher, he blasted me: "You wouldn't be here if you couldn't do B work or better. Of course you can—and in anything you choose. Are you here just to waste your time or to learn something?" I do not know how much of what he said "took," but that I might be wasting my time when I had already lost so much of my life struck a responsive chord. Though angry at him for his tirade and what I took to be his lack of sympathy for my financial needs, I stormed out of his office resolved not to waste any more of my time.

COLLEGE

All my subsequent time at Harvard was spent exploring. The natural sciences held little attraction (perhaps through lack of exposure, perhaps still through fear), but I stood in awe of the humanities. Gradually I began to taste, and having tasted I became a devourer. Introduced to Hemingway, I read everything he wrote. And so it went with Faulkner, Lewis, Fitzgerald. Howard Mumford Jones was my early guide and Albert Guerard, Jr., my later one. I surprised myself by doing well in humanities courses, but I felt the papers I wrote were more analytically skillful than of any literary merits, so a humanities major did not seem a wise choice. Social Relations, on the other hand, though considered a "gut" major, attracted me more. It consisted of four separate areas—sociology, social anthropology, social psychology, and clinical psychology and personality—and this intellectual breadth appealed to me. The requirements were minimal: eight courses, two of which could be used for thesis work. Yet I really backed into my major. As a freshman I had taken Social Relations 1A, and though I did well enough, the course was a disaster. Not only was it enormous in size, but the material seemed terribly pedantic, the exams multiple choice, and the principal lecturer, the famous Gordon Allport, boring. (He subsequently became one of my favorite graduate teachers.) The eccentric anthropologist Clyde Kluckhohn, however, prompted a second look. He was everything I had expected. Back and forth across the podium he ranged, often strikingly outfitted in a green flannel shirt and a red tie. His topics ranged further than his restless movements, from the Navaho hunter to the Russian emigré, from the ancient shaman to the modern psychoanalyst. By the final exam, when I was asked to apply what I had learned about culture to some experience in my own life (I wrote about Dorchester and Haym Saloman A.Z.A.), I knew I had found my subject.

My accident had proved little obstacle to my intellectual explorations. From my bed I studied the history of religions, theories of personality, modern American literature, the Russian novel. But it seemed time to settle down when I returned to school. Another year of my life had been taken away, and soon I would have to earn a living.

Two events during my senior year, both enormously pleasurable, gave my studies coherence and a sense of purpose. My previous forays into literature had seemed encapsulated and maybe a little frivolous. During my confinement the previous year, however, I had taken a magnificent course which introduced me to the great Russian writers of the nineteenth century. It was a literature that suited all my tastes; it was epochal, social, political, psychological, and even appealed to my Boston Latin training—keeping all the characters in place was a delightful game. Also, though I was unaware of it then, the literature put me in touch with aspects of my Eastern European heritage. I was so stimulated by this venture that I decided to take a follow-up course. The only one available that fall dealt with twentieth century Russian literature. The course was small, with only a dozen students. By virtue of the relative unavailability of the texts, each week's assignment required reading one of six choices. Thus rarely did more than two of us read the same book. The lectures, instead of focussing on the works themselves, were devoted to the broad social history of the time. Instead of writers, Professor Murphy spoke of circles; instead of individual plots, he described historical and social themes. I was made acutely aware of the effect of political conditions on what is called "culture." My working-class background had conditioned me to think of them as completely unrelated phenomena. Culture, I had thought, was the product of individual efforts, not social conditions. In the long run, this insight has justified my long-term interest (and trivia expertise) in popular culture (a student once claimed that the only book I read from cover to cover was *TV Guide*). But in the short run it provoked me to learn everything I could about the social and political conditions of the Soviet Union.

Over the next two years (1955–57, my senior and first year of graduate study) I took every available course on Russian government (Fainsod), history (Malia), development (Moore), social structure (Feldmesser) and culture (Kluckhohn). I even took an intensive Russian language course and toyed with applying to Harvard's Russian Research Center. But a second event proved more powerful and sealed my choice of career.

During the summer of 1955, I began to gather graduate school catalogues. At one point I was considering brochures for business, law, and psychology. The choices they offered did not seem incongruous. In some broad way I wanted to work with people. In business it would be personnel work and in law, criminal practice. Psychology, ironically, was less simple. At various times I'd thought of myself as a possible psychiatrist-psychologist, but I had worked for a while in a mental hospital and found both the physical conditions depressing and the long-term nature of therapy unsatisfying. Then as now I was in no mood to postpone gratification. I wanted to see the results of my labor in more immediate terms. Graduate study in psychology seemed equally disappointing. Few indeed were the courses on personality and psychodynamics; most focussed on cognition, perception, physiology, and experimental methods.

An alternative began to present itself—academic life. However, while I had some idea what business and law were like, the life of a professor when outside the classroom was a mystery. But for my disability I might have considered becoming an anthropologist or an archaeologist. And so began my first systematic excursion into what I later realized was "participant-observation."

The mid-fifties were still a time of scant financial resources for social scientists. With this fact in mind, I approached several junior faculty in the Department of Social Relations with a straightforward offer. I suggested that each must have some special project which he wished to undertake, but lacked the money or resources for. I offered to be a "free" research assistant for at least eight hours a week for the duration of the academic year. In return, I wanted the following: the option to use part or all of the data I might collect for an undergraduate honors thesis; a detailed explanation of the whys and wherefores of what they wanted me to do; and continued access to them in their role as professors and social scientists, so that I could discover what academia was really like.

Several were interested, but it was William McCord I came to work for. As a teacher he was charismatic—handsome, articulate, wide-ranging; moreover, he and his colleague/wife, Joan, always made me feel comfortable and valued. I thought their project fascinating—an objective outcome study of the Cambridge Somerville Youth Study. I think I was particularly interested because I knew the Cambridge-Somerville area so well and because I again had been able to use some personal Dorchester experience in McCord's course on criminology.

The Cambridge Somerville Youth Study was perhaps the most famous intervention program in the 1930s (Powers and Witmer 1951). It was initiated by Dr. Richard Cabot, a physician at Massachusetts General Hospital, a professor of social ethics at Harvard, and one of the spiritual predecessors of the Department of Social Relations. Long family and social histories had been kept on both the "control" group, which received no counseling, and the experimental group, which did. These histories, which had never been analyzed, provided a unique source of data. Since we did not know which group an individual belonged to, we were able to objectively rate the boys and their families on dozens of attitudinal and behavioral scales, and then see how they turned out twenty years later.

I took to this work like the proverbial duck to water. Buried amidst the dusty records in the fourth floor of Emerson Hall, I spent far more than my promised eight hours. The experience far exceeded my expectations: it became my honors thesis and earned me a *magna*; it garnered the praise of Robert White and Gordon Allport, who dubbed my thesis a true social relations project; it led to my first publication (an acknowledged collaborator on the McCords' *Origins of Crime* [1959]); it also impressed the admissions committee of graduate schools, gaining me acceptances and fellowships wherever I applied. Most of all, it showed me that I could do work that was relevant, appreciated, and gratifying. It thus wedded me forever to a career in social science.

Where I might pursue that career was not immediately clear. Though I majored in social relations, I had taken only three formal courses in sociology. I thus had little idea of the differences between the various schools, and looked for a program that would allow me to pursue my interests in the broadest possible way. By that standard, Harvard was the obvious choice. But I'd also heard that Harvard was notoriously reluctant to accept its own undergraduates. For this reason I also applied for a Fulbright to study at the Adorno Institute in Frankfurt. I had found Adorno and his colleagues' work (1950) on the authoritarian personality much to my liking; this is both multi-disciplinary and socially relevant. Though a Jew, I had no deep-seated dislike of Germans and Germany. In fact, my fluency in Yiddish helped me survive the first round of rejections. After a long conversation in which an examiner spoke German and I responded in Yiddish, he judged the latter an adequate enough starting point. At about this time I received an informal query from the Harvard Admissions Committee as to whether I was serious enough about Harvard to forego a possible Fulbright. I said I was and they accepted me.

The months before entering graduate school were spent tooling up. My work with the McCords had been so rewarding that I sought similar opportunities. Two part-time jobs came my way. The first required skill and patience with case records, and involved a certain amount of detective work. Under the general directorship of Ralph Notman (1956), a psychiatrist, we were to trace the admission and discharge patterns of former mental patients. A bonus of this job was its location. First, the records were on the grounds of Boston State Hospital, a short distance from my home in Mattapan; second, the experience strengthened my disinclination to work in a mental hospital (it was not yet apparent to me that I had a limited view of both mental illness and therapy). My second job involved library work, assisting A. Paul Hare (1967) who was then forming a compendium of small group research. One of the greatest payoffs of this job was the opening it provided to the stacks of Widener Library. I spent as much time reading adjacent materials as I did the ones I was assigned. This job introduced a new subject area in which I quickly felt competent. It had a drawback, however. I felt like a data bank; I could tell the effect of many variables but lacked even the vaguest of analytic schemas to make the material comprehensible. In my remaining time I took a Russian language course at night and worked weekends at Staple-Belt, a factory where I had been employed part-time and during summers of my college years. I thought I was in the process of bidding goodbye to my old world and saying hello to my new one.

My first encounter with Harvard Graduate School in the fall of 1956 left me intimidated. I felt incredibly young, much as I had on entering Boston Latin School at the age of eleven. Then I was overpowered by the physical size of everyone around me; now I was overpowered by the size of my classmates' intellect. As we introduced ourselves and shared our interests I felt smaller and smaller. They spoke easily of Hegel, Marx, and Weber, and even more upsetting was how they spoke of Parsons, Homans, and Bales. "Do you think Parson's theory of action will really lead anywhere?" asked the person sitting adjacent to me. I didn't even know where his office was, let alone what he was working on.

The sense of intimidation eventually narrowed. It became confined to tests but not papers, to written examinations but not oral presentations, to concern whether professors might think me adequate as opposed to my own assessment of my competence.

Actually, this period was the golden era of the Social Relations Department—a marvelous blending of the old and new. To me it was an intellectual feast and I tasted whatever I could. We were required to take general introductory courses in social psychology (Gordon Allport and Richard Solomon), sociology (Talcott Parsons and Freed Bales), clinical psychology (David McClelland) and social anthropology (William Caudill). To me the requirements were no problem; I would have taken the courses regardless. It was particularly fascinating to see the different sides of these great figures. Allport, although generally uninspiring in his lectures, was enthralling in his seminar on prejudice. Parsons, who was always mystifying (through three general courses and two directed studies) in his theoretical excursions, was crystal clear when he dealt with concrete phenomena such as American social structure. I found the same true of his writing, always preferring *The Social System* (1951b) and his *Essays* (1954) to his more grand schema (Parsons, Bales, and Shils 1953). I heard the retiring members talk of their current interests—Henry Murray on *Moby Dick* and Pitrim Sorokin on moral altruism—

and listened to the newer arrivals discuss their latest breakthroughs—David McClelland on N-achievement, Freed Bales on Interaction Process Analysis. Everywhere I turned someone was opening a new door. Jerome Bruner was examining social perceptions and the development of learning; Clyde Kluckhohn concerned himself with the integration of psychoanalysis and social science; Alex Inkeles was systematically outlining where personality and social structure intersect. Fred Mosteller and Dick Hyman were demystifying statistics while Sam Stouffer was patiently demonstrating what one could learn from social surveys. With so much to learn from the "great" authorities, I postponed working with the younger faculty till my postresident years (Harvard only required two years of residency—nearly half of which were required courses). It was only when the pressure of requirements had passed that I became free to explore courses in social structure and personality with Eleanor Maccoby, Richard Alpert, John Whiting, Timothy Leary, or study more specialized aspects of social problems such as deviance and social control with Stan Wheeler, Ted Mills, John Spiegel, Herb Kelman, Tom Pettigrew.

My academic record at Harvard was mixed. My grades are singularly unrevealing, a mix of A's and B's and "Satisfactory." Most surprising was that I lost (I think forever) my knack for taking exams. On the other hand, my writing took wing. If I did well in a course, the grade either was based chiefly on a paper or the exam questions were so general as to constitute a paper. Most scary was the fact that the required course in which I performed worst was sociology. My "B" necessitated retaking the exam the following year. I did little better in comprehensive exams, and received the lowest possible pass. I am sure it was a mystery to the faculty how I could do so well on papers and research and so poorly in my exams. I imagined they assumed, as I did, that acute social observation compensated for whatever skills I lacked in academic sophistication. That I was already "published" as a graduate student may also have counted in my favor.

ACADEMIC RESEARCH

Puzzles have always interested me, whereas riddles do not. I like jigsaw puzzles most. Though less intellectually demanding than crossword puzzles, for example, jigsaws seem to draw on more parts of me. Not only must I keep the total picture in mind, but its minute details as well. Not only must I think about how pieces fit together, but continually experiment with both my hands and eyes. I think the same dimensions characterize my interests in research.

I had a chance to learn this lesson from my first research experience, but I did not. During my sophomore year I took a course from George Homans. For my final project I decided (as I had on the anthropology exam of the year before) to draw on the world around me. This time I focussed on the garment factory in downtown Boston where I had already been working for three years. First I mapped out what I already knew, and then I spent a few days diagramming the physical layout and observing it. All this I supplemented with a series of informal interviews. The grade I received did not compare with the satisfaction I derived from the reactions of my employer. Even though I had described the big boss as a benevolent tyrant, he was so taken with the general description that he showed it around for years afterwards. Only much later did I realize that I had fulfilled a fundamental task of good descriptive anthropology—to map out an area with sufficient clarity that the "natives" accepted it as accurate.

Not until my first year of graduate school did I again consciously draw on my own life for a research project. I was taking Bob Feldmesser's course on social stratification when he casually dropped a remark about the decreasing importance of religion and ethnicity in American life. His comment did not ring true to me. Certainly I was very aware of my own ethnic background. Moreover, most of my friends and classmates also came from distinct, defined communities and were self-consciously Jew and Catholic as well as Rumanian, Polish, Irish, and Italian. Though Feldmesser was convinced of his claim, he admitted that we knew relatively little about how people identified themselves. And so for my final term project I decided to find out "a little" about this complex subject. The study as well as its aims were quite modest. I created an anonymous questionnaire which asked age, gender, area of residence, occupation, education, religion, and the birthplace of the respondent, his/her parents, and that of both maternal and paternal grandparents. The key question inserted among the others was simply a request for the respondent's "nationality." I preferred this term to "ethnicity," which I felt, was too academic for most people, at least in 1956.

My sampling was hardly random. My purpose was to gather sufficient numbers of different religious, economic and ethnic groups to permit cross tabulations. I sampled students from three Harvard courses, a group from Boston University, visited two factories in downtown Boston, distributed it at several gatherings and to people

I met during the next few weeks (I was limited by the usual requirements of a term paper). In all I collected data on nearly three
hundred people.

Though all of my respondents were born in America, the results
were quite interesting. A third identified themselves in some way
other than American. Although education, generation, and class had
some effect on how individuals identified themselves, it was the
influence of religion which fascinated me. "Nationality" seemed to
mean three different things to Jews, Catholics, and Protestants. No
Jews in my sample, regardless of generation, identified themselves
through their family's country of origin. If they did not describe
themselves as Americans, which the majority did, they called themselves Jewish, Jewish-American, or Hebrew. The Catholics responded
quite differently; depending on generation, they identified themselves in terms of their homeland or that of their parents or grandparents. They most commonly saw themselves as "hyphenated-
Americans." The Protestants in turn were concerned about
something still different—what one might call "ancestry." Most of
them were already fourth generation American, but their answers
reflected no loyalty to a single homeland. If their answer was other
than "American," they usually presented a multiple listing—English
and French, Swedish and German, etc. However, Anglo-Saxon
ancestry was inevitably cited first.

The lessons of this research were several. It taught me to trust my
social instincts, even when they conflicted with academic or expert
opinion. I also gained respect for what one could learn by questioning large samples of people, and particularly by simple forays—what
has later been called "quick and dirty" research. There was also a
serendipitous finding, which revealed either how hard-boiled a
"show-me" empiricist I was or perhaps just how naive. Despite my
upbringing and the years spent at Harvard, it was only with this
survey that I began to realize my family's "working-class" background. In each Harvard class I sampled, I filled out the questionnaire
myself. Mine was always easy to identify. I was the only respondent
whose father was a blue-collar worker!

For a long moment during my Harvard years, I was fascinated by
educational administration. I once asked the current Dean of
Students, Delmar Leighton, how one got into the field. He said the
traditional route lay through schools of education and learning the
necessary skills; in the "Harvard way," however, one acquired solid
academic credentials and then gradually took on administrative
responsibilities. If I was on either path it was the latter, but I still

liked to "learn by doing." An opportunity soon presented itself. Ted Wilcox, who had recently been placed in charge of the Harvard Office of Advanced Standing, needed an assistant to compile mounds of statistics. I found the work boring, which dimmed my interests in a career in education, but the people I met were fascinating. In particular I marvelled at what it took to be a dean. Seeing McGeorge Bundy run a committee meeting made me realize how such a man might ultimately run the Ford Foundation, or want to run the entire country.

Earlier I mentioned how intimidated I'd been during my early graduate years at Harvard. Two people in particular helped me overcome this problem. The first was my wife, Lee, who was herself pursuing a doctorate in clinical psychology at Boston University (we married in 1957). That both of us were undergoing similar experiences was a tremendous source of support. The second person was the new assistant professor who supervised the introductory seminar for graduate students—Phil Slater. Though I never formally took a course from Phil I learned (and am still learning) much from him and his writing. It will probably shock some readers that it was under his aegis that I, as well as several other graduate students, received our most systematic exposure to quantitative methods. In 1957 Phil became the research director of the Age Center of New England. Toward the end of my first year of residence, he invited me and several other graduate students to work under him. I was doubly pleased. In addition to his personal regard, which I highly valued, the work forced me to *do* what I was learning and what I did best, research.

The data itself were not particularly interesting, but the challenge they provided was. Most consisted of already collected responses to a lengthy series of questionnaires on elderly people's life experiences. Our job was to make sense out of them. And much of the next two years was spent doing just that. From the questions we created codes, from the codes came scales, and from the scales numbers. These we analyzed. Computers were available but expensive. Thus most of the nitty-gritty statistics were done by hand on a desk calculator including the then esoteric techniques of factor analysis and multiple regression. Our team included Bernard Bergen, Harry Scarr, Phil and myself (Fritz Mosher joined us later). Though each of us took several pieces of the data for our own there were projects for which we were jointly responsible. In our daily meeting we discussed not only our own progress but the more general methodological and substantive issues arising from the work. It was here that we puzzled over inconsistencies and where we spent time, some of it playfully, inventing elegant names for the dimensions that our latest statistical toy, factor analysis, kept spewing forth.

This experience led to many firsts—including exposure to myriad statistical techniques and a bewildering array of different kinds of data, experience in report and grant writing, my first convention presentation, and also my first solo publication. This published paper, although it occupied a rather small part of my activities, proved particularly significant. Its implications were substantive as well as professional. A concern that began to surface in my earlier works, first in delinquency and later in ethnicity, now emerged more fully: how people tended to view themselves. In this case, I focussed on whether or not people thought of themselves as "elderly." According to the data I had available, their self-descriptions were not related to age, physical, marital, or economic status. Instead, the variables that explained the major differences were all related to familial dynamics. It was this key element that got me into some professional difficulty.

Pleased with the reception that my paper received at the 1959 American Sociological Association convention, I submitted it for publication. The *American Sociological Review* showed interest and we corresponded for the next several months. Yet succeeding drafts never fully satisfied them. Although they had many criticisms, their most consistent objection fell on my interpretive framework, in particular, psychoanalysis. I was furious. Anyone was free to interpret my data how they wished, but changing the framework which stimulated the key hypothesis seemed intellectually dishonest. I composed a blistering letter which Phil toned down. I nevertheless withdrew the article and published it elsewhere (Zola 1962a). This contretemps, however, proved a forerunner to what I have experienced several times since—a long series of publisher or editorial rejections preceding ultimate publication.

For a time I thought of doing my dissertation on other data from the Age Center. I also collected more material on how people thought of themselves, read much about the concepts of socialization and identification, wrote term papers about group identity and social movements and went back to Harvard to study "self-concepts" with Stan Wheeler and "reference-group theory" with Herbert Kelman. But nothing really clicked. When the money for the Age Center grant began to run out in the spring of 1959, it became time to move on.

I interviewed for several jobs, but the one that best fit my combination of quantitative and qualitative skills was the West End Research Project. The principal investigator and creator was Erich Lindemann, the Chief of Psychiatry at Massachusetts General Hospital. The project director and implementer was a psychologist, Marc Fried. Originally, I thought I'd work on the systematic interviewing, and later shift to data analysis. But since that position was not immediately available, I was temporarily assigned to work with Ed Ryan, an anthropologist who was directing a parallel field study. The West End Project had apparently always been conceived as two-tiered. Lindemann was concerned, in many previous projects, with how people dealt with crises. He saw the so-called "redevelopment" of the West End as an opportunity to pursue these issues in a more systematic and socially relevant manner. The tearing down of the West End was already underway when he received funding, a fact that helped determine his methodology. A study of the effects over time of this "dislocation" on the former residents (three separate interviews were planned) required an understanding of what it was like to live in the West End (Duhl 1969; Fried 1973). Herbert Gans had previously been hired to collect such information. But although he turned out a brilliant analysis of working class and lower class life (*The Urban Villagers* 1962), his data did not suit the perceived needs of this project. A second attempt was undertaken under Ed Ryan.

I remember vividly being reintroduced to the West End by Ed. It was an area familiar to me from childhood, but now to be examined from a sociological perspective. Sport-jacketed, button-downed, thin-tied, brief-cased and Harvarded, I surveyed my new domain. Ed pointed out the sites where I would be interviewing "informants." Casually he suggested, "If you can, over the weekend, why don't you come down and spend some time at these places? Nothing special, just mill aroung to get a sense." It seemed a good idea, so I agreed.

That night, my wife Lee and I celebrated my new job at a graduate school party. Unaccustomed to heavy drinking, I woke the next morning with a hangover. That is my only explanation for what followed. I put aside my standard Harvard costume and put on what was near at hand: khaki slacks, a sports shirt and a raincoat. Fearing that in my unsteady state I'd slit my own throat, I even forsook a shave. So into my Saab I went and headed wearily for the West End. "Pinky's" was the place Ed had suggested for a start; it was a major hangout for the younger residents. I parked my car, sauntered in, took a corner table and buried myself in the morning newspaper. It took a few moments for the ludicrousness of my position to sink in. As the only customer on this rainy morning, how could I "mill around"?

Instead of leaving, I made a decision which affected the rest of my life. Like the jigsaw puzzles of which I am so fond, I looked at myself as an odd piece which nevertheless must fit in somewhere. But where? My stomach provided an answer—I needed something for my hangover. The next question was how to broach this. As I approached the counter, Pinky turned toward me. She was a muscular young woman. From her short hair to the cigarette dangling from her lips she exuded toughness. "Yeah?" she said as she towelled the counter in front of me. In those seconds as she awaited my reply, my Harvard years slipped away. I fell back to my years working at Staple-Belt, a factory in Boston's garment district.

The words sounded foreign to my lips but out they poured. "I don't know what the fuck's really bothering me, but whatever shit I drank last night is sure eatin' the hell out of my stomach."

She smiled knowingly, "I got just the thing." As she brought over a bowl of soup, she said too casually to be real, "Ain't seen you around here lately?"

"Ain't been around."

"Oh yeah, where have you been?"

"Oh, here and there," I answered, hoping this would be enough. It wasn't.

She leaned on the counter. "I'm living in Dorchester now. Do you know it?"

"Do I know it!" I exclaimed. I began to describe in detail the Dorchester of my childhood. When I realized that I knew the area far better than she did, I claimed it as my current home.

Over the next few hours she fed me more soup and other soothing drinks. She also mentioned how the neighborhood was changing. Of course, this was the kind of material the West End project was most interested in, so I gently reinforced her reminiscences. Where it seemed appropriate I probed. But probing has a cost, for she also wanted to know more about me. I let her supply the clues, pretending to be as closemouthed about my past as I was about my comings and goings. Gradually, building on my own past, I created a viable present. I admitted a Jewish heritage, alluded to certain "familiarity" with crime, and claimed part-time employment as a factory worker and painter. By the end of the morning, she was embellishing my story as she introduced me to later customers as a former West Ender.

With great excitement I called Ed Ryan and related my adventure. He agreed that the material I gathered that morning was rich, but was unsure whether I could continue to pull off my "cover." But I was really excited and sought another test. On Monday I showed up at Mario's bar to try out my new identity. There too I passed and continued to do so for the next several months.

This period as an "undercover" sociologist was intense. It caused some difficulty with my wife because I spent strange hours, including many evenings, away from home. My mother was unconvinced that this was what she'd trained her son for. My father, however, was delighted at all the new skills—betting systems, pool, billiards—that he could finally teach his "Harvard professor." Yet I felt ambivalent myself. In addition to the ethical issues implicit in my disguise, I was afraid of what my "informants" might do if they discovered who I really was; moreover, what if the police discovered all the blatantly illegal activities my new friends were getting me involved in? All this was complicated by the fact that I couldn't believe it possible to have so much fun and draw on so much of myself while performing as a professional sociologist.

In another paper I delineated some of the substantive, methodological, and even personal issues that emerged from this experience (see "When Getting into the Field Means Getting into Oneself," which is included in this collection). At present I want to discuss some aspects untouched on elsewhere. My research findings again reflected how people thought of themselves, but this time I began more explicitly to contrast social "labels" (particularly what society thought "deviant") with the respondents' own conceptions. I gained an even deeper respect for participant observation, especially for its unique ability to draw out aspects and textures of daily living.

My findings led to another professional clash. I wrote up the experience, presented it a few times publicly, and then submitted it for publication. Aside from long delays in response—one journal kept me waiting nine months—their opinions were unanimous (no thank you) but contradictory: the paper was too short or too long, insufficiently documented or oversaturated with quotes, atheoretical or inappropriately generalized; and most infuriating, "It's all been done before." My guts told me otherwise, but several rejections diminished my self-confidence. Nearly three years after my participant observation had begun, I saw that Howard Becker had just become editor of *Social Problems*. I knew his work so I once more submitted the article. Within three weeks he accepted it. Vindication! I was later to see the article, "Observations on Gambling in a Lower-Class Setting" (Zola 1963a), translated into foreign languages, reprinted in several collections, and included as one of the early works of the "societal-reaction" or "labelling" school of deviance (Becker 1964).

My work on the West End project ended with the West End itself—that is, with the demolishment of the places I hung out. My original job in the study never materialized, and I was about to search for another position when Erich Lindemann had an idea (he was a man of many ideas. A few of those he committed to writing are found in *Beyond Grief* [1979]). One of his pet projects was to bring social scientists and physicians together, and I turned out to be his latest means. He suggested that I visit the Massachusetts General Hospital medical clinics and spend some time with two young physicians. One was a psychiatrist named Gerald Davidson, the second was John Stoeckle, an internist. And so in the fall of 1959 began a collaboration with John and an affiliation with Massachusetts General which continues to this day.

Although I finally wrote my dissertation on "sociocultural factors in the seeking of medical aid" (the details of the Massachusetts General Hospital experience appear in subsequent sections of this volume), I hardly thought the project would propel me into the world of medical sociology. Quite the contrary, I conceived of myself and was conceived of as a specialist in deviance. Thus, when the McCords left Harvard for the greener pastures of Stanford, and Bud's criminology spot was filled by Stan Wheeler, I quickly sought his tutelage. For the next several years (1958-62) I worked with him as a student teaching assistant and research associate; in between (1959-61) I taught several criminology courses at Boston University. During this period Talcott Parsons and then Ted Mills helped broaden my perspective; I came to see that my work in criminology, and then later in aging, gambling, and medical care could be analytically subsumed under the general rubric of deviance. All my intellectual parts again felt integrated.

Thus though the years 1957-62 seemed filled by three major projects—at the Age Center of New England, the West End and Massachusetts General—I still worked on what I thought were my more general interests. Interested in the definition of deviance, I decided to examine its definers more closely. My first step was a journey across Mass Avenue to the Harvard Law School, where I spent a year in a general course in criminal law. Within another year I was able to apply this knowledge in a study with Stan Wheeler, Richard Cramer, Joe Hozid on "agents of social control" (Wheeler et al. 1968).

My job in the study was to interview juvenile court judges. Again, although the data were interesting, the contextual learning proved more enlightening. Merely seeing the wide range of choices open to the judges both organizationally (how they ran their courts) and jurisdictionally (what they could do to those who appeared before them) was both awesome and disquieting. Despite all the admirable behavior I saw many judges display, it was scary to realize how little curb there was on their discretion and how little recourse any juvenile appearing before them had. Sometime later I began to see similar issues emerge between doctors and patients.

My Mass General research, of course, took up most of my time. But when this data collection was finished in February 1961, I returned to my earlier interests. A Ford Foundation grant seemed to offer an excellent opportunity to investigate even more probingly the "agents of social control." I already knew about their professional training. Now I wanted to *see* what they really did, and what they said they did on the job.

Building on the extensive contacts made through the previous "agents of social control" study, I decided to follow the path of a juvenile through the system from court to incarceration. My aim was to see through the eyes of the controllers—what they thought they were doing and why. My previous contacts with the juvenile court system had established a certain legitimacy. Permission was remarkably easy to get. At each step I presented myself as a future teacher of courses in criminology and delinquency. I claimed, rightly I think, that I had a great deal of theoretical knowledge about the causes of crime and its treatment but little firsthand experience. Thus I wanted to know how it felt to deal with such issues daily. I asked to take notes about what I saw, but I promised I was interested neither in systematically evaluating what they did nor (more importantly) in publishing any results. Perhaps because they liked the idea of teaching a teacher and also because of my vow of written silence, I received permission at every level of administration.

In March 1961 I began a tour of juvenile courts in eastern Massachusetts—the same courts in which I had interviewed the judges. At each I took extensive notes on all aspects of the proceedings, including the physical setting. I then accompanied the judge into his chambers as he met with probation officers, the family, and the boy himself. I watched as he made his disposition. After each decision, I was able to spend a few minutes with the judge, asking him about the decision he made. After touching bases with all these courts, I proceeded to the next stop: the Youth Service Board Detention Center. Male juveniles arrived here if they were declared to be "delinquent." The boys were usually held for a couple of weeks until a decision was made on a suitable placement. My method of participant-observation was more varied in this setting. Over a several week period I worked at every position the organization offered, from recreation supervisor to lunchroom supervisor, from night shift caretaker to psychological tester. And, of course, I read all the reports and attended the meetings where the final dispensations were made. From the center I went to the end-point—the institutions, often called residential guidance centers, where the boys were sent to be rehabilitated—or, as they themselves put it—"to serve their time." At Lyman, the "school" for preteenagers, I again took over all the jobs available, expanding my repertoire to include assistant teacher and dorm counselor. At one point I replaced a vacationing counselor and moved in to assume responsibility for a group of eight boys. By the end of August 1961, my "internship" was completed. I possessed several hundred pages of field notes and an unchartered list of memories and contacts which has since helped me teach and guide students in this and related areas.

The study also served as a needed respite. I returned with renewed energy to the coding of my Massachusetts General Hospital data. The process took several months, and afterward I might have moved on to a new project but for the unexpected death of my mother. For two years she had been diagnosed as having uterine cancer, though in the "infinite wisdom" of her doctor, I had been the only one deemed strong enough in the family to know the full facts. Everyone, including my mother, agreed to ask no questions about the weekly X-ray treatment to which I drove her. I felt torn, but warned of the consequences should I blurt out the truth, I reluctantly kept my silence. In any case, she seemed to be doing well, so there appeared no need for a confrontation. She was experiencing neither pain nor major side effects from the treatment. She was even able to continue working, so none of us thought much about it when some minor preventative surgery was suggested to eliminate the possibility of urinary blockage. The night before the operation, which was my twenty-seventh birthday, my wife and I visited her. We talked about rather mundane matters and joked that soon she would number two doctors in the family—Lee and myself. We left and promised to see her the next day. We did not. She never regained consciousness after surgery and died the following morning.

The grief that we experienced bordered on hysteria. She was only fifty-two years old. We had lost a mother, wife, daughter, and friend without ever having a chance to say goodbye. I was furious and at the same time overwhelmed by a sense of impotence. During the period of mourning, the first-run analysis of my data came off the computer.

The results were striking, and Phil Slater, my now absent thesis advisor (he was an assistant professor at Brandeis), suggested that the data looked good enough to write up. I leaped at his idea. Over the next two months I wrote and revised my dissertation. It was a way of retaining my sanity and working out my anger as well as making a belated present to my mother.

Such a rush had its costs. The dissertation was uneven. As one reader commended, "Chapter 3 is so good that the others pale by comparison." In the course of the committee's deliberations I received a phone call. I learned of several criticisms, all relatively minor, but an awkward pause followed. "You know, Irv, the general feeling is that if you took another year to bring all the chapters up to the level of chapter 3, then this would be a really publishable thesis."

I thought about it for a moment and answered, "If you are asking me whether I will voluntarily take another year to work on the thesis, my answer is no. If, of course, the committee decides that such revision is necessary I will have to abide by their decision." Then I added, "Besides, no one is ever going to read this version of the thesis. They will judge the work by the published papers which I will inevitably get out." The committee, perhaps reluctantly, agreed and approved my dissertation. In June of 1962 my life as a graduate student came to an end.

PUTTING IT ALL TOGETHER

With my silent promise to my mother completed, it was time to fulfill my promise to myself and my committee to "put it all together." After consulting with my wife, who was in the midst of her own dissertation, I decided not to put myself immediately on the job market. Instead I created a year (1962-63) of postdoctoral study, which I sometimes think of as my sabbatical. With the advice and help of Erich Lindemann, I decided to use this time for writing and exploration. He agreed to support me as a part-time consultant to the Departments of Psychiatry and Medicine. This meant that I could continue my collaboration with John Stoeckle (this book itself contains examples of our collaboration), and also try to implement some of what we'd learned. I could also begin to write up some results of my own research and decide at leisure what new directions I wanted to pursue.

At the same time I had other interests to pursue. In particular, I wanted to work in a less isolated environment than Massachusetts General, one with other fellow social scientists. At the time, Greater

Boston was abuzz with such opportunities, and one of the best known was again an offshoot of the work of Erich Lindemann, at the Social Science Unit at the Harvard School of Public Health. This center was then headed by Ben Paul, known as the editor of a stimulating book on the integration of social science and medicine (Paul 1955). With a recommendation from Erich Lindemann in hand, I sought work at Ben Paul's shop. At the time Sydney Croog was seeking help on two projects—one a study of Children's Hospital and the second an organization analysis of the work of public health nurses. Although I possessed much informal knowledge about the first study, it was the latter that proved the most involving. First, it extended my ability to analyze someone else's data; unlike the Age Center material, however, the basic data were qualitative. The second was the confirmation the work gave to a niggling doubt. My own personal experience with patients as well as Davis's *Passage Through Crisis* (1963) made me feel that medicine *per se* was overemphasized at the expense of other elements in medical care. So I welcomed the opportunity to focus solely on the work of nurses.

The professional workers around me proved equally stimulating. Seeing Ben Paul, Sol Levine and Norm Scotch develop ways of making social science concepts relevant to health workers was an adventure in teaching. And sitting in as they discussed research with the likes of Elliot Mishler, Jack Geiger, Howard Freeman, Sydney Croog, and Paul White was an adventure in conceptualization. That my fellow research assistants were Jean Litman-Blumen and Elliot Krause is further testimony to the intellectual atmosphere. As good an experience as Massachusetts General had been, I realized that for my own intellectual growth I had to move on.

That same year I returned to Boston University, this time to the faculty of the School of Social Work. My job was to direct a group of second year students on their theses. They did so well and the work was so satisfying that I felt teaching would provide me with the most consistent intellectual gratification.

In the winter of 1963 I put myself on the job market. Though I considered research positions, a university appointment to Brandeis seemed more attractive. The appeal of Brandeis stemmed from several sources. My wife was still working on her thesis and also gaining a reputation as a clinician, so she had little desire to leave the Boston area. My closest friend, Phil Slater, taught at Brandeis and I knew the work of several other department members—Morris Schwartz, Maurice Stein, Kurt Wolff, and Lew Coser. In fact, I had many years before accompanied a student to one of Lew Coser's senior tutorials. Sitting on the floor with several others, I heard him discourse on the differences between Merton and Mannheim. And as he talked about their characters and the times they were part of, I was reminded most pleasantly of that Russian literature course which had awakened my own interest in social history and social conditions. It was only as a colleague that I learned of Coser's own interest in the Soviet Union (an article on the Soviet family in 1951), the links he saw between sociology and literature (1963), and his growing work on intellectual history (1965). In short, from all I knew it was a good department. In many ways I was still naive. I had little sense of competing "schools" of sociology and certainly less of what was so special about the Brandeis department.

I did, however, know something about Brandeis in general, and that made me wary. In the eyes of the world it was a Jewish university. Despite my deep identification as a Jew, my living and working so long in the gentile world of Harvard and Massachusetts General made me fear the trip to Brandeis as one which might take me closer to my roots than I wished. The second doubt came from a most unlikely source—a group of anthropologists at the Society for Applied Anthropology Convention. This was the year of the famed Kennedy-Khruschev eyeballing, and apparently one Brandeis anthropologist, Kathleen Gough, had spoken out against the American strategy. She was supposedly being harassed by the Brandeis administration because of her remarks, and my fellow anthropologists were bewailing this restriction of academic freedom. That hardly boded well for my personal and professional expansion.

Were I more politically aware at the time or less comfortable with my Jewishness, I might have accepted a rather large three-year grant from the then National Institute of General Medical Sciences to continue my research on patient decision-making (I have written more about this grant and the dilemmas it presented in other sections of this volume). But the opportunity to explore still another side of me proved too enticing.

Although I thought of myself as a specialist in deviance, Everett Hughes valued my skills in qualitative methods. He had read several of my papers, including the one on gambling in the West End, and thought that I was "a natural field worker." He decided that I'd make a good field supervisor of the newly funded National Institue of Mental Health field training program at Brandeis. However, though I had taken many anthropology courses, none focussed explicitly on its methodology. When I expressed this anxiety to Everett, he calmly assured me that we'd work it out together. And we did.

This section of the present chapter should be the longest, for it tells of a process that is still going on. I stop here for several reasons. My purpose has been to chart my intellectual origins—to tell how I embarked on a career of sociomedical inquiry, but not fully explain how I became or am still becoming the sociologist I am. In part I will deal with other issues of my development as I introduce the selections in this volume. Yet in truth the process of selecting material for my biography has become more difficult at this point. Since the late 1960s my life has become less compartmentalized; it has become more difficult to speak easily of discrete events and people who influenced my intellectual life. In fact, I have written about this period of my life at length elsewhere (Zola, 1982a. See the epilogue for more details). In the next several pages, however, let me give an overview of where I've been and where I think I'm going.

The Brandeis Sociology Department remains my intellectual home base. Brandeis let loose my potentialities, and I began here another round of learning. Over the next several years I sat in on the courses of my senior colleagues. With Coser, Stein, Wolff, and Vic Walter I lost forever my awe of theory. I became less concerned with trying to understand any theory's derivation and true meaning and more interested in what it meant to me, how I could use it. Bob Weiss, who glided back and forth between qualitative and quantitative methods, helped me feel less schizophrenic about my research approaches. From courses, conversations, and contact with Morrie Schwartz, Maurie Stein, and Jack Seeley, I let myself be drawn into the importance of self-involvement in what one professes as well as what one studies. And I got to work with and learn again from my colleague and friend Phil Slater.

Ever since my undergraduate work with Paul Hare I'd been fascinated with small groups. I was also interested in therapy. I once observed a long-term counseling group and even toyed with the idea of applying to the Boston Psychoanalytic Institute. I also found that I was spending more and more time in my office counseling students. And so in 1967 the offer to colead a group process seminar with Phil seemed an excellent opportunity to deal with all these issues. Some three years later Phil, myself, Morrie Schwartz, and several others founded Greenhouse, a Cambridge-based personal growth and counseling center.

But in both content and style I am especially grateful to Everett Hughes. I cannot easily specify why—perhaps it was osmosis—but I know I learned much from him. One day after years of coteaching and colleagueship, I realized that I was thinking about problems differently, asking different questions and feeling extraordinarily more confident in my ability as a researcher, teacher, and fieldworker. There was no one at Brandeis with whom I had more run-ins, disagreements, and even one infamous temper tantrum. And yet there was also no one at Brandeis who I felt saw me more totally and communicated more consistently the respect he had for me and my work.

A group, however, is more than the sum of its parts, and it is from its esprit in general that still another important step in my intellectual growth began—my politicization. My teachers and colleagues at Harvard had not been especially apolitical, but politics seemed as separate from our intellectual careers as were our love lives. It was assumed that each of us possessed both a political and sexual dimension, but its expression was certainly not to be demonstrated within academia. This was hardly the case at Brandeis. And though there was wide disagreement in the department as to tactics, there was agreement that we should be not only politically concerned, but involved. It started with the signing of protest petitions, became more forceful in a formal statement we released to the newspapers in the early 60s about segregation in Boston public schools, and culminated in our very long and active participation in both the civil rights and anti-Vietnam movements. I am sure we were less radical than many would have liked, but for me it gave new meaning to the word "relevance."

What started as statements of merely personal convictions eventually filtered into my work—first in my writings on medicine as an institution of social control, and later in my working to create a grass roots counseling and advocacy organization, The Boston Self Help Center. In fact, this change in consciousness probably solidified my personal identification as a "medical sociologist." For not only was medicine becoming an area in which I could pursue my research and theoretical interests in deviance, but I gradually began to see it as a microcosm of important social issues.

One other lesson sunk in from these Brandeis years, a sad yet sobering one. During this period I was being interviewed for a senior position at another university. The dean, looking over my now fat and impressive vita, eyed me rather suspiciously. "This resume is filled with lists of your experiences and accomplishments in research, teaching, administration, writing, and clinical work. Just how do you manage to do it all?" "I don't do it equally well all of the time," I replied. I got the job, but the lesson sunk in. It was becoming impossible to keep up with all my interests. Though a voracious reader, I had no desire to hole up in the library and read journals to keep up. There was another consequence. Much as I liked research, I had lost my desire to devote myself for any significant time to any single enterprise. I wished neither that kind of responsibility nor that kind of commitment.

My work with Everett Hughes provided an unwitting answer to my dilemma. I began to let myself appreciate how much I could learn simply from daily living. In short, I began living out what Everett had once said in his introduction to a class: "My name is Everett Cherrington Hughes and I do field work all of the time." Thus I consciously started to take advantage of who I was; I put myself into situations in which, though I was ostensibly the teacher-consultant, I was learning as much as I was teaching.

Every Thursday, for example, I would venture into Boston and spend the day wherever anything interesting was happening. It might mean travelling to a university research center to talk about a current project. It could mean settling in with John Stoeckle as he wrestled with some issue in medical education or ambulatory care. Or it might mean sitting in on a class or attending a clinical discussion—sometimes a case presentation, sometimes "grand rounds." With some this developed into long-term collaborations. For nearly a decade I worked with Edith Lenneberg at the Stoma Rehabilitation Clinic of the New England Deaconess Hospital and learned first hand the clinical and political meaning of self-help. With John Kosa and Aaron Antonovsky I spend endless hours talking about socioeconomic aspects of health care, a series of conversations which eventually developed into our editing of two books (Kosa, Antonovsky, and Zola 1969; Kosa and Zola 1975). With a group from the Beth Israel Hospital and the help of Lincoln Laboratories, I developed a series of instruments which helped paramedics do the work of physicians (Zola 1970a). But most of the time the contacts were short—a good talk, a good lunch—and more data and experience filed away in my retentive memory. This has proved so worthwhile a gambit that I've continued it even on various leaves, sabbaticals and trips to Europe.

But chiefly I have learned from my students. I hesitate to use the words "my" and "students," because they imply ownership and superiority, concepts I want no part of. Bear with me as I acknowledge a little of what I owe to so many. My earlier students deepened my appreciation of the institutions of social control (Alex Liazos on halfway houses, Ruth Jacobs on high schools, Lea Baider on long-term care hospitals, Barbara Carter on women's prisons, Claire Lang on community mental health centers, Aline Zoldbrod on nursing homes); about the training of professional helpers (Jane Jones on female medical students, Miriam Sonn on nurses, Lilly Offenbach on social workers, Donald Light on psychiatrists, Norman Mirsky on rabbis); and how they dealt with on-the-job dilemmas (Fran Portnoy on hospital nurses, Rachel Kahn-Hut on clinical psychiatrists, Michael Yedidia on nurse practitioners). Others deepened my understanding of areas I naively thought I knew quite well (Sam Black on experimental education, Susan Dibner on "integrated vs segregated" institutions, Robert Emerson on juvenile courts, Harvey Feldman on drug use, Lynda Holmstrom on dual career families, Elsbeth Kahn on the elderly, Charlotte Schwartz on the notion of trouble, Harriet Skillern on juvenile law, Kelly Weisberg on urban communes). Some have been and are still taking me into areas where I'd have no easy access either as a man (Natalie Allon on diet workshops, Louise Levesque and Nancy Shaw on childbirth, Norma Swenson on women's self help, Kathleen MacPherson on menopause and Beth Shub Pessen on the concerns of first-time mothers), or as a white (Gilberto Lusero on Chicano alcoholism, Tahi Mottl on black education, Joan Harris on ethnic problems in retardation, Marie Zuniga on the Chicano elderly), or just for lack of a better term, psychophysically (Jim Kelly on the gay elderly, Doug Harper on hoboes). Still others have led me into places where I would not go alone, such as political economic analysis (Naomi Aronson on food production, Phil Brown on the mental health movement, Susan Bell on DES research). And still others have taught me how to look more deeply at my own data (Elizabeth Hartwell Harvey and Rachel Spector) as well as my own experience (Shulamit Reinharz). To all of these and numerous others, I acknowledge a great and unpayable debt.

Finally, there is a more difficult subject to discuss or relate, my acknowledgments to women I have known and loved. (So that I will not be more unclear than necessary, let me note that I separated from my wife in 1971 and did not marry again till 1981.) Almost everyone I've been involved with has been an important source of intellectual support. The dedications on my papers and books are genuine acknowledgments of debt. For many there was a tradeoff; as we read, commented on and criticized each other's intellectual creations. But equally important was an influence of another kind. I believe it no accident that the vast majority of women with whom I sustained a relationship have considered themselves (at least partly) therapists and counselors. This pattern started early and intensely at the age of twenty. My former wife is a clinical psychologist and my mother-in-law a social worker.

Uncomfortable as it is to examine my personal life very closely, I do see several implications for my intellectual development. First, by their very work the women I have known never let me forget the importance of individuals, their complexity, and their variety. Second, their embeddedness in very applied activities never let me stay abstract for long. Third, they offered a daily education (through osmosis) in what counseling and helping were all about. And lastly, I know I was a fiercely independent person who could not admit vulnerability; they helped me work on my personal problems, making it possible that I need not seek (nor admit the need of) professional help. Their help also contributed to a gradual loosening up of my thinking as well as my writing. All in all, they kept my work multidisciplinary and grounded, and eventually opened up for me a second career in counseling.

At a public lecture several years ago, someone obviously familiar with my writing asked if my biting criticism of medicine was rooted in my own personal disillusionment and experiences in the medical area. Many people in the audience were offended by the question, and I was taken aback. The question seemed to imply that my criticisms were a sort of personal vendetta; a way of getting back.

I am not about to engage in a debate over whether or not I am really "antimedicine." Throughout this essay I have claimed that my sociology is in fact closely linked to my biography. Some of these connections are obvious, and where I am aware I have noted them. It is certainly not accidental that I long resisted thinking of myself as a medical sociologist. That identification was too personal. It seemed unscientific if not unhealthy to dwell on or use my own experience. The reversal of this principle was by no means sudden. My teaching, particularly my individual work with graduate students, seemed to push me to share more of myself. Slowly it crept into my undergraduate teaching, still later into my counseling, and finally into my research and writing. And when I let life in, it seemed to deepen and sensitize what and whom I teach, research, and write about.

There is, however, a special way in which much of my work has been influenced by having experienced polio and a serious car accident. Like many others I wondered and cried aloud, "Why me?" "Why me?" For reasons beyond my comprehension I gradually broadened my concern. First it became a more philosophical "Why anyone?" and eventually a more sociological "Why some and not others?" Still later I became less interested in why people "got" the problems they had and more in why some "troubles" were "problems" and others were not.

The asking of such questions has been accompanied by the continual search for answers. From personal feelings of dependency and impotence I have sought to examine the bases of power and control; and in so doing I to hope to reinstate them where they once existed, or to establish them where they never did.

Part Two

Why Should Anyone Listen? Audiences and Justifications

2 *My Introduction to Research in the Medical World*

From the streets of the West End to the corridors of Massachusetts General Hospital is a physical distance of about a hundred yards. In every other way they are distant worlds. Hence it was with a certain reluctance that I shed the casual informality of the neighborhood for the rigid formality of the clinics in the fall of 1959. Though I now had to be jacketed, necktied, and brief-cased once more, it didn't bother me as it once might have. All clothes began to feel like costumes befitting an occasion, with less effect on the real me.

Being at Mass General also marked my return to the world of hard research. Erich Lindemann liked the way John Stoeckle, Gerald Davidson, and I were collaborating and so agreed to support me financially (a $3000 fellowship) for at least a year. This reduction of financial pressure enabled us to learn about each other, share our general experiences, and slowly explore our research options.

The formulation of our investigation went through five distinct phases. The first was to determine the general area of inquiry. The second was to delineate our specific theoretical concerns. The third was to agree on a general research strategy. The fourth was to develop the specific methodology to deal with the questions we had raised. The fifth was to secure the permission and cooperation of the administration, the staff, and the patients.

In the beginning we thought there was nothing in the world of medicine that we could not explore. We soon learned better. By inclination and interest we were all fascinated by what transpired when a doctor and patient came together. We read and discussed our readings, shared insights, and developed hypotheses, but we soon found ourselves at a dead end. A previous group of social scientists had studied doctor-nurse interaction, and the hospital staff was still reeling from the experience. Not only was the staff unclear about the relevance of that work, they clearly disliked being placed under any more scrutiny. Though a few physicians expressed interest in our observing their encounters with patients, the vast majority stated that such observation would be a "violation of the doctor-patient relationship" (Stoeckle and Zola 1964b). Reluctantly we postponed such a query to another day.

Thus our first decision was made for us. Politically and methodologically it seemed best to study the world of the patient. Our specific theoretical focus, however, came from more academic concerns. One of the most lively debates among my Harvard colleagues concerned the definition of "normality." In the late 1950s there was a growing suspicion that our notions of conformity and deviance were hardly universal, but rather socially conditioned. In research this suspicion emerged as an increasing dissatisfaction with how problems were conceptualized. For example, suppose you accepted that the standard by which one was labelled a "deviant," be it homosexual, criminal, or schizophrenic, was objective and scientific. To investigate such concerns you then got two populations—one possessed of the "deviant" characteristic and one not—and then asked how these groups differed. The usual focus was on how one became "deviant" more than on how one remained "conformist." The full sociological and political implications of such questioning were still several years ahead. We were more in the throes of trying to develop the legitimacy of even asking such questions. Since many of us had interests in the mental health area (partly because the Social Relations Department as a whole seemed fascinated with psychiatry and psychoanalysis, and partly because everyone knew that the National Institute of Mental Health was the largest single source of funding for social scientists) it was here that our discussions were most informed. We were intrigued by new findings which showed how widely mental illness varied not only in social prevalence and incidence, but also in perception in cultures around the world as well as within our own.

All of these reinforced the notion that deviance was socially created, yet we shared a niggling methodological concern. Even without our sociological doubts, much of the world was already suspicious of psychiatry and its tools. One prominent critic, Thomas Szasz, had begun to accuse psychiatry itself of being a misguided child of medicine (1959). To me this seemed uncomfortably *ad hominem* and limited, though it took more than a decade for me to make my disagreement with Szasz more explicit (Zola 1972a). If blame should be placed anywhere it was on some basic structural fault in American society. For me the debate culminated one night at a graduate student party. In answer to some probably unasked question, I blurted out, "We need to find some form of deviance which everyone accepts as real, objective, scientific, and then show how that is socially conditioned."

"Like what?" asked someone.

"Like physical disease," I replied.

The next day my insight still felt right, and I shared it with my medical colleagues. With their encouragement it was easy to apply the findings and controversies about mental illness to the field of physical illness. We soon realized that the so-called "objectivity" of signs and symptoms not only influenced how we delivered our services (i.e. if anyone was sick enough they would eventually be seen), but also how we did any patient research (i.e. we inevitably studied people's *information* about specific diseases, rarely if ever their attitude or perception of them). I, however, wanted to do more than merely document that lay people perceived illness differently than did professionals. I wanted to see what difference such perceptions made behaviorally. Thus our theoretical concern was not only specified but operationalized. Specifically, I decided to investigate how someone decided that "the trouble" they had was "important enough" to make them enter the outpatient clinics of Massachusetts General Hospital.

Now it was necessary to develop a specific research strategy. I eagerly devoured the "literature"—from specific studies describing the use of services to general treatises and experiments on decision-making. As the dimensions of an approach emerged, I found there were at least three teams of investigators working on similar issues. None had yet published and all were located in New York City. With the financial backing of Walter Bauer, then Chief of Medicine, I sought them out. I quickly discovered that though each (Bernard Kutner, Eliot Freidson, and Sylvia Gilliam) was using a different strategy, all three were working with what Freidson later called the lay referral system (1960, 1961). (Kutner ultimately published only one article from his work [Kutner and Gordon 1961], though Gerald Gordon [1966] used data from the study for an analysis of the sick role. Gilliam died during the course of the project; some of her data was later analyzed by Suchman [1964, 1965a,b].) I was impressed by both the wealth of material and its sophistication. All three researchers willingly shared their instruments with me, and in some cases the data they had already collected. It did not seem worthwhile to repeat their approaches in Boston, so I focussed instead on one aspect, namely the decision to seek medical aid—what I called "the why now" question and what others have since dubbed "triggers to action."

The fourth step, determining the specifics of my methodology, is fully described in papers reprinted in this volume. Let me conclude then, with the final and most time-consuming step of all: gaining the necessary permission to do the study. First I had to prove to our medical colleagues that the general issue of decision-making was worth investigating. I documented a series of medical conditions for which there was an unexplained discrepancy between people who did and did not seek treatment. Then I was able to show that failure to seek treatment was related neither to the availability of services nor to the medical seriousness of the condition. From other evidence I argued that neither patients' ignorance nor dissatisfaction with medicine helped explain the phenomenon either. I concluded that the explanation might lie in a series of social, psychological, and cultural factors which influenced people's very perception of their body, and therefore the kind of attention they paid to it.

After several presentations the staff guardedly accepted the value of the project. But there was an increasing suspicion that such an extensive investigation would interfere, at least in terms of time, with the doctor-patient relationship. Back to the drawing boards I went, and returned a month later with a time study of the clinics. I proved that since the average waiting time for patients was over an hour, I had ample time to do my interviewing. Several argued that my finding was unusual and that many doctors worked much faster. I promised that a doctor's readiness to see the patient would always take precedence over my interviewing (as it turned out I only "lost" one patient. That the loss occurred during the first week of my study led me to believe that I was being tested). A third stumbling block presented itself: how could I be assured of a meaningful number of respondents, and how could I devise a system that would not interfere with the basic out-patient admitting process? Again I returned to the "field," did a one-month demographic-epidemiological survey of all new patients to the outpatient clinics. From this I learned several things: first, that by sampling only three clinics—the Eye; the Ear, Nose, and Throat; and the Medical—I could cover the vast majority of new patients and a wide range of disorders; second, that a short demographic questionnaire and tagging system would not interfere with general procedures; and third, that as in any other situation I should be wary of stereotypes. Prior to the survey I'd been assured by several "knowledgeable" staff members that Jews and Hispanics were major ethnic groups served by Massachusetts General. Although both of these groups were clearly visible, they came to the clinics (as new patients) at so slow a rate compared to the Irish, Italian and Anglo-Saxons that statistically they were not worth sampling.

Perhaps exhausted by my persistence and by mushrooming support, the administration and the research committee gave me permission to do the study. But that only meant that the hospital administration and research committee thought the project was worth doing. I still needed the cooperation of the chiefs of staff for each of the respective services, and I needed it on two levels. All patients "belonged" to specific doctors, and only they could give permission for their patients to be interviewed. Secondly, I needed physicians to supply certain medical information on each patient I interviewed. I quickly learned that permission from the chiefs was not enough in itself. It was the head nurse who ultimately controlled the flow of patients, and who thus had the power to determine if *my* work was interfering with *the* work of the clinics. And so still another round of conversations took place. By this time I decided to eliminate all conceivable administrative blockages, I independently sought "clearance" for my study from still another rung of staff—all the clerks and secretaries who handled the most basic procedural matters.

Of course, there was still another group whose cooperation I would desperately need—the patients. There seemed no a priori way to secure both their permission and cooperation, so I decided to learn by doing. With the permission of the administration I was allowed once more to become a participant-observer. After John Stoeckle advised me how to display medical symptoms which would eventually get me to the Medical clinic, I once more donned my West End identity and presented myself at the out-patient admissions office. Two days later I possessed far more information than I'd anticipated. In addition to learning why many patients arrived both angry and suspicious at their physicians' doors (the many confusing and contradictory instructions they received were enough to drive anyone crazy), I also learned what I could do to enhance their cooperation. I explained about hospital procedures and the likely waiting period, my own role, and my research. Finally I told them they could smoke if they wished and that the decision to participate in the study was theirs alone. I did add, however, that staying with me might prove more interesting than waiting for their turn. Over three hundred patients agreed.

It took nine months of gestation before Stoeckle, Davidson, and I "delivered" a research project into the field. From July 1960 through February 1961 I spent every morning collecting data on the project, which had now become both my doctoral dissertation, and the forerunner of many publications in the sociomedical field.

As with my other research, I learned almost as much from the experience as from the data I collected. The difficulty I had in getting the study approved served me very well when I ultimately aired my research to the medical world. I had learned a great deal about the functioning of hospital administrations, medical bureaucracies, and out-patient clinics; this knowledge powerfully informed much of my later research, teaching, and consulting. But probably my greatest joy was seeing the changes effected by my work. With the close collaboration of John Stoeckle, we were able to make alterations over the years in the operation of the clinics—from the medical forms to the seating arrangements, from the physical structure of the examining rooms to the education of the medical, nursing, and social service staff.

Publishing the results was the next step. Though the findings seemed significant we still had to justify their importance. So in a three year period a number of general papers quickly emerged (Stoeckle and Davidson 1962a & b, Stoeckle and Davidson 1963, Stoeckle and Zola 1964a & b, Stoeckle, Zola, and Davidson 1963, 1964). I included two which are the best examples of our efforts at outreach.

The first paper, written with my two physician colleagues, has a clinical perspective. "On Going to See the Doctor" was primarily a review of the relevant literature. We were trying to explain to doctors not only how important it was to understand the patient's point of view but also what social science could contribute to this understanding. We intentionally published in *The Journal of Chronic Diseases* because we thought we might reach more "socially-oriented" physicians. I think we achieved our aims. The article was widely cited and we received over a thousand requests for offprints.

"After Everyone Can Pay for Medical Care" was also written with John Stoeckle, but its aim was hardly clinical. It was our attempt to deal with some of the issues arising out of the early 1960s debate over Medicare. In particular we argued that although we personally favored such legislation, it would in no way deal with some of the basic problems underlying the current distribution and organization of medical care. The paper is personally gratifying, though politically disillusioning. Some ten years after its publication, we received three separate requests to reprint it in collections because the dilemmas we had postulated about Medicare were still relevant to the currently proposed legislation on national health insurance.

A final note to these articles is necessary. I am and always have been of two worlds—the applied and the academic. This section illustrates the personal, professional, and political implications of this stance. First, I found myself in a position to influence people politically if I got my results out quickly. Thus I jumped at the opportunity to publish papers with my medical colleagues and to present my work at conferences which guaranteed quick publication. I was also aware that publishing with physicians in medical journals would lend legitimacy to my findings, my interpretations, and even my later work. Professionally, this decision kept me visible while I continued to write up my research for more scholarly audiences in my own field. And personally it appealed to my need for short-term gratification. After the long struggle of delivering the study into the field, it was very important to receive some immediate feedback. The mere fact that a medical journal would decide on the merits of an article within a few weeks (whereas a social science journal often took months) had considerable appeal.

3

On Going to See the Doctor: The Contributions of the Patient to the Decision to Seek Medical Aid

A Selective Review

Our national statistics report the volume, the frequency and the costs of medical visits to the doctor (U.S. National Health Survey 1958). This actuarial account, however, does not tell us about the human situations and contributions which the patient brings to his decision to go to the doctor. There are, of course, many players in this common scene of the visit to the doctor and many variables which each player contributes. The actual coming to the doctor may be initiated not only by the patient but by his family, by persons in his social life and by institutions that may demand medical attention: for example, in selecting, placing and retiring employees or as a perquisite and norm of executive employment. When the patient makes the decision, his act of coming and his particular choice of medical help is influenced, in turn, by the structure and availability of medical practices, by his knowledge of particular doctors and medical institutions, and by opinions among his social contacts—what Freidson (1961) has called the "lay referral system."

Much information on the subject of seeking medical aid is part of the physician's store of clinical knowledge, folklore, and gossip

Originally appeared as "On Going to See the Doctor: The Contributions of the Patient to the Decision to Seek Medical Aid: A Selective Review," by John D. Stoeckle, Irving Kenneth Zola, and Gerald E. Davidson, *Journal of Chronic Diseases* 16 (1963): 975–989.

about patients, practice, and the vicissitudes of the doctor-patient relationship. But such experience is likely to have its own clinical bias and, by itself, is hardly a broad enough view of the patient's world. Even though every practitioner feels he already knows about people seeking medical aid, the actual literature on this subject is, itself, not large. The considerable information that can be found about patients, about doctors, and about diseases can only provide us with an unfinished sketch of several features which contribute to the decision to seek medical aid. Social scientists and clinicians are, however, increasingly concerned with gathering a more systematic description of these features, for the decision to see a doctor is not only germane to the kind, quality, and quantity of treatment which the individual patient receives, but further knowledge of the bases of such decisions can no doubt influence the organization of the doctor's practice, as well as the directions of medical education and of public health programs in medical care. Since so few empirical studies have been done on the specific process of seeking medical aid, we have undertaken a selective review of three factors which seem particularly important to the patient's decision. When the patient initiates the process, he contributes at least three important features: (1) his objective clinical disorder and symptoms, as well as his perception, knowledge, beliefs and attitudes about having a particular disorder or symptom; (2) his attitudes and expectations of the doctor and medical services; and (3) his definitions of "health," "sickness," and when medical care is necessary.

THE PATIENT'S PARTICULAR CONCERN

One of the most obvious factors to consider in examining the patient's decision is the objective clinical disorder. A person with a bleeding traumatic wound can hardly avoid going to the doctor or being taken there. On the other hand, a patient's knowledge and beliefs of his clinical disorder, especially when it is chronic and insidious may or may not be a reason for seeking help. Community surveys have repeatedly noted large numbers of individuals, both aware and unaware of their disorders, who were not under medical care (Commission on Chronic Illness 1957). So widespread, in fact, is the prevalence of both symptoms and signs of disease that these circumstances may, in fact, be regarded as the normal condition of the population. The absence of complaints and signs of disease may be exceptional even for the "healthy" members of the population who do not attend the doctor. For example, in a population of Peckham, London, pre-selected to the "healthy," 91 per cent had a physiologic or bodily disorder when interviewed and medically examined (Pearse and Crocker 1949). A more recent report of multiphasic examinations carried out in 10,709 apparently healthy subjects showed that 92 per cent had disease or clinical disorder which was amenable to diagnosis and treatment (Schenthal 1960). If sickness, judged by the prevalence of symptoms and signs, is, in fact, the rule rather than the exception in the "healthy" population, then the individual's response to symptoms by seeking aid may be a more objective or operational definition of "sickness" than our usual clinical emphasis on the fact of symptoms and signs alone. All of these studies, as well as the countless ones focussing on "unmet" physical needs suggest that important factors besides the fact of medical disorder must intervene in bringing the patient to the doctor or in keeping him away.

That something besides the presence of a medical disorder *per se* is influencing the patient's perception of symptoms and is illustrated by the many observations on how often the patient's chief complaint differs from other medically significant features of his clinical problem. For example, among patients with the nephrotic syndrome, Derow (1958) has pointed out that "edema" is the "illness" both for the patient and for the patient's family; and it is the symptom for which the patient seeks advice regardless of other symptoms of his renal disease. For many patients with bronchitis and emphysema the "cigarette cough" is a norm and not a reason to consult the doctor. Such patients come only in advanced stages when dyspnea occurs and, even then, often only when this interferes with the performance of some of their usual tasks. Among acromegalic patients, localized complications of vision, arthritis, diabetes, and lactation are more often the presenting reasons for medical aid rather than the obvious gross facial disfigurement. Similarly, many observers have commented on how differently obesity is viewed by patients and nonpatients alike so that by itself it is rarely the chief presenting symptom (Bruch 1957).

Social workers' case reports of their working-class clients contain similar accounts of the patient's reaction to or "meaning" of his disease (Bartlett 1940). Quite often the basis for coming for medical care may be due more to a specific impairment of an equally specific social role (e.g., as breadwinner) rather than concern with any broad underlying medical problem (Freidson 1961).

On the other hand, some recognition, knowledge or beliefs about the fact of disease does not automatically guarantee positive action. One of the reasons people with heart disease (Bertrand and Storla

1955) or cancer (Aitken-Swan and Patterson 1955; Titchener et al. 1956) delay in seeking medical aid is that they view the disease as incurable and therefore avoid the doctor so as not to find out the "truth" and also because they feel he can really do nothing for them. Other investigators have noted that ulcer patients who under-emphasized or misunderstood the causative importance of gastric acidity in their disease were also unable to conceive of the rationale and necessity of undertaking therapeutic and preventive programs in terms of "acid neutralization" (Roth et al. 1962).

Two studies are particularly relevant here not only because they studied the different reactions to similar symptoms but also because they attempted to examine the sources of such differences. Zborowski (1952) studied *hospitalized patients* who were suffering from back pain due mainly to herniated discs and spinal lesions. He found that while both the Jewish and Italian patients were more disturbed by pain and more vocal in their concern than the Anglo-Saxons, their reactions stemmed from different problems and required differing solutions. For example, the Italian patients seemed to be mainly concerned with the immediacy of the pain experience and were disturbed by the actual pain sensation while the Jews focussed mainly upon the diagnostic meaning of pain and upon the significance of pain in relation to their own future health, and eventually for the welfare of their families. The Anglo-Saxon considered pain bad, unnecessary, and therefore to be immediately taken care of. Such observations also had implications for their medical care. Sophisticated treatment would require more attention to concerns about the source of pain among Jewish patients and more attention to actual relief of the pain sensation among Italian patients. Zola (1966), on the other hand, studied ambulatory patients *in the process* of seeking aid at an out-patient department. The sharpest difference in response to symptoms occurred between Italian and Irish patients with the Anglo-Saxons occupying an intermediate position, more closely resembling the Irish in virtually all instances. Italians tended to be more disturbed by pain and to a greater extent felt that it was present in, and an important part of, their distress. The Irish tended to place the locus of their symptoms in specific body locations such as the eye, ear, nose or throat. This could not be attributed to the objective nature of their disorders but the data suggested that the Irish were more concerned with specific problems of body dysfunction or impairment while the Italians were more concerned with the diffuse physical and social effects of being sick. If, as these two studies claim, there is a differential reaction to, and concern with, similar symptoms, one may infer (1) that it would take different symptoms to bring these patients to the doctor and (2) that the presence of the same symptom in these populations would lead to vastly different courses of action, e.g. from immediate concern and therefore early consultation to complete ignoring and perhaps "infinite delay" in seeing a doctor.

In general, however, the individual has no clear idea of his disorder and must rely on *critical symptoms* that he considers worthy of medical attention and treatment. It may be "coughs," "fevers," "pain," "bleeding," "rheumatism," "nerves," or the location, intensity and frequency of symptoms. Reports on "delay" in cancer patients contain examples of the relationship of specific localized symptoms and clinical disorders to late decisions to come "to the office." One observation is the long delay in recognized superficial skin lesions for which self-treatment was common (Leach and Robbins 1947; Pack and Gallo 1938; Robbins et al. 1950). Kutner and Gordon (1961) found that patients with general medical symptoms, i.e. multiple complaints, delayed less than those with the "seven danger signals" of cancer. They also noted that low education and socioeconomic status have much more markedly affected delay for cancer symptoms than for general medical ones.

What may be operating in the above-mentioned differing perceptions is not only a matter of relative attention to certain physical signs but also a difference in the very definitions of what constitutes a symptom. Social scientists have frequently noted that physical signs or behavior which in one society may be considered symptomatic or evidence of disease, may not be so in another society (Paul 1955; Opler 1959). Several observers have examined the health and medical beliefs of Mexican and Spanish Americans and found them markedly different from the dominant Anglo-Saxon model. For example, Clark (1958) found that Mexican-Americans sometimes showed grave concern over the significance of unusual bodily states which physicians viewed as "functional variations" within the normal range. A child with "sad eyes" or one who "didn't sleep enough" may be taken for medical treatment whereas one with diarrhea, a common condition in the population studied by Clark, might not be considered particularly ill. Even within the more ordinary urban population of an American city, Koos (1954) found striking differences in what physical symptoms were deemed worthy of medical attention. The lower classes seemed to ignore many symptoms for which the upper classes sought aid. It thus appeared that the lower classes had to have more medically serious and manifest symptoms (e.g., lump, bleeding) before seeing a doctor than did the upper or middle class respondents. Such differences in definitions of symptoms have been noted more often in research on "mental illness." For example, several studies on "treated" populations noted the greater tendency for suburbanites and those of higher education and income to be troubled by and to consult doctors for problems related to "nerves" than were less affluent and mobile populations (Gordon and Gordon 1958; Gordon, Gordon and Gunther 1962; Martin, Brotherston and Chave 1957). Others have noted the clustering of more "serious" disorders in lower socioeconomic classes (Hollingshead and Redlich 1958).

Recently, however, there has been speculation as to whether this difference in rates might, in part, be due to differences in what social classes define as appropriate for medical treatment. Two recent surveys of mental health have documented that the tendency of the lower social classes to seek therapy less often *is not* a function of the lack of distress among them (Gurin, Veroff, and Feld 1960; Srole et al. 1962). Gurin, Veroff, and Feld (1960) have contended that this tendency is due to the fact that this psychological distress is not defined as a mental health problem and that treatment for such distress is not deemed appropriate.

The above studies have tried to demonstrate that the reason why a particular patient comes for, or focuses on, some symptoms rather than others, or why patients with the same underlying disorder may focus on different symptoms or concerns, is not due solely to objective features of the clinical disorder. Several observers have gone further and noted that this is not a purely idiosyncratic problem but may be related to more global social factors such as social class or ethnic group membership.

Most of the investigations presented here are highly retrospective. They are based on the responses of people who were not in the process of coming to the doctor nor in the process of making a decision to come. While it must be remembered that the use of recall and the reported response to anticipated and projected symptoms may not have the same significance when the individual actually decides to go to the doctor, such responses may, nevertheless, offer some clues as to the importance of these concerns in the general decision to seek medical aid.

THE PATIENT'S INTENTIONS, AND
HIS EXPECTATIONS OF THE DOCTOR

It is not popular to view the patient as a person with purposeful intent in seeing the doctor. Such considerations may distract the physician from important clinical issues of whether the patient is helplessly "sick" or not, whether he has a medical disease or not. If intentions are examined, often they are reduced to generalized clinical concepts of gratification of instinctive needs by medical care and attention and the repetition of child-parent patterns in the doctor-patient relationship. Allport (1960) has reminded us that the ongoing intentions of the individual may also be usefully examined. Going to the doctor may thus be treated on its own terms as a special institutional relationship by studying the patient's attitudes toward and expectations of the doctor and medical services.

Research has usually been based on patients' estimate of very general qualities of a "good" doctor, especially of his technical competence versus his personal "interest in patients" (Hassinger and McNamara 1958, 1960; Reader, Pratt and Mudd 1957).

In groups who have been surveyed, personal interest, though it is a highly valued expectation in general, seems to rate higher among groups with less education and income. Bott (1957), however, observed in her intensive study of the social network of twenty ordinary urban families that they regarded the doctor not unlike an "educated plumber," a view out of keeping with common professional conceptions. Other studies have included not only attitudes towards the doctor, but towards different health personnel within medical institutions. Such reports (Koos 1955) have examined the patients' satisfaction-dissatisfaction with, and acceptance-nonacceptance of, the doctor, the nurse, the social worker, and other medical personnel providing care. Freidson's study (1961) of a health supervision for insured families indicated greater acceptance of the doctor and the nurse over the social worker, even for problems within the latter's competence. While some studies have examined changes in attitudes toward medical personnel with different phases of illness, this has not been usual. One study of patients in various phases of recovery from poliomyelitis (Davis 1963), reported that they regarded the doctor with less importance and looked more to the physiotherapist for advice during hospital convalescence. Medical practice suggests that such phases as "health supervision," acute injury, convalescence, chronic disability or recovery are important in the decision to seek aid, and in the choice, acceptance and use of particular caretakers.

Other reports of the significance of the doctor himself can shed indirect light on the patient's expectations, and thereby also his use of medical personnel. Parson's description of American medical practice (1951) is a very general outline of several aspects of the doctors role vis-à-vis his patient. It includes the social aspects of his technical functions. Certain general expectations apart from those concerning his technical skills, such as confidentiality, may be important in deciding to come. Field's study of the physician in Russia (1957) indicates that there the doctor is a key person in sanctioning "excuses" from the work demands of the state. But such descriptions do not include the particular patterns of patients in using confidentiality and many unique role expectations the patient often has of the doctor. As a pediatrician Yudkin (1961) has illustrated the clinical importance of the mother's intentions in seeing the doctor regardless of what symptoms her child brings, while Balint (1957), as a psychoanalyst generalizing from case conferences with general practitioners in England, has emphasized the doctor's actual psychotherapeutic role in the light of the patient's implicit and purposeful intention to discuss personal problems with the medical practitioner. Yudkin (1961) considers that therapeutic intervention of any type is handicapped without a knowledge of intention. Balint (1957) is concerned with the doctor's responses to the patient, how the doctor can make the initial relationship therapeutic, using the techniques of advice, suggestion, exhortation, abreaction, reassurance, clarification, and manipulation in aiding the patient with the predicaments in his social and intrapersonal relationships.

Observations on the differing roles and expectations of doctors have also been documented in other papers. Reader, Pratt and Mudd (1957) noted that patients attending their medical clinic expected very little other than reassurance about medical disease and symptoms. Stoeckle and Davidson (1962b), from a similar setting, noted more varying role expectations among medical patients who often presented with depression. The doctor was alternately perceived as medical expert, substitute affiliation, sanctioning authority, intermediary between other family members, and a person for communication of aggrieved feelings, to mention a few of his roles.

Research in "mental health" reports the frequent use of the medical doctor, as well as other caretakers, by people with acknowledged emotional problems. In one study 30 per cent of patients with acknowledged problems first sought the aid of a medical doctor (Gurin, Veroff, and Feld 1960). Such explicit use, documented by surveys, indicates definite expectations of the doctor to deal with the psychological and social quandaries of the patient. Besides such surveys of physician-patient contacts, however, there is little information on variations in the patient's actual expectations of the doctor when first deciding to come. It is not even known if the concept of "personal" or "family" doctor exists for patients in this modern day of specialization or what kinds of relationships actually develop between patients and their "personal" doctor (Fox 1960), who is traditionally looked upon as the initial source of medical aid. Actual knowledge of where personal concerns are treated is missing.

In the realm of expectations there is also evidence of the influence of sociocultural factors. The previously mentioned anthropological works, as well as a recent book by Blum (1960) have documented the great diversity of conceptions of medical practice. The centuries-old perception of the hospital as a place to die and not to be helped is one that is found even today within the borders of our country. Though the most systematic work on the doctor-patient relationship has been done in the field of psychotherapy and psychoanalysis, there are major implications for general and even specialty medical practice. One such study is particularly interesting because it utilized the insights of social science, notably the value orientation analysis of Kluckhohn (1958). Thus, Spiegel (1959) felt that some of the Irish values on reticence, present-time orientation, and the consideration of certain topics as taboo led to great difficulty in treatment and presumably in seeking help in the first place. It was particularly acute in the fathers of disturbed children. Spiegel noted that such patients often were not used to working on their own problems for the sake of vague personal gains. The patient is accustomed to being told what to do, right now and if he is not told he feels paralyzed, that nothing is happening and he is wasting his time. So, too, many medical patients expect the magic pill, the instant cure. Another example of contrasting values and expectations was noted by Clark (1958). In general, the medical practitioner is trained to foster impersonal objectivity, to place a premium on efficiency—maximum output in minimum time—and to assume that his status as a specialist gives him prestige, authority, and final judgement in medical matters. The Mexican-Americans, however, expect and require him to share certain informal niceties—to drink, eat and chat before examining the patient, even an unconscious one as reported in one case. As a result, they find it difficult to trust a doctor with impersonal manners. Moreover, with their background of familiar authority and joint decision-making, they cannot acknowledge even his medical opinion as final and so often refuse to comply with his on-the-spot instructions. The doctor's continued insistence on immediate action that the individual make up his *own* mind is thus incomprehensible, and is regarded as discourteous and, ironically, as signs of the doctor's inadequacy and inefficiency. One such encounter is often sufficient to preclude further consultation. Zborowski (1952) and Zola (1963c) also noted that their patients had expectations of the doctor not necessarily in line with his own conception of his role and that these fears and misconceptions might and did lead to instances of mutual distrust and hence reluctance to continue in treatment at the time or to seek advice in the future.

RATIONALE: THE NEED FOR MEDICAL CARE

Given that the individual perceives something wrong with himself and has certain expectations, there still remains the problem of what he does about it. Freidson (1961), Gilliam (1961) and Spiegel and Bell (1959) have pointed out that there are stages in this process, from symptom recognition to the final choice of a physician or healer. Studies have focussed on various aspects of this process but few have dealt with the actual final decision.

What the patient does about his objective clinical symptoms may well be rooted in cultural and social definitions of "health" and "sickness." In sharing these, the individual may rationalize the importance of and general necessity for medical care and attention from doctors. For example, Parson's (1958) clinical observations of American social attitudes state that "health" is equivalent to "achievement," a belief more common to the upper social classes, provides the individual with a *rationale* for seeking professional aid. There is the corollary proposition that coming to the doctor may help maintain one's capacities for achievement. The frequency of "check-ups" among certain groups tends to confirm this social observation. But, variant definitions of "health" in our own country may also be important in determining whether the patient comes. Such definitions may be inferred from observations on the differential rate of visiting the doctor among various social classes reporting symptoms; for example, the lesser rate among the lower class families. Apathy about "health" and a lack of any definition for action have been found in such families (Weeks, Davis, and Freeman 1958). In a study of older people, health was found to be equated with interpersonal competence (DiCicco and Apple 1960), while in a second study, worry about anticipated or real impairment of this competence, not achievement, was found to be critical in patients who have come or come frequently for medical visits (Marmor 1958). Apple's study (1960) is indicative of the implications of variant definitions. She found that, to middle-class Americans, to be ill means to have an ailment of recent origin which interferes with one's usual activities. She was quick to point out, however, that this idea may be an example of cultural lag, since the idea seems more appropriate to an earlier period when infectious diseases with obvious symptoms were a greater threat to life than they are today. Since chronic diseases are increasingly common, and often have a slow and insidious onset, with symptoms persisting and not necessarily limiting activity, the criterion of "interference" is not an adequate impetus to seek aid. Such a standard may, in fact, be detrimental where early consultation for diagnosis is essential to the treatment and prevention of potential complications.

SPECIFIC TIMING OF THE DECISION

Thus it seems that while there is awareness as to the importance of the patient's perceptions and definitions of health and illness requiring medical action, systematic empirical research is scant. Even less is known about the particular set of circumstances which determine *when* the patient comes, although this is of great concern particularly to those studying "patient delay." This is the "Why now" question. Balint's account of case histories (1957) from the doctor's office practice calls attention to the immediate and chronic psychological problems of the patient irrespective of the critical bodily symptom which he "offers" the doctor as his "chief complaint." However, Balint does not distinguish the effects which recent psychological stress may have on bringing the patient to the doctor from the effects on the development of the clinical disorder or symptoms itself. Mechanic and Volkart (1961) have called attention to the analytic importance of distinguishing between the effects of "stress" in producing clinical disorder and symptoms (i.e. headache) from the effects on the act of seeking aid or "tendency to adopt the sick role."

Lindemann (1956) and others interested in social definitions of "mental health" have used the idea of "crisis" as a social psychological concept to describe a temporary disequilibrium in an individual's usual capacity to adapt to new life situations. The occurrence of a "crisis" may be the time when the individual with a clinical disorder "calls for help," and also the time when he is most prepared to receive it. This idea emphasizes a primary interest in the psychosocial adaptation of the individual to his social roles. It expands traditional psychosomatic interest in the etiology of bodily disease and disturbances and clinical interest in the patient's psychopathological traits. In a crisis situation, coming to the doctor may be a way of dealing with the crisis or the disturbances arising from it, and a time when the individual is prepared to accept outside help (Stoeckle and Davidson 1962a). The observations of Hinkle and Wolff (1958) are also suggestive on this point. Their periodic inventories of reported "illness" in selected groups with common work experiences or occupations suggest a "clustering" of illnesses with periods of life stress. Such life stresses have been related to clustering itself, not to etiology of specific disorders nor to coming to the doctor.

Recently workers in the field of "mental health" have also attempted to examine how and why the decision to seek help from psychiatric institutions and professionals was made. The most common research focus has been on the turning-point for the family, their limits of tolerance (Linn 1961; Schwartz 1957). Though the clinical problems in "mental health" are not unlike those of medical practice, this orientation has been used less often to study decisions to seek aid for "physical" complaints at medical institutions and in medical practices. By studying new ambulatory patients in the process of seeking medical aid and by interviewing them prior to their being seen by an examining physician, Zola (1973) attempted to delineate some specific circumstances under which the decision to seek medical aid was made—the trigger, the last straw, the patient's or his family's limit of tolerance. Moreover, by restricting the sample to certain socio-cultural groupings, attempts were made to discover whether the "bases for decision" varied in any systematic way, i.e., whether they might be, in part, socially conditioned, as suggested by the findings of the previously cited works. The analysis of patient decisions showed that even where serious and great debilitation were present, the decision was based on extra-physical grounds.

While these works give us some understanding of the decision to seek medical aid, a caution is necessary. For though some incident or crisis was necessary to get these people to overcome their resistance to seeing a doctor, it does not follow that the occurrence of such crisis or incidents automatically leads to a medical visit. O'Neil (1959) soberly reminds us that the individual has his own ordinary paths to friends, bartenders, and quasi-professionals for dealing with his distress and "crisis." Clinical observations suggest that for some the decision to complain to the doctor may be quite idiosyncratic, like a shopper in a supermarket, an impulse to go to the doctor because the office is near and he is quite accessible. For others it may be like the check-ups of pediatric practice, a scheduled conventional routine of child rearing practice, at least for those who use them. As Mechanic and Volkart (1961) caution, whether or not a person under stress goes to a doctor is more likely to reflect their patterns of *illness behavior* than the nature and quality of stress. It is in the area of patterns of illness behavior that remarkably little is known.

DISCUSSION

This paper has been a highly selective review of some important features in the patient's decision to seek medical aid and as such there are many omissions. Largely ignored are the many studies of patients' utilization of doctors and of their participation in clinics or therapeutic programs. Most participation and utilization studies, while seemingly similar to the initial process of seeking medical advice, are really the repeated use or re-use of the doctor-patient relationship. A selected group of frequent users may bias such studies. This re-use factor reflects as much the demands and concrete influence of the doctor about therapy and "coming back" as the patient's own immediate attentions and needs. "Going back to the doctor" is thus a central problem of chronic care and treatment and a special subject of its own receiving much attention in current studies. Another source of data related to the decision to see a doctor and yet barely touched is the particular choice of physician. In some cases this choice involves the decision between Shaman, minister, herbalist, chiropractor, homeopath, pharmacist, osteopath or physician. In others, it is the choice between types of medical service, between public or private care, general practitioner or specialist, clinic group or solo practice, Doctor X or Doctor Y— choices in medical service about which there is great debate on what is good, better or best. While such research on the medical service market is of great interest in the choice and planning of medical services, space has necessarily limited its review.

Several purposes are served by this limited review. First, it is hoped that avenues of future research have been indicated. This paper is primarily a review of some of the factors influencing the decision to seek medical aid: the perceptions of and beliefs about symptoms, the expectations of medical personnel, and the rationale of the need for medical care. The presentation of so many social science and clinical studies is an attempt to demonstrate this decision is not necessarily idiosyncratic but often rooted in the patient's social background. Such research may also give empirical backing and put in proper perspective the current interest in comprehensive medicine and the possibility, value and need of "treating the total patient." Equally important are the implications of this review for our general thinking about health and illness and thus the structure of medical practice. Much of patient care has been organized on the assumption that those patients coming to the doctor are "the sickest" of the total population. Thus, if an institution or doctor "lost" patients (finding that many did not continue in treatment) or if studies showed many "unmet" medical needs, these facts were easily rationalized; such untreated people were considered not to be very sick nor to need immediate care. If, however, as the above studies document, the characteristic that differentiates patient from non-patient *is not* the seriousness of his complaint nor its treatability then this basic assumption about patient care can hardly be true. Future health care programs, in turn, may be directed towards the non-attending population and attempts to rationalize and plan medical organizations along technical lines may have to bend to social considerations of how the patient sees and uses them. Finally, even though few broad generalizations are possible, this review may make the nature of clinical work more explicit. The studies presented here and clinical experience itself suggests that knowledge of the patient's path to the doctor is an important part of clinical diagnosis and treatment, the doctor's usual implicit considerations which cannot be described by any convenient one-word from the nomenclature of psychiatry and medicine. These facts about the patient often determine whether the individual becomes available for the exercise of clinical skill and treatment. For example, who comes from among those at risk, and then when, where, and what therapeutic intervention is possible? Needless to say, the doctor cannot always treat the etiologic agents of disease or psychopathological trends themselves. Specific therapies as such are limited. But he may more intelligently intervene in the patient's own efforts to cope with his disorder with knowledge of the patient's views of "health," "sickness" and "coming to the doctor." Further descriptions and understanding of these "other" diagnostic features may also help extend the scope of patient care and the maintenance of treatment.

4   *After Everyone Can Pay for Medical Care: Some Perspectives on Future Treatment and Practice*

One of the most important concerns about being sick is how to pay for it. But through legislation and the mass consumption of private insurance, largely financed by industry in exchange for wages on the job, everyone will soon become a paying patient at the doctor's office, the hospital and nursing home and then purely economic barriers to medical care will disappear. In reality, however, financing medical care is only the top portion of an iceberg. As in so many other social, economic, and political problems (our foreign policy being a prime example), money is only a step in the solution of more basic and fundamental problems.

In medical care, even with everyone a paying patient, at least four important problems remain submerged from recognition and debate. (1) Do we want treatment to reach everybody? (2) Does everyone get the best possible treatment? (3) Do we care who treats us? (4) Do we care about the size and location of our hospitals and practices?

Originally appeared as "After Everyone Can Pay for Medical Care—Some Perspectives on Future Treatment and Practice," by John D. Stoeckle and Irving Kenneth Zola, *Medical Care* 2 (1964): 36–41.

DO WE WANT TREATMENT TO
REACH EVERYBODY?

Our treatment institutions, our hospitals, clinics and medical practices, have traditionally viewed the public who did not seek medical aid as being relatively healthy or certainly not very sick. For, if they really were, they would come to the doctor. Similar views have been expressed about patients who did not regularly keep their appointments, who broke off in the midst of treatment or who did not wait around in a waiting-room or on a waiting list. Yet many studies and observations of those who are not going to the doctor have revealed a high prevalence of sickness, disease, and disability. In one recent industrial survey some 90 percent of the workers were found with treatable but untreated disorders. No one knows how large is this population with unmet needs that does not seek medical aid, that is apathetic about getting treatment, that procrastinates in going to the doctor; but it has been estimated at near some 40,000,000 Americans. What is more important is the fact that this population of non-users, slow users, treatment drop-outs, is found predominantly, but not only, in our lower socio-economic classes. The irony of unmet medical needs in a country of plenty was shown in a recent survey of one ef our major cities, where it was noted that those with greatest medical care needs for example, the elderly and other low income, and "minority" groups—have the lowest recognition of their medical needs and the longest duration of care once it is initiated.

REASONS FOR NON-ATTENDANCE

Again and again health surveys have demonstrated that the section of our population that does not participate in immunization campaigns or take preventive action—cancer check-ups, going to the doctor early, mass X-rays—is not a random one. Investigators have emphasized the potential patient's contribution to this problem and have studied the characteristics of this non-attending population. They have pointed out their lack of psychological readiness, their lack of medical knowledge, their fear of seeking medical aid, their negative views of treatment and of the doctor, clinic or hospital delivering medical services, and finally, their personal (that is, idiosyncratic) and very unscientific ideas about being sick or healthy.

Too often, however, it appears as if this delay or unwillingness to seek help is all the patient's fault. Yet some of it is fostered, at least indirectly, by the health professions. The reasons, of course, are manifold. One is our activist overemphasis on dramatic "cures" fostering unrealistic expectations on the part of much of our population. Either one does not have to worry because the illness can easily be cured, or the condition is hopeless and nothing can be done. These black and white expectations have not only blinded us to the necessity and appreciation of the importance of preventive measures but have also led to considerable unwillingness to embark on any long-term course of treatment which will not lead to a "complete cure." The potential patient is often unenthusiastic about continuing in a course of long-term treatment which guarantees at most only remission, control, or relief, and physicians, trained in a framework of specific techniques and skills to cure or remove certain acute conditions, may find the treatment of chronically ill patients unsatisfying and so neglect it.

Another reason treatment may not reach everyone is professional reliance on the lay decision to go to the doctor. The patients who come to see him may not be all the people who can be treated. Medical advances appear more and more capable of detecting disease or its precursors in asymptomatic populations. To rely on testing only those coming to the doctor will not, of course, find all the treatable cases. Large-scale mass testing will be necessary. So often, too, medical seriousness of a patient's symptoms may not be the major factor getting him to the doctor. In fact, he may be unaware of or ignore early symptoms of sickness.

Since there may also be a general reluctance to see a doctor, it may be necessary to reevaluate what aspects of health and illness can truly be left to individual initiative and to what extent the health professions are willing and able to assume more initiative and responsibility for the initial steps in detection and treatment. Just sitting in the office waiting for the patient will not reach all the public. In the same way as getting alcoholics into treatment, some people will have to be educated, some coaxed, some led, and some sought out.

SOLUTIONS TO THE PROBLEM

Today the social-welfare value of making medical services available to everyone is generally accepted. While removing financial barriers to such services will help to make them more accessible, this will not lead automatically to mass participation. As we have stressed, more attention will have to be paid to the segment of unrecognized treatable illness and the reasons for the lack of action by many of us in seeking medical aid. Such facts will provoke questions about how our treatment institutions can work better and how our population's views of sickness and seeking help might be changed. But easy solutions and answers are not at hand. They will have to encompass (1) realistic health education, particularly of children, which would result in realistic expectations of patients and their families, particularly regarding the more chronic disorders, (2) development of treatment techniques and services acceptable to and able to reach different segments of the population and illness groups who may customarily avoid treatment, and (3) improving the availability of treatment, not just for the individual patient in the doctor's office but for everybody in his group— whether at school, the company office, the factory plant, his housing project or home—whatever medical resources of detection, prevention, diagnosis and treatment can practically be brought to bear.

DOES EVERYONE GET THE BEST POSSIBLE TREATMENT?

Up to this point our concerns have been what illnesses or potential patients do not come to the attention of a doctor when we aim that treatment should reach everyone. But what of those that do come? Does everyone get the best of our services or are there differences in treatment and services unrelated to the patient's diagnosis? We do not have to look very far for objective examples of different treatment. A walk around our cities will often reveal how marginal are the facilities of many municipal hospitals compared to the superior facilities of private voluntary ones. Even the historical basis of our private voluntary hospitals with their built-in differential service to "charity" patients is only slowly disappearing, hastened a bit by the paying status of the consumer. What confronts the patient here may still run the gamut from shabby surroundings, detailed questioning on his "means" and resources, to delays and inconvenient scheduling of diagnostic and treatment service.

DIFFERENTIAL TREATMENT

Other examples of differential treatment have been documented. In a recent survey of hospital care in New York City, experts rated privately owned, proprietary, profit-making hospitals poorer in standards of care than voluntary or government hospitals. That treatment was not solely related to the patient's need based on psychiatric diagnosis but also to his social class has been documented in Hollingshead and Redlich's much quoted study of psychiatric care. With the same diagnosis higher-class patients received psychotherapy while lower class patients were given more organic forms of treatment.

Similar observations about bias in the medical diagnosis have been made among patients from different ethnic backgrounds. Among patients seen at three medical clinics, *despite* the same objective degree of psychological difficulties, emotionally caused symptoms were diagnosed more often in Italian as compared to Irish and Anglo-Saxon patients. Such problems of communication between patient and doctor may lead to under-diagnosis of treatable medical diseases. And some observers feel that when patients are treated in any bureaucratic and institutional setting they get less treatment—that is, less personal attention—than when they are treated in a private office. All these studies demonstrate that the quality of treatment in our country is not only uneven but that it is influenced by important historical and sociological conditions.

SOCIAL-PSYCHOLOGICAL FACTORS

Even our legislation has a narrow orientation toward medical care, in spite of evidence to the contrary that good care and treatment is not just medical. It has become clearer, but often not an acknowledged fact, that the problems of patients presenting at medical institutions and medical practices are social and psychological in important respects. Many recent studies have shown that the patient's decision to see a doctor is rarely based only on his medical symptoms or his knowledge about diseases, but more often on important events and factors in his family situation and social relationships. Other studies have shown similar influences in the decisions to undergo surgery, to re-hospitalize mental patients, and to place old people in nursing homes. Likewise, it is becoming increasingly difficult to ignore the widespread prevalence of emotional and psychological distress and disability. Whether we take the results of national opinion surveys on where people take their acknowledged personal concerns, reports of mental distress in morbidity surveys of residents in mid-town Manhattan, the Jersey suburbs and rural America, or the experience of doctors in practice, social-psychological factors in illness and patient care are large. When such factors are unrecognized and untreated by the physician it prevents rational diagnosis and handicaps the patient treatment.

The scientific understanding and handling of these aspects of illness, so important for future practice in the community, are still a matter of much debate in the education and training of the doctor.

The curriculum and training experiences are already crowded with medical subject matter and medical orientation for practice in the hospital. Since training for practice in the community is not in itself an acknowledged aim and since hospital clinical care and research departments play so large a role in what is taught, curriculum additions dealing with the psychosocial study of illness and patient care are, in spite of their documented need, considered unnecessary.

Solutions to differential treatment (like making sure that everyone receives treatment) will have to encompass the patient, the public, and the professions. Where education contributes to professional treatment skill there is need not only for upgrading traditional medical teaching in some schools but for greater recognition of their responsibility to the community and of the need for newer programs in the social study of illness and disease. Yet, as George Silver (1958) argues, education alone may not be translated into an improvement of treatment unless an appropriate organization—the family medical team—is developed to apply social skills and preventive medicine.

DO WE CARE WHO TREATS US?

Our nation's professional journals carry endless definitions of professional specializations, of limited and exclusive enclosures of competence, of the role of doctor, nurse, social worker and a host of sub-specialists within the professions themselves. No role, in turn, is more discussed than that of the doctor, and that of various types of doctors. Much of our thinking and planning of patient care centers on the transfer of the doctor's functions into an institutional setting, a big clinic or a group practice, or the division of his functions among various practitioners in the community. Complaints are frequently made that there is too much division of treatment labor among specialists, that there is no one doctor for everyone in the family, that there is no "personal doctor" to deal with the more intimate problems and concerns, that no one practitioner is available for initial medical aid, advice, and direction to other sources for help, that physicians are too busy to give "physicals" to healthy individuals or to be interested in the early detection and prevention of disease, that the doctor's office is located farther and farther away from the neighborhood and home, or that emergency round-the-clock help is no longer available. These are important care-taking and treatment functions of the family doctor, who has largely disappeared in fact but not in fancy.

To want a family doctor may no longer be a question of choice.

The question that needs to be asked is how are his functions being met in our organizations and patterns of specialization. Many of these essential functions are now in several hands. Much of the public, at least in the middle-class suburbs, seems to be using multiple "specialists" for health care needs at different periods of life: the pediatrician for the children and the baby; the obstetrician-gynecologist for delivery and the mother's check-ups; and the internist for the mother's, father's and grandparents' "medical troubles." Every "specialist" may be expected to take on some of the functions of the family doctor at times, and yet their professional training and orientation does not acknowledge this and their own definition as specialists deals only with technical diagnostic questions about the patient.

This problem becomes exacerbated as medical men increasingly specialize and as the lay population becomes more medically sophisticated and so goes directly to specialists or asks to be referred. This will not be "bad" if the patient's "other problems" and concerns are recognized and he is directed to a suitable source of help. But since there will often be no family physician to whom the specialist can return such patients when these other problems arise, he will have to deal with them himself—a situation for which his medical education may have left him largely unprepared.

ANCILLARY PROFESSIONS

While much debate is centered on how the various medical specialists should be related, a still more fundamental issue concerns the transfer and division of functions among other health professions, who may do diagnostic and therapeutic work. It is in this area that what is truly "team medicine" may develop. The expectation, however, that the doctor, as "the specialist" of the team, will deal only with the complicated medical aspects of the patient, leaving personal concerns to the nurse and social worker, and ordinary diagnostic skills to the technicians, is not a likely possibility. This might seem a rational division of the technical skills of the team, but there will be social limits. For example, the patient, in seeking help, will not always view the professions as they see themselves nor be able to diagnose his illness and choose or accept the right kind of help. Called to see a patient vomiting at night, the doctor may come upon a family quarrel and a crisis over the behavior of a child. Some would argue that the family called the wrong person, that it should have called the psychiatrist or the social worker. But since the call for help was in response to a child's vomiting, it is unlikely that anyone other than a medical man would have been called and expected to cope with such a crisis.

There is, however, another side to this coin: it concerns the limits of competence of the community practitioner. Psychosomatic complaints and physical symptoms of behaviour disorders are most likely to come to the attention of physicians and may require some medical surveillance and be subject to rational psychological treatment. Yet there is no evidence that more general behavioral problems are most appropriately treated by "medical men" as they are now trained. Some would even contend that the psychological training of a Ph.D. clinical psychologist is often more extensive than that of many psychiatrists and certainly of most physicians. Whether behavioral problems such as delinquency, malingering, anti-social acts and even much of what is called neurotic should be considered "illness" and therefore under the sole dominion of the medical professions has been questioned by at least one psychiatrist, Thomas Szasz.

PUBLIC HEALTH NURSE

A less noticeable transfer and fractionization of medical duties is taking place in still another sphere. As our professions specialize and centralize—for example, at hospitals and medical centers—as they limit the hours they work and the calls they make—for example, no house calls—and as we fail to train enough doctors or to organize health personnel for the needs of the population, makeshift solutions in treatment develop. For instance, the public health nurse is filling a doctor-gap for large segments of our lower socio-economic classes, as well as for still larger populations abroad. She has become a sort of second-choice-doctor—giving some emergency treatment, teaching health care and prevention, and doing a considerable amount of family counseling. Since it is rarely recognised or acknowledged that she is engaged in such tasks, she is often without connecting links to any chain of medical practice and lacks the face-to-face communication with colleagues that is important in patient care. One of the dangers of being outside any network of medical practice is the lack of informal supervision of the quality of patient care which ordinarily occurs through mutual consultation and interchange among professional staffs. Whether she will ultimately become the "family doctor" of choice is inextricably entwined with the degree to which doctors will continue to withdraw from and reject such duties.

Thus, who takes care of the patient—the division of labor of medical practice—will utlimately depend on the patients' views of their illness and of the professionals they seek to treat them as well as on the internal needs of professionals themselves. Fractionization of medical care has already and inevitably taken place. Much of the current dissatisfaction is due more to ineffective communication between therapists and their lack of coordination and "team-work" than to any inherent "badness" in a division of treatment itself. Unwillingness to recognize this phenomenon has resulted in scant attention being paid to how immediate medical aid can be organized, what treatment can and should be coordinated, who can treat personal concerns and behavioral problems, how exclusively "specialistic" should a specialist's training and education be—to what, in fact, is the appropriate use of other professions whether they be behavioral scientists, human relations experts, or public health nurses. As long as these problems are not even acknowledged, effective planning of treatment is impossible.

DO WE CARE ABOUT THE SIZE AND LOCATION OF OUR HOSPITALS AND PRACTICES?

Not because of "specialization" but because of rising costs, the work of hospitals has also been scrutinized. Demands are made to restrict the hospital as a sick-bed institution only to the performance of technical procedures required in complicated diagnosis and treatment of acute illness. At the same time, the hospital has been taking on other functions besides bed care and maintaining a "sick room away from home." For example, all phases of illness— from the acute attack to convalescence, rehabilitation, chronic care, and terminal stages—have increasingly become hospital functions. There has also been a greater recognition of the care and treatment which can be organized for a patient without hospitalization. Certainly more medical care is possible with ambulant patients, in out-patient clinics and offices, although such functions rarely receive the public, professional, or institutional support which the bed functions do.

All these trends make the hospital a bigger and bigger "center," a diversified organization with more care-taking services on its grounds. However, the mere bringing of all care-taking services to hospital grounds does not guarantee that nursing home, chronic disease treatment, and ambulatory care will, in turn, get better facilities, better professional staff, better organization of treatment, and more investment. The hospital as an institution has its own priorities and can just as well neglect certain treatment functions as the community at large.

PROCESS OF CENTRALIZATION

How the bigger hospitals grow will also determine the future existence of our small local hospitals and local practices where much general care is given and where many patients prefer to attend. It will depend on whether there is merely centralization of facilities and services and practices—witness the private practice office buildings moving to hospital grounds—or whether there is growth through more effective integration and alliance with and among smaller local community institutions and practices. The trend to add and centralize more and more activities in the hospital grounds will certainly make some of our traditional local hospitals and practices less important, but growth by cooperation and integration should not have this effect. "Reorganization" has become the shorthand for this cooperative organization of medical services in a community. Unfortunately, in some situations it has only meant dividing up clientele area, thus limiting medical competition among big hospitals. It may, however, mean a brake on duplication, on the purchase of expensive equipment by each of several hospitals, and the selected development of expensive therapies. And it can mean even more—such as the development of working relationships among institutions and medical practices, for the management of illness and disability in an urban treatment area. An important yet intangible by-product could be the informal supervision of the quality of patient care in the community that can occur through mutual consultation and interchange among professional staffs, managers and the lay boards alike. Now they so often work in relative isolation.

MENTAL HEALTH CARE

Finally, we might want our hospitals to grow in still another way. For example, a major concern of our hospital staffs, managers and boards might be whether our traditional medical institutions, whose practices are in reality concerned as much with mental health, should include treatment departments, divisions, and even special hospital units for social and psychiatric care. Such health care has long been an implicit function of the work of the personal doctor or "GP," but as a hospital function, it has developed into special mental institutions parallel to but separate from our general medical ones. Large-scale psychiatric services, particularly in in-patient care, is still a comparatively rare phenomenon in a general hospital.

Some would say that to join these traditionally separate systems is too difficult an alliance both idelogically and practically. For example, mental institutions and psychiatric care have been financed through taxes and thus have a history and background different from that of the community's general voluntary hospitals with their history of private financing. However, even these differences are disappearing. As voluntary hospitals rely more and more on patient-care receipts and government programs, they are becoming increasingly like traditional public institutions, at least in financing. Another similarity is administrative management. Mental hospitals are taking on discharge and treatment policies and practices like general hospitals, returning many chronic patients to the community. Recent studies have shown that for many psychiatric patients hospitalization in a general hospital has distinct treatment advantages and that their care can be managed with minimal disruption of hospital routine. Notwithstanding differences that still exist, if demands and needs for health care are not just medical but also psychosocial, then the integration of these parallel services is a major public concern.

SOLO PRACTICE

The question of centralization of functions in the hospital has its counterpart in the current debates about medical practice. Perhaps in fear of the growing tentacles of the hospital or medical center, there is concern about whether solo *entrepreneurial* practice, a more dominant style of organization in our country, is suitable for the complexities of patient care as opposed to group practice where medical specialization is formally organised for treatment. Will the solo practitioner, the individual firm, the medical small business, like the corner grocer, be swallowed up by or affiliate with a big chain like a group practice or clinic? And, if he does join, will he contract his skills to the group or *entrepreneur* within it?

The alternatives in organization have always been pictured as either one system or another, private practice or "government medicine," solo or contractual practice. For example, it seems clear that even individual solo practice has already done many things which make ideological views outdated—it has remained as an informal network of colleague practices, it has formed into group practice units, and even contracted for medical care of groups. Some have also located on the hospital's grounds as a big private *entrepreneurial* business, alongside more contractual forms of group practice and clinics. Large clinics with contractual practice have also sprung up in response to the needs of the blocks of consumers found in industry, unions, and colleges. Harvard, for example, has organized a pre-paid in-plant medical service for students, faculty and employees with contractual services of doctors.

This retail view of practice and organization may not appeal to us when we are dealing with such charged transactions as our own health, illness and treatment. However, it may caution us against too ideological a commitment to one form of practice for everybody. It may also modify views which regard only our own consumer choice as ideal and all others as undesirable, without a real respect for other choices in the domestic scene. When it comes to actual facts about what organization is best, we often adhere to traditional concepts with little evidence as to what actually works best for whom.

But there are many other public concerns about organization of medical practice. Equally important is its location—at the hospital, the school, the plant—in addition to the traditional location in the neighborhood or downtown. Medical practices at these institutional sites, in contrast to the *entrepreneurial* organization of private practice, have usually been contractual, with the doctors as employees. Practitioners at these sites have always been ambivalent about the scope and depth of their medical services to their clientele. Should they provide personal and comprehensive health services or restrict themselves to job-related injuries and employment examinations? The uneasiness in deciding to do the former has been due to the fear of competing with private practice. To add to the dilemma, recent research has documented the importance of the work situation in the individual's physical and psychological health. Surely, if we hope to reach everyone, these on-the-spot sites may be realistic ways of offering personal and preventive medical services, and our traditional ambivalence about competition will have to give way to concern about availability and consumption of services.

EPILOGUE

Remembering the high prevalence of treated and untreated symptoms and disorders, cited previously, there are those who claim that we cannot treat everything. There are others who note that there is probably a great deal we should not treat such as many self-limiting disorders—for example, minor burns, some communicable childhood diseases, unnecessary tonsillectomies. The task of treatment is indeed monumental, for the very progress and development of man introduces new dangers, new agents of disease. Man experiments with synthetic products and changes his diet; he constructs cities that breed rats and infection; he builds automobiles, factories, and bombs which pollute the air. When one disease or disorder is controlled, its control mechanism may produce the breeding ground for still another disease. As Rene Dubos contends, the goal of complete freedom from disease and struggle is almost incompatible with the progress of living; so also with medical care. Whether we should strive to provide medical care for everything is impossible to say. Until we recognize that illness and health is more than the mere presence or absence of symptoms, that seeking medical aid is more than reactive behavior to symptoms, and the health professions' responsibility is more than to wait for patients and then to treat these symptoms, our solutions for providing medical care will only be stopgaps.

With more and more possibilities of therapeutic intervention for everything, a philosophy of medicine is needed to define what is "good medical care," comprehensive care or the "best medical care in the world." While medical care experts can furnish us with measurements of the quality and quantity of treatment, we also need to consider our directions, for example, the other problems produced by the technical capacity to prevent death at any cost in old age, the values of genetic counselling particularly in regard to the problem of treating congenital defects, or the use of the medical services to meet personal needs—that is, as a "refuge in a storm"—as much as we need to consider utilitarian demands of keeping people healthy and on the job.

Finally, it is often complained that the government will set the policies regarding medical care and practice. The basic problems besetting medical care, however, are neither financial nor administrative, but the professional and public needs and aspirations. In this commentary specific solutions have not been suggested but several important issues, often submerged from view, have been discussed. Only when such issues are recognized can solutions be found: and only then can we claim to provide not only the best medical care but the best possible medical care.

Part Three

The Proof Is in the Tasting: Empirical Data and Generalizations

5 *Data, Data, Data*

The following articles contain the major empirical findings of my first study on patient decision-making —my Massachusetts General Hospital work. Their publication dates are deceptive; the wide discrepancies reflect the exigencies of publishing more than anything else. As the reader is aware, the work was essentially completed in 1962. Why then the long delay in getting it out? First of all, the pressure was off. We had published the earlier papers hoping to influence people in the medical field. Also, I'd published pieces of it elsewhere (Stoeckle, Zola, and Davidson 1963, 1964; Zola 1963 b,c, 1964), so much of the work was already made public. A second set of factors related to my career. In the fall of 1963, I became an assistant professor in the Department of Sociology, Brandeis University. As with so many young academics, the responsibilities of a first full-time teaching position were more overwhelming that I had anticipated. Not only was I faced with creating new under-graduate courses, but also with supervising the work of many graduate students in the required first-year field work course. This was particularly scary since many of the students were my own age. In addition, the department was rapidly growing (this was the 1960s—a time when we thought universities would continually expand), and I found myself appointed to various committees. There were other responsibilities. I had long been interested in educational administration, and during my second year at Brandeis I accepted the invitation of Morrie Schwartz, then Chair, to be his administrative assistant. I continued in this post under his successor, Jack Seeley. Were this not enough, I had been awarded a large research grant. Aside from the time required to be its Principal Investigator (chapter 11), I was for awhile lulled into thinking that this new data would update my previous work, and that all of it together would make an impressive book. When in 1965 I realized that these hopes were false, I hastened to publish the original work.

"Culture and Symptoms" (chapter 6), which some regard as my best and "most scholarly" piece, was based heavily on Chapter 3 of my dissertation. Although I recognize its academic quality, it is by no means my favorite article. It is far too dry. Moreover, I have always been more interested in decision-making than in symptomatology. I did realize, however, that this article provided the scholarly, empirical legitimation for much of my later work. Yet professional acceptance was neither swift nor easy, even for this so-called "classic." When I first presented the findings, some accused me of being racist because the results could be used to perpetuate ethnic stereotypes. Even fellow sociologists were rather critical, and the paper required considerable revision before the *American Sociological Review* deemed it worthy of publication.

"Pathways to The Doctor" (chapter 7) was written as a companion piece to "Culture and Symptoms," but expressly for oral presentation in a lecture series. This accounts both for its less formal style and its speedy acceptance for publication in a collection of essays. Two years later, however, the book was withdrawn from publication. In the meantime I was receiving frequent invitations to deliver the essay as a speech. When one of these occasions resulted in an invitation to publish in still another collection of original articles, I accepted. Again I was to be disappointed. After a delay of three years this book also failed to appear. Resubmitted a third time, some seven years after being written, it finally saw daylight. I never really revised it, however, and though its data remained relevant, the references were hardly up-to-date.

The next article, "The Problems of Communication. . ." (chapter 8) is one of my favorites because it enabled me to range far beyond the original research, and in particular to use much of the observational data I had collected by virtue of merely being present at Massachusetts General. It was also the major empirical precursor to my later work on medicine as an institution of social control. For the first time I was able to document the tremendous power of doctors to use labels, and the generally nonmedical grounds on which some of their diagnoses were based. My smugness (but not my pride) was punctured about fifteen years afterwards when I reread this article and saw a significant finding that I had missed. That finding is related in chapter 9.

The following article, "The Mirage of Health Revisited" (chapter 10), resulted from what I call a throw-away insight. In "Culture and Symptoms" (Zola 1966, p. 616) I made the following statement:

> Such data as these give an unexpected statistical picture of illness. Instead of it being a relatively infrequent or abnormal phenomenon, the empirical reality may be that illness, defined as the presence of clinically serious symptoms, is the statistical *norm*.

Though I thought I was merely restating an insight of Edwin Lemert (1951), its application to the field of medicine was and still is controversial. In subsequent years I expanded upon the point in various papers and continued to collect data bearing upon it. In 1972 an opportunity arose to assemble all this information in one piece, which appears here as my most extensive discussion of that issue.

Part III concludes with "An Error in Research Judgment," (chapter 11) a rather chastening reflection on follow-up research that got out of hand.

6   *Culture and Symptoms: An Analysis of Patients' Presenting Complaints*

THE CONCEPTION OF DISEASE

In most epidemiological studies, the definition of disease is taken for granted. Yet today's chronic disorders to not lend themselves to such easy conceptualization and measurement as did the contagious disorders of yesteryear. That we have long assumed that what constitutes disease *is* a settled matter is due to the tremendous medical and surgical advances of the past half century. After the current battles against cancer, heart disease, cystic fibrosis and the like have been won, Utopia, a world without disease, would seem right around the next corner. Yet after each battle a new enemy seems to emerge. So often has this been the pattern, that some have wondered whether life without disease is attainable (Dubos 1961).

Usually the issue of life without disease has been dismissed as a philosophical problem—a dismissal made considerably easier by our general assumptions about the statistical distribution of disorder. For though there is a grudging recognition that each of us must go sometime, illness is generally assumed to be a relatively infrequent, unusual, or abnormal phenomenon. Moreover, the general kinds of statistics used to describe illness support such an assumption. Spe-

Originally appeared as "Culture and Symptoms—An Analysis of Patients' Presenting Complaints," *American Sociological Review* 31 (1966): 615–630.

cifically diagnosed conditions, days out of work, and doctor visits do occur for each of us relatively infrequently. Though such statistics represent only treated illness, we rarely question whether such data give a true picture. Implicit is the further notion that people who do not consult doctors and other medical agencies (and thus do not appear in the "illness" statistics) may be regarded as healthy.

Yet studies have increasingly appeared which note the large number of disorders escaping detection. Whether based on physicians' estimates or on the recall of lay populations, the proportion of untreated disorders amounts to two-thirds or three-fourths of all existing conditions. That these high figures or disorder include a great many minor problems is largely irrelevant. The latter are nevertheless disorders, clinical entities, and may even be the precursors of more medically serious difficulties. The most reliable data, however, comes from periodic health examinations and community "health" surveys. At least two such studies have noted that as much as 90 percent of their apparently healthy sample had some physical aberration or clinical disorder (Pearse and Crocker 1949; Schenthal 1960). Moreover, neither the type of disorder, nor the seriousness by objective medical standards, differentiated those who felt sick from those who did not. In one of the above studies, even of those who felt sick, only 40 percent were under medical care (Pearse and Crocker 1949). It seems that the more intensive the investigation, the higher the prevalence of clinically serious but previously undiagnosed and untreated disorders. [See chapter 10 for more detailed discussion as well as references on this issue.]

Such data as these give an unexpected statistical pictrure of illness. Instead of it being a relatively infrequent or abnormal phenomenon, the empirical reality may be that illness, defined as the presence of clinically serious symptoms, is the statistical norm. Consider the following computation of Hinkle et al. (1960). They noted that the average lower-middle-class male between the ages of 20 and 45 experiences over a 20-year period approximately one life-endangering illness, 20 disabling illnesses, 200 non-disabling illnesses, and 1,000 symptomatic episodes. These total 1,221 episodes over 7,305 days or one new episode every six days. And this figure takes no account of the duration of a particular condition, nor does it consider any disorder of which the respondent may be unaware. In short, even among a supposedly "healthy" population scarcely a day goes by wherein they would not be able to report a symptomatic experience.

What is particularly striking about this line of reasoning is that the statistical notions underlying many "social" pathologies are similarly being questioned. A number of social scientists have noted that the basic acts or deviations, such as law-breaking (Murphy et al. 1946), addictive behaviors, sexual "perversions" (Kinsey et al. 1953), or mental illness (Srole et al. 1962; Leighton et al. 1963) occur so frequently in the population that were one to tabulate all the deviations that people possess or engage in, virtually no one could escape the label of "deviant."

Why are so relatively few potential "deviants" labelled such or, more accurately, why do so few come to the attention of official agencies? Perhaps the focus on how or why a particular deviation arose in the first place might be misplaced; an equally important issue for research might be the individual and societal reaction to the deviation once it occurs (Becker 1963; Erikson 1962; Goffman 1963). Might it then be the differential response to deviation rather than the prevalence of the deviation which accounts for many reported group and subgroup differences? A similar set of questions can be asked in regard to physical illness. Given that the prevalence of clinical abnormalities is so high and the rate of acknowledgment so low, how representative are "the treated" of all those with a particular condition? Given further that what *is* treated seems unrelated to what would usually be thought the objective situation, i.e., seriousness, disability and subjective discomfort, is it possible that some selective process is operating in what gets counted or tabulated as illness?

THE INTERPLAY OF CULTURE AND "SYMPTOMS"

Holding in abeyance the idea that many epidemiological differences may in fact be due to as yet undiscovered etiological forces, we may speculate on how such differences come to exist, or how a selective process of attention may operate. Upon surveying many cross-cultural comparisons of morbidity, I concluded that there are at least two ways in which signs ordinarily defined as indicating problems in one population may be ignored in others. The first is related to the actual prevalence of the sign, and the second to its congruence with dominant or major value-orientations.

In the first instance, when the aberration is fairly widespread, this, in itself, might constitute a reason for its not being considered "symptomatic" or unusual. Among many Mexican-Americans in the Southwestern United States, diarrhea, sweating, and coughing are everyday experiences (Clark 1958), while among certain groups of

Greeks trachoma is almost universal (Blum 1960). Even within our own society, Koos (1954) has noted that, although lower back pain is a quite common condition among lower-class women, it is not considered symptomatic of any disease or disorder but part of their expected everyday existence. For the population where the particular condition is ubiquitous, the condition is perceived as the normal state (Ackerknecht 1947; Raper 1958). This does not mean that it is considered "good" (although instances have been noted where not having the endemic condition was considered abnormal) but rather that it is natural and inevitable and thus to be ignored as being of no consequence. For example, Ackerknecht (1947) noted that pinto (dichromic spirochetosis), a skin disease, was so common among South American tribes that the few single men who were not suffering from it were regarded as pathological to the degree of being excluded from marriage. In such instances where the "symptom" or condition is omnipresent (it always was and always will be) there simply exists for such populations or cultures no frame of reference according to which it could be considered a deviation. It is no doubt partly for this reason that many public health programs flounder when transported *in toto* to a foreign culture. In such a situation, when an outside authority comes in and labels a particularly highly prevalent condition a disease, and, as such, both abnormal and preventable, he is postulating an external standard of evaluation which, for the most part, is incomprehensible to the receiving culture. To them it simply has no cognitive reality.

In the second process, it is the "fit" of certain signs with a society's major values which accounts for the degree of attention they receive. For example, in some nonliterate societies there is anxiety-free acceptance of the willingness to describe hallucinatory experiences. Wallace (1959) noted that in such societies that fact of hallucination *per se* is seldom disturbing; its content is the focus of interest. In Western society, however, with its emphasis on rationality and control, the very admission of hallucinations is commonly taken to be a grave sign and, in some literature, regarded as the essential feature of psychosis. In such instances it is not the sign itself or its frequency which is significant but the social context within which it occurs and within which it is perceived and understood. Even more explicit workings of this process can be seen in the interplay of "symptoms" and social roles. Tiredness, for example, is a physical sign which is not only ubiquitous but a correlate of a vast number of disorders. Yet amongst a group of the author's students who kept a calendar noting all bodily states and conditions, tiredness, though often recorded, was rarely cited as a cause for concern. Attending school and being among peers who stressed the importance of hard work and achievement, almost as an end in itself, tiredness, rather than being an indication of something being wrong was instead positive proof that they were doing right. If they were tired, it must be because they had been working hard. In such a setting tiredness would rarely, in itself, be either a cause for concern, a symptom, or a reason for action or seeking medical aid (Carter 1965). On the other hand, where arduous work is not gratifying in and of itself, tiredness would more likely be a matter of concern and perhaps medical attention. Such a problem is often the presenting complaint of the "trapped housewife" syndrome (Friedan 1963; Gordon, Gordon, and Gunther 1962). I realize, of course, that tiredness here might be more related to depression than any degree of physical exertion. But this does not alter how it is perceived and reacted to once it occurs.

Also illustrative of this process are the divergent perceptions of those bodily complaints often referred to as "female troubles." Nausea is a common and treatable concomitant of pregnancy, yet Margaret Mead (1950) records no morning sickness among the Arapesh. Her data suggest that this may be related to the almost complete denial that a child exists, until shortly before birth. In a Christian setting, where the existence of life is dated from conception, nausea becomes the external sign, hope and proof that one is pregnant. Thus in the United States, this symptom is not only quite widespread but is also an expected and almost welcome part of pregnancy. A quite similar phenomenon is the recognition of dysmenorrhea. While Arapesh women reported no pain during menstruation, quite the contrary is reported in the United States (Mead 1949). Interestingly enough the only consistent factor related to its manifestation among American women was a learning one— those that manifested it reported having observed it in other women during their childhood. The fact that one has to learn that something is painful or unpleasant has been noted elsewhere. Mead reports that in causalgia a given individual suffers and reports pain because she is *aware* of uterine contractions and not because of the occurrence of these contractions. Becker (1963) and others studying addictive behaviors have noted not only that an individual has to learn that the experience is pleasurable but also that a key factor in becoming addicted is the recognition of the association of withdrawal symptoms with the lack of drugs. Among medical patients who had been heavily dosed and then withdraw, even though they experience symptoms as a result of withdrawal, they may attribute them to their general convalescent aches and pains. Schacter and Singer (1962) have reported a series of experiments where epinephrine-injected subjects defined their mood as euphoria or anger depending on whether they spent time with a euphoric or angry stooge. Subjects without injections reported no such change in mood responding to these same social situations. This led them to the contention that the diversity of human emotional experiences stems from differential labelling of similar physical sensations.

From such examples as these, it seems likely that the degree of recognition and treatment of certain gynecological problems may be traced to the prevailing definition of what constitutes "the necessary part of the business of being a woman." That such divergent definitions are still operative is shown by two studies. In the first, 78 mothers of lower socioeconomic status were required to keep health calendars over a four-week period. Despite the instruction to report *all* bodily states and dysfunctions, only 14 noted even the occurrence of menses or its accompaniments (Kosa et al. 1965). A second study, done on a higher socioeconomic group yielded a different expression of the same phenomenon. Over a period of several years I have collected four-week health calendars from students. The women in the sample had at least a college education and virtually all were committed to careers in the behavioral sciences. Within this group there was little failure to report menses. Very often medication was taken for the discomforts of dysmenorrhea. Moreover, this group was so psychologically sophisticated or self-conscious that they interpreted or questioned most physical signs or symptoms as attributable to some psychosocial stress. There was only one exception—dysmenorrhea. Thus, even in this "culturally advantaged" group, this seemed a sign of a bodily condition so ingrained in what one psychiatrist has called "the masochistic character of her sex" that the woman does not ordinarily subject it to analysis.

In the opening section of this paper, I presented evidence that a selective process might well be operating in what symptoms are brought to the doctor. I also noted that it might be this selective process and not an etiological one which accounts for the many unexplained or over-explained epidemiological differences observed between and within societies. For example, Saxon Graham (1956) noted a significantly higher incidence of hernia among men whose backgrounds were Southern European (Italy or Greece) as compared with Eastern European (Austria, Czechoslovakia, Russia or Poland). Analysis of the occupations engaged in by these groups revealed no evidence that the Southern Europeans in the sample were more engaged in strenuous physical labor than the Eastern Europeans. From what is known of tolerance to hernia, I suggest that for large segments of the population, there may be no differences in the actual incidence and prevalence of hernia but that in different groups different perceptions of the same signs may lead to dissimilar ways of handling them. Thus the Southern Europeans in Graham's sample may have been more concerned with problems in this area of the body, and have sought aid more readily (and therefore appear more frequently in the morbidity statistics). Perhaps the Southern Europeans are acting quite rationally and consistently while the other groups are so threatened or ashamed that they tend to deny or mask such symptoms and thus keep themselves out of the morbidity statistics.

There may even be no "real" differences in the prevalence rates of many deviations. In studying the rates of peptic ulcer among African tribal groups Raper (1958) first confirmed the stereotype that it was relatively infrequent among such groups and therefore that it was associated (as many had claimed) with the stresses and strains of modern living. Yet when he relied not on reported diagnosis but on autopsy data, he found that the scars of peptic ulcer were no less common than in Britain. He (Raper 1958 P.544) concluded: "There is no need to assume that in backward communities peptic ulcer does not develop; it is only more likely to go undetected because the conditions that might bring it to notice do not exist."

Selective processes such as these are probably present at all the stages through which an individual and his condition must pass before he ultimately gets counted as "ill." In this section I have focussed on one of these stages, the perception of a particular bodily state as a symptom, and have delineated two possible ways in which the culture or social setting might influence the awareness of something as abnormal and thus its eventual tabulation in medical statistics.

SAMPLE SELECTION AND METHODOLOGY

The investigation to be reported here is not an attempt to prove that the foregoing body of reasoning is correct but rather to demonstrate the fruitfulness of the orientation in understanding the problems of health and illness. This study reports the existence of a selective process in what the patient "brings" to a doctor. The selectiveness is analyzed not in terms of differences in diseases but rather in terms of differences in responses to essentially similar disease entities.

Specifically, this paper is a documentation of the influence of "culture" (in this case ethnic-group membership) on "symptoms" (the complaints a patient presents to his physician). The measure of "culture" was fairly straightforward. The importance of ethnic groups in Boston, where the study was done, has been repeatedly documented (Handlin 1959a). Ethnicity thus seemed a reasonable urban counterpart of the cultures so often referred to in the previous pages. The sample was drawn from the outpatient clinics of the Massachusetts General Hospital and the Massachusetts Eye and Ear Infirmary; it was limited to those new patients of both sexes between 18 and 50 who were white, able to converse in English, and of either Irish Catholic, Italian Catholic, or Anglo-Saxon Protestant background. These were the most numerous ethnic groups in the clinics; together they constituted approximately 50 percent of all patients. Ethnicity was ascertained by the responses to several questions: what the patients considered their nationality to be; the birthplaces of themselves, their parents, their maternal and paternal grandparents; and, if the answers to all of these were American, they were also asked from whence their ancestors originated. The actual interviewing took place at the three clinics to which these patients were most frequently assigned (the largest out-patient clinics): the Eye Clinic; the Ear, Nose, and Throat Clinic; and the Medical Clinic.

In previous research the specific method of measuring and studying symptoms has varied among case record analysis, symptom check lists, and interviews. The data have been either retrospective or projective, that is, requesting the subjects either to recall symptoms experienced during a specific period or to choose symptoms which would bother them sufficiently to seek medical aid. Such procedures do not provide data on the complaints which people actually bring to a doctor, a fact of particular importance in light of the many investigations pointing to the lack of, and distortions in, recall of sickness episodes (Feldman 1960). An equally serious problem is the effect of what the doctor, medicine man or health expert may tell the patients on the latter's subsequent perceptions of and recall about their ailment (Kadushin 1966). I resolved these problems by restricting the sample to new patients on their first medical visit to the clinics and by interviewing them during the waiting period *before* they were seen by a physician. This particular methodological choice was also determined by the nature of the larger study, that is, how patients decided to seek medical aid, where the above mentioned problems loom even larger. While only new admissions were studied, a number of patients had been referred by another medical person. Subsequent statistical analysis revealed no important differences between this group and those for whom the Massachusetts General Hospital or the Massachusetts Eye and Ear Infirmary was the initial source of help.

The primary method of data-collection was a focused open-ended interview dealing with the patient's own or family's responses to his/her presenting complaints. Interspersed throughout the interview were a number of more objective measures of the patient's responses—checklists, forced-choice comparisons, attitudinal items, and scales. Other information included a demographic background questionnaire, a review of the medical record, and a series of ratings by each patient's examining physician as to the primary diagnosis, the secondary diagnosis, the potential seriousness and the degree of clinical urgency (i.e., the necessity that the patient be seen immediately) of the patient's presenting complaint (Zola, 1962b).

THE PATIENT AND HIS ILLNESS

The data are based on a comparison between 63 Italians (34 female, 29 male) and 81 Irish (42 female, 39 male), who were new admissions to the Eye, the Ear, Nose, and Throat, and the Medical Clinics of the Massachusetts General Hospital and the Massachusetts Eye and Ear Infirmary, seen between July, 1960 and February, 1961. (Forty-three Anglo-Saxons were also interviewed but are not considered in this analysis. They were dropped from this report because they differed from the Irish and Italians in various respects other than ethnicity: they included more students, more divorced and separated, more people living away from home, and more downwardly mobile; they were of higher socioeconomic and educational level, and a majority were fourth generation and beyond.) The mean age of each ethnic group (male and female computed separately) was approximately thirty-three. While most patients were married, there was, in the sample, a higher proportion of single Irish men—a finding of other studies involving Irish and not unexpected from our knowledge of Irish family structure (Arensberg and Kimball 1948). Most respondents had between 10 and 12 years of schooling, but only about 30 percent of the males claimed to have graduated from high school as compared with nearly 60 percent of the females. There were no significant differences on standard measures of social class, though in education, social class, occupation of the breadwinner in the patient's family, and occupation of the patient's father, the Irish ranked slightly higher. The Italians were overwhelmingly American-born children of foreign parents: about 80 percent were second generation while 20 percent were third. Among the Irish about 40 percent were second generation, 30 percent third, and 30 percent fourth.

With regard to general medical coverage, there were no apparent differences between the ethnic groups. Approximately 62 percent of the sample had health insurance, a figure similar to the comparable economic group in the Rosenfeld (et al. 1957) survey of Metropolitan Boston. Sixty percent had physicians whom they could call family doctors. The Irish tended more than the Italians to perceive themselves as having poor health, claiming more often they had been seriously ill in the past. This was consistent with their reporting of the most recent visit to a doctor: nine of the Irish but none of the Italians claimed to have had a recent major operation (e.g., appendectomy) or illness (e.g., pneumonia). Although there were no differences in the actual seriousness of their present disorders (according to the doctor's ratings), there was a tendency for the examining physician to consider the Irish as being in more urgent need of treatment. It was apparent that the patients were not in the throes of an acute illness, although they may have been experiencing an acute episode. There was a slight tendency for the Irish, as a group, to have had their complaints longer. More significantly, the women of both groups claimed to have borne their symptoms for a longer time than the men.

In confining the study to three clinics, we were trying not only to economize but also to limit the range of illnesses. The later was necessary for investigating differential responses to essentially similar conditions. Yet at best this is only an approximate control. To resolve this difficulty, after all initial comparisons were made between the ethnic groups as a whole, the data were examined for a selected subsample with a specific control for diagnosis. This subsample consisted of matched pairs of one Irish and one Italian of the same sex, who had the same primary diagnosis, and whose disorder was of approximately the same duration and was rated by the examining physician as similar in degree of "seriousness." Where numbers made it feasible, there was a further matching on age, marital status, and education. In all, thirty-seven diagnostically-matched pairs (18 female and 19 male) were created; these constituted the final test of my finding of the differential response to illness.

These pairs included some eighteen distinct diagnoses: conjunctivitis; eyelid disease (e.g., blepharitis); myopia, hyperopia, vitreous opacities; impacted cerumen; external otitis; otitis media; otosclerosis; deviated septum; sinusitis; nasopharyngitis; allergy; thyroid; obesity; functional complaints; no pathology; psychological problems.

To give some indication of the statistical significance of these comparisons, a sign test was used. For the sign test, a "tie" occurs when it is not possible to discriminate between a matched pair on the variable under study, or when the two scores earned by any pair are equal. All tied cases were dropped from the analysis, and the probabilities were computed only on the total number excluding ties. In our study there were many ties. In the nature of our hypotheses, as will appear subsequently, a tie means that at least one member of the pair was in the predicted direction. Despite this problem, the idea of a diagnostically-matched pair was retained because it seemed to convey the best available test of our data. Because there were specific predictions as to the direction of differences, the probabilities were computed on the basis of a one-tailed sign test. This was used to retest the findings of Tables 6-1 through 6-6 (Siegel 1956).

LOCATION AND QUALITY OF PRESENTING COMPLAINTS

In the folklore of medical practice, the supposed opening question is, "Where does it hurt?" This query provides the starting-point of our analysis—the perceived location of the patient's troubles. The first finding (Table 6-1) is that more Irish than Italians tended to locate their chief problem in either the

Table 6-1
Distribution of Irish and Italian Clinic Admissions by Location of Chief Complaint

LOCATION OF COMPLAINT	ITALIAN	IRISH*
Eye, ear, nose or throat	34	61
Other parts of the body	29	17
Total	63	78

Note: $x^2 = 9.31$, $p < .01$.
*Since 3 Irish patients (two women, one man) claimed to be asymptomatic, no location could be determined from their viewpoint.

eye, the ear, the nose, or the throat (and more so for females than for males). The same tendency was evident when all patients were asked what they considered to be the most important part of their body and the one with which they would be most concerned if something went wrong (Table 6-2). Here, too, significantly more Irish emphasized difficulties of the eye, the ear, the nose, or the throat. That this reflected merely a difference in the conditions for which they were seeking aid is doubtful since the two other parts of the body most frequently referred to were heart and "mind" locations, and these represent only 3 percent of the primary diagnoses of the entire sample. In the retesting of these findings on diagnostically-matched pairs, while there were a great many ties, the general directions were still consistent. For the prediction that the Irish would locate their chief complaint in eye, ear, nose, or throat, and the Italians in some other part, 8 matched diagnostic pairs were in favor of the hypothesis, 1 against, 28 ties (p = .02); for the same with respect to most important part of the body there were 12 in favor of the hypothesis, 2 against, 23 ties (p = .006). Thus even when Italians had a diagnosed eye or ear disorder, they did not locate their chief complaints there, nor did they focus their future concern on these locations.

Pain, the commonest accompaniment of illness, was the dimension of patients' symptoms to which I next turned. Pain is an especially interesting phenomenon since there is considerable evidence that its tolerance and perception are not purely physiological responses and do not necessarily reflect the degree of objective discomfort induced by a particular disorder or experimental procedure (Chapman and Jones 1944; Hardy, Wolff, and Goodell 1952; Melzack 1961; Olin and Hackett 1964). In this study not only did the Irish more often than the Italians deny that pain was a feature of their illness (Table 6-

Table 6-2
Distribution of Irish and Italian Clinic Admissions
by Part of the Body Considered Most Important

MOST IMPORTANT PART OF THE BODY	ITALIAN	IRISH
Eye, ear, nose or throat	6	26
Other parts of the body	57	55
Total	63	81

Note: $x^2 = 10.50$, p<.01.

3) but this difference held even for those patients with the same disorder. For the prediction that Italians would admit the presence of pain and the Irish would deny it, 16 matched diagnostic pairs were in favor of the hypothesis, 0 against, 21 ties (p = .001).

When the Irish were asked directly about the presence of pain, some hedged their replies with qualifications. "It was more a throbbing than a pain . . . not really pain, it feels more like sand in my eye." Such comments indicated that the patients were reflecting something more than an objective reaction to their physical conditions.

While there were no marked differences in the length, frequency or noticeability of their symptoms, a difference did emerge in the ways in which they described the quality of the physical difficulty embodied in their chief complaint. Two types of difficulty were distinguished: one was of a more limited nature and emphasized a circumscribed and specific dysfunctioning; the second emphasized a difficulty of a grosser and more diffuse quality. Complaints of the first type emphasized a somewhat limited difficulty and dysfunction best exemplified by something specific, e.g., an organ having gone wrong in a particular way. The second type seemed to involve a more attenuated kind of problem whose location and scope were less determinate, and whose description was finally more qualitative and less measurable. When the patients' complaints were analyzed according to these two types, proportionately more Irish described their chief problem in terms of specific dysfunction while proportionately more Italians spoke of a diffuse difficulty (Table 6-4). For the prediction that the Italians would emphasize a diffuse difficulty and the Irish a specific one, there were 10 diagnostically-matched pairs in favor, 0 against, 27 ties (p = .001). Once again, the findings for diagnostically-matched pairs were in the predicted direction.

Table 6-3
Distribution of Irish and Italian Clinic Admissions
by Presence of Pain in Their Current Illness

PRESENCE OF PAIN	ITALIAN	IRISH
No	27	54
Yes	36	27
Total	63	81

Note: $x^2 = 10.26$, p<.01.

Table 6-4
*Distribution of Irish and Italian Clinic Admissions
by Quality of Physical Difficulty Embodied in
Chief Complaint*

QUALITY OF PHYSICAL DIFFICULTY	ITALIAN	IRISH*
Problems of a diffuse nature	43	33
Problems of a specific nature	20	45
Total	63	78

Note: $x^2 = 9.44$, p<.01.
*Since 3 Irish patients (two women, one man) claimed to be asymptomatic, no rating of the quality of physical difficulty could be determined from their viewpoint.

DIFFUSE VERSUS SPECIFIC REACTIONS

What seems to emerge from the above is a picture of the Irish limiting and understating their difficulties and the Italians spreading and generalizing theirs. Two other pieces of information were consistent with this interpretation: first, an enumeration of the symptoms an individual presented—a phenomenon which might reflect how diffusely the complaint was perceived; second, the degree to which each patient felt his illness affected aspects of life other than purely physical behavior.

The first measure of this specific-diffuse dimension—number of distinguishable symptoms—was examined in three ways: (1) the total number presented by each patient; this number could be zero, as in a situation where the patient denied the presence of any difficulty, but others around him disagreed and so made the appointment for him or "forced" him to see a doctor (Table 6-5); (2) the total number of different bodily areas in which the patient indicated he had complaints, e.g., back, stomach, legs; (3) the total number of different qualities of physical difficulty embodied in the patient's presenting complaints. Qualities of physical difficulty were categorized under nine headings. The ethnic differences were consistent with the previous findings. Compared to the Irish, the Italians presented significantly more symptoms, had symptoms in significantly more bodily locations, and noted significantly more types of bodily dysfunction. The distributions for these two latter tables closely resemble those of Table 6-5 (p = .018 for bodily locations; p = .003 for types of bodily dysfunctions).

Table 6-5
Distribution of Irish and Italian Clinic Admissions
by Number of Presenting Complaints*

NUMBER OF PRESENTING COMPLAINTS	ITALIAN	IRISH
Zero	0	3
One	5	21
Two	15	22
Three	14	16
Four	10	7
Five	9	7
Six or more	10	5
Total	63	81

Note: p<.001.
*The Mann-Whitney U-test was used. Probabilities were computed for one-tailed tests. They are, however, slightly "conservative"; with a correction for ties, the probabilities or levels of significance would have been even lower.

The second analysis, the degree to which a patient felt his illness affected his more general well-being, was derived from replies to three questions: (1) Do you think your symptoms affected how you got along with your family? (2) Did you become more irritable? (3) What would you say has bothered you most about your symptoms? For the latter question, the patient was presented with a card on which were listed eight aspects of illness and/or symptoms which might bother him. One of these statements was, "That it made you irritable and difficult to get along with." An admission of irritability scale was created by classifying an affirmative response to any of the three questions as an admission that the symptoms affected extra-physical performance. As seen in Table 6-6, the Irish were more likely than the Italians to state that their disorders had not affected them in this manner. Here again the asides by the Irish suggested that their larger number of negative responses by the Irish reflected considerable denial rather than a straightforward appraisal of their situation.

To examine these conclusions in a more rigorous manner, I turned again to our subsample of matched diagnostic pairs. In general, the pattern and direction of the hypotheses were upheld. For the prediction that the Italians would have more symptoms in all instances, there were for total number, 24 matched diagnostic pairs in favor of

Table 6-6
Distribution of Irish and Italian Clinic Admissions
by Responses to Three Questions Concerning
Admission of Irritability and Effect of Symptoms
on Interpersonal Behavior

RESPONSE PATTERN	ITALIAN	IRISH
No on all three questions	22	47
Yes on at least one question	41	34
Total	63	81

Note: $x^2 = 7.62$, $p < .01$.

hypothesis, 7 against, 6 ties ($p = .005$); for number of different locations, 16 in favor, 5 against, 16 ties ($p = .013$); for number of different qualities of physical difficulties, 22 in favor, 9 against, 6 ties ($p = .025$). For the prediction that Italians would admit irritability and Irish would deny it, there were 17 in favor, 6 against, 14 ties ($p = .017$). Thus even for the same diagnosis, the Italians expressed and complained of more symptoms, more bodily areas affected, and more kinds of dysfunctions than did the Irish, and more often felt that their symptoms affected their behavior.

The following composite offers a final illustration of how differently these patients reacted to and perceived their illnesses (Table 6-7-. Each set of responses was given by an Italian and an Irish patient of similar age and sex with a disorder of approximately the same duration and with the same primary and secondary diagnosis (if there was one). In the first two cases, the Irish patient focussed on a specific malfunctioning as the main concern while the Italian did not even mention this aspect of the problem but went on to mention more diffuse qualities of his condition. The last four responses contrast the Italian and Irish response to questions of pain and interpersonal relations.

What has so far been demonstrated is the systematic variability with which bodily conditions may be perceived and communicated. Until now the empirical findings have been presented without interpretation. Most of the data are quite consistent with those reported by other observers. The whole specific-diffuse pattern and the generalizing-withholding illness behavior dovetails neatly with the empirical findings of Opler and Singer (1956), Fantl and Schiro (1959) and Barrabee and von Mering (1953). The specific emphasis

Table 6-7
Irish and Italian Reactions to and Perceptions of Illness

DIAGNOSIS	QUESTION OF INTERVIEWER	IRISH PATIENT	ITALIAN PATIENT
1. Presbyopia and hyperopia	What seems to be the trouble?	I can't see to thread a needle or read a paper.	I have a constant headache and my eyes seem to get all red and burny.
	Anything else?	No, I can't recall any.	No, just that it lasts all day long and I even wake up with it sometimes.
2. Myopia	What seems to be the trouble?	I can't see across the street.	My eyes seem very burny, especially the right eye . . . Two or three months ago I woke up with my eyes swollen. I bathed it and it did go away but there was still the burny sensation.
	Anything else?	I had been experiencing headaches, but it may be that I'm in early menopause.	Yes, there always seems to be a red spot beneath this eye . . .
	Anything else?	No.	Well, my eyes feel very heavy . . . at night they bother me most.
3. Otitis externa A.D.	Is there any pain?	There's a congestion . . . but it's a pressure not really a pain.	Yes . . . if I rub it, it disappears . . . I had a pain from my shoulder up to my neck and thought it might be a cold.
4. Pharyngitis	Is there any pain?	No, maybe a slight headache but nothing that lasts.	Yes, I have had a headache a few days. Oh, yes, every time I swallow it's annoying.
5. Presbyopia and hyperopia	Do you think the symptoms affected how you got along with your family? your friends?	No, I have had loads of trouble. I can't imagine this bothering me.	Yes, when I have a headache, I'm very irritable, very tense, very short-tempered.
6. Deafness, hearing loss.	Did you become more irritable?	No, not me . . . maybe everybody else but not me.	Oh, yes . . . the least little thing aggravates me . . . and I take it out on the children.

on expressiveness has been detailed especially by Zborowski (1952) and the studies of Italian mental patients done by Anne Parsons (1960 and 1961). Finally the contrast on number of symptoms has been noted by Croog (1961) and Graham (1956). Although no data were collected in our investigation on the specific mechanics of the interplay between being a member of a specific subculture and the communication of "symptoms," some speculation on this seems warranted.

In theorizing about the interplay of culture and symptoms particular emphasis was given to the "fit" of certain bodily states with dominant value orientations. The empirical examples for the latter were drawn primarily from data on social roles. Of course, values are evident on even more general levels, such as formal and informal societal sanctions and the culture's orientation to life's basic problems. With an orientation to problems usually goes a preferred solution or way of handling them. Thus a society's values may also be reflected in such preferred solutions. One behavioral manifestation of this is defense mechanisms—a part of the everyday way individuals have of dealing with their everyday stresses and strains. I contend that illness and its treatment (from taking medicine to seeing a physician) is one of these everyday stresses and strains, an anxiety-laden situation which calls forth coping or defense mechanisms. From this general reasoning, I would thus speculate that Italian and Irish ways of communicating illness may reflect major values and preferred ways of handling problems within the culture itself.

For the Italians, the large number of symptoms and the spread of the complaints, not only throughout the body but into other aspects of life, may be understood in terms of their expressiveness and expansiveness so often cited in sociological, historical, and fictional writing. And yet their illness behavior seems to reflect something more than lack of inhibition and valuation of spontaneity. There is something more than real in their behavior, a well-seasoned, dramatic emphasis to their lives. In fact, clinicians have noted that this openness is deceptive. It only goes so far. Thus this Italian overstatement of "symptoms" is not merely an expressive quality but perhaps a more general mechanism, their special way of handling problems—a defense mechanism I call dramatization. Dynamically dramatization seems to cope with anxiety by repeatedly overexpressing it and thereby dissipating it. Anne Parsons delineates this process in a case study of a schizophrenic woman. Through a process of repetition and exaggeration she was able to isolate and defend herself from the destructive consequences of her own psychotic breakdown. Thus Anne Parsons (1961, p.26) concludes:

> Rather than appearing as evidence for the greater acceptance of id impulses the greater dramatic expression of Southern Italian culture might be given a particular place among the ego mechanisms, different from but in this respect fulfilling the same function as the emphasis on rational mastery of the objective or subjective world which characterizes our own culture (U.S.A.).

While other social historians have noted the Italian flair for show and spectacle, Barzini (1965, p. 104) has most explicitly related this phenomenon to the covering up of omnipresent tragedy and poverty, a way of making their daily lives bearable, the satisfactory *ersatz* for the many things they lack:

> The most easily identifiable reasons why the Italians love their own show . . . First of all they do it to tame and prettify savage nature, to make life bearable, dignified, significant and pleasant for others, and themselves. They do it then for their own private ends; a good show makes a man *simpatico* to powerful people, helps him get on in the world and obtain what he wants, solves many problems, lubricates the wheels of society, protects him from the envy of his enemies and the arogance of the mighty—they do it to avenge themselves on unjust fate.

Through many works on the Southern Italian there seems to run a thread—a valued and preferred way of handling problems shown in the tendency toward dramatization. The experience of illness provides but another stage.

But if the Italian view of life is expressed through its fiestas, for the Irish it is expressed through its fasts. Their life has been depicted as one of long periods of plodding routine followed by episodes of wild adventure, of lengthy postponement of gratification of sex and marriage, interspersed with brief immediate satisfactions like fighting and carousing. Perhaps it is in recognition of the expected and limited nature of such outbursts that the most common Irish outlet, alcoholism, is often referred to as "a good man's weakness." Life was black and long-suffering, and the less said the better.

It is the last statement which best reflects the Irish handling of illness. While in other contexts the ignoring of bodily complaints is merely descriptive of what is going on, in Irish culture it seems to be the culturally prescribed and supported defense mechanism—singularly most appropriate for their psychological and physical survival. Spiegel (1964) states that the Irishman's major avenue of relief from his oppressive sense of guilt lies in his almost unlimited capacity for denial. This capacity, he claims, is fostered by the perception in the rural Irish of a harmonic blending between man and nature. Such harmonizing of man and nature is further interpreted as blurring the elements of causality, thus allowing for continually shifting the responsibility for events from one person to another, and even from a person to animistically conceived forces. Thus denial becomes not only a preferred avenue of relief but also one supported and perhaps elicited by their perception of their environment. When speaking of the discomfort caused by her illness, one of my respondents stated, "I ignore it like I do most things." In terms of presenting complaints this understatement and restraint was even more evident. It could thus be seen in their seeming reluctance to admit they have any symptoms at all, in their limiting their symptoms to the specific location in which they arose and finally in their contention that their physical problems affected nothing of their life but the most minute physical functioning. The consistency of the Irish illness behavior with their general view of life is shown in two other contexts. First it helped perpetuate a self-fulfilling prophecy. Thus their way of communicating complaints, while doing little to make treatment easy, did assure some degree of continual suffering and thus further proof that life is painful and hard (that is, "full of fasts"). Secondly, their illness behavior can be linked to the sin and guilt ideology which seems to pervade so much of Irish society. For, in a culture where restraint is the *modus operandi*, temptation is ever-present and must be guarded against. Since the flesh is weak, there is a concomitant expectation that sin is likely. Thus, when unexpected or unpleasant events take place, there is a search for what they did or must have done wrong. Perhaps their three most favored locations of symptoms (the eyes, ears, and throat) might be understood as symbolic reflections of the more immediate source of their sin and guilt—what they should not have seen; what they should not have heard; and what they should not have said.

In these few paragraphs, I have tried to provide a theoretical link between membership in a cultural group and the communication of bodily complaints. The illness behavior of the Irish and the Italians has been explained in terms of two of the more generally prescribed defense mechanisms of their respective cultures—with the Irish handling their troubles by denial and the Italians theirs by dramatization.

QUALIFICATIONS AND IMPLICATIONS

The very fact that I speak of trends and statistical significance indicates the tentativeness of this study. In particular, the nature of sample selection affected the analysis of certain demographic variables since the lack of significant differences in some cases may be due to the small range available for comparison. Thus, there were no Italians beyond the third generation and few in the total sample who had gone to college. When comparisons were made within this small range (for example, only within the second generation or only within the high school group) there were, with but one exception, no significant differences from previously reported findings (Zola 1964). Despite the limitations cited, it can be stated with some confidence that, of the variables capable of analysis, sociocultural ones were the most significant. When a correlational analysis (and within this, a cluster analysis) was performed on all the codable and quantifiable material (including the demographic data, the health behaviors and attitude scales) the variable which consistently correlated most highly with the "illness behaviors" reported in this study was ethnic group membership.

There is one final remark about our sample selection which has ramifications, not for our data analysis, but rather for our interpretation. I am dealing here with a population who had decided to seek or were referred for medical aid at three clinics. Thus I can make no claim that in a random selection of Irish, they will be suffering primarily from eye, ear, nose, and throat disorders or even locate their chief symptoms there. What I am claiming is that there are significant differences in the way people present and react to their complaints, *not* that the specific complaints and mechanisms I have cited are necessarily the most common ones. (I would, of course, be surprised if the pattern reported here did not constitute one of the major ones.) Another difficulty in dealing with this population is the duration of the patients' disorders. Since the majority of these patients have had their conditions for some time, one may wonder if similar differences in perception would exist for more acute episodes, or whether the very length of time which the people have borne their problems has allowed for coloration by sociocultural factors. As a result of this we can only raise the issues as to whether the differences reported here between members of a cultural group exist only at a particular stage of their illness, or reflect more underlying and enduring cultural concerns and values.

While there has long been recognition of the subjectivity and variability of a patient's reporting of his symptoms, there has been little attention to the fact that this reporting may be influenced by systematic social factors like ethnicity. Awareness of the influence of this and similar factors can be of considerable aid in the practical problems of diagnosis and treatment of many diseases, particularly where the diagnosis is dependent to a large extent on what the patient is able and willing, or thinks important enough, to tell the doctor. The physician who is unaware of how the patient's background may lead him to respond in certain ways, may, by not probing sufficiently, miss important diagnostic cues, or respond inappropriately to others [see chapters 8 and 9 in this volume].

The documentation of sociocultural differences in the perception of and concern with certain types of "symptoms" has further implications for work in preventive medicine and public health. It has been found in mental health research that there is an enormous gulf between lay and professional opinion as to when mental ilness is present, as well as when and what kind of help is needed (Cumming and Cumming 1957; Gurin, Veroff, and Feld 1960; Nunnally 1961; Roper 1950; Woodward 1951). If my theorizing is correct, such differences reflect not merely something inadequately learned (that is, wrong medical knowledge) but also a solidly embedded value system. Such different frames of references would certainly shed light on the failure of many symptom-based health campaigns. Often these campaigns seem based on the assumption that a symptom or sign is fairly objective and recognizable and that it evokes similar levels of awareness and reaction. My study adds to the mounting evidence which contradicts this position by indicating, for example, the systematic variability in response to even the most minor aches and pains.

The discerning of reactions to minor problems harks back to a point mentioned in the early pages of this report. For, while sociologists, anthropologists, and mental health workers have usually considered sociocultural factors to be etiological factors in the creation of specific problems, the interpretative emphasis in this study has been on how sociocultural background may lead to different definitions and responses to essentially the same experience. The strongest evidence in support of this argument is the different ethnic perceptions for essentially the same disease. While it is obvious that not all people react similarly to the same disease process, it is striking that the pattern of response can vary with the ethnic background of the patient. There is little known physiological difference between ethnic groups which would account for the differing reactions. In fact, the comparison of the matched diagnostic groups led me to believe that, should diagnosis be more precisely controlled, the differences would be even more striking.

The present report has attempted to demonstrate the fruitfulness of an approach which does not take the definition of abnormality for granted. Despite its limitations, my data seem sufficiently striking to provide further reason for re-examining our traditional and often rigid conceptions of health and illness, of normality and abnormality, of conformity and deviance. Symptoms, or physical aberrations, are so widespread that perhaps relatively few, and a biased selection at best, come to the attention of official treatment agencies like doctors, hospitals, and public health agencies. There may even be a sense in which they are part and parcel of the human condition. I have thus tried to present evidence showing that the very labelling and definition of a bodily state as a symptom or as a problem is, in itself, part of a social process. If there is a selection and definitional process, then focusing solely on reasons for deviation (the study of etiology) and ignoring what constitutes a deviation in the eyes of the individual and his society may obscure important aspects of our understanding and eventually our philosophies of treatment and control of illness.

Pathways to the Doctor:
From Person to Patient

The problem on which we wish to dwell is one about which we think we know a great deal but that, in reality, we know so little—how and why an individual seeks professional medical aid. The immediate and obvious answer is that a person goes to a doctor when he is sick. Yet, this term "sick," is much clearer to those who use it, namely the health practitioners and the researchers, than it is to those upon whom we apply it—the patients. Two examples may illustrate this point. Listen carefully to the words of a respondent in Koos' study of the Health of Regionville (1954, p. 30) as she wrestled with a definition of this concept.

> I wish I really knew what you meant about being sick. Sometimes I felt so bad I could curl up and die, but had to go on because the kids had to be taken care of and besides, we didn't have the money to spend for the doctor. How could I be sick? How do you know when you're sick, anyway? Some people can go to bed most anytime with anything, but but most of us can't be sick, even when we need to be.

Even when there is agreement as to what constitutes "sickness," there may be a difference of opinion as to what constitutes appropriate action, as in the following incident:

Originally appeared as "Pathways to the Doctor—From Person to Patient," *Social Science and Medicine* 7 (1973): 677-689.

A rather elderly woman arrived at the Medical Clinic of the Massachusetts General Hospital three days after an appointment. A somewhat exasperated nurse turned to her and said, "Mrs. Smith, your appointment was three days ago. Why weren't you here then?" To this Mrs. Smith responded, "How could I? Then I was sick."

Examples such as these are not unusual occurrences. And yet they cause little change in some basic working assumptions of the purveyors of medical care as well as the myriad investigators who are studying its delivery. It is to three of these assumptions we now turn: (1) the importance and frequency of episodes of illness in an individual's life; (2) the representativeness of those episodes of illness which come to professional attention; and (3) the process by which an individual decides that a series of bodily discomforts he labels symptoms become worthy of professional attention. Together these assumptions create an interesting if misleading picture of illness. Rarely do we try to understand how or why a patient goes to the doctor, for the decision itself is thought to be an obvious one. We postulate a time when the patient is asymptomatic or unaware that he has symptoms, then suddenly some clear objective symptoms appear, then perhaps he goes through a period of self-treatment and when either this treatment is unsuccessful or the symptoms in some way become too difficult to take, he decides to go to some health practitioner (usually, we hope, a physician).

The first assumption, thus, deals with the idea that individuals at most times during their life are really asymptomatic. The extensive data pouring in from periodic health examination has gradually begun to question this notion. For, examinations of even supposedly healthy people, from business executives to union members to college professors, consistently reveal that at the time of their annual check-up, there was scarcely an individual who did not possess some symptom, some clinical entity worthy of treatment (Siegel 1963; Meigs 1961). Such data begins to give us a rather uncomfortable sense in which we may to some degree be sick every day of our lives. If we should even think of such a picture, however, the easiest way to dismiss this notion is that the majority of these everyday conditions are so minor as to be unworthy of medical treatment. This leads to our second assumption; namely, the degree of representativeness, both as to seriousness and frequency, of those episodes which do get to a doctor. Here too we are presented with puzzling facts. For if we look at investigations of either serious physical or mental disorder, there seem to be at least one, and in many cases several, people out of treatment for every person in treatment (Commission on Chronic Illness 1957). If, on the other hand, we look at a doctor's practice, we find that the vast bulk is concerned with quite minor disorders (Clute 1963). Furthermore, if we use symptom-check-lists or health calendars, we find that for these self-same minor disorders, there is little that distinguishes them medically from those that are ignored, tolerated, or self-medicated (Alpert et al. 1967; Kosa et al. 1965, 1967).

With these confusions in mind, we can now turn to the third assumption. On the basis that symptoms were perceived to be an infrequent and thus somewhat dramatic event in one's life, the general assumption was that in the face of such symptoms, a rational individual after an appropriate amount of caution, would seek aid. When he does not or delays overlong, we begin to question his rationality. The innumerable studies of delay in cancer bear witness.

If we examine these studies we find that the reason for delay is a list of faults—the patient has no time, no money, no one to care for children, or take over other duties, is guilty, ashamed, fearful, anxious, embarrassed, or emotionally disturbed, dislikes physicians, nurses, hospitals, or needles, has had bad medical, familial or personal experiences, or is of lower education, socioeconomic status, or an ethnic or racial minority (Blackwell 1963; Kutner et al. 1958; Kutner and Gordon 1961). As the researchers might put it, there is something about these people or in their backgrounds which has disturbed their rationality, for otherwise, they would "naturally" seek aid. And yet there is a curious methodological fact about these studies for all these investigations were done on *patients*, people who *had* ultimately decided to go to a physician. What happened? Were they no longer fearful? Did they get free time, more money, outside help? Did they resolve their guilt, shame, anxiety, distrust? No, this does not seem to have been the case. If anything the investigators seem to allude to the fact that the patients finally could not stand it any longer. Yet given the abundant data on the ability to tolerate pain and a wide variety of other conditions, this notion of "not being able to stand it" simply does not ring true clinically.

We can now restate a more realistic empirical picture of illness episodes. Virtually every day of our lives we are subject to a vast array of bodily discomforts. Only an infinitesimal amount of these get to a physician. Neither the mere presence nor the obviousness of symptoms, neither their medical seriousness nor objective discomfort seems to differentiate those episodes which do and do not get professional treatment. In short, what then does convert a person to a patient? This then became a significant question and the search for an answer began.

At this point we had only the hunch that "something critical" must ordinarily happen to make an individual seek help. Given the voluminous literature on delay in seeking medical aid for almost every conceivable disorder and treatment, we might well say that that statistical norm for any population is to delay (perhaps, infinitely for many). The implementing of this hunch is owed primarily to the intersection of two disciplines—anthropology and psychiatry. The first question to be faced was how and where to study this "something." Both prospective and retrospective studies were rejected. The former because as Professor H. M. Murphy noted there is often an enormous discrepancy between the declared intention and the actual act. The retrospective approach was rejected for two reasons—the almost notoriously poor recall that individuals have for past medical experiences and the distortions in recall introduced by the extensive "memory manipulation" which occurs as a result of the medical interview. Our resolution to this dilemma was a way of studying the patient when he was *in the process* of seeking medical aid. This process was somewhat artifically created by (1) interviewing patients while they waited to see their physician; (2) confining our sample to new patients to the Out-Patient Clinics of the Massachusetts General Hospital who were seeking aid for their particular problem for the first time. Thus, we had a group of people who were definitely committed to seeing a doctor (i.e. waiting) but who had not yet been subject to the biases and distortions that might occur through the medical interview (though some patients had been referred, we included only those on whom no definitive diagnosis had been made). This then was where we decided to study our problem.

In what to look for we were influenced by certain trends in general psychiatry away from defining mental illness solely in terms or symptoms possessed by a single isolated individual and instead conceptualizing it as a more general kind of disturbance in interpersonal behavior and social living. (The resemblance that this bears to early classical notions of health and illness is quite striking. For then illness was conceived to be the disturbance between ego and his environment and not the physical symptom which happens to show up in ego [Galdston 1956].) On the empirical level we were influenced by the work of Clausen (1955) and his colleagues at the National Institute of Mental Health on the first admission to the hospital for male schizophrenics. Most striking about their mateial was the lack of any increase in the objective seriousness of the patient's disorder as a factor in this hospitalization. If anything, there was a kind of normalization in his family, an accommodation to the patient's symptoms. The hospitalization occurred not when the patient became sicker, but when the accommodation of the family, of the surrounding social context, broke down. A translation of these findings could be made to physical illness. For, given all the data on delay, it seemed very likely that people have their symptoms for a long period of time before ever seeking medical aid. Thus one could hypothesize that there is an accommodation both physical, personal, and social to the symptoms and it is when this accommodation breaks down that the person seeks, or is forced to seek, medical aid. Thus the "illness" for which one seeks help may only in part be a physical relief from symptoms. The research question on the decision to seek medical aid thus turned from the traditional focus on "why the delay" to the more general issue of "why come *now*." This way of asking this question is in itself not new. Physicians have often done it, but interestingly enough, they have asked it not in regard to general physical illness but rather when they can find nothing wrong. It is *then* that they feel that the patient may want or have been prompted to seek help for other than physical reasons.

The sample consisted of patients completely new to the out-patient clinics who were seeking medical aid for the first time for this particular problem, who were between the ages of 18 and 50, able to converse in English, of either Anglo-Saxon Protestant, Irish Catholic or Italian Catholic background. The data-collection took place at the three clinics to which these groups were most frequently sent— the Eye Clinic, the Ear, Nose and Throat Clinic, and the Medical Clinic, which were, incidentally three of the largest clinics in the hospital. The interviewing took place during the waiting time before they saw their physicians with the general focus of the questioning being: Why did you seek medical aid now? In addition to many such open-ended questions, we had other information derived from the medical record, demographic interviews, attitude scales and check lists. We also had each examining physician fill out a medical rating sheet on each patient. In all we saw over two hundred patients, fairly evenly divided between male and female.

All differences reported here are statistically significant. Given that there are no tabular presentations in this essay it may be helpful to remember that for the most part we are not stating that all or necessarily a majority of a particular group acted in the way depicted but that at very least, the response was significantly more peculiar to this group than to any other. Moreover, all the reported differences were sustained even when the diagnosed disorder for which they sought aid was held constant. For details on some of the statistical procedures as well as some of the methodological controls, see Zola, 1966.

The crux of the study is, however, the decision to see a doctor. One of our basic claims was that the decision to seek medical aid was based on a break in the accommodation to the symptoms, that in the vast majority of situations, an individual did not seek aid at his physically sickest point. We do not mean by this that symptoms were unimportant. What we mean is that they function as a sort of constant and that when the decision to seek medical aid was made the physical symptoms alone were not sufficient to prompt this seeking. Typical of the amount of debilitation people can tolerate as well as the considerable seriousness and still the decision to seek medical attention made on extra-physical grounds is the case of Mary O'Rourke.

> Mary O'Rourke is 49, married and is a licensed practical nurse. Her symptom was a simple one, "The sight is no good in this eye . . . can't see print at all, no matter how big." This she claimed was due to being hit on the side of the head by a baseball 4 months ago, but she just couldn't get around to a doctor before this. Why did she decide now, did her vision become worse? "Well . . . about a month ago I was taking care of his (a client's) mother . . . he mentioned that my eyelid was drooping . . . it was the first time he ever did . . . if he hadn't pointed it out I wouldn't have gone then." "Why did you pay attention to his advice?" "Well it takes away from my appearance . . . bad enough to feel this way without having to look that way . . . the same day I told my husband to call." Diagnosis—Chorioretinitis O.S. (permanent partial blindness) "lesion present much longer than present symptoms." Incidentally, no "drooping" was noticeable to either the interviewer or the examining physician.

Case after case could be presented to make this point but even more striking is that there is a "method underlying this madness." In our data we were able to discern several distinct nonphysiological patterns of triggers to the decision to seek medical aid. We have called them as follows: (1) the occurrence of an interpersonal crisis; (2) the *perceived* interference with social or personal relations; (3) sanctioning; (4) the *perceived* interference with vocational or physical activity; and (5) a kind of temporalizing of symptomatology. Moreover, these five patterns were clustered in such a way that we could characterize each ethnic group in our sample as favoring particular decision-making patterns in the seek of medical aid.

The first two patterns, the presence of an interpersonal crisis, and the perceived interference with social or personal relations were more frequent among the Italians. The former, that of a crisis, does not mean that the symptoms have led to a crisis or even vice-versa, but that the crisis called attention to the symptoms, caused the patient to dwell on them and finally to do something about them. Two examples will illustrate this.

Jennie Bella was 40, single, and had a hearing difficulty for many years. She said that the symptoms have not gotten worse nor do they bother her a great deal (Diagnosis: Non-suppurative Otitis Media) and, furthermore, she admitted being petrified of doctors. "I don't like to come . . . I don't like doctors. I never did . . . I have to be unconscious to go. . . ." She can nevertheless not pinpoint any reason for coming at this time other than a general feeling that it should be taken care of. But when she was questioned about her family's concern, she blurted out, "I'm very nervous with my mother, up to this year I've been quiet, a stay-at-home . . . Now I've decided to go out and have some fun. My mother is very strict and very religious. She doesn't like the idea of my going out with a lot of men. She don't think I should go out with one for awhile and then stop. She says I'm not a nice girl, and I shouldn't go with a man unless I plan to marry . . . she doesn't like my keeping late hours or coming home late. She always suspects the worst of me. . . . This year it's just been miserable . . . I can't talk to her . . . she makes me very upset and it's been getting worse. . . . The other day . . . last week we (in lowered tones) had *the* argument." Miss Bella called for an appointment the next morning.

Carol Conte was a 45-year-old, single, bookkeeper. For a number of years she had been both the sole support and nurse for her mother. Within the past year, her mother died and shortly thereafter her relatives began insisting that she move in with them, quit her job, work in their variety store and nurse their mother. With Carol's vacation approaching, they have stepped up their efforts to persuade her to at least try this arrangement. Although she has long had a number of minor aches and pains, her chief complaint was a small cyst on her eyelid (Diagnosis: Fibroma). She related her fear that it *might* be growing or could lead to something more serious and thus she felt she had better look into it now (the second day of her vacation) "before it was too late." "Too late" for what was revealed only in a somewhat mumbled response to the question of what she expected or would like the doctor to do. From a list of possible outcomes to her examination, she responded, "Maybe a 'hospital' [ization]. . . . 'Rest' would be all right . . ." (and then in a barely audible tone, in fact turning her head away as if she were speaking to no one at all) "just so they [the family] would stop bothering me." Responding to her physical concern, the examining physician acceded to her request for the removal of the fibroma, referred her for surgery and thus removed her from the situation for the duration of her vacation.

In such cases, it appeared that regardless of the reality and seriousness of the symptoms, they provide but the rationale for an escape, the calling-card or ticket to a potential source of help—the doctor.

The second pattern—the perceived interference with social or personal relations—is illustrated by the following two Italian patients.

John Pell is 18 and in his senior year of high school. For almost a year he's had headaches over his left eye and pain in and around his right, artificial, eye. The symptoms seem to be most prominent in the early evening. He claimed, however, little general difficulty or interference until he was asked whether the symptoms affected how he got along. To this he replied, "That's what worries me . . . I like to go out and meet people and now I've been avoiding prople." Since he has had this problem for a year, he was probed as to why it bothered him more at this particular time. "The last few days of school it bothered me so that I tried to avoid everybody [this incidentally was his characteristic pattern *whenever* his eyes bothered him] . . . and I want to go out with . . . and my Senior Prom coming up, and I get the pains at 7 or 7:30 how can I stay out . . . then I saw the nurse." To be specific, he was walking down the school corridor and saw the announcement of the upcoming Prom. He noticed the starting time of 8 p.m. and went immediately to the school nurse who in turn referred him to the Massachusetts Eye and Ear Infirmary.

Harry Gallo is 41, married, and a "trainee" at a car dealers'. "For a very long time my trouble is I can't drink . . . tea, coffee, booze . . . eat ice cream, fried foods. What happens is I get pains if I do have it." [Diagnosis: peptic ulcer]. He becomes very dramatic when talking about how the symptoms affected him. "It shot my social life all to pieces . . . we all want to socialize . . . and it's a tough thing. I want to go with people, but I can't. Wherever we go they want to eat or there's food and I get hungry . . . and if I eat there, I get sick." Of course, he has gone off his "diet" and has gotten sick. Most of the time he watches himself and drinks Maalox. He saw a doctor once 2 years ago and has been considering going again but, "I kept putting it off . . . because I got lazy . . . there were so many things. I've just been starting a new job and I didn't want to start taking off and not working, but this last attack was *too much*!" He then told how day after day the "boys at work" have been urging him to stop off with them for a few quick ones. He knew he shouldn't but he so wanted to fit in and so "It was with the boys and the other salesmen . . . I drank beer . . . I knew I was going to have more than one . . . and . . . *it* happened on the way home." Storming into his home, he asked his wife to make an appointment at the hospital, stating almost exasperatingly, "if you can't drink beer with friends, what the hell."

In these cases, the symptoms were relatively chronic. At the time of the decision there may have been an acute episode, but this was not the first such time the symptoms had reached such a "state" but rather it was the perception of them on this occasion as interfering with the social and interpersonal relations that was the trigger or final straw.

The third pattern, sanctioning, was the overwhelming favorite of the Irish. It is, however, not as well illustrated by dramatic examples, for it consists simply of one individual taking the primary responsibility for the decision to seek aid for someone else. For many weeks it looked as if one were seeing the submissive half of a dominant-submissive relationship. But within a period of 6 months, a husband and wife appeared at the clinics and each one assumed the role of sanctioning for the other.

> Mr. and Mrs. O'Brien were both suffering from myopia, both claimed difficulty in seeing, both had had their trouble for some period of time. The wife described her visit as follows: "Oh, as far as the symptoms were concerned, I'd be apt to let it go, but not my husband. He worries a lot, he wants things to be just so. Finally when my brother was better he (the husband) said to me: "Your worries about your brother are over so why can't you take care of your eyes now?" And so she did. Her husband, coming in several months later, followed the same pattern. He also considered himself somewhat resistant to being doctored. "I'm not in the habit of talking about aches and pains. My wife perhaps would say 'Go to the doctor,' but me, I'd like to see if things will work themselves out." How did he get here? It turns out that he was on vacation and he'd been meaning to take care of it, "Well I tend to let things go but not my wife, so on the first day of my vacation my wife said, 'Why don't you come, why don't you take care of it now?' So I did."

Thus in these cases both claimed a resistance to seeing a doctor, both claimed the other is more likely to take care of such problems, and yet both served as the pushing force to the other. Interestingly enough, the dramatic aspect of such cases was not shown in those who followed the general pattern which was often fairly straight-forward, but in those cases which did not. Two examples illustrate this. One was a woman with a thyroid condition, swelling on the side of the neck who when asked why she came at this time blurted out almost in a shout, "Why did I come now? I've been walking around the house like this for several weeks now and nobody said anything so I *had to come myself*." Or the almost plaintive complaint of a veteran, kind of grumbling when asked why he came now, begrudged the fact that he had to make a decision himself with the statement, "Hmm, in the Navy they just take you to the doctor, you don't have to go yourself." It is not that these people are in any sense stoic, for it seemed that they were quite verbal and open about complaining but just that they did not want to take the responsibility on themselves.

There is a secondary pattern of the Irish, which turns out to be also the major pattern of the Anglo-Saxon group. It was almost straight out of the Protestant ethic; namely a perceived interference with work or physical functioning. The word "perceived" is to be emphasized because the nature of the circumstances range from a single woman, 35 years old, who for the first time noted that the material which she was typing appeared blurred and thus felt that she had better take care of it, to a man with Multiple Sclerosis who despite falling down and losing his balance in many places, did nothing about it until he fell at work. Then he perceived that it might have some effect on his work and his ability to continue. The secondary Anglo-Saxon pattern is worth commenting on, for at first glance it appears to be one of the most rational modes of decision-making. It is one that most readers of this paper may well have used, namely the setting of external time criteria. "If it isn't better in 3 days, or 1 week, or 7 hours, or 6 months, then I'll take care of it." A variant on this theme involves the setting of a different kind of temporal standard—the recurrence of the phenomenon. A 19-year-old college sophomore reported the following:

> Well, it was this way. I went into this classroom and sat in the back of the room and when the professor started to write on the blackboard I noticed that the words were somewhat blurry. But I didn't think too much about it. A couple of weeks later, when I went back into that same classroom, I noted that it was blurry again. Well, once was bad, but twice that was too much.

Now given that his diagnosis was myopia and that it was unconnected with any other disease, we know medically that his myopia did not vary from one circumstance to another. This imposition of "a first time, second time that's too much" was of his doing and unrelated to any medical or physical reality.

By now the role that symptoms played in the decision to seek medical aid should be clearer. For our patients the symptoms were "really" there, but their perception differed considerably. There *is* a sense in which they sought help because they could not stand it any longer. But what they could not stand was more likely to be a situation or a perceived implication of a symptom rather than any worsening of the symptom *per se*.

I now would like to note some of the implications of this work. When speaking of implications, I ask your indulgence, for I refer not merely to what leads in a direct line from the data but some of the different thoughts and directions in which it leads me. What for example are the consequences for our very conception of etiology—

conceptions based on assumptions about the representativeness of whom and what we study. We have claimed in this paper that the reason people get into medical treatment may well be related to some select social psychological circumstances. If this is true, it makes all the more meaningful our earlier point about many unexplained epidemiological differences, for they may be due more to the differential occurrence of these social-psychological factors, factors of selectivity and attention which get people and their episodes into medical statistics rather than to any true difference in the prevalence and incidence of a particular problem or disorder (Mechanic and Volkart 1960). Our findings may also have implications for what one studies, particularly to the importance of stress in the etiology of so many complaints and disorders. For it may well be that the stress noted in these people's lives, at least those which they were able to verbalize, is the stress which brought them into the hospital or into seeking treatment (as was one of our main triggers) and not really a factor in the etiology or the exacerbation of the disorder.

Our work also has implications for treatment. So often we hear the terms "unmotivated, unreachable, and resistance" applied to difficult cases. Yet we fail to realize that these terms may equally apply to us, the caretakers and health professionals who may not understand what the patient is saying or if we do, do not want to hear it. Again and again we found that where the physician paid little attention to the specific trigger which forced or which the individual used as an excuse to seek medical aid, there was the greatest likelihood of that patient eventually breaking off treatment. Another way of putting this is that without attention to this phenomenon the physician would have no opportunity to practice his healing art. Moreover, this problem of triggers, etc. brooked no specialty nor particular type of disorder. So that being a specialist and only seeing certain kinds of problems did not exempt the physician from having to deal with this issue.

Such data alone supports those who urge more training in social and psychological sophistication for *any* physician who has contact with patients. With chronic illness making up the bulk of today's health problems it is obvious that the physicians cannot treat the etiological agent of disease and that the effect of specific therapies is rather limited. Nevertheless the physician may more intelligently intervene in the patient's efforts to cope with his disorder if he has the knowledge and awareness of the patient's views of health, sickness, his expectations and his reasons for seeking help.

To the social scientist we have tried to convey the somewhat amazing persistence of certain cultural characteristics which we in our cultural blindness have felt should have died and disappeared. The reason for their survival is that such behaviors may well be general modes of handling anxiety, sort of culturally prescribed defense mechanisms and probably transmitted from generation to generation in the way that much learning takes place, almost on an unconscious level. If this be true, then they constitute a group of behaviors which are much less likely to be changed as one wishes or attempts to become more American.

Finally, this is not meant to be an essay on the importance of sociological factors in disease, but rather the presentation of an approach to the study of health and illness. Rather than being a narrow and limited concept, health and illness are on the contrary empirically quite elastic. In short, it is not merely that health and illness has sociological aspects, for it has many aspects, but really that there is a sense in which health and illness *are* social phenomena. The implication of this perspective has perhaps been much better put by the Leightons (though quoted out of context [1963 pp. 135-136]):

> From this broad perspective there is no point in asking whether over the span of his adult life a particular individual should or should not be considered a medical case—everyone is a medical case. The significant question becomes how severe a case, what kind of case.

I myself would add—how does one become a case and since of the many eligible, so few are chosen, what does it mean to be a case. In an era where every day produces new medical discoveries, such questions are all too easily ignored. The cure for all men's ills seems right over the next hill. Yet as Dubos (1961) has cogently reminded us, this vision is only a mirage and the sooner we realize it the better.

8   *Problems of Communication, Diagnosis, and Patient Care: The Interplay of Patient, Physician, and Clinic Organization*

As every beginning medical student learns, history taking is a major diagnostic tool. Such interviewing requires a great deal of skill and understanding, and when there are reasons for reticence and fear, such as in an initial medical visit, even greater demands are placed on the doctor and the patient in their attempt to communicate with one another (Kahn and Cannel 1957; Magraw and Dulit 1958). The nature of this communication, moreover, is determined by a number of nonmedical factors, three of which will be delineated in this paper: the patient's ethnic background, the physician's medical specialty-orientation, and the clinic's spatial design and organization. An attempt will be made to demonstrate how each of these may operate to prevent or limit communication between patient and doctor and thus affect ultimate diagnosis and treatment.

THE PATIENT'S ETHNIC BACKGROUND

A number of studies have noted that both the diagnosis and treatment which psychiatric patients received were related to their social class (Hollingshead and Redlich 1958; Kahn,

Originally appeared as "Problems of Communication, Diagnosis and Patient Care: The Interplay of Patient, Physician, and Clinic Organization," *Journal of Medical Education* 38 (1963): 829–838.

Pollack and Fink 1959). There has, however, been little speculation about the effect of social background on the diagnosis and treatment of medical patients and their physical disorders. During a study on the decisions of lower-class Italians, Irish, and Anglo-Saxons to seek aid at the Medical, Eye, Ear, Nose, and Throat (ENT) Clinics of a large urban hospital, proportionately more Italians were found to be labeled "psychiatric problems" by their physicians. This was despite the fact that there was no evidence that psychosocial problems were more frequent among them.

In obtaining a measure of the amount and nature of psychosocial problems in the study population, all the patients were rated on three categories: (1) Note was made of the spontaneous mention by the patient of being "very nervous," or of "Nerves" being one of his greatest problems. (2) Note was made of the spontaneous mention of very pressing and difficult vocational, personal, or interpersonal situations (e.g. in the process of getting a divorce, having to care for a mentally ill husband or child, hating present work and life, etc.) and (3) A clinical psychologist rated the patient's interview responses as to the "presence of obvious psychological problems interfering with adequate functioning." On these three general ratings, there were no statistically significant differences between the ethnic groups and thus no objective reason to expect the greater frequency of "psychiatric diagnosis" in one group over another.

Such differences in diagnosis might, however, be related to how the patients presented themselves and thus how they were perceived and ultimately diagnosed and treated. In the larger study, basic differences were found between the Italians and the Irish (the Anglo-Saxons occupied a middle position but more often resembled the Irish) in the way they presented their chief complaints and illnesses and in the specific circumstances surrounding the decision to come to a doctor. The over-all study is reported elsewhere, but some specific findings on the Italians are pertinent: they tended to show more diffuse reactions to being sick; they reported more symptoms and stated more often that the symptoms made them irritable and difficult to get along with; and, in describing the specific circumstances bringing them to a doctor they more often felt that their symptoms interfered with social and personal relations, or mentioned the presence of an interpersonal crisis. In another study of Italians Zborowski (1952) felt that their "uninhibited display of reactions" to pain and their overinvolvement with symptoms would tend to provoke distrust in the doctors treating them. Since the Italians in our sample might also be perceived as "overacting," we speculated that this might have influenced the high number of psychiatric diagnoses.

The hypothesis that the patient's social background (i.e., ethnicity) and thus the way he presented himself influenced his diagnosis was tested by examining a group of cases where no medical basis for the symptoms had been found. It was felt that in these cases the operation of nonmedical factors would be most clear. So that we might err on the side of conservatism, a number of diagnoses which did little more than describe the patient's symptoms were excluded. (For example, "vitreous opacities" referred to the fact that the patient saw spots in front of his eyes, while "tinnitus" meant he heard hums, rings, buzzing, etc. It is interesting to note, however, that these "descriptive" diagnoses were attributed primarily to the Anglo-Saxon and Irish patients.) Because the number of males which fit this criteria was too small for statistical comparisons, the hypothesis was only tested on a subsample of women: ten Italians, thirteen Irish, and six Anglo-Saxons.

When the previously mentioned ratings of psychosocial problems were applied to the above three groups, no statistically significant differences were found. Each of these three groups were then further subdivided by the implied etiology of their symptoms. The first category, "psychogenesis implied," were patients with one of three diagnoses: tension headache, functional complaint (e.g. functional pain in the left arm) and emotional disorder (e.g. anxiety, depressed, neurotic etc.). The second category consisted of patients where no explicit psychogenesis was implied. It included only those women in whose cases the physician had explicitly stated there was "no pathology" and a few cases of asthenopia (meaning tired eyes). Table 8-1 shows how the doctors diagnosed patients where no organic

Table 8-1
*Physician Diagnoses of Female Patients with No
Organic Basis for Symptoms*

	ITALIAN	IRISH	ANGLO-SAXON
Psychogenesis implied	11	2	2
No psychogenesis implied	1	9	4
Total	12	11	6

Italian vs. Irish, X^2 equals 10.60 (corrected for continuity), P <.01.

basis for their complaints had been found. It is worth noting that the two "psychogenesis" cases of the Anglo-Saxons had the most obvious psychopathology in the entire sample of two hundred. One of these presented herself as being "mentally ill" and had been referred by the local Mental Health Association. The second entered the interview reeling and unsteady, accompanied by the distinct aroma of liquor and was subsequently diagnosed by her physician as "alcoholic."

In short, when no medical disease was found, the Italians were diagnosed as having a psychological problem while the Anglo-Saxons and Irish were not. Since psychosocial problems were equally present in all groups, there was no reason to expect one of the three ethnic groups to have more diagnoses in the "psychogenesis implied" category. Thus one can only conclude that the patient's ethnic background, which influenced the way she presented herself and her complaint, may have inordinately and inappropriately influenced the diagnosis by the examining physician.

THE PHYSICIAN'S SPECIALTY-ORIENTATION

The forces which affect the doctor-patient communication stem from attributes of the doctor as well as the patient. What the patient tells the doctor is influenced, for example, by what cues and interests he perceives and thus what he thinks the doctor wants to hear. What the doctor wants to hear is, in turn, the product of his own background, training and specialty-orientation.

When attention was focused on the doctor's recognition of patient concerns directly related to his symptoms and his decision to seek aid, evidence was found of a barrier in doctor-patient communication. Our material indicated that not only were there many instances where such concerns were not considered but that recognition, or lack of recognition, of these concerns was more marked at one clinic than another. While more patients with psychosocial problems appeared in the Medical Clinic population, proportionately fewer were acknowledged at either the Eye or the ENT Clinics. (Incidentally, the tendency toward giving the Italians, rather than the Anglo-Saxons or Irish, diagnoses which implied a psychogenic basis was most evident at the Eye Clinic, least at the Medical, with the ENT intermediate.) Thus, a person, regardless of the nature of his presenting complaint had the best chance of his personal and psychosocial problems being recognized if he was first seen by a doctor in the Medical Clinic, and the worst chance if seen by a doctor in the Eye

Clinic. This seemed to imply that there was a differential tendency on the part of specialty-orientations to be aware of the present personal concerns of the patient.

Unfortunately, no objective statistical material was collected on what transpired between the patient and his doctor. The research situation, however, often permitted the author to speak with both the doctor and the patient after the latter was seen. By systematic record review, it was also possible to check the nature of his treatment (including mention of reassurance, guidance, etc.) and his medical progress. From this information and from the more systematically collected interview data, it was possible to create a fairly complete picture of the patient's concerns, both medical and otherwise, surrounding his decision to seek aid. The following cases are illustrative of instances where the psychosocial concerns of the patient were not recognized.

NO ORGANIC PATHOLOGY

Mary B. was twenty-three, married and in her seventh month of pregnancy with her first child. She felt she was nearsighted and that it had been too long since her last check-up (i.e., three years). In recent months she had suffered from headaches in and around her eyes and some dizziness. On examination, the doctor found "no visible problem" and told her to return PRN. Since she was pregnant he explained to the author that he did not think it necessary to check her glasses since the prescription would only change once she had delivered. "I told her to return then if she was still bothered by them (i.e., headaches). Her vision was 20/20 with glasses." Why then did this patient come in with such minor problems? The research interview revealed that she was extremely embarrassed about her appearance and felt that this was affecting all her relationships. About three months ago, she broke her glasses (they were presently taped together), but "we didn't have the money with my husband out on strike." "The other day my cousin was over at the house and I was talking about being ashamed of the glasses and how I look 'cause we were going to a wedding." When asked about the general effect of her symptoms (i.e., headache, etc.) she responded. "Well I might have stayed home when I could have gone out . . . or go to bed rather than go out . . . I couldn't go to a movie or anything like that (the way I looked) . . . and so my husband had to go with his brothers." Again and again, she somewhat defensively told how much her husband was against her coming to this clinic but she felt that she could not wait any longer and so went against his wishes.

In understanding this case, it is irrelevant whether the embarrassment and her anxiety stem really from the taped and broken glasses or is related more to her pregnancy; the point is that she has come to the doctor. While he has examined her calling card (i.e., the symptoms) and quite correctly dismissed her ocular symptoms as minor and inconsequential, he did not recognize her more pressing concerns. Knowledge of these might have led to their discussion, a prescription for a new pair of eyeglass frames, or a referral elsewhere. The patient, however, returned empty-handed and discouraged to a husband who told her not to come here in the first place.

MINOR ORGANIC PATHOLOGY

Carol C. was a forty-five year old, single, bookkeeper. Within the past year, her mother died and shortly thereafter her relatives began insisting that she move in with them, quit her job, work in their variety store and nurse their mother. With her vacation approaching, they have stepped up their efforts to persuade her to try this arrangement. Although she had a number of minor aches and pains, her chief complaint was a small cyst on her eyelid (Diagnosis: Fibroma). She feared that it might be growing or could lead to something more serious and so felt that it should be checked now (the second day of her vacation) before it was too late. It was only in a somewhat mumbled response to the question of what she expected or would like the doctor to do that she made a connection between the stress she was undergoing with her family and her present insistence on taking care of the cyst. From a list of possible outcomes to her examination, she chose, "Maybe a hospital (ization) . . . Rest would be all right . . . (and then in a barely audible tone) just so they (family) would stop bothering me." The examining physician acceded to her request for removal of the fibroma and referred her to the out-patient operating room. The cyst, however, was only her calling-card and its removal only temporarily alleviated her difficult and threatening interpersonal situation. Her subsequent pattern of medical care bore this out.

Within two weeks after recovery from the operation, she returned to the Eye Clinic still claiming that something was wrong with her eyes. She was sent to Refraction but the tests revealed that glasses were unnecessary. Four months later, she returned again to the Eye Clinic, this time presenting headaches in and around her eyes as the chief complaint. Once again she was examined by an opthalmologist and once again she was refracted. This time, the doctor noted in the record, "Headaches not thought to be on an ocular basis." He did, however, prescribe Collyrium 26 and told her to see her local medical doctor for a more complete examination. (According to her replies in the research interview, she did not really have one.) Seven months later, she appeared at the Emergency Ward with "terrific headaches." She was examined by the attending physicians and given a skull series. The final report states there was no pathology, "though possibly increased intracranial pressure." Several weeks later, she turned to still another avenue of help and asked for an appointment at the Medical Clinic. Here again she presented chiefly the complaint of headaches but this time accompanied by a great deal of bloating and belching. After a series of tests, there appeared in the record the first documented awareness of an underlying psychogenic problem.

The final diagnosis was functional headache and epigastric distress. In the course of the last two years, this woman has presented herself at the clinics of the hospital on five separate occasions, involving some ten visits, with as many doctors and technicians and countless tests and examinations.

MAJOR ORGANIC PATHOLOGY

Paul W. was thirty-nine, married, a college graduate and presently between assignments as a waiter. A week prior to this visit, his face had become chapped when he had gone for a long walk on a windy, rainy day. He applied cold cream and almost immediately his face began to swell. At about the same time, he noticed a loss of vision in his right eye but he decided to wait awhile before doing anything. As he put it, "I like to feel self-sufficient." When asked when he considered himself sick enough to go to a doctor, he replied, "I don't know . . . something obviously calling for medical aid, like appendicitis . . . I feel most people go too frequently, magnify their symptoms out of proportion . . . If they had greater knowledge of self and physical functions, they wouldn't go as often . . . I only go when I can't help myself." As an example, he cited a recent incident. "Last summer I cut my foot and allowed it to become poisoned . . . It became pretty bad . . . When the glands in my groin started to swell and pain, it was time to see a doctor . . . and that was the first time in years." When he asked what made him come now, he replied, "Every man has a dream . . . and this (symptoms) affected mine. You see, I do some writing and that's why we follow the resorts. In between jobs I'm able to do this (writing), but if my eyes go, I couldn't drive to the resorts . . . My worry reached a peak last night. It was the first time that it (symptoms) became so prominent that it affected my continuity, my ability to concentrate and do my work." The physician, however, did not recognize his concern about self-reliance and independence reflected both in his general pattern of medical care and in his delay in seeking help for his current visual problem. Instead he told him that it was necessary to come back for further tests. Paul W. took the appointment slips and never returned. The probably major diagnosis of optic neuritis or multiple sclerosis only emphasizes the implications of this break in treatment.

While it is expected that there would be instances where the patient's psychosocial concerns would go unnoticed, two conclusions may nevertheless be drawn. (*a*) Lack of recognition was in large part due to the doctor's orientation and communication (or lack thereof) with his patient; and (*b*) this lack of attention was more frequent among the practitioners of one specialty rather than another (Eye and ENT vs. Medical). Perhaps the clinician cannot be concerned with the patient's psychosocial problems in this global and general dimensions. Nevertheless, it seems apparent from these cases that he must at least be concerned with those problems which pertain to the patient's presenting complaint and his decision to seek aid. If he does not recognize these concerns, the examining physician may lose an opportunity to treat his patients effectively.

THE CLINIC'S SPATIAL DESIGN AND ORGANIZATION OF WORK

While the organization and physical structure of a clinic is often thought to be determined by the nature of the disorders, the number of patients, and the most efficient mode of treatment, this very structure can also contribute to the dilemma of the physician in attempting to deal with the patient's "problems."

The clinics, for example, differed in physical structure. At the time of this study, each patient in the Medical Clinic was led by his doctor into a private examination room, in most instances, a room not visible to the other patients. In the ENT Clinic, only a curtain and a partition (open at the top) closed out the world of the doctor-patient from the world of the "waiting." The other patients were relatively near, sitting on benches only a yard or two away. The Eye Clinic, both in the screening room and the clinic proper, was the most open of all. No doors, screen or walls—only six feet of space separated the patient being seen from those who were waiting. In many instances, he may be within "touching distance" of the patient being examined next to him.

An innovation at the Medical Clinic indicates that the physical setting of a clinic has more to do with a basic philosophy of patient care than with the limitations set by the disease under treatment. Though the medical examination rooms insured physical privacy (an enclosed room), the new chief felt that they did not insure psychological privacy and so had the walls extended to the ceilings. He felt that it was essential to better medical treatment to facilitate communication between the doctor and the patient and that by insuring complete privacy, he was removing one of the barriers.

The flow of patients and thus the demands on a doctor determine, in part, the amount of time he can spend with each individual. In the Medical Clinic, a modified block appointment system was in operation and limited numbers of patients are assigned to the staff. On the other hand, in both the ENT and the Eye Clinics, a sizeable proportion of patients were seen without appointment (Eye more than ENT). The majority of these "walk-in" patients were not strictly emergency cases, a fact well known to the staff.

Another organizational feature is worthy of mention which was, however, peculiar to the Eye Clinic—the utilization of paramedical personnel. The pattern of this use was especially crucial in the case of the patient who came in for such complaints as headaches, blurriness of vision, or difficulty in reading or seeing objects and whose final diagnosis indicates that "nothing is physically wrong." Initially, they were seen in the screening room or in the clinic proper. Upon examination, no ocular disease was detected. The doctor, however, felt that their eyes should be tested more thoroughly or that their glasses should be checked and so referred them to the Refraction Clinic. There they were seen by an optometrist and told that there was nothing wrong with their vision (20/20) or that there was no necessity to change the prescription of their glasses. Unless the patients requested it (they rarely if ever did), they were not referred back to their examining physician but sent along, still with their headache, their blurriness, their difficulty in seeing. The last person to see these patients was an optometrist, who by training and organizational role in this clinic, functioned primarily as a technician and thus was perhaps the one least likely to be in a position to help them, as well as the one least likely to be asked by these patients for further help.

Thus the utilization of paramedical personnel, the flow of patients, and the use of physical space served to make the Medical Clinic most suited to the recognition of the patient's psychosocial concerns and the Eye Clinic least well suited. More importantly, these features illustrate how the differing spatial structure and organization of the clinics implicitly supported the differing orientations of their physicians.

DISCUSSION

Originally, clinics began as dispensaries to screen patients for hospital admission and therefore were not conceived as treatment centers themselves (Washburn 1939). The increasing number of chronically ill patients and the nature of their medical problems make it evident, however, that more and more patients will be treated in out-patient facilities. In one sense, then, this paper is an extension of previous studies (Grobin 1958; Mannucio, Friedman and Kaufman 1961; Shepherd, Fisher, Stein and Kessel 1959; Tyler 1950) which have called attention to the presence and importance of psychosocial problems in out-patient or ambulatory populations.

The major observations of this study suggest that the recognition of and attention to such problems are influenced by an interplay of several non-medical factors: the patient's ethnic group membership as shown in the way he presents himself and communicates to the doctor; the examining physician's specialty-orientation as it is reflected in his tendency to overlook the patient's psychosocial concerns; and the clinic's spatial design and organization which can be either a stimulant or a barrier to communication. Particularly in cases where the medical condition is not clear-cut, these factors will influence the diagnosis and treatment which a patient receives.

None of these factors are immutable. The physical and spatial structure can be changed to assure more communication. Organizational changes are also possible. For example, in the special instance of the Eye Clinic, refractions might routinely precede the regular examination or some arrangement might be devised whereby patients are referred back to the examining physician, especially when nothing organic is found to account for his symptoms. All clinics could, without sacrificing emergency coverage, regulate the intake and flow of patients and thus allow more time for physician-patient contact. If an individual's condition goes untreated and therefore worsens or becomes more difficult to manage, or if, though untreated, he continues to seek a solution through different avenues, the total costs in time and money would certainly outweigh the costs of an extended or more thorough initial visit.

Physical and organizational changes are, however, only part of the story. Regardless of the degree of privacy, the patient may be unwilling to talk. Findings of the larger study indicated that patients differed in the way they presented themselves to the doctor. It may also be inferred that they differed in what they thought relevant to their illness and what they deemed necessary to tell the doctor. In this paper, it has been demonstrated that, in reality, patients of all three ethnic groups studied had major psychosocial problems and concerns which either caused or exacerbated their conditions or interfered with effective treatment. Yet, in part because of the way the patient initially presented his complaint (which differed by ethnic groups), the recognition of such problems was confined inordinately to one ethnic group. Thus greater attention must be given to the fact that illness or disease is not a purely physical and isolated problem but arises, is perceived, and treated within a social context and this, in turn, will affect the nature of all communication about it.

Doctor-patient communication is, however, a two-way street and evidence has been presented showing that physicians themselves were often unwilling to listen to or probe the patient. Moreover, it seems evident that the doctor's clinical training is at least partly responsible for his difficulty in recognizing and treating such problems and that the training for some specialties prepares one less well than does others. This last observation assumes greater importance as we realize that with the increasing sophistication of the lay population (as well as the increasing specialization of medical personnel) more and more people go directly to specialists or are referred to him at their own request (Williams et al. 1960). While the specialist is necessarily concerned with the treatment of a specific organ or disease, the dilemma arises over what his responsibility is to the patient. In an ever growing number of cases, there simply is no "family doctor" to whom he can return the patient who has pressing psychosocial problems.

CONCLUSION

The question now becomes, should all medical practitioners be capable of recognizing and treating the psychosocial concerns and complaints of the patient? Some feel that this should be the task of other professionals or the task of a special group of medical specialists. To emphasize this point, Churchill (1961, p. 1172) cited the following example:

> a conscientious doctor responded to the call (re: a sick child) but found that the real reason for the vomiting and pain was an angry dispute between the child's parents. After a long day he (the doctor) has to stay until long past midnight in an effort to straighten matters out. An experienced visiting nurse or trained social worker or even the wise neighbor next door might have handled this situation.

While it is problematical to speculate who could best have helped these parents, it is completely unreasonable to expect that any professional or semi-professional other than the physician would have been called in under any circumstances where the immediate problem was a child's vomiting and pain. A similar situation often confronts the specialist. With increasing sophistication and regardless of the "true" or underlying concerns of the patient or the etiology of his specific condition, patients with visual symptoms are more likely to consult an eye specialist; with a nasal condition, an ENT man; with a limb or back ailment, an orthopedist, etc. This has led men like Balint (1957), Magraw (observations on general practice 1959), and Yudkin (observations on pediatric practice 1961) to claim that psychosocial conerns and problems are part of most illnesses and that attention to them is integral to the effective practice of any medical specialty. Thus, while we cannot expect all specialties to be equally interested in the global and general concerns of the patient, we should expect the physician to be aware of those concerns which affect the patient's presenting complaint, his decision to come, and his subsequent willingness to continue in treatment.

If, as Coleman (1962, p. 37) contends, the emotional distance and the barrier to patient-doctor communication

> . . . is not a necessary or inevitable result, nor the price the physician must pay for calling—it's merely the price he pays for the neglect of this aspect of his training,

then it is within the realm of medical education that a solution will have to be found. Certainly, there is ample evidence both in this paper and in other investigations, that the vast majority of patients are reticent, anxious, and even fearful of consulting a doctor. In other words, there is probably a general tendency toward delay. Cognizant of this phenomenon, physicians in general, regardless of the seriousness of the patient's presenting complaint, could acknowledge this anxiety and attempt to reinforce his openness as well as the very fact of his coming at all. There is too little awareness of the two-sidedness of the doctor-patient relationship (Apple 1960, p. 224):

> The roles of the doctor and patient are complementary, and it would be most unusual if ideas in role behavior held by patients were not interlocked with and reinforced by expectations of patients which are held by doctors.

Perhaps the major step toward such awareness is the not-so-simple realization that the doctor can block or reject the patient's communication by his very reaction, or lack of reaction, to the patient's concerns and that this will have profound effects on how much he can help and treat his medical condition.

While the comments in this paper have relevance for the handling of all disorders, they seem to have particular relevance in the treatment and management of chronic illness. With the overwhelming majority of such disorders there is at present no instant cure, no miracle drug, no medical surgical procedure and yet there are continual requests and demands for help and support made by the patient. Treatment has become a question of controlling, maintaining and rehabilitating—processes in which the patients themselves play the major role. With awareness of himself as well as of the patient, the doctor would be in a position to more intelligently intervene and support the patient's own efforts to cope with his disorder.

9

On What Happens When One's Consciousness Gets Raised: A Reflection on "The Problems of Communication . . ."

For years, I used the findings in the previous article to demonstrate the subtle but awesome power of medical labels. Hence I was particularly familiar with the details of the data and the argument. And yet I suffered a significant blindspot until the women's movement changed my consciousness. A look at Table 8-1 demonstrates a diagnostic bias of the physicians with a sample of women. A single clause buried in the text explains this: "Because the number of males which fit this criteria was too small for statistical comparisons . . ." By its placement in the text (i.e. in the introductory paragraphs) and by its terminology, the implication was clear. The issue was described as simply methodological, as commonplace as the statement so often appearing in empirical studies, i.e. "the cells were too small to permit adequate. . ."

One day in the mid 1970s, while presenting this data for the thousandth time, a warning signal went off in my head as I was about to introduce these findings. The class was about to end, so I said, "Tune in Wednesday for the next exciting episode in this research series." Later, for the first time in fifteen years, I reexamined the basic data. I found what turned out to be a curiously prophetic statement early in the original text:

So that we might err on the side of *conservatism* [italics added], a number of diagnoses which did little more than describe the patient's symptoms were excluded.

Although it was true that the responses of the males in the sample could not be easily coded either as "psychogenesis implied" or "no psychogenesis implied," they were indeed, significantly overrepresented in those "descriptive" diagnoses. In other words, where no organic pathology was obviously present, a very convenient nonjudgmental diagnosis was found for male patients. There was no such option for females. In the same situation their complaints were "dismissed" as being either psychological or of no clinical significance, depending on their ethnic group.

To the question I have always been asked subsequently, Yes, all the examining physicians were white males and those that weren't Anglo-Saxon Protestant acted as if they were. Thus I had indeed "erred on the side of conservatism." In addition to the ethnic, organizational, or specialty biases which influenced certain diagnoses, there was also (thanks to the hindsight of history) a sexist bias.

10

The Mirage of Health Revisited: On the Omnipresence of Illness

HISTORICAL BACKGROUND

In the mid 1950s three medical scientists began a critque of the American and Western way of medicine. They were Hans Selye, Thomas Szasz, and Rene Dubos. The respective titles of their books indicate both their concern and their tone: *The Stress of Life* (Selye 1956), *The Myth of Mental Illness* (Szasz 1961) and *The Mirage of Health* (Dubos 1961). They were not necessarily the first to make their particular critique but they were certainly the most articulate. Perhaps because of their eminent positions or their very persistence (each has been "accused" of making the same point since in many different ways), they were also the first to command a wide hearing.

Each in his own way was criticizing the implications of a medical model which conceived of illness as an objective, limited and finite entity. In pointing out the restrictiveness of our notions of clinical entity, Selye noted that differential diagnosis is based on a very small number of characteristics peculiar to that disease and no other, and that by far the largest number of signs and symptoms of any disease are shared with a wide variety of disorders and physiological malfunctioning. Furthermore, the limited success that this notion has

Rewritten from a chapter in *de medische macht: de invloed van de gezondheidszong op de maatschappij*, translated by Marius Vellema (Amsterdam: Boom Meppel, 1973).

had with a few infectious diseases has led to a focussing on disease causation as "invasion from the outside" and to a neglect of the "breakdown" in adaption which takes place within the host. The latter is a more generally diffuse phenomenon which, he argues, is what disease is "really" all about. Szasz was concerned that the supposed "objectivity of illness and its practitioners" has allowed that label to be applied to a whole host of phenomena he called "problems in living." In a long series of books, he has gone on to show not only the social implications of the label "mental illness" but the political motivations that seem to be associated with its use and acceptance. Perhaps the best known critic of all is Rene Dubos. In a series of books (Dubos 1961, 1965, 1968a, b) he criticized our static notion of disease and pointed out that such notions of fixity and finiteness have given us a misplaced and false hope in our attempts to cope with illness. Over the next hill lies no Utopia. After the conquest of cancer or heart disorder lies no world without disease or suffering. Quite the contrary;

> Organized species such as ants have established a satisfactory equili-
> brium with their environment and suffer no great waves of diseases
> or changes in their social structure. But man is essentially dynamic,
> his way of life constantly in flux from century to century. He ex-
> periments with synthetic products and changes his diet; he builds
> cities that breed rats and infection; he builds automobiles and fac-
> tories which pollute the air; and he constructs radioactive bombs. As
> life becomes more comfortable and technology more complicated,
> new factors introduce new dangers; the ingredients for Utopia are the
> agents of new disease. (Dubos 1961, flyleaf)

And thus he coined the expression, "the mirage of health."

All these names and their viewpoints are increasingly well-known to American audiences—even on a certain popular level. Dubos (1968b) has won a Pulitzer Prize and Szasz continues to make the rounds of American TV "talk" shows.

Yet I would contend that twenty years after they first offered their messages—while widely quoted and even lampooned—they have made little headway where it operationally counts: in medical prac-tice, education, expenditures, and research priorities. Perhaps it *is* coming, but I think we can safely agree that it is *not yet here* and thus at very least this lack provides the rationale for this paper.

THE COGNITIVE MAP OF "ILLNESS"

As I proceed to illustrate the omnipresence of disease, you will probably note an interesting irony. For the very same researchers who are providing me with my data on the preva-

lence of illness, at the same time continue in their traditional research directions unimpeded by the implications of their own
remarks. At very least this shows the power of models and what
Gouldner calls "domain assumptions" and how data *per se* is insufficient to change the commitments and orientations even of scientists.

As Dubos, Selye, and Szasz pointed out, the notion of illness as a
discrete, fixed, infrequent entity goes deep. In fact it goes so deep
that it has become part of our cognitive map, built not only into our
thinking but our very tools—namely the way we tabulate and record
the presence of disease. I take as typical the reports of "health
statistics" regularly reported by most governments. For we count
such things as days of disability, doctor visits, and specifically diagnosed conditions, and when we do we are confirmed in our belief
that illness is a relatively infrequent phenomenon. From a handy
compendium of "vital statistics" in the United States I culled the
figures for Table 10-1.

In the same volume, the rates of separate specifically diagnosed conditions are so small that they are usually computed in numbers per
thousand. None of these rates is particularly high and since cross
tabulations are rarely if ever made except in very select populations
(i.e. to demonstrate the existence of multiproblem families), we
never get any total picture. When a realization intrudes on an investigator that people indeed are "sicker" than he was led to believe,
he does not change his orientation but may regard it as an interesting
methodological problem. This was illustrated quite vividly in a study
of coping reactions to a first myocardial infarct. The sample was
quite large, in the hundreds, but the investigator was perplexed
when he discovered that in the vast majority of cases, a myocardial
infarct was not the only major medical problem of his patients. He

Table 10-1
*U.S. Department of Health, Education, and
Welfare Statistics*

MEASURES OF DISABILITY (1959-60)	
Ages 17 or over days out of work	5.6 days per year
Ages 6-16 days out of school	5.3 days per year
All ages bed disability	6.0 days per year
MEDICAL VISITS (1958-1959)	
All ages physician	4.7 visits per year
All ages dental	1.4 visits per year

thus spent most of the next several months in designing a way of "controlling" this fact out of existence. To me, he was doing more, he was controlling reality. For by trying to ignore the fact that a myocardial infarct was just one of many medical and other problems with which his patients had to cope, he was altering their reality and was compromising the practical utility of his findings.

The operation of assumptions about "frequency" and "fixity" is more pervasive than a single example and is reflected in much of the sociomedical research formulated through the late 1960s. To heighten this phenomenon, look at the contrast between some research trends in "mental" versus "physical" illness (See Table 10-2). The behavior of mental patients, if not the very state itself, is usually regarded as problematic, not so in regard to physical illness. There a quite contrary set of assumptions creates an interesting if misleading picture of physical illness and the way it is handled. Rarely do investigators or clinicians try to understand how or why patients go to the doctor, for the decision itself is thought to be an obvious one. We thus postulate a time when the patients are asymptomatic or unaware that they have symptoms. Then suddenly some clear symptoms appear, perhaps followed by a period of self-treatment, and when either this treatment is unsuccessful or the symptoms are in some way too difficult to live with, the "patients" decide to go to some health practitioner.

A "TRUER" EMPIRICAL VIEW OF ILLNESS

Let me piece together what I think is the "real" empirical picture of disorder. I can start with mental illness, which has a long tradition of case-finding in the community. In the 1930s data began to be reported indicating that for every individual hospitalized for mental illness, there was one or more "ambulatory" in the community who perhaps should not be. Gradually, more sophisticated measurements and surveys were created resulting in the two best known studies, The Midtown Manhattan Study and the Stirling County Study. Both were published in the early 1960s and both documented a rather high level of psychosocial disturbance; scarcely 20 percent of the population appeared free from distress (Leighton et al. 1963; Srole et al. 1962). In a separate substudy of the Midtown Manhattan investigation the finding that 75 percent of the total sample manifested "significant symptoms of anxiety" led them to the conclusion that

> anxiety is not only highly prevalent in our population but given that it is completely independent of so important a factor as socio-

Table 10-2
Trends in Illness Research

THE PROBLEM	MENTAL ILLNESS	PHYSICAL ILLNESS
	THE DATA EXAMINED OR QUESTIONS ASKED	
The state or amount of illness in a society	Epidemiological—studies or attempts to measure the *untreated*, often assuming that most or a significant portion do not get into treatment, and a concern with the issue of what is a case	Epidemiological—based on *treated* cases—on the implicit assumption that the vast majority eventually get into treatment and are thus counted, or stated another way, that those untreated do not represent a significantly different population. A clear definition of what a case is.
What is illness? (laity view)	The studies of attitudes toward and perception and *definition* of mental illness	Measures of the accuracy of *knowledge* about certain physical disorders (CA, Heart Disease, Arthritis, Diabetes, etc.)
Doctor usage	The single instance—why do you come now?	Utilization—how often does one go?
Decision to seek	Why he/she comes? (*motivation* for treatment?)	Why he/she delays? (*barriers* against treatment)

economic status, it must be regarded as a highly generalized psychological phenomenon as well. (Rennie et al. 1957, p. 834)

The reactions to such claims have been mixed. They have been criticized on methodological grounds, taken as further proof that the concept "mental illness" is too amorphous a one and that psychiatrists seem to see illness everywhere. Surely it is claimed this does not apply to what we know as "physical illness" and surely not to the perspectives of medical practitioners.

Well, it all depends on where you look for your data. For in a most unlikely place, figures on a similarly high prevalence of physical illness have been accumulating. The repositories I refer to are journals of industrial and occupational medicine and the myriad health reports which businesses and large-scale institutions publish. The data is from their "periodic health examinations." From business executives to union members, from college students to college professors, the reports note that at the time of their annual check-up, there was scarcely an individual who did not possess some symptom or clinical entity worthy of treatment. The figures range from 50 percent to 90 percent of all "examinees." And yet these statistics describe a supposedly healthy population, people both employed and financially secure (Meigs 1961; Siegel 1963).

My favorite illustration of this point, mostly because of its detailed reasoning, is a rather old study named The Peckham Experiment (Pearse and Crocker 1938, 1949). During the late thirties in London, England, a group of physicians specializing in preventive medicine grew concerned with the problem of how people stay healthy. They did not want to study the problem of ailments; they wanted to learn how to institute good preventive medicine programs. To do this they created a center in Peckham, which is just outside London. They chose this area because in that locale all the statistics on morbidity, mortality, juvenile delinquency, and other social problems were relatively low. The residents were described as being of "good working class stock," "good lower middle class," clerical, and white collar. They were neither the very poor nor the very rich. The physicians organized a recreational center where people could congregate. Since the researchers were interested in how this population maintained its good health, however, they required that everyone coming to the center had to submit to a physical examination at least once a year, and that in addition to this examination, medical care would generally be available for them. The researchers' aim here was to gain a baseline measure of the general health of the people. With this as a standard they could later note change. They were very strict about their criteria. They started with an assumption: "Biology is concerned with the function of the living organism and any deviation from this function that is observable is worthy of note" (Pearse and Crocker 1938, p. 50ff.).

Then they gave the following definitions.

A. In this survey we have dealt only with those conditions which are universally recognized as clinical entities. Symptoms such as constipation, headaches, rheumatism or the milder forms of dysmenorrhea, our knowledge of which depended only on the testimony of the member, have not been included in this list.

B. Again conditions such as the milder catarrhs, bronchitis, sinusitis, vaginitis, though accompanied by some visible manifestation have been excluded.

C. Moreover where an appendix has been removed, a hernia repaired, teeth stopped, the repaired lesion does not count.

D. Neither is any mention made of the various psychological conditions or social maladjustments.

E. Eye conditions are also omitted.
   The schedule of diseases given here is thus to be read in the straightforward clinical sense. It represents active or progressive lesions of one kind or another of a definite clinical nature. It is not a list of biological shortcomings measured by any theoretical standard.

Two further definitions were used: Disorder was the presence of clinical entities, as determined by a professional diagnostician, while disease was the subjective state of discomfort verbalized by the individual. With all these qualifications, the results of their first examination of this supposedly healthy population were as in Table 10-3. In the total study sample of 3,911 people of all ages, 3,553 or 91 percent were diagnosed upon complete examination as having some

Table 10-3
Disorder: Relationships between Males and Females

TYPES OF DISORDERS	MALES		FEMALES	
	NO.	PERCENT	NO.	PERCENT
I Disorder accompanied by disease	165	21	163	21
II Disorder without disease	484	63	568	75
III Without disorder	123	16	33	4

Source: Pearse and Crocker 1949, p. 97

physiological defect or aberration. After examining 9 percent of the population that had no problem, they noted two qualifications—an over-representation of children under the age of five, and people in good general condition under normal circumstances but not necessarily under certain unexpected emergency conditions (e.g. a person who had been given a "clean bill of health" dying soon after of a heart attack). Thus an enormous number of symptoms and conditions occurred in this population, conditions which doctors would doubtlessly label sickness if they appeared in patients seeking aid.

DOES WHAT IS "MISSED" MATTER?

Before turning from this data it is necessary to deal with some obvious criticisms. The first is that the bulk of this high prevalence figure is made up of relatively minor problems. It is worth noting, however, that minor does not mean insignificant, for many of these problems, such as obesity, are regarded by the medical profession as the potential precursors of much more serious conditions. Moreover, studies of doctors' practices reveal that the bulk of the problems they daily confront are of the "minor" variety. Thus doctors have traditionally argued that while they miss many such conditions, what they miss is unimportant, "not serious." Logan and Cushion (1958), engaged in one of the largest surveys of morbidity, claimed that "for practical purposes it can be assumed that the general practitioner sees, during the course of a year, virtually all the significant illnesses in his practices." But does he? In the above mentioned Peckham study every type and seriousness of disorder was found in the class of individuals who are unaware of or disregard their symptoms—from multiple sclerosis to cancer to tuberculosis, including various vorms of heart disease. J. Morris (1967, p. 122) put this into statistical terms. From available epidemiological data and clinical surveys he estimated that "in an average British general practice of 2,250 persons, for every 8 in one year he sees, there are 69 with 'latent diabetes. . . . and for every 5 he sees with ischeamic heart disease there are 15 more undetected."

The final "fall back position" is representativeness. Some will admit that the physician never sees some cases, including some serious cases, but the argument was that those he does see and treat are representative of the universe of such cases. But now even this most unquestioned of assumptions (and therefore uninvestigated) is being called into doubt. All studies must deal with the problem of those not included in their sample—the nonrespondents—and researchers often go to great lengths to show that the missing are just like or at least "not significantly different" from the included. In medicine, because of many of the assumptions I have already delineated, this justification was never thought necessary. But now there exist data which show that those individuals who did go into treatment were in certain important ways unrepresentative of all those who had the disease. Let's look at some examples and their implications.

Sometimes this unrepresentativeness may lead to an over- or underestimation of a disease's extent and seriousness. May Clarke's *Trouble with Feet* (1969) is instructive. She notes that between 55 and 90 percent (patient report versus chiropodist examination) of her sample of 1,100 adults had something the matter with their feet. The conditions ranged from corns to skin infections, from ingrown toenails to hammer toes. Yet only 17 percent of these problems had ever been treated, although they were often painful and inconvenient; ironically, they are often functionally crippling for the aged, though clinically not "serious." But most people regard them as an ordinary consequence of life and worthy only of "self-treatment." In this way neglect is perpetuated. In a similar vein, scarlet fever was thought to be a relatively mild disease without serious complications because the early reporters like Sydenham primarily dealt with wealthy patients (Rosen 1967). A case of over-estimation of seriousness is histoplasmosis, which until the late 1940s was thought to be a rare tropical disease, with a uniform, fatal outcome. Recently, however, it was discovered that it is widely prevalent, and with fatal outcome or impairment extremely rare (Schwartz and Baum 1957).

Sometimes the lack of representativeness leads to invalid generalizations. Thus it was formerly believed that Buerger's disease was prevalent in Eastern European Jews. Later it was discovered that this conclusion reflected less the nature of the disease than fact that Dr. Buerger made his observations at Mount Sinai Hospital in New York City—an institution which served predominantly Jewish patients (Schmideberg 1961). A study by Cobb (1963) has shed doubt on the traditional emphasis on arthritis as being a predominantly female disease. When all the employed males in a factory were surveyed for prodromal arthritic symptoms, their rates were as high as any of those traditionally reported for women. It thus seems that the oft reported gender difference in arthritis reflects a greater tendency for women to seek aid for arthritic-like symptoms.

The prevalence of peptic ulcer provides a final example. Raper (1958) first confirmed the stereotype that peptic ulcer was relatively infrequent among African tribal groups and therefore concluded that it was associated (as many had claimed) with the stresses and strains of modern living. Yet when he relied not on reported diagnosis but on autopsy data, he found that the scars of peptic ulcer were no less common than in Britain.

Occasionally, the lack of representativeness may lead to questioning the very conceptualization and measurement of the disease. For example, it was discovered with some surprise that a fair proportion of the general population outside the consulting room manifests the signs of high blood pressure without any apparent complaint or ill effects (Freidson 1970, p. 270). Similarly, a community study searching for undetected diabetes revealed a great many cases which by clinical standards should have resulted in much more serious impairment if not in a comatose condition; Butterfield (1968) wondered if the very clinical criteria of diabetes, based as they are on treated cases, might need to be changed.

Thus I conclude that illness, instead of being a relatively infrequent or abnormal phenomenon, is the statistical *norm*!

THE OPERATION OF THE CLINICAL PERSPECTIVE

Assuming that this prevalence of disease is "real," how did it come to be? At very least we are dealing with an interplay of the clinical perspective and a new population awareness. We will turn to the what Freidson has called "the professional construction of illness" first.

An analogy: the priest in his confessional assumes that none are without sin; the physician in his office assumes that none are without disease. From another perspective: in an American courtroom the defendant is assumed innocent until proven guilty; in a doctor's office, the patient is assumed sick until proven healthy. The priest, the doctor, the judge—all make decisions. Thomas Scheff (1964) argues that members of professions (including medicine) are frequently confronted with uncertainty in their routine diagnoses. Informal norms, based on the assumption that some errors are more to be avoided than others, have developed for handling this uncertainty. Doctors, he claims, believe that judging a sick person well is more to be avoided than judging a well person sick. At least one consequence is labelling some healthy patients sick.

Is there evidence for such a bias? Disagreement over diagnoses is common, but I am concerned with the "directionality" of such disagreement. Garland (1959) reports that out of 14,867 X-ray readings for tuberculosis, 1,216 were initially interpreted as providing positive indication of TB but were subsequently interpreted as negative (false positive); only twenty-four of those interpreted as negative were later declared positive (defined as false negatives). But perhaps most illuminating is a report by Bakwin (1945) of a 1934 survey by the American Child Health Association of doctor's judgments on the advisability of tonsillectomy for 1,000 schoolchildren. Some 611 of this thousand had already had their tonsils removed. The remaining 389 were then examined by another set of physicians, who selected 174 for tonsillectomy. This left 215 children whose tonsils were apparently normal. Another group of doctors then examined these 215 children and judged 99 in need of tonsillectomy. Still another group of doctors examined the remaining children, and nearly one-half were recommended for operation.

According to Freidson (1970a, p. 259), American medicine displays

> the thrust toward active intervention that is inherent in clinical practice as such. While the physician's job is to make decisions, including the decision not to do anything, the fact seems to be that the everyday practitioner feels impelled to do something, if only to satisfy patients who urge him to do something when they are in distress.

Friedson cited two studies in support of this thesis. The first is a survey finding that a prime reason why physicians prescribe is the reported fear of not doing anything (Dowling 1963). The second is a study of surgical decisions which concluded that virtually every diagnosis of de Stetin-Leventhal syndrome is erroneous (Peterson, Barsamian and Eden 1966). That mistaken diagnosis is apparently popular because the syndrome represents the only type of infertility that benefits from surgery. By making the diagnosis the doctor encourages the patient to feel that everything is being done in order to help. A more serious outcome of this clinical perspective emerges from a study which took place beyond the borders of the United States. Sigrid Lichtner and Manfred Pflanz (1971) decided to focus on the epidemiology of appendectomy because it represented such a well-defined disease. Observing first that the death rate for appendicitis was three to four times higher in German-speaking countries (Federal Republic of Germany, German Democratic Republic, West Berlin, Austria) than elsewhere in Europe, they then noted a similar high rate within the Federal Republic of Germany itself. There the rate was two to three times higher than in non-German-speaking countries. At this point they made a detailed comparison between Oxford, England, and Hannover, West Germany. In Oxford, 12.7 percent of all males and 12.1 percent of all females will undergo an appendectomy prior to their 75th year; in Hannover the percent will be 33.7 for males and 46.2 for females. And so Lichtner and Pflanz naturally wondered what was going on. Nothing they knew led them to think these percentages reflected any true incidence of disease. Local findings bore out this negative conclusion, for on the basis of pathological-anatomical findings,

> acute appendicitis led to surgery in only one out of three men and in one out of five women. The biggest fraction is accounted for by "recurrent scarred appendicitis" which practically represents a normal status. It may be assumed further that the terms "neurogenic appendicitis" and "chronic appendicitis" stand for more or less normal findings. Thus there has been no strict indication in almost two thirds of the operations performed. (p. 322)

The disease also seems to display a nonorganically explainable demographic distribution in Hannover—namely, it hardly occurs on weekends and afflicts white-collar workers three times more often than blue-collar workers. Lichtner and Pflanz offer several explanations for these findings. They mention first the possibility of certain psychosomatic conflicts, perhaps "favored" among Germanic peoples, which may result in abdominal pains and a resulting pressure for surgery. Somehow, however, one feels that they place little credence in this explanation; they devote very little space to it. A more likely cause lies in the orientation of the physician:

> In face of the lack of characteristic symptoms in uncomplicated acute appendicitis, it would not be surprising if fashion trends played a great part especially in this disease. There is only one sound reason why surgeons in the Federal Republic should perform appendectomies voluntarily for their own interest, i.e. if in order to obtain the certificate as a specialist of surgery, the applicant is required to perform a nonspecified but relatively large number of appendectomies. According to some word of mouth communications, 40 to 60 appendectomies are the absolute minimum but many applicants can boast more than 200 cases. (p. 327)

Serious consequences can evolve even when overdiagnosis and overtreatment do not result in surgery or medical intervention. Meador (1965) writes of this in describing "nondisease"—a diagnostic label applied when someone is incorrectly diagnosed as ill of a particular disease is later found free of it.

All false positives become potential nondiseases. Superficially, it would seem that having a nondisease is hardly more serious than the cost, temporary worry, and annoyance incurred between the initial and final diagnoses. In any case, medical opinion holds that it is more serious to miss a disease, even if a "temporary" diagnosis results in surgery. But Freidson (1970a) notes that the label "illness" has other implications, not all of which are supplied or controlled by the diagnosing physician. For all too many people, merely being suspected of a particular illness proves damaging. This is true not merely in cases of mental illness (all too often the questions on medical forms ask whether you have ever consulted a psychiatrist or been in a mental hospital—but not your final diagnosis or treatment), but for cases in which benign tumors were not caught, in which vitreous opacities did not indicate neurological damage, for the all too many conditions described as "low" or "high," as the case may be, but which lie "within normal limits," and for all those signs and bodily states which "one should keep an eye on though they are nothing to be alarmed or worried about." "Don't worry," when expressed by a physician, must be among the most noncomforting messages in the Englishg language. Thus Warren and Walter (1954, p. 78) conclude:

> The physician, by calling attention to a murmur or some cardiovascular abnormality, even though functionally insignificant, may precipitate (symptoms of heart disease). The experience of the work classification units of cardiac-in-industry programs, where patients with cardiovascular disease are evaluated as to work capacity, gives impressive evidence regarding the high incidence of such functional manifestations in persons with the diagnosis of cardiac lesion.

THE PUBLIC'S PERCEPTION

It is not merely professionals who hold somewhat inconsistent attitudes concerning the prevalence of illness. Although public opinion surveys report that most people describe themselves as feeling healthy, substantial numbers—from 50 to 75 percent—report having experienced a recent medical difficulty. "Recent" used to mean within the last year, but now surveys often specify the last two weeks or even the last 24 hours. A current study in England noted that of 2,153 adults, only 5 percent had no complaints during the fourteen days before the interview (Wadsworth, Butterfield, and Blaney 1971). Even this finding does not give a clear picture, for it perceives and reports the illness that occurred as a one-time event.

A clearer picture of illnesses' statistical omnipresence can be illustrated by the following computation of Hinkle et al. (1969). The authors noted that over a twenty-year period the average lower-middle-class male between the ages of twenty and forty-five experiences approximately one life-endangering illness, twenty disabling illnesses, 200 nondisabling illnesses, and 1,000 "symptomatic" episodes. The total amounts to 1,221 episodes over 7,300 days, or one new episode every six days. This figure however, takes no account of the duration of a particular condition; nor does it consider any disorder of which the respondent may be unaware. In short, even among members of a supposedly "healthy" population scarcely a day goes by without a "symptomatic experience."

A study by Kosa and his colleagues (1965) makes this point even more vividly. Seventy-eight families who kept a health calendar for an average of 25.9 days, reported 834 medical symptoms, 136 upsetting events, 12 chronic stress situations and 11 crises. And some recent data culled by myself indicates that even these figures may be too low. For when I assigned a group of college students (supposedly among the most healthy of population samples) to keep a health calendar of their bodily discomforts, I found that the more structured I made my questioning—for example, by having them take notes on their bodily states at specific time intervals instead of only at the end of the day—the more symptoms they described. Thus there was virtually no one who did not experience one or more bodily discomforts a day, severe enough for them to notice and require some behavioral response.

We used to rationalize that this high level of prevalence did not translate itself into action because medical rates are astonishingly high and still rising. Some recent studies, however, indicate that we may have been looking in the wrong place for this medical action. It has been noted by both American (White et al. 1967) and British investigations (Dunnell and Cartwright 1972) that from 50 to 80 percent of the adult population has taken one or more "medical drugs" within any given 24–36 hour period.

I think we are seeing just the beginning. For the public is like a sleeping giant awakening to more and more bodily awareness. As I noted previously, part of this awakening is related to a rising standard of living and a consequent decline in mortality. For when "the here and now" begins to expand, when men and women can live to fifty, sixty, or seventy and suffer diseases they never dreamed of, then this life and its most concrete embodiment, the human body, becomes of increasing interest and concern. Yet this concern need not express itself in merely a negative fashion, as in emphasizing how "unhealthy" we really are. As my colleague Egon Bittner pointed out, it may lead to interest in how to make one feel, look, or function better. The health food movement in the United States, for example, has emphasized not only our previously ill-nourished state but that our health can be improved with purer foods. Yoga and related disciplines emphasize the oneness of mind and body, and the necessity to get back in touch with our deepest inner thoughts and bodily states. Finally, the human growth potential movement as well as women's liberation continually emphasize how culture has repressed our potential to experience our own bodies (from bodily sensations to bodily contacts).

From still another, though certainly not independent source, the fourth estate, comes a further negative focussing on the human body. Anyone reading the scientific, pharmacological, and medical literature will find a growing litany of "unhealthy" life activities. From sex to food, from aspirins to clothes, from driving your car to riding the surf, it seems that under certain conditions, or in combination with certain other substances or activities, or if done too much or too little, virtually anything *can* lead to medical problems. It seems that living is injurous to health—a facetious remark with an element of truth: every aspect of our daily life has in it elements of risk to health.

OVERVIEW

The general argument of this paper is that belief in the fixity, finiteness, and infrequency of illness allows us to think of it as controllable, and therefore of minor concern. On the other hand, viewing illness as fluid, infinite, and very frequent (by whatever clinical standards are currently practiced) opens us to its pervasiveness as well as its lack of objectivity. This in turn means several things. The pervasiveness of symptoms and the infrequency of medical attention provide still further reasons to study what people do to and for themselves (Zola 1972b,c and chapters 13–16 in this volume). Since people clearly respond to bodily discomforts, often in ways that work (Dunnell and Cartwright 1972), it is time to stop dismissing all "folk remedies" and self-medications as quaint practices. We must recognize them for what they are—existential and viable alternatives to orthodox medical care. There are also political implications. On the one hand, illness and symptoms are experienced by all of us all of the time. On the other hand, the diagnosis, the treatment, and even the very legitimation of their existence has been restricted largely to physicians, both legally and economically (Zola 1972a). Thus the practitioners of medicine possess great power to intervene in our lives. And when, as in the latter part of the twentieth century, health and illness become of increasing importance, when parts of everyday life become increasingly medicalized (Zola 1972a), this group gains increasing control and influence over what we should and should not do to our bodies (Freidson 1970a, Zola 1975a). For this reason their work, their judgments, and their assumptions must be open to systematic inquiry, study, and even criticism.

11   *An Error in Research Judgment*

"Follow what I say, not what I do" was advice my mother gave me to deal with her contradictions. It is the same advice I would give readers who are interested in the follow-up to the previous research.

I am often asked, in regard to many of my writings, "What have you done further on . . . ?" It is an easy question to deal with, and I usually answer that something else has caught my interest, that I really am a bit of an intellectual dilettante, or simply that I have carried the issue as far as I can. Glib answers, but usually true. But occasionally the questioner probes deeper; "I thought you had a grant to follow up your earlier work on decision-making. But I've never seen it referred to. What happened?" Then I have no glib responses. Here is the sad answer: I screwed up.

The problem began with an embarrassment of riches. The early 1960s was a golden age for the funding of social science, and I took advantage of it. Partly to give myself more options while I looked for an academic position and partly because I wanted to follow up my research on "seeking medical aid," I applied to the National Institute of General Medical Sciences for financial support. Shortly after accepting a position as an assistant professor at Brandeis, I was awarded a three-year (1963–1966) federal grant. The advice which I was given and which I unfortunately followed was to take it with me, to retain the principal investigatorship, and to hire a project director. I was told that the grant would supplement my income (true), increase my independence of academia (partly true), enhance my clout in the department (hardly), add immeasurably to my general status (false), and be relatively easy to do (impossibly naive). And so I took the grant to Brandeis and proceeded to hire a project director and a staff. At one time there was in addition to myself, a full-time project director, secretary, one senior research associate, two research assistants, three part-time coders and data analysts, and a part-time interviewing staff of nearly a dozen.

In re-reading the grant application I see that the confidence of the awarding committee was not entirely misplaced. Though one reviewer later confided that the committee thought I promised more for the money than I could ever deliver, my lack of delivery was due to factors other than money. On the whole the project was well-conceived, well designed, methodologically sophisticated, and ingeniously implemented. However, it subsequently disintegrated in the stages of execution, coding, analysis and interpretation. Let me state it another way. We indeed designed the study I promised, got it into the field, collected all the necessary data on over a hundred respondents. But we took in much more material than we could use or comprehend, and it took longer to collect than expected. Moreover, we overcoded the material, underanalyzed what we did code, and essentially interpreted little.

Of course, I could draw on the usual reasons to defend this failure: money ran out prematurely; key staff members left unexpectedly; and so forth. The basic problem, however, was that I tried to reassert control over the study when it was already too late. I could no longer make sense out of many research decisions and thus was at a loss how to formulate appropriate analyses. In short, I had lost control long before I realized it. I had pushed too quickly in designing the study. In fact, I had applied for the grant (1962) long before the previous data was fully analyzed. Had I remained full-time on the project I would have designed it differently. In the original investigation, I was close to the data. Not only was I the collector, but I was in many ways preanalyzing it. Thus when I sensed something missing I could alter my strategy by adding or dropping questions. As it was, I had other people implementing my (sometimes) half-baked hunches and making decisions on methodological rather than substantive grounds. Thus when I finally got involved, it was in a real sense no longer my study. In retrospect I could have handled it as data collected by someone else. But I did not. Money ran out, and the granting agency, satisfied with its final report, refused further funding. I was already pursuing other academic and research interests, so I cut my losses and filed the data for some later time. Of course, that later time has never really come and the data remains largely in crates, some of it destroyed by mould and age.

There is, however, an "on the other hand." Although much of the data has been forever lost, the experience was not. On the most mundane level, the project provided income for a number of good people as they struggled through undergraduate and graduate school. At least one doctoral dissertation emerged from the data, Elizabeth Hartwell's (1967), as did several undergraduate papers. Nor should anyone suspect that there were "professional" reasons for dumping the data. The data from Hartwell's work as well as the undergraduate papers again confirmed the persistence of some basic ethnic patterns (for example, the basic thesis of "Culture and Symptoms"). My general reading of the marginals and the raw interviews confirmed the earlier patterns of "symptom presentation" and "medical decision-making." There were some interesting new findings on how people used check-ups. This is reported in "Studying the Decision . . ." reprinted in Part IV of this volume. But the most important benefit was what this experience told me about doing research. In the ensuing decades, I have taught methodology courses, supervised countless dissertations, been a frequent reviewer for governmental agencies and a long-term consultant to several epidemiological investigations. Thus "my error in research judgment" was to bear fruit not only in such forays but also in the papers reproduced in Part IV.

Part Four

So Where Do We Go From Here? Research Directions and Applications

I think that much of my writing reflects the example of an American singer who was making his European debut in a renowned Italian opera house. After performing a particularly difficult aria, the audience responded, "Encore! Encore!" He repeated the passage. "Encore! Encore!" shouted the audience. So again he resung the aria. After several repetitions of this sequence, he turned to the people, "Thank you! Thank you! Thank you for your appreciation. But I am exhausted. I simply cannot do it again." "What appreciation?" yelled someone from the second balcony. "You gonna sing it till you get it right!"

Like the American novice, I sometimes present my material prematurely, before it is a finished product. And like him I may have to redo it until I get it right. Thus a characteristic of my work is that many ideas start out as a footnote, a memorandum, or an observation in a book review. They may go through several published versions as I continue to explore their implications.

In that sense the following series of essays may appear both self-indulgent and problematic; they contain ideas still in the process of formulation. Most of the papers have not circulated widely (some might say, "Thank God") and some are but fragments written in outline form. I reproduce them here because they are the product of over a decade of research consulting.

Between 1965 and 1972 I was involved in the design of several large-scale health surveys. None were academically based. Each pushed me to create instruments for very different populations, and each of the projects were directly tied to pragmatic and policy concerns. Two were conducted inside the United States and two outside its borders. In the American studies (one for the Kaiser-Permanente Health Plan and a second for the United States Public Health Service) I was most active in the design phases; in the other two I was involved in various stages of implementation. Indeed, I had time for greater involvement, for I spent two separate years as consultant in residence, first to the World Health Organization in Geneva (1968–69) and later to the Netherlands Institute of Preventive Medicine in Leiden (1971–72).

The first two papers grew directly out of my stay with the World Health Organization. Some social and political background about this organization will prove helpful. Founded in 1948, WHO is the largest public health organization in the world. Though revolutionary in scope, I found it to be very traditional in approach. Until the late 1960s, for example, WHO gave little more than lip service to the importance of cultural factors in the countries it served. Perhaps this is not such a surprise. The varying suborganizations which comprised it, the placing of countries in certain regions, and the tasks assigned to particular regions were born of political compromise. Moreover, many of its staff, particularly members away from the home office in Geneva, had been trained in medical care as part of the British, French, or other European colonial medical services— not necessarily the best training ground for understanding a population they were supposed to serve. Thus when a special division, Research in Epidemiology and Communications Science, was created in 1967, it should be no surprise that its very organization, its membership (based on "quotas" from certain countries), its research mandate and ultimately its usefulness were politically circumscribed. Ray Elling (1976, 1978) among others has described how these issues affected the specific design of research.

It was thus with some uncertainty that I arrived in Geneva in the fall of 1968 as a research consultant on "cultural" issues. I was a 33-year-old man from Dorchester who had traveled outside American borders on only one previous occasion. My expertise on "culture" was based on a series of ethnic comparisons between Irish, Italians, and Anglo-Saxons who (like me) lived in the suburbs of Boston. I was overwhelmed. And so at first I complied with the suggestion of my superiors to bury myself "in the literature" as preparation for a report on "the importance of cultural issues in the delivery of medical services." However, when my initial anxiety subsided, my general wish to *see* and *do* reemerged. Besides, I discovered that my colleagues at the division were not waiting with bated breath for my report. In fact, they were already in the process of putting studies in the field. Thus, even if I wrote a report they later considered brilliant, it could have no affect on their current research. For this reason I convinced my superiors as well as my colleagues to let me join several research studies already in progress, and make my contributions in that way. In this way began one of the most exciting and adventurous years of life. Not only were my colleagues genial and intelligent, but they came from all over the globe. Not only was I to design investigations for countries in Africa and South America, but I was to visit and implement research in Israel, Iran, and India. And in the end, borne out of practical experience, I ultimately wrote my report.

How Sick Is Sick: Working Notes and Reflections on the Cross-Cultural Study of Illness (1970c) was the formal title of the technical report I submitted to WHO. The two essays which open Part IV were originally part of that document. Chapter 13, "The Concept of Trouble," arose directly from the need to create a schema for the study of health and illness which was not culture-bound. This was my theoretical and research attempt in that direction. The second essay, "studying the Decision . . ." (chapter 14), arose from a debate within a research team as to the "best" measure of illness. I believed there was no single best index. Each measure would tell us something different. It all depended on our specifying *why* we wanted to know *what* we wanted to know. In other words, the most important measure of illness depended on the level of action/intervention we were capable or willing to undertake. As with much of my writing, the publication dates of these articles are deceptive. Basically they were all written in the summer of 1969, revised and resubmitted to WHO in the winter of 1970. However, on my return to the United States in 1969 I presented the report to a conference. When a decision was made to publish the proceedings they asked permission to reprint my work. Well over a year later the editor felt that more concise articles were appropriate, and returned the manuscript. I then excerpted and submitted "The Concept of Trouble" (1972b) for publication elsewhere. It was accepted. "Studying the Decision" (1972c) came in response to a request from Z. J. Lipowski to contribute an essay to a volume he was editing for *Advances in Psychosomatic Medicine*. I reviewed the literature on "decision-making" and then offered a reconceptualization of the problem—an update and revision of my original research memo to WHO.

The next two pieces (chapters 15 and 16) are even more specific in their research focus. Both were alluded to in my work, but it was not until I returned to the Netherlands that I made explicit what had to this point been implicit. At the end of my stay I again wrote a consultant's report, *Issues and Suggestions in the Study of Health and Illness Behavior* (1972e), which I submitted to the Netherlands Institute of Preventive Medicine in June of 1972. Though neither has ever been published, they formulated important material I have been "peddling" for well over a decade. Part IV concludes with a quite general article, "When Getting into the Field . . ." (chapter 17) which grew out of an invitation to reflect on the relationship of an investigator to his data. It represents my attempt to apply a personal perspective, to justify the subjective involvement of a researcher in the people and material he seeks to understand. It also embodies the point of view that stimulated the creation of this book.

The Concept of Trouble and Sources of Medical Assistance: To Whom One Can Turn, with What and Why

Disease of one kind or another has afflicted mankind in all times and places. Thus, in all human groups there exists a body of belief about the nature of disease, its cause, cure, and possible avoidance, as well as a whole range of therapeutic practices many of which are the exclusive property of, and are dispensed or supervised by a group of men or women who vary both in their degree of technical (a particular method or disease) and occupational (part-time, full-time) specialization.

It is this last observation—the occupational specialization—which has caught the eye and at the same time misled sociomedical investigators in their attempts (both historically and cross-sectionally) to describe and analyze medical care. For while such a high degree of occupational specialization (e.g. the standard medical degree in Western societies) can be rightly interpreted as meaning that *this* source of medical aid is the society's officially mandated one, the legal one, the most respected one, and by some standards even the "best" one—it does not necessarily mean that it is the *only* one nor that it treats the majority or most significant illnesses which trouble the doctor's potential clientele.

Originally appeared as "The Concept of Trouble and Sources of Medical Assistance—To Whom One Can Turn, with What and Why," *Social Science and Medicine* 6 (1972): 673-679.

While many of these untreated conditions may be subliminal or unacknowledged by their bearer, the majority are not—the people have the symptoms, are aware of them, and either decide to do something about them or not. The remainder of this section will be devoted to the action of others—"medical" and non-medical and the question—if they do not go to the orthodox or generally provided medical care system, where do they go? (This, interestingly enough, is a relevant question even in a well-staffed and fully financed medical care system [i.e. where the patient has to pay little or no fee], as pointed out by Freidson's (1961) observations of the Montefiore Demonstration Plan and the general observations made about the British Health Service.) The extent to which the orthodox (or in today's phraseology, establishment) medicine is functionally ignorant or blind to any alternative sources of medical care is illustrated by a personal experience. During 1967 and 1968 I was a consultant to a large metropolitan teaching hospital which had decided to make a special effort to provide medical care to the ethnic minority of its catchment area—largely Negro, Cuban and Puerto Rican. It was not merely that the staff did not know of the existence of the local marginal practitioners (e.g. healers, curandisimos, etc.), they did not even know the local "orthodox" medical practitioners who were not affiliated with the hospital and were primarily members of the ethnic minority to be served. The case for identifying and studying non-orthodox, medical practitioners in developing countries is even more straightforward, for there it is patently obvious that the bulk of medical services is being provided by just such "marginal doctors."

Saying that it is important to study such phenomena is, however, easier said than done. For there is in reality a large body of data, one might even say tradition, which has long recorded the existence of such practices and practitioners. The problem is *how* such observations were reported and interpreted. Missionaries spoke of barbaric and cruel remedies, anthropologists of esoteric, exotic, and occasionally erotic practices, and Western medical men of unscientific theories and treatments. Even today such evaluations are at very least latent in our continual insistence in talking about scientific-modern medicine versus popular traditional medicine or civilized rational beliefs versus primitive magical thinking. This very terminology not only embodies an evaluative component, but a normative one as well—we could only describe and understand such "medicine" by comparison with our brand, we could not (or did not) literally make any effort to understand it neutrally or in its own right, in its own context. But gradually and almost imperceptibly a shift or at least a broadening of perspective has occurred. As mentioned, the practices continued and even flourished, and though the list of successes and acceptances of Western medicine was impressive, the area of rejection or distortion was disturbing (Paul 1955; Saunders 1954a & b).

On the research level a similar shift was also taking place. While there was a continuing tradition of describing the cultural differences in what is normal and abnormal between them and us (Devereux 1956; Opler 1959), there was a newer concern with studying the possible efficacy of many of the traditional practices (Efron 1967; Kiev 1964, 1968). While most of the time the standard of comparison for normalcy or efficacy was still to be found in the West, recently even these standards have come into question. Thus whether it be medical researchers (Dubos 1961), or clinicians (Ratner 1962) or psychiatrists (Szasz 1961) or historians (Foucault 1965; Rosen 1944, 1968), the objectivity and the "value-freeness" of the Western notion of disease has been called into question and several social scientists have spleculated as to what these values might be (Goffman 1961; Scheff 1966). The recent statements of "radical" physicians at the 1969 American Medical Association Convention went even further and accused orthodox medicine of purveying some basically anti-social and discriminating policies and treatments.

The final step is seen in the more specific contextual awareness of all medical beliefs and practices. (Much of the following pages was suggested by the writings of Lucy Mair [1969]). For instance, some of the differences between Western and African belief systems can be seen in the differential concerns each have for understanding the nature of human suffering—the why me and nobody else phenomenon. While for some highly educated and sophisticated it is perceived as best a philosophical problem for many others it is a real existential issue. For despite all our technical explanations of the mechanism of disease, the question always remains—Why me? Why just then? For all sick persons do not die, all persons exposed to an infection do not catch it, all who smoke do not suffer from lung cancer, several others went up the ladder before it broke, and all who fall in skiing do not break their legs etc. As Mair and others have pointed out, in many African societies the belief in magic and witchcraft is associated with just this kind of "injustice." To them events like the aforementioned are caused, accident is simply and literally incomprehensible. Mair (1969 p. 240) further speculates that the Western situation may not be so radically different:

So perhaps the world of modern technology is too complacent in its attitude towards the belief in witchcraft. With the advance of knowledge has come an understanding of physical causes that are unknown in the countries where the belief is still an indispensable element of cosmology. Few members of technologically developed countries now see events that affect them directly as expressing the plans of a personified deity, even fewer envisage the existence of a personified evil spirit and none suppose that such a spirit makes human beings his tool. It is easy to look down on societies, contemporary or historical, in which remedies or revenge for disasters are sought in terms of this kind of world view. But in reality we do not stoically accept that a misfortune either has a rational cause or is explicable—that we either know what to do about it or must endure it—and we are no more willing than primitive folk to recognize our own responsibility for our failures. When these are private failures, we are no longer allowed to seek out the person responsible and make him suffer; we have to be content with grumbling about anonymous jealousies or prejudices.

Even the specific content of "modern" versus "primitive" etiology is not so markedly different as the terms "modern-scientific" or "primitive-magic" would imply. It is not so surprising that different peoples have different responses to what causes disease, for each of the beliefs of any society is founded to a large extent on the "faith" that the lay population have in our respective and somewhat distant experts in health affairs. We scoff at the invisible mechanisms—soul loss, spirit possession, spells—which the diviner-healer-"witchdoctor" claims to be operating and readily accept the force of equally invisible (to the laymen) mechanisms—filterable viruses, microbes, bacteria, cells, chromosomes, the unconscious. We are amused at their image of the internal struggle of soul and spirit and seriously discuss the image of (and occasionally the location of) instincts as well as the eternal ego/id/superego struggle. We laugh at their notion that people through hatred, envy and jealousy (with the aid of sorcery) could make one sick and then speak of people's hatred, envy and jealousy (with aid of "pull") which makes us sick. And finally, we smirk at their historical search for etiological clues in broken taboos, frightening sights, sins of, or offenses to, ancestors and we seriously search historically for etiological clues in earlier mistakes, childhood traumas, environmental influences as well as the deprivations, feelings, and emotions toward and by our parents. Empirical analysis of belief systems has further illustrated these basic points. Thus Apple (1960) and others have pointed out that what passes for contemporary scientific rational thinking is that only in its most superficial aspects. Similarly Harley (1941) has noted that if we study the medical action of African medicine *in toto* and not merely the public and the more esoteric aspects, we would find that there are indeed many levels of practices which are quite pragmatic and based on as much practical experience as our daily medicating of our everyday symptoms and complaints. Indeed the claims that there is even a hierarchy of disease causation and that much of the more magical thinking is concerned with the more major unexplainable disorders—just as it is with us. The point of this discussion is not to state that there have been no important differences between historical eras or between different societies. Rather it is that the variance is much more on a continuum and not necessarily an evaluative one, and where we can read in an evaluative component, the current Western solutions are not wholesale advancements over previous eras and other societies. While not necessarily advocating ecumenicalism, a religious analogy may have meaning in this context. The religion or ideology with a one and only answer is rarely interested in other answers except to refute them. It usually is in continual conflict with what it regards as competitors, cannot learn from them, and regards any compromise as heresy. On the other hand, the religion which views many paths to salvation, rarely seeks converts, regards other faiths with at least an open mind and tolerance, and with some of the basic reasons for conflict absent may easily adapt to, add to, or itself be modified by adjacent influences. What is true of the ancient sacred religions, may also be true of other modern (and often thought sacred) medicine.

To partly free us of our own biases, it thus seems especially necessary to collect the following kinds of information.

1. CONCEPTIONS OF TROUBLE

a.) *Epidemiology of Bodily Complaints and Image*

We have much too fragmentary a grasp on the empirical nature of health and illness. Documented time and again is the difference between the orthodox physician's interpretation of illness and that of the lay population. So far most attempts to study what illness is, or unmet medical needs are, have been too dominated by a medical orientation.

To better understand what comes into awareness, perhaps the best preliminary method is the use of open-ended health diaries or calendars:

—whatever the individual defines as a bodily discomfort is the

starting point for data collection and analysis
—if symptom check lists strike the investigator as more reliable, then they should be as simple as possible, unencombered by adjectives, modifiers, qualifiers—e.g. headaches, pain, cough, appetite, appearance
—the focus for questioning is first the epidemiology of such   phenomena and then the action he takes

—the focus for questioning is first the epidemiology of such phenomena and then the action he takes
—the absence of modifiers, etc., is to learn what concerns the "average individual" and not what is of medical relevance
—putting the two perceptions together (the medical and the lay) is a later stage of research and analysis
—the use of proxy respondents could be done in accordance with the suggestions outlined. Special focus on certain bodily parts and processes
—subjective: what the individual feels is his weakest, most vulnerable body part and why
—worst disease condition that could happen to one and why
—degree of satisfactions with bodily parts and states
—measures of bodily concern and bodily cathexis

b.) *Historical and Cultural Approaches*
The socio-historical study of the development of a particular disease includes:

—when it was recognized
—how it was treated and who was responsible for its treatment what were the different theories of cause and categorization through which it passed both in time and space (Zinsser 1935)

On the contemporary study of nature and conception of disease:

—medicine seems continually to be increasing its "relevance" now it seems one of the major, if not the major, institution of social control and arbiter of social problems in the United States and also in other Western nations (Zola 1972a)

The historical and cross-cultural study of the place of health and illness in a society involve:

—in particular the differentiation between the various forms of trouble and deviation in a given society
—What it takes to become noticed, reacted to, by "official" agencies
—what is the basis of differentation between "illness and other troubles":

—the key elements
—examples of change
—a preliminary attempt on this might be done through the use of Human Relations Area Files
—the historical study of the development of specialties (Ackerknecht 1942a,b, 1949, 1967; Galdston 1958, 1959; Rosen 1944)
—the within-culture division of labour
—the rigidity of the very blurring of "specialties"
—the basis of differentiation
—the exclusiveness which will yield important clues on the general saliency and handling of illness in a society

2. THE SOURCES OF MEDICAL ASSISTANCE

There are a large number of potential sources of medical assistance to whom one can turn besides the general physician, ranging from a series of "medical" sources to essentially non-medical ones. Thus one of the first orders of business is to map out these "other" practitioners, including:

—a study of their practices" within a limited period of time as well as their relationship with other "practitioners," including the orthodox, and the stage when referrals are sought and received (Cunningham 1970).

An additional concern is the issue of how "cases" are counted. This does not merely refer to age-old confusion of failing to distinguish between patients and visits, disease and episodes, etc. A recent study of medical visits (Zola 1972c) has noted that many "symptomatic" cases are masked and thus essentially "uncounted" in check-ups, visits for someone else (mother for her child), visits with an ostensibly set purpose (injections, visits for ante-natal and postnatal care); and nonvisit consultations via telephone (a prime source in pediatric care).

3. THE WHYS AND WHEREFORES OF UTILIZATION AND ACTION

● Surprisingly few published studies exist on why an individual uses everything but the orthodox medical services, so at very least we need some preliminary data on such usage (Bender 1965; Mills 1964; Cassee 1970):

—usually covering a specific time-period in the course of an episode, how one got there, learned of him etc., previous usage by self and family (Freidson 1961)
—most delicate is why at all (here we have the preliminary work on what it is that patients seek and when it is they seek it) and whether

and how they think it helped (Balint 1957; Kadushin 1969; Mechanic and Volkart 1961)

• The users' theories of cause for specific conditions and what the relationship of this is to a specific set of actions including self-medication. This may also provide clues why one practitioner rather than another is used (as well as when) in the course of handling a particular condition (Gurin, Veroff, and Feld 1960)

• A short, hard and fairly quick method of getting relevant data on action in a relatively unknown situation is as follows: find several of the most *prevalent* ailments (i.e. such that most respondents are likely to have had them) but potentially ambiguous (i.e. such that it is not absolutely clear what one should do), and then trace out in detail on a sample of respondents what they did the last time they suffered the complaint from ignoring it to self-medication, from seeking advice to seeking some "professional" help.

14   *Studying the Decision to See a Doctor: Review, Critique Corrective*

THE STATE OF THE ART

The serious application of the behavioral science perspective to the practice of medicine is barely a decade old. Each of the early investigators opened vast areas for questioning: Parsons (1951a) perhaps cast his net most widely in his analysis of the place of health in a social system as well as his now classic model of the doctor-patient relationship. Merton et al. (1957) and Hughes (1958, 1961), each from very different perspectives, delineated the nature and power of medical school training. Stanton and Schwartz (1954) studied the social structuring of a medical service, Hollingshead and Redlich (1958) reported the biased nature of the distribution of such services, and Goffman (1961) described the awesome potential of such services for disservice.

Large-scale epidemiological studies (Commission on Chronic Illness 1957; Koos 1954; Srole et al. 1962) documented the unmet and unknown medical needs; Opler (1959), Ackerknecht (1942a, b, 1946), and Zborowski (1952) analyzed the variations in perceiving and reporting of needs and symptoms; Clausen and Yarrow (1955)

Originally appeared as "Studying the Decision to See a Doctor: Review Critique, Corrective," in *Advances in Psychosomatic Medicine*, edited by Z. Lipowski 8 (1972): 216–236.

and Freidson (1960) described the complex process in seeking help and Mechanic (1959) the factors which influenced that seeking. Finally, A. Lewis (1953), Szasz (1959), Selye (1956) and Dubos (1961) began to cast doubt on our most basic assumptions about health and illness. Admittedly this is just a sampling of the early seminal work. The point is that from the beginning and continuing through today virtually every aspect of medicine—from its mandate (Freidson 1970a) to the very nature of its therapy (Bakan 1969) is under scrutiny, if not attack.

My appointed task in this volume was to assess one of these new directions—the current state of knowledge about how people get to physicians, or triggers for medical action. However, as I began to assemble and analyze the literature two things became apparent. Firstly, several excellent analytic reviews were already available (Stoeckle, Zola and Davidson 1963; Kasl and Cobb 1966; Rosenstock 1966; Mechanic 1968; McKinlay 1972), and secondly, that there was something awry about the direction and assumptions of all this work (including my own). It is to this latter concern that this paper is devoted.

Let us briefly review "the state of the art." In what seems almost like "parallel invention," very old data or data previously ignored began to be examined in a new light. As Mechanic (1959, p. 37) simply put it:

> not all organically "sick" people define themselves as ill and there-
> fore often do not come under medical scrutiny—a fact which suggests
> that how people come to receive medical attention is itself a research
> problem.

There had prior to this insight been a long history of delay studies (reviewed in Blackwell 1963; Kutner et al. 1958) and of noting the discrepancy between lay and professional definitions (Star 1955, 1957, Pratt et al. 1957; Woodward 1951). New meaning was given to such observations as investigators began to speculate that doing something about one's state of health was complex and analytically separable into health, illness, and sick-role behavior—see Kasl and Cobb (1966) for a general statement and the works of Baric (1969), Rosenstock (1966), Mechanic (1959, 1962, 1964, 1966, 1968) and Gordon (1966) for specifics—but also that any of these behaviors might be delineated into a series of stages. For coming to a doctor, see the illustrative works of Suchman (1964, 1965a,b) and Zola (1964, 1973a). In regard to seeking help, Freidson (1960, pp. 377-378) provides one of the earliest and still most trenchant descriptions:

Indeed, the whole process of seeking help involves a network of potential consultants, from the intimate and informal confines of the nuclear family through successively more select, distant authoritative laymen, until the "professional" is reached. This network of consultants, which is part of the structure of the local lay community and which imposes form on the seeking of help, might be called the "lay referral structure." Taken together with the cultural understandings involved in the process, we may speak of it as the "lay referral system." . . . Insofar as the idea of diagnostic authority is based on assumpted hereditary or divine "gift" or intrinsically personal knowledge of one's "own" health, necessary for effective treatment, professional authority is unlikely to be recognized at all. And, insofar as the cultural definitions of illness contradict those of professional culture, the referral process will not often lead to the professional practitioner. In turn, with an extended lay referral structure, lay definitions are supported by a variety of lay consultants, when the sick man looks about for help. Obviously, here the folk practitioner will be used by most, the professional practitioner being called for minor illnesses only, or, in illness considered critical, called only by the socially isolated deviate, and by the sick man desperately snatching at straws.

The opposite extreme of the indigenous extended system is found when the lay culture and the professional culture are much alike and when the lay referral system is truncated or there is none at all. Here, the prospective client is pretty much on his own, guided more or less by cultural understandings and his own experience, with few lay consultants to support or discourage his search for help. Since his knowledge and understandings are much like the physician's he may take a great deal of time to treat himself, but nonetheless will go directly from self-treatment to a physician.

Justifying which piece of the help-seeking process to investigate created little difficulty, for so little had been previously documented that one could literally jump in anywhere and make an empirical contribution. Thus some focussed on the perception of symptoms (Apple 1960 and Zola 1966) others on the readiness for action (Rosenstock 1966; Kegeles 1963; Hochbaum 1958) some on the expection and delineation of pathways (Freidson 1960, 1961, Gurin et al. 1960; Mishler and Waxler 1963; Kadushin 1969) others on how pathways vary (Suchman 1964, 1965a), some on the psychosocial determinants of general illness behavior, delaying (Kutner and Gordon 1961) or going (Mechanic and Volkart 1961) and still others on the psychosocial determinants and mening of specific illness behavior (Balint 1957; Zola 1964, 1973a). This work is still in its infancy and as the many investigators and reviews note there are still many important unanswered questions. It is how these unanswered questions are framed to which we now turn.

The proceedings of a very recent and impressive conference, now dubbed colloquially the Boiling Springs Conference on Medical Education, may serve as an illustration of this aforementioned framing of research. While the entire proceedings are filled with suggestions for interdisciplinary research, the most straightforward statement of the social science perspective occurs early on (Behavioral Sciences and Medical Education 1969, p. 11):

> They [socially-oriented behavioral scientists] are trained to look at broader questions:
> How is health or ill health perceived?
> How and when and why do people go to doctors?
> How do they find health care facilities?
> How do they get there?
> Do they really get the care they need?
> Do they accept it?
> Do they get satisfactory results?
> Quite aside from narrow biological concerns, what are the social, psychological, cultural, and economic characteristics of patients that affect the kinds of health care they want or need?
> What sorts of instruments exist to measure the characteristics and qualities of medical students that might help to guide their career choices?
> What sorts of physicians are most effective in dealing with what sorts of patients?

Good questions all, and yet they represent a rather significant narrowing of focus. For while a critical attitude to the current practice and organization of medicine is implicit in the vast majority of such question-studies, their wording and emphasis indicate a basic acceptance of the primacy of the institution of medicine. Put another way, it was usage of the doctor we were trying to understand and in some sense improve. For when we divide a population along the criteria of high or low doctor utilization we are implicitly saying there is some "correct," appropriate level of utilization, and that "correct" utilization consists of seeing a doctor. Freidson (1970a,b) has convincingly delineated how medicine came to such a dominating position, though there is some recent questioning as to how long this exclusivity will continue to be maintained (Zola and Miller 1973). In any case, it is not unreasonable to assume that sociomedical investigators, creatures of the same culture as the public, also "bought" medicine's claims. And to the degree they did, it may help explain how these investigators were consistently able to ignore another implication of their studies. For in justifying their focus on psychological, social, economic, ecological, etc., etc. factors in the utilization of, or decision to seek medical aid, they often cited data to emphasize that not all the organically ill were under medical care. A few examples will illustrate how extensive the number of untreated were. One of the more conservative estimates of what is missed was stated by White et al. (1961, p. 89):

> Data from medical-care studies in the United States and Great Britain suggest that in a population of 1,000 adults (16 years of age and over) in an average month 750 will experience an episode of illness and 250 of these will consult a physician . . .

This means that the physician has no medical contact with two out of every three illness episodes. More intensive studies of select populations, the aged (Williamson et al., 1964), mothers with young children (Alpert et al. 1967; Kosa et al. 1965, 1967) and young college students (Zola 1966), raise this figure to nine out of ten or higher. Nor can it be contended that such "untreated by a physician" conditions are necessarily minor. Whether we take the results of an old study (Pearse and Crocker 1938, 1949) or a newer one (Commission on Chronic Illness 1957), the focussing on a minor medical problem, feet (Clarke 1969), a potentially serious one, streptococcal pharyngitis (Goslings et al. 1963, Valkenburg et al. 1963) or a major one, diabetes (Butterfield 1968), by either functional or clinical criteria an equal number if not a majority of such conditions are simply unseen and untreated by the "available" medical services. Yet even this kind of medical evidence led investigators to phrase their research in some variation of the following (Zola 1973a, pp. 678-679):

> We can now restate a more realistic empirical picture of illness episodes. Virtually every day of our lives we are subject to a vast array of bodily discomforts. Only an infinitesimal amount of these get to a physician. Neither the mere presence nor obviousness of symptoms, neither their medical seriousness nor objective discomfort seems to differentiate those episodes which do and do not get professional treatment. In short, what then does convert a person to a patient? This then became a significant question and the search for an answer began.

And when answers indeed started to come in, the data was used to delineate how and who got stuck, delayed, perhaps even ignored or passed in their seeking of help. When the data was sufficiently detailed, the aforementioned stages (Suchman 1964, 1965a,b) were documented. Yet somehow these stages—though it was empirically obvious that the majority of all people and illness episodes never reached the end point, i.e. the doctor—were viewed as way stations, and inappropriate ones at that. To paraphrase another professional credo, there seems to have been the acceptance that "he who has himself (or a friend, or a chiropractor, or once an osteopath) for a physician has a fool for a doctor." In this light it is not surprising that there have been few published studies of self-medication (Jefferys et al. 1960; Kessel and Sheperd 1965; Knapp et al. 1966), virtually none on the utilization of nonorthodox practitioners (Bender 1965; Cassee 1970), and the merest beginnings of how illness is managed without resort to medicine (Alpert et al. 1969). There is a history of looking at these issues not in Western industrial settings but amongst more "backward," "underdeveloped" nations (Cunningham 1970; Harley 1941, Kiev 1968; Hughes 1968), which implies that the practices themselves are perceived to be "backward" and "underdeveloped." Mechanic (1968, p. 135) could justly and perhaps too calmly maintain:

> We know very little about how people use their friends and acquaintances to cope with distress, and not much more about the use of a great variety of non-medical practitioners such as clergymen and lawyers, semi-medical persons such as druggists, and marginal practitioners such as chiropractors and faith healers.

This is the state of the art.

TOWARD A RECONCEPTUALIZATION

This section is an attempt to apply a corrective to the bias outlined previously. Our goal is to outline the various places and ways in which "illness" is measured, counted, and handled as well as some of the implications of any particular handling. To give perspective, we start with the most objective measures of illness and proceed through to the most subjective, giving less emphasis to more commonly documented indices and more to poorly articulated ones.

The Measures

A.   The Clinical-Epidemiological Field Survey

Clinical exams: scars, residuals, lesions, autopsies, for past history.

Laboratory tests, X-rays: physiological measures may be used which, while themselves not the equivalent of disease, may be designated as indicators, prodromal signs, "high risk" characteristics, etc.

B. The Utilization of a Medical Facility, Office, Clinic, Hospital

Derived from medical records, hospital and surgical records (admissions diagnosis or discharge diagnosis is sometimes an issue).

Use of the above facilities but in ways which do not necessarily lead to the recording of either the visit or the symptom: consultations undertaken during the visit of someone else; telephone consultations; consultation with a very specialized medical service—psychiatrist, dentist, ophthalmologist, dermatologist, gynecologist, etc., check-ups.

C. The Utilization of "Other Medical" Personnel

Use of nonmedical (i.e. MD) "specialists"—podiatrist, chiropodist, optometrist, midwives.

Use of allied personnel or paramedicals—office nurses, medics, public health nurses, physiotherapists, "trainees."

Use of pharmacists, chemists.

Use of "marginal practitioners"—a list cannot be given, for the alternatives vary greatly from society to society; from chiropractors, osteopaths, naturopaths in the West to hakims, diviners, injection doctors, ayurvedic healers in other parts of the world.

Use of personnel with no formal medical knowledge, but with some "attributes and medical expertise": social workers and the clergy and occasionally lawyers are often people to whom people bring their problems; people with attributed medical knowledge such as people who work in hospitals, clinics, doctors' offices; people with life experiential qualifications—from sheer age, to having suffered the disorder or known others who had; people associated with the current health food movement—the sales people, clerks, etc.

D. Withdrawal Behavior

Withdrawal from activity due to illness (commonly registered): absence from work; absence from school; absence from military service; absence from other captive or compulsory activity (e.g. in a prison).

Withdrawal from activity due to illness (not commonly registered): done outside ordinary working, school hours, etc. (weekends, evenings); done in a normally nonregistered activity or context: (a) "house-wife"; (b) child out of nursery or preschool 0-5 years; (c) man in part-time, unskilled activity; (d) man in full-time, independent professional activity.

E. Self-Medication

Use of ethical prescribed drugs where records of such purchase can be or are kept recorded, etc.

Use of ethical prescribed drugs already bought or available for other purposes.

Use of "patent" proprietary medicines.

Use of other "medical" cures—folk or home remedies.

F. Subjective Lay Appraisal

Self-appraisal: where the respondent answers either systematically or unsystematically about the state of his past or present health.

1. A list of diseases: did (do) you have . . . ?
2. A list of symptoms: either directly indicative of a specific disorder; or simply a list of common or serious symptoms.
3. Open-ended: the respondent defines the state of his health by his own criteria.
4. Illness-related behavior other than withdrawals or self-medications.

Other or proxy appraisal: for certain conditions and for certain limited periods of time.

1. Informants may be able to report on a whole host of diseases or indicators.

The immediate question is whether one measure is not somehow better than another. And the immediate answer is that it depends on what one wants to know. Thus the clinical-epidemiological field study will for most disorders provide the most accurate picture of the prevalence and incidence of a particular disease entity, but it may be entirely misleading data for the purposes of health planning based on "unmet medical needs." For what does it tell us if we can detect that a person has had a specific condition (either by autopsy, X-ray, laboratory test, or examination) if he has never sought treatment for it, and if indeed there is no evidence that he at least in his own mind has suffered from it. Or take the opposite extreme where a person "suffers" (i.e. subjective lay appraisal) but no organic-disease entity can be found. Eliminate for the moment that he is "malingering": what or how would his case be counted? Moreover, if we were trying to estimate demand in terms of health services or the economic-social losses to a society, on what basis could we consider such subjective appraisals irrelevant?

Now we can, a bit more systematically, speak of some essential strengths and weaknesses of each of these measures.

It is only within recent years that the clinical field study (A) has gained increasing importance. For the study of most entities such a large-scale enterprise was regarded as an almost academic frill. As mentioned in the previous pages, there was no need to do such studies since it was long held that utilization figures represented a close enough approximation to the prevalence and incidence of most disorders. While more and more doubt has been cast on this position, from studies of arthritis (Cobb 1963), to studies of mental illness (Srole et al. 1962), it was rarely questioned as to whether treated cases might not be representative of the disease under study. Thus Butterfield (1968) in his epidemiological study of diabetes was shocked not only at the number of untreated cases but at the fact that many of the untreated were so clinically different from the treated as to cast doubt on the current diagnostic criteria for diabetes.

To the degree that there is a fit between the clinical epidemiological survey (A) and utilization data (B) it will tell us something about the degree of fit between medical and lay standards. At best, both sets of data may give important clues for the study of etiology and the minimal demand to be placed on medical services. As far as general utilization data is concerned, it will tell who uses what (but not why—what the doctor thinks is wrong and what the patient thinks is wrong may not coincide), and it will give some indications of what (and with what frequency) the lay population thinks the medical profession is able or willing to treat.

In addition, there are a whole series of "utilizations" which are either not counted or not given sufficient weight in understanding the why's and wherefore's of medical usage. The first of these is medical consultation that takes place while the physician is essentially treating someone else. This usually takes the form of "While we [usually family members] are here [i.e. at your office] I wonder if you would take a look at . . ." or "While you are here [at the home of the patient], would you take a look at . . ." The latter apparently was quite common when house calls were a major part of the doctor's activity. It is still true apparently in some settings and constitutes a great deal of the public health nursing job as well as of the new "family health worker." In the latter instances, the professional uses the presenting patient quite consciously as an entree to other problems in the family (Zola and Croog 1968). The second category, telephone conversations, while always considered a routine (though unrecorded) part of medical practice, has become for some practices institutionalized. Thus pediatricians in many locales set aside an hour or more in the morning to dispense advice and even drugs to the mothers of their patients. The full extent of this practice is unknown, but there is potential benefit in getting answers to questions like: "Should I keep . . . home from school or bring . . . to you, or have you visit us?" The use of the telephone—at least as a preliminary screening device is also being explored in many settings as a preliminary treatment device—from the Poison Control Information Centers to the Suicide Prevention Centers to the new "hot lines."

The third grouping, consultation with recognized medical specialists, is duly recorded, but some clinical observations as well as my own unpublished data indicate that under the guise of specialist consultation a great many other problems are handled. Thus in a long series of postnatal check-ups, it was found that the visit was used by the patient (treated and unrecorded by the physician) for a whole host of essentially un-OB-GYN problems. This point becomes even more pertinent if we were to extend our definition of medical problems to include social and psychiatric, for here there is ample anecdotal material to document how often such problems either arise or are part of standard medical treatment (Balint 1957; Stoeckle, Zola and Davidson 1964).

Finally, we turn to the most neglected and thus least fully appreciated of medical consultations: the check-up. Here again I must rely on my unpublished data. My claim is that except for required, prearranged check-ups, few patients arrive at the doctor's office merely for the annual physical. The preliminary analysis of our data indicates (1) that even for those who go for regular check-ups, the timing is related to something that they "do not regard as serious but is worth looking into, so why don't I get my check-up"; (2) that the check-up is a way of handling and presenting complaints which put the burden on the physician. We recorded many cases of pressing complaints which the patient did not verbalize if the physician, during the course of the examination, indicated that the appropriate body system is "in good working order"; (3) that the check-up for an individual is also a way of bringing up a complaint analogous to the aforementioned visitor consultation ("Oh yes, by the way while I'm here I wonder if you think this is serious"); (4) that even when the check-up is prescheduled as a follow-up, one of the major differentiating features between those that do and do not keep these appointments is having a series of "other" complaints which concern them. Needless to say none of the above four findings concerning check-ups are discernible in the medical records. And on the whole all of the medical encounters in the above series represent data which is uncounted and thereby ignored in our understanding of ordinary medical visits.

There is really not much commentary to add to our listing of "other medical" personnel (C). At the very least they represent a conscious use of sources outside the accepted system. Their use is, however, so unsystematically documented that one can little more than speculate whether such use precedes, follows, or, as in some underdeveloped countries, parallels that of regular physicians. No doubt one of the more illuminating studies would be where the comparison is made between specialties treating similar problems, e.g. the oculist, optometrist, opthalmologist, the podiatrist, chiropodist, orthopedist, as well as their changing relationship with the patient during the course of an illness (à la F. Davis 1963).

The recording of withdrawals (D) is essentially a way of inferring illness by a negative response—the absence of the individual from some regular activity. As currently used, they are cited as indices of the economic loss to the society through disease. Ironically, these most commonly registered absences represent both a capitalist as well as a sexist bias. The former is clear insofar as the activities whose absence we record are essentially occupationally linked. On the other hand, if interference/disability were what we were primarily interested in, then the list of activities should be expanded from the individual (not the medical or "social") point of view. Thus such activity withdrawals would include many nonvocational activities (withdrawal from religious participation, social and leisure-time activities—from reading to sports to sexual relations). Interestingly enough, in a secure economic system with heavy "illness compensation" or health insurance schemes, it may be these kinds of activities which are most important to the individual. There is also a sexist bias on two levels. First, there is the usual lack of recognition of income equivalence for the work of the housewife. Second, even where studies allow for the difficulty in temporarily leaving the responsibilities of children and household, it is easy to infer from the words of a respondent in Koos' study (1954) that some more subtle or different measure of interference might be required:

> I wish I really knew what you meant about being sick. Sometimes I felt so bad I could curl up and die, but had to go on because the kids had to be taken care of and besides, we didn't have the money to spend for the doctor. How could I be sick? How do you know when you're sick, anyway? Some people can go to bed most anytime with anything, but most of us can't be sick, even when we need to be.

Finally, measures of withdrawal are best at supplying data about illness at its most general level—whether or not someone was sick and how often, rather than what specifically he had. It is exceedingly difficult from such data to create rates for any but the most general category of specific diseases. For while such records may be replete with diagnoses—the latter may reflect more acceptable diagnoses for the purpose of legitimizing withdrawal, than the primary diagnoses or even the major complaint of the respondent (Field 1957).

Self-medication (E) represents one of the least understood and yet most prevalent of medical actions. In this general area we are indeed in virgin territory. While there has been a continuing tradition of research into the patient's keeping to a prescribed regimen (Davis and Eichhorn 1963; Roth and Caron 1968) and occasional studies on physicians' prescribing patterns (Coleman et al. 1966; Lee 1964, Lee et al. 1965; Martin 1957), there have been few systematic studies and even fewer publications of what the lay individual does to, and for, himself. An example of this is seen in the recent publication *Home Medication and the Public Welfare* (Whipple 1969). This document, despite the thirty-plus articles, panel discussions and a welter of references, fails to cite a single published study of self-medication. Virtually all the data on which they base their conclusions is inferred from general statistics on drug sales and purchases. There have been many studies past and ongoing which include some data on the issue (Hassinger et al. 1959; White et al. 1967), but since the primary purpose of such studies was quite different, the relevant information was not indexed and is thus unavailable to all current methods of data retrieval. It is only within the last year or so that the *Index Medicus* has begun to classify studies under the rubric of self-medication, etc. Thus to most investigators (as judged by the references cited in their publications and research proposals) the literature is functionally nonexistent. Moreover, the word "published" should be emphasized, for as seen in the recent pamphlet *Without Prescription* (Office of Health Economics 1968), such data does exist and may well have existed for a long time. It is, however, reposing in the coffers of the marketing divisions of the pharmaceutical firms or in the files of market research firms which have specialized in drug research. The one exception to these comments is the study by Jefferys et al.— done in the 1950s but published in 1960—but it took over a decade for similar research to be done in the United Kingdom and even longer in the United States (Cartwright 1969; Knapp 1968).

The reason for such a vacuum in this all-important area of medical care is not hard to understand. As elsewhere, in regard to several other areas of sociomedical investigation (Zola 1966), it is related to several hidden and inarticulated assumptions about the prevalence (how much of it exists) and the process (why it takes place) which tend to play down the existence of any "real" issues to study. Here, however, there was additional overlay. For such phenomena—self-treatment as well as the use of "quacks," or anyone who did not have an M.D.—was "bad" in and of itself and therefore not worth investigating except to "expose" it. Perhaps as seen today in regard to certain drug investigations (Efron 1967), there was the fear that to even investigate it systematically would give the phenomena some air of legitimacy or, at the very least, publicity and therefore unintentionally encourage the "evil" practice.

A current reversal of both "research policies" is due in part to the penetration of some long-standing observations: (1) that in no predictable future will there be in either the developed, the developing, or underdeveloped countries sufficiently qualified (by current standards) physicians to service adequately the populace; (2) that despite massive educational and legal efforts, people continue to self-medicate and go outside the orthodox medical services; (3) that perhaps such forms of doctoring do or can do some good (Cargill 1967); (4) that for an increasing number of conditions the treatment of choice is the patient management and administration of a particular regimen. Regardless of these practical forces there are a number of other pushes (particularly in the self-medication area) such as the current scares concerning drug abuse in general, and the more limited but equally dramatic area of adverse drug reactions (Goulston and Cooke 1968; Mintz 1967; Moser 1964). All lead to a desire to learn more about how and why people use drugs. In the case of adverse drug reactions, the situation is even more complex, pharmacologically and sociologically. For here, too, an old reality is coming to the fore: it is not merely the effect of a single drug which is of major concern (for further laboratory testing with longer and more extensive field studies along this line is at least possible), but of incorrect and multiple dosage. For in today's society (at least in the United States, and other nations are probably not far behind), people are not merely taking one drug for one disease, but (1) are not following the doctor's direction as to timing and dosage, (2) are using drugs prescribed for other (or previous) conditions or even for other people, (3) are taking more than one ethical drug at a time (e.g. a birth control pill and something else) for more than one condition (often though not necessarily prescribed by more than one physician), (4) are taking an ethical drug in combination with some non-prescription proprietary, each of which may be innocuous but in combination might be dangerous, and finally, (5) are taking patent medicines which ordinarily are harmless but taken in excessive dosages or for extended periods of time or in certain combinations lead to toxic effects (Goulston and Cooke 1968). Some countries (really the physicians and pharmaceutical firms of such countries) by their very prescribing patterns allow or unwittingly encourage such overtreatment. This is seen in the practice of prescribing and hence dispensing drugs in standard units or sizes which have only a limited relationship to the required regimen. Thus, even if a patient adheres rigidly to the regimen outlined by his physician, he will inevitably have some left-over drugs.

On the most general level, self-medication reflects the treatment of conditions which the individual, or his immediate social circle, thinks will not get better by themselves. They may also reflect conditions which he thinks are too minor (and occasionally too serious) for medical consultation. The data that does exist on this subject may be calming to the medical profession, for it indicates that high self-medicators are also high doctor utilizers (Jefferys et al. 1960).

Now we turn to type (F) measures—the softest, the most unreliable, and what some might contend are the most worthless of all: lay appraisals. First, let us examine the appraisal by others; in such cases our data is obtained secondhand. There is little doubt that in some instances such recall will be the only data that we are likely to get. This is especially true where we are trying to get a historical picture of phenomena which are no longer verifiable, such as cases of certain types of mental illness, certain physical deformities, mental deficiency, etc. (Eaton and Weil 1955). It is virtually the only source of data we are likely to get on very young children, where mothers will be the best reporters. Such appraisals can also be useful where the respondent himself is unable (what he cannot usually see or observe —from snoring or body odor to bad breath to certain stages of decompensation) or unwilling (because of assessments potentially damaging to the ego—from assessments of sexual compatibility to disposition to some generally stigmatized medical conditions) to report them.

The most difficult data to assess, of course, is the individual's self-appraisal (his estimation of his health, etc.) or self-reporting (the symptoms he has experienced). It is, however, the most unreliable primarily because of how we collect it or ordinarily want to use it. It is most easily dismissed (and perhaps rightly) when it is used to directly reflect disease states, i.e. where the symptom which the respondent is asked to recall is directly diagnostic (e.g. pain radiating around the heart and up the left arm). It is also of questionable diagnostic use where the time and frequency is clear to the doctor-diagnostician (*frequent* urination, *persistent* cough, *severe* pain, *considerable* loss of appetite, weight, etc.), but where these simply do not mean the same to the patient. Signs and symptoms are also subject to faulty recall: the longer the time period (over 24–48 hours), the greater the likelihood that it was not accompanied by an action (e.g. withdrawal from some activity), the less dramatic (coughing versus bleeding) the symptom, and the less frequently it appears to occur (he or others have it all the time versus rarely).

One could list other criticisms of self-appraisal, but let us now turn briefly to some of its strengths. Assuming one has solved, or more adequately than most, dealt with these methodological issues, at the very least it will provide a more adequate picture of the nature of the ills, sufferings, bodily discomforts that afflict mankind, for it will probably show a prevalence figure which will be staggering in dimension. It will thus be a baseline, a background for trying to understand (and perhaps change) an individual's ordinary response to physical trouble and a further appreciation that only an infinitesimal amount of this ever comes to the attention of orthodox medical authorities. The latter observation should have great implications for the future training and role of physicians, including some sharper delineation of what cannot or should not be the exclusive province of the physician. Such data will also provide some extraordinary insights cross-sectionally (for people and groups), and I would make the prediction that the most significant differences (what they will be, I wish I knew) will be found between (1) the untreated conditions, (2) self-treated conditions, and (3) those where some external help is sought. Still another reason for collecting such data is its direct medical implications. As shown in one recent study (Reidenberg and Lowenthal 1968) which focussed on the adverse effects of certain drugs, many of the supposed side effects were indistinguishable from the respondent's general bodily discomforts as well as the very illness for which he was being treated. As regards the latter, it is well to bear in mind Selye's observation (1956) that diagnosis and the notion of clinical entity are based on a very small number of characteristics peculiar to that disease and no other, and that by far the largest number of signs and symptoms of any disease are shared by a wide variety of disorders and physiological malfunctioning. Morris (1967) has some similar comments on the uses of epidemiology to delineate syndromes. Finally, such data should give a much better empirical base to our understanding of the true nature of chronicity and should provide an infinitely better picture of the nature of delay (Kutner and Gordon 1961).

There is, however, a final type of self-report which to my knowledge has never been systematically collected. For paralleling any list of symptoms should logically be a list of actions. While investigators are studying two types of patient behavior—withdrawals and self-medication—there is at least from common-sense observation a whole series of other actions individuals take to cope with a symptom-problem: rest, stop what we are doing, exercise, get fresh air, eat something, analyze the reasons why we might be suffering from discomfort. That we have ignored them intellectually (though not in daily living) probably reflects our verbalized evaluation of them as unefficacious. To date, their study has been left more in the hands of psychologists (Bakan 1969) and those who, reflecting on the wisdom of the East, are beginning to ponder over our ability to cure ourselves. This in itself is ironic since it has been literally generations since we have accepted those aspects of the psychosomatic approach which emphasize how well we are able to harm ourselves.

EPILOGUE

With so many "illnesses" pressing on man, the traditional view of illness as being automatically bad and therefore worthy of elimination is being challenged. Putting aside the social use of illness labels (Foucault 1965; Leifer 1969; Szasz 1959; Zola and Miller 1973), the title of Dubos' book, *The Mirage of Health* (1961) is finally being attended to. Thus Ratner (1962) has questioned our zeal in immunization and Jones (1960, p. 358) has speculated in a similar vein about the so-called diseases of civilization, wondering if they represent a kind of

> . . . balanced polymorphism: [since] such conditions as obesity, diabetes, hypocholesterolaemia and ischaemic heart disease are so frequent—and so often associated—because they represent the survival of genes that could withstand famine, and other privation, from times when such genes were advantageous to age and affluence (to times) when manifestly they are not.

There is also some limited evidence that at least in the psychic realm such symptoms as anxiety are not necessarily all bad, related as they may be to certain kinds of achievement and adaptational as they are under certain situations of acute crisis (Janis 1958). Perhaps being "ill" may at times be positively functional for the continued long-run health and performance of the individual and the group. Ironically, it may be treating certain phenomena as basic disorders rather than as ephemeral or adaptive episodes which leads to their being maladaptive and dysfunctional for the individual and society. Hopefully our research orientation will provide a beginning answer to such issues. On the other hand, we are not merely calling for new research, although that is surely needed; the import of our message is for a reorientation in perspective. For we hope that the expanded notion of medical behavior will help us see more clearly the growing roles of paramedicals and self-help groups in treatment and rehabilitation as well as the enormous amount of activities people engage in to "doctor" themselves—something that future medical care programs hopefully can build upon technically, educationally, and therapeutically.

15   *The Educational and Political Implications of Studying One's Own Body*

In many papers (most directly in the "Concept of Trouble" and "Studying the Decision . . .") I have recommended that serious attention be given to the study of "the epidemiology of bodily complaints." Though I have never undertaken a large-scale study of the topic, I have over the years created a pedagogical tool which provided me with much useful information on the subject. In the following pages I will describe the procedure and what some people have learned from it.

On the first day of class in selected undergraduate courses and in most graduate seminars I distribute the following assignment:

ASSIGNMENT 1

Starting immediately, each student is expected to start a health diary. He or she is to record any physical or general episodes experienced during the day and their reactions. Do not discriminate between what you think is or is not worth recording, any bodily state which *comes to your attention* is worth recording—anything which you feel or would classify as noticeable *regardless* of how minor.

It is suggested that these incidents be noted as close as possible to the actual event. Start by noting how you felt when you arose that morning.

Your notes should be primarily a description of the condition and what you did about it. I am not particularly concerned about your interpretation of the dynamics underlying the symptom, *except* as it related to what you did about it.

"I got up and felt rather lousy, my stomach was upset. I know that I was anxious about the exam coming up, *so* I decided to ignore it."

"My head started to bother me at about 3:00. It wasn't too bad so I decided to wait until I got home. When I got home at 5:00 it was pretty well gone *but since* I had a lot of reading to do, I decided to take a couple of aspirins."

These are sample descriptions. Yours can be longer or shorter, as you see fit.

The diary should be kept for a minimum of *four* weeks; the termination date will be set in class. Within a week or so after this termination date, each student is expected to turn in a paper analyzing the diary in the light of the readings, class discussion, and any other relevant data and knowledge.

In format, the paper should be in *two* parts—a first section confined to the data and the second to include the analysis.

The analysis starts with a rereading of all you have written. Your task is to try and understand what you have recorded—what does it tell you about yourself, your health, your pattern of health care and what does your pattern of care tell you about more general phenomena: being a man, woman, student, worker, or about health and illness in general.

You may bring to bear on this analysis not only material from this course but any other source which seems appropriate, including your own understanding of yourself.

All material will be held in strictest confidentiality—available to, and readable by, the instructor alone.

Two copies of the assignment are to be submitted. One will be returned with comments, and with your permission one will be retained for my file anonymously, i.e., all identifying correspondence will be removed.

The format was purposefully loose, partly because I wished to see how they interpreted the assignment and partly because it seemed the best way to assure their cooperation. I did, of course, meet with much resistance, particularly around issues of privacy and confidentiality. Ironically, this led me to share more of myself in the classroom. For if I expected my students to share part of their intimate life with me, a stranger, then I at least should do something similar in return—share my own personal and medical experience with them.

Responding to the diaries was also a ticklish matter. Though trained as a counselor, this seemed no place to "psychologize" about behavior patterns. My comments were thus more limited than usual, confined to the most general phenomena and to their organization, presentation and analysis. Partly to make up for my sparse comments, I instead analyzed their papers both statistically and thematically, reporting my findings in the class sessions. Where feasible I also reported time trends. It is of note, for instance, that since the 1960s psychological states (depression, anxiety, nervousness, etc.) have become the most often reported condition in the health diaries. Over the years, sexual issues and problems have been increasingly reported, with women far exceeding men in this regard. By the late 1970s, however, with the decreasing use of the birth control pill, certain conditions (e.g. sore breasts) as well as issues, were decreasingly noted. Otherwise the ranking of conditions is as follows: tiredness-energy level, gastro-intestinal, upper respiratory, headaches, musculoskeletal, GYN and GU, and skin conditions. The women consistently reported more symptoms and more detail than the men, with the exception of musculoskeletal (often athletic injuries) and any complaint in which "pain" was the predominant symptom. During the class discussion I also reported the kinds of causal explanations they used, the responsibility they felt for their own bodies, how effectively they described different conditions and parts of the body, and what this told us about health and illness in general.

A student summed up a part of the learning experience very well when he said.

> As I look back over this diary, I feel like a complainer or a hypochondriac, I'm just never made aware of little ailments. There is something artificial about concentrating on them like this, that makes one look at them more carefully, and take things seriously that would otherwise go unnoticed. I am finding it very interesting.

At its best, the assignment "worked" by its very process. Almost everyone who has ever begun this assignment thought themselves in excellent health with relatively few or any "troubles." At first they were resentful (often at me) at "the symptoms" they produced, their frequency, and occasionally their intensity. Gradually they began to see how difficult it was to record *all* the details and how vague and unspecific their "complaints" often were. When this happened they began to grow more suspicious of the studies on patients' symptoms, of their own difficulties in communicating the onset and course of their own conditions to health personnel and how from this perspective, many health campaigns (as well as studies) presented an unreal picture of the specificity and clarity of certain physical syndromes. Some students, of course, steadfastly denied the presence of any complaints, almost defiantly turning in blank pages. Even they contributed something to our understanding, since they tried to explain in their analysis why they never pay attention to their bodies.

For most diarists there was hardly a day that went by without something to record.

The diaries generally had a sobering effect on the students. They began to realize (and I reinforced their realization with my overall report) that there were indeed patterns that underlay their "troubles" as well as their reactions—patterns conditioned by their family, personal history, ethnic, racial, and religious group, age, gender, and current status. It was also a demystifying experience. For all too many, no one but a doctor had ever paid so much attention to their body—which (they realized) reinforced the rather Anglo-Saxon notion that such attention was "bad" or at least only necessary when some issue of "pathology" was at stake. In short, paying little attention to one's body until it "breaks down" is a weak position from which to gain knowledge. (This attitude is documented more fully in "Structural Constraints . . . " in Part V of this volume.) Many thus realized that they had trivialized their body and, more important, the significance of some actions, particularly nondrug actions, they took in regard to it. This helped them understand the overly-narrow perspective of many who study "health and illness behavior." They also realized that merely becoming more aware was an important action, often with beneficial implications. In short, many found the experience an empowering one.

In a still broader way this assignment had a political aim. Survey after survey has attempted to estimate the number of symptoms/conditions not seen by doctors. Once found they are most often labelled "untreated." Both the labelling and the fact that the number of "unmet needs" are often presented in quite precise terms (i.e. *one* of 3, or 4, or 5 syndromes never reach a physician) lull us into a false sense of security. It encourages health planners, for instance, to assume that mere increases in "person power" can meet these needs. My point is that most such "guesstimates" are so far off as to prove useless. I am sure that fewer than one hundredth, maybe even one thousandth, of all the bodily complaints or medical episodes that come (or can come) to an individual's attention ever come to a physician's (For the "medical significance" of such episodes, that is, those the doctor misses, please see "The Mirage of Health Revisited" in Part III).

To put it boldly, the most infrequent response of an individual to a bodily complaint is to seek medical help. For this reason there will never be sufficient health personnel to cover all "untreated" conditions. Nor should there be. We would be far better off if we studied not only who goes to a doctor and who does not (as in traditional utilization studies) but also what people do in their everyday lives to prevent, treat, and rehabilitate certain conditions *they* define as worthwhile—and why. Finally, it is a misnomer as well as a disservice to label these conditions "untreated," for what the investigators really mean is "untreated by established medical authority."

Out of frustration that sound data on self-medication was still scarce in the early 1970s, I embarked on a small-scale project to collect my own. I asked any class I taught in medical sociology to detail their "drug and medication" use during the last thirty-six hours. I started with a general question about drugs, medicines, tablets, and pills and followed that with a series of specific probes. Had they used:

any throat lozenges, cough drops, syrups, etc.?
anything for indigestion, heartburn, diarrhea, stomach cramps, etc.?
any salves, ointments, powders, body lotions?
anything for a cold, stuffiness, congestion? any nasal sprays?
any medical product for the eyes?
any medical product for mouth or teeth?
any vitamins?
birth control pills or any other contraceptive devices?
any medical drug ordinarily taken, regularly or at special times, but
  not taken in the last thirty-six hours?
any other "medicated" products not previously listed?
any chemical substance, herbal or other preparation, regarded as
  relevant to the student's health?

For each yes, the student noted whether the substance was prescribed and for what condition he used it. Over the years I had added other items. Off and on I ask about psychotropic drug use, cigarettes, and more often about the use of alcohol and caffeinated products such as coca-cola, tea, coffee. The respondents were asked to identify themselves only by age and gender. The administration of the survey takes about half an hour of class time.

As with the health diary, the impact was many-sided. The mere act of doing it was often a learning experience. Many were shocked that they used so many "drugs." Although they dismissed many of the medicines as being of little consequence, they were nevertheless taken aback by the sheer amount of medical products they used.

In the following class session I would usually report the results in sheer statistical terms. Let me state some of the most consistent findings. In this generally healthy segment (ages 18–21) of the American population, at least 70 percent have self-medicated (using the most conservative definition of "medicine") within the last thirty-six hours! In every survey I have done more women self-medicate (even after discounting birth-control methods) and do it more frequently. The drugs most often used were aspirin, vitamins, and cold pills. The conditions treated more or less followed the pattern of the health diaries—colds, headaches, energy level, stomach. There were however, some interesting differences. No medicines were taken directly to deal with psychological states (the number one condition in the health diary) and less attention was given to musculoskeletal conditions. Since neither of these conditions, were treated primarily by drugs, (at least in the diaries) this omission is not so surprising. On the other hand, the syndrome most often treated by medicines related to skin conditions. Though women far exceeded men in total as well as frequency of treatment, it was still the third most treated condition by men. These findings remained true even when the analysis was restricted to prescriptions. The relatively low ranking of skin condition in the health diaries may reflect the fact that it was so endemic (i.e. they had to "treat" it every day) as to be "invisible" (i.e. not worth mentioning).

When these results are presented to a class they often provoke a discussion similar to but more focussed than that stimulated by the health diaries. Again it seems to have a personal as well as "political" impact. It lets them again see how much they do to and for themselves—information they could utilize in reenforcing or changing their own behavior. Once again it helped demystify medicine. It also demonstrated "in living color" how much medical action takes place outside the doctor's office and purview. And maybe, as Ivan Illich (1975) claims, that's as it should be!

17

When Getting into the Field Means Getting into Oneself

My first sabbatical year came in 1971-72, and I was spending it as a consultant-in-residence at the Netherlands Institute of Preventive Medicine in Leiden. Trying to speak Dutch was difficult enough, but hearing them use "my" language in unaccustomed ways was often unsettling. A particular shock was their pronunciation of the word "invalid." They enunciated it in accord with its derivation—the word "valid." To my Dutch friends, this was the natural way to refer to a reality—the difference between healthy people and the handicapped lay in the latter's invalidity. To me, it was a chilling revelation of the complicity of language and those who use it. Every time I heard it—and given my work at a medical institution, that was often—it made me feel very uncomfortable. The pain it stirred was very deep, but I put it aside until a series of chance events catalyzed me to greater probing.

Through one of my colleagues at the Institute, Dr. Willem Metz, I was invited to see Het Dorp, a 65-acre village, specifically designed to house 400 severely disabled adult Netherlanders. I approached Het Dorp as I do many things—exploring and uncommitted. I went first as a professional tourist for a day in January 1972, but waited five months before returning for a week as a resident visitor. I sub-

Originally appeared as "When Getting into the Field Means Getting into Onself," *New England Sociologist* 1 (1979): 21-30.

sequently went for three days in August 1974 and again for a weekend in June 1976.

"Visit" was the appropriate word for my original mind set. I was not fully conscious of what drew me back for an additional week. As was my practice in such situations, I expected merely to take notes for my own general purpose. To get "a feel" for Het Dorp, I relied pretty much on an experiential approach. Although I was quite capable of getting around the Village, I decided that, for a week, I would "resume" the role of a functional paraplegic. My personal medical experiences (two separate years of confinements: one with polio at sixteen and the second at twenty because of a shattered femur) led me to believe that this was a condition with which I was quite familiar. In any case, I was quite confident of my ability to handle the ordinary problems of being physically restricted.

So, for a week, back into a wheelchair I went. I did everything from that position. I travelled, ate, washed, shaved, and, ultimately, at the end of every day, hoisted myself wearily into bed. All I had hoped was to gain some greater *physical* awareness of being a resident and perhaps some greater ease of communication with them.

Time collapsed during these seven days. Phases of acceptance that, in previous circumstances, had taken weeks and months, here took minutes and hours. Socially, I became so quickly involved in a network of relationships that I occasionally felt part of a speeded up movie. During the week, I visited all facilities where the residents spent their time. But most importantly, they let me into their homes and into their lives. No resident whom I wanted to see ever refused my request, and many more sought me out.

I began this experience thinking of myself primarily as a foreigner and a professor, but to them, the far more overriding identification was as a curiously different handicapped person. My very "differentness" also proved to be an asset. My being an American and a successful one in terms of status (being a professor) and family (having been married with two children), made me as much a fund of information to them as they were to me. Thus, the burden of starting conversations or even probing sensitive areas (by my standards, sensitive, not necessarily by theirs) was largely mitigated. Many of our meetings began with their questioning me about my handicap and how I managed. To ask them in turn about theirs was not only fair but natural.

They asked me all manner of questions. Many could be dubbed "mechanical." They were concerned not only with how I "made" it physically, but how I "made" it sexually. Not only did they ask what devices I used in helping me walk, but whether I needed any help in having sexual relations. And for each question they asked of me, I found myself asking a dozen more and surprising myself with the answers.

And yet I never felt so comfortable in an interviewing situation. It was as if, for the first time, I were truly able to pay back respondents for what they had shared with me. In so equal but atypical a research situation, I began to understand recent writings of some social scientists who claimed that any research situation had the potential of exploitation (i.e. where one gets a great deal, but returns very little).

My acceptance by the residents was also expedited by a number of other factors. My refusing a special guest room and insisting on a wheel chair furthered my physical equality with the residents. My using a hand-operated rather than an electric wheel chair proved particularly important. Not only was this appropriate to my "resumed condition," but also it further committed me physically as well as psychologically to "living it like it was." Though I had not fully realized it at the time, it probably also showed to the villagers that I would not take the easy way out. In fact, as I write this, it becomes clear to me that during my whole stay, I never consciously took the easy way.

Put more strongly, I never "cheated." This was important to me for several reasons. To have cheated when no one was around would not only have seemed unfair and dishonest, but it would also have cut me off from some very important behavioral and psychological data. I was only alone when in my room, and to have been my old self there would have deprived me of a fuller appreciation of the physical aspects (i.e. the details of daily hygiene) and the emotional aspects (i.e. the feelings of loneliness) of living in the Village. In this sense, I had gone farther than many investigators who, in their private, out-of-the-field space, tried to create a bit of their old home.

I was also proving something to myself, though I am not yet sure what it was. Perhaps it was the only way to get back in touch with a part of myself that I had for so long rejected—my physical disability. What I had done at the Village was to live out, in a totally unexpected way, one of my favorite denial mechanisms. For most of the past twenty years I had, at least once a day, "mislaid" my cane, usually in some other room or behind some chair. I then had to search all about for my lost "appendage." As a professor, I integrated this into the "absent-mindedness" supposedly characteristic of my occupation. At Het Dorp, I had *really* lost it and had to do without it. But instead of feeding my denial, it served to reinforce, if not validate, my dependence on it.

Whatever else this experience had been, it was one of the most exhausting and intense experiences of my life. I was *always* "on." In this sense, perhaps my experience was a bit atypical. Every minute was an opportunity to observe and learn something. If it was not appropriate to talk with someone, then it was appropriate to examine my own behavior and reactions. I felt I retained my "true self," much truer than I would ordinarily be in a research situation. While I was no more active or passive than usual, all my senses felt "finely tuned." But it did take a tremendous amount out of me psychologically. As anticipated, it unearthed old anxieties and generated new ones. But my anticipation had been only theoretical. I had no idea what core would be touched or how deeply I would feel it.

I was also totally unprepared for the bodily strain. All the trips around the Village took their toll. My arms and back continually ached. I had been unaware of how difficult and complex were tasks that "in my previous life" had been so simple. My bouts with illness and my hospitalizations were not as directly relevant as I had expected. In those situations, there was almost always someone on hand—a nurse, an aide, a friend, a relative—to help me with every task. Here I was expected to do much more on my own. It was in many ways a much less sheltered environment. As a result, I had to expend considerable energy, both physical and psychological, on mundane tasks such as washing clothes, opening doors, and travelling any distance.

For all these reasons, it was a real pleasure to follow an old field work dictum, namely to spend almost as much time recording as observing. For me, it served a double function. On the one hand, a great deal was happening and needed to be transcribed. This period of recording thus became an occasion for reflection and interpretation of the day's events. On the other hand, the intensity of the experience was often so great that I needed some release. The time devoted to detailed writing thus also had the cathartic value of allowing me to get it all out and, in the act of transcription, not only work through some of the issues, but also get some protective distance from them.

This last statement gets me in touch with something that pervaded all my observations—the shattering of a certain smugness I never thought I had, about the ease in trying to communicate the way it looked from "the other side." Again and again I recorded in my notes my tripping over prejudice I never thought I had. I can best convey my new appreciation by contrasting two experiences—Het Dorp and the one that started me on the field-work road some thirteen years earlier.

In the spring of 1959, I was hired as a staff member of the anthropological research team studying the redevelopment of the West End of Boston (Duhl 1969; Fried 1973; Gans 1962). Through a series of fortuitous circumstances, I found myself converted from the position of interviewer to that of "undercover" field observer (Zola 1963a). In this role, I spent nearly four months passing as a former resident, never revealing fully who I was, and eventually leaving the scene as did many real residents when the last of our hangouts was destroyed. It was an adventure in many senses of the word, but what has stayed with me over the years is not the escapades I engaged in (good for cocktail party conversation), but the identification I felt with those I studied. For instance, one day in a bar, the owner, angry at several of us for being too loud, picked up a wet rag and flung it at no one in particular. It hit me square on the face. As it lay draped across my head, I picked up a glass of beer to toss back. As I raised my hand, she looked at me defiantly and said, "*You!* You're just like all the *rest!*" With a sense of pride, more to do with the issue of belonging than imitation, I said a silent thank you, smiled, and put down the glass.

The West End was an extraordinary experience, in part, because it drew upon so many facets of my life that had been submerged as I climbed the academic ladder. In 1959, I was a third year graduate student in the Harvard Department of Social Relations with a Harvard B.A. behind me and a Ph.D. looming ahead. At the time, it seemed quite an accomplishment for a Dorchester boy, not so much in terms of my immediate circle of friends (of forty-five boyhood chums, almost all had gone to Boston Latin School, and thence onto Harvard, other Ivy League colleges, and finally toward graduate degrees), but certainly from the point of view of the Zola family group. My father was the youngest of eleven children, and at the time I was only the third Zola to get any college education and the first to go further.

By contrast, my involvement in the West End project created strong reaction from my immediate family. While my mother was distressed by this "sinking" into the lower classes which she was trying so desperately to escape, my father was absolutely delighted. For the first time since I was a little boy, he could not only share an activity with me, but also transmit specific skills. It was with great pride that he took me to a local pool room, introduced me as his Harvard professor son, and then told how he was instructing me in the fine art of billiards and "eight-ball." In addition, he reschooled me in the ins and outs of gambling, barroom slang, and behavior. All this made my mother so upset that she never wanted to hear about my work, and for the first time in her life stopped asking, "How are you doing in school?"

My West End work also crystallized other issues. First, though trained in survey and statistical methods, I had always a gnawing doubt about their limitations. As a graduate student, I was a close admirer of C. Wright Mills and of the psychoanalytic insights scattered interestingly enough by my anthropological (William Caudill, Clyde Kluckhohn) and sociological mentors (William McCord, Ted Mills, Talcott Parsons, Phil Slater). The West End gave substance to this doubt, as I, for the first time, felt a texturing and depth of understanding of what I was studying.

Secondly, it gave me a taste, albeit a guilty one, of what it meant to use every facet of my being in my work. Not only was I able to use my senses—what *I* saw, felt, heard—but also I could draw on parts of me that traditional participant observation had not ordinarily mentioned—my background. Having grown up in Dorchester and Mattapan of working-class origins, being Jewish, having had polio and having worked at manual labor for several years in a factory were not merely interesting things to talk about with my fellow West Enders but were directly drawn upon in my work. This was so contrary to the trained objectivity of current social science that I could only relish the feeling of totality very privately, feeling guilty that I was betraying my training by using such extraneous and personal factors to enhance my grasp of the situation.

There was, however, a final dimension to this experience, which in some ways simmered within me for a decade, for there was a real surprise in what I *learned*. I don't mean merely the excitement of *learning* something new, but rather, the shock of discovering something that I thought, by the very virtue of who I was, I should have known. For, after all, I was not really investigating an alien culture. What fascinated me was why, in some ways, it had become that. Starting then, and culminating in Het Dorp, was the disturbing fact that my socialization (courtesy of two loving, pushy Jewish parents), my education, and all the energy devoted "to overcoming" my polio and my accident had indeed made me distant and separate from part of myself. (It wasn't until I got to college that I even thought of myself as working-class. Only then did I discover that I alone of my closest friends had a father who was a blue-collar worker.) Knowing what I do about psychology, I am not completely sorry that this process took place. I'm not sure that I could be where I am (largely happy in my work and life) if I had not been able to regard certain elements of my life as something alien to me, to be overcome, to be put behind me. But it did have a cost, one I am only now beginning to appreciate and understand.

My Het Dorp experience in many ways paralleled, heightened, and reawakened the West End issues. Once more I saw how incomplete had been previous accounts of people with chronic illnesses and physical handicaps. (In a sense, the more statistical the accounts were, such as the studies of sexual ability and capacity, the more unrepresentative they were of the experience.) Once more, I was reaffirmed in what can be captured by experiential methods. Once more, I was able to draw upon many aspects of my personal and social background. Never so fully involved, *every* aspect of my being seemed relevant to the task of understanding "the nature of being invalid." And all of it was done knowingly and without guilt. This time I was no undercover observer with all attendant ethical issues. This time, the biggest secrets were those hidden from myself. But most of all, this capped of what had begun thirteen years previously— the awareness once again of how much of my experience and adaptational processes had distanced me from myself and the phenomena I wanted to understand.

While the details of my blind spots may be unique, I am not sure about the general process of distancing and the results thereby engendered. In particular, I am having serious doubts about how much social and emotional spearation *is* necessary from those we study. Much, now I suspect too much, has been written about the problems of "going native" or "becoming overidentified" with the people or phenomenon one is investigating. At a historical moment, this was probably a very important issue, for the tendency might well have been to glorify more than to understand nonliterate groups, exotic cultures, quaint customs. But today, awareness rather than noninvolvement seems our best defense against such overstepping.

There is an analogy here to the current conflict between doctors and patients. Much has been made about the social and emotional distance "necessary" for physicians and therapists to treat their patients. As in the above example, this "separation" might once have been quite functional. With no anaesthesia and with death a common outcome of serious illness and hospitalization, without such "steeling," few would have been able to continue their work. Though the realities that produced this distancing have long since passed, the educative process that brought it about still remains. And thus we now hear about cold, unfeeling doctors and therapists who are so removed from the patients they wish to help that they cannot understand and thus help them (i.e., the patients) deal with their pain, their suffering, their chronic loss, and their eventual dying.

Social scientists are beginning to note how difficult, if not impossible, it was and is to be value-neutral or to divorce oneself completely from one's values, one's personal and social history. The new admonition, then, is to at least acknowledge and state explicitly what these are.

I would go further. We can make use of these realities continually to ask what and how one is like or different from what one is observing. It is no longer enough to be aware that, as a researcher, one is part of the research situation and thus altering it. As part of the research situation, the researcher him/herself is worth studying. To fully comprehend the texturing of everyday life, it is not sufficient to relegate to a methodological appendix or later memoirs "what this experience meant to the investigators" (Bowen 1964; Mead 1972).

Rather, we must look at that experience—the anxieties, fears, delights, repulsions—as part of the very situation we are trying to understand. Thus, while social and emotional distancing once provided us with important objectivity and noninvolvement, it has now come to overemphasize the dissimilarities of human experience. Perhaps through the kind of self-examinations I have suggested, we can bridge the gap of understanding and restore some of the universality of the human condition.

In many ways, I am neither the same person nor the same fieldworker I had been in the past. Perhaps now I am only more conscious of something that was always there. I am certainly not the value-free observer. Part of this I have fully incorporated into my research style, sharing not only experiences with the residents, but also ideas as to how to change their situations. I felt then and now, truly on someone's side—the side of the Village against the world.

Part Five

What Are We All Doing? Patients, Practitioners, and Researchers

18

Getting Involved
as Well as
Concerned

The next three essays in Part V are in many ways similar to those in Part IV, but whereas the previous papers emerged in response to a set of research questions, these grew out of a series of clinical and social concerns. "Helping One Another..." (chapter 19) stemmed from a depressing discussion with several people who were trying to form a self-help organization. They were bewailing all the difficulties that seemed to stand in their way. When Edith Lenneberg later invited me to address the 1970 United Ostomy Convention, it seemed a good opportunity to try out my ideas before one of the largest self-help groups in the country. The reception was warm. As a result I was encouraged not only to publish the paper but also to participate in the creation of a self-help group. The latter was eventually incorporated in 1978 as the Boston Self Help Center, a counseling, advocacy, resource, and educational center devoted entirely to, and staffed primarily by, people with chronic diseases, disabilities, and handicaps. The paper in its present form has benefited from that experience and been expanded from two earlier published versions (Zola 1971a,b, 1972d).

"Structural Constraints..." (chapter 20) was stimulated by a concrete clinical issue. During much of the 1970s I participated with Dr. John Stoeckle and others at the Massachusetts General Hospital in the development of a "primary care curriculum." Aside from general lectures, much of our time was spent in small group discussions trying to bring a social science perspective to bear on clinical concerns. Over the weeks and months I began to notice that one issue arose in clinical discussions far more than any other. It was usually verbalized as "Why can't I get Mrs. X to take her medicine?" In medical terms, this was traditionally referred to as "patient noncompliance." I took on the task of discovering what social scientists and others had written on the topic, and when I completed my search I presented my findings to the work group. The paper here has been through several published and unpublished versions (Zola 1976, 1977a).

Not only is the current version in my opinion the best reasoned and most articulate, it also represents a gradual shift in emphasis from an analysis of the literature of noncompliance to a more systematic analysis of the structural features in the doctor-patient relationship which may contribute to patient noncompliance. It is one of my favorite pieces. More than any other article I have written it has given me an entrée to the medical world. For one whose work is often cited this may seem ironic, but my point is a simple one. In almost every other issue I have had to convince the medical world (sometimes successfully and sometimes not) of the importance of my arguments as well as of the issue itself. Not so in this case. For here I deal with a problem of great interest to the practicing physician, the supposed failure/unwillingness of patients to follow the prescribed regimen. This "success," however, brought in its wake certain problems which I delineate in Part VII.

The last paper, "Oh Where, Oh Where Has Ethnicity Gone?" (chapter 21), is a recent favorite because it gave me the opportunity to speculate on something that concerned me—the continued "popularity" of my now nearly two decade-old "ethnic research." It seems to me that both the work of Zborowski (1952) and my own have been cited endlessly but with little impact on the delivery of services or even on other research. When I recently did a bibliographic computer search on what the ensuing decades had produced, I was astonished by the meager results. The bulk of published papers extended our documentation of "ethnic factors" to other groups, but did little to advance our conceptualization. Embarrassed once more by the invitation to speak again on my "old" research, I asked if I could deal with a question that really intrigued me—why after twenty years has there been so little progress? With my sponsors' support, I thus produced "a sociopolitical history of ideas . . . a reflective and admittedly speculative interpretation of the development of ethnic and cultural research in the field of health care."

19

Helping One Another: A
          Speculative History of the
          Self-Help Movement

HISTORICAL ANTECEDENTS

The roots of mutual-aid groups reach back to the frontier days of the United States. Alexis de Toqueville (1961) noted the American penchant for joining groups, and by 1900 a directory listed over 250 independent, national, voluntary lay organizations. For most of these organizations, whether Rotarians, Lions or women's clubs, the goal of helping, though often central to their reason for being, did not mean that members helped each other. Those to be helped were the community in general, some specific problem or disease.

The development of mutual-aid organizations in which the members help each other came slowly. Though some have cited examples of such activities in early agricultural cooperatives (Katz and Bender 1976), the mass waves of immigration of the late nineteenth and early twentieth century were the clearest stimuli to their proliferation (Handlin 1959b). Thrust into a nation in which there were few formal services to aid in their survival, the new arrivals turned to one another. Their response was the creation of mutual-aid societies whose membership was based primarily on sharing

Originally appeared as "Helping One Another: A Speculative History of the Self Help Movement," *Archives of Physical Medicine and Rehabilitation* 60 (1979): 452–456.

some explicit social characteristic, such as race, religion, or country of origin. Interestingly, by far the most "popular" of their benefits were burial and funeral rites. A far distant second service was the lending of money. Thus, in these early self-help groups the aid given to one another was of the most material sort. From such tangible service, aid of a more social and psychological nature was truly a giant step.

How difficult this step was is illustrated in the history of that best known of illness-oriented voluntary organizations, the March of Dimes. Although the rehabilitation problems of young children afflicted with polio were enormous as well as controversial, there was no "coming together" of the afflicted. When we consider that polio patients were not isolated from one another, that clinics, wards, and hospitals were devoted to their exclusive treatment, it is even more surprising that no support organization, however informal, ever arose or was encouraged to form. In retrospect it seemed to have been considered inappropriate. Everything that could be done was being done *for* you. If the recent slogan "do your own thing" fits the atmosphere today, "do your own suffering and keep your problems to yourself" suggests the atmosphere then. In this way disabled people were kept isolated and powerless—separated from others who might share similar concerns, and organized in such a way (i.e. to provide money for research) as to at least inadvertently prevent them from seeing what if anything they could do about their own situation.

THREE BARRIERS TO SELF-HELP

Background reading plus my own experience suggest that a number of barriers impeded the development of health-related self-help organizations. Three that seem most basic were the nature of the problems which such groups addressed, the nature of the help required in dealing with the service they provided, and the nature of the personnel best suited to give that service.

In the first place, the problems with which mutual-aid societies dealt were long considered socially unacceptable. These groups address issues of loss and deficiency, from a missing bodily part or function—the ability to walk, to see, to hear, to speak, to urinate, to defecate—to the most taboo of psychological traits, the inability to control one's behavior, whether in gambling, drinking, drugs, sexuality, mental illness or obesity. There is no doubt a hierarchy of taboo problems; for instance, problems of hearing, seeing or walking are far less stigmatized than facial disfigurement or undergoing a colostomy. But toleration for anything less than normal functioning is a very recent phenomenon. "Boys never make passes at girls who wear glasses" is a ludicrous taunt found only in the current generation of teenagers. On the other hand, we (the older generation) are still uncomfortable with even the most socially accepted of handicaps: we scream at those with no hearing, avoid mentioning the beauty of scenes to the blind, and reprimand our children for being curious about someone with a limp.

All of this is complicated by an American belief that *all* problems can be ultimately overcome. Thus unsolved problems or diseases come to represent a failure, and the bearers become constant reminders of inadequacy. As such, the general response has been to put them as far out of sight and mind as possible (Zola, 1981a).

The nature of the help that such problems entailed, was a second barrier hindering the growth of mutual-aid organizations. For the idea of being in need of help is not an accepted theme in the Western world and certainly not in the United States. No aphorism was known so well as "The Lord helps those who help themselves." Independence was the byword, achievement against all odds the measure of success. The fiction of Horatio Alger embodied this American ideal—the boy (never the girl) who overcame his background to attain success. So, too, the folk heroes of disability and chronic disease were not the millions who merely came to terms with their problems, but those few who overcame them spectacularly—the polio victim who broke track records, the one-legged pitcher who played Major League baseball, the great composer who was deaf, the famous singer who had a colostomy. They were all so good that no one knew, and therein lay part of their glory.

In fact, the emphasis on such successes may have done more harm than good for the majority of people with disabilities. For it masks the kinds of help that those with chronic conditions really need. Management in daily living does not involve doing dramatic tasks, but mundane ones. And these examples of someone overcoming their handicap *once and for all* obscures the time required for such help. Most of this aid cannot be given in even a short series of encounters. And for the majority of us the problem is not temporary, but one that will last for life. That is what chronic means! How uncomfortable this makes people feel is frequently seen in the negative response to mutual-aid organizations which state this life-time commitment explicitly, such as Alcoholics Anonymous, Synanon, Re-Evaluation Counseling and the current Independent Living Movement.

The third barrier to any widespread acceptance of mutual aid was the nature of the personnel involved in giving help. For modern medical care has been, and to a large extent still is, the exclusive province of the technical expert, the doctor. It has been hard enough for the physician to give up tasks, and inevitably some responsibility, to a growing army of paramedics. But these health workers were at least nominally under his authority. Self-help organizations, on the other hand, were essentially lay groups and as such largely outside medical control. As a result, any good that they could do was scarcely examined. Even when positive results of mutual aid were reported, as in group therapy and encounter groups, they were given little professional recognition. At best they might be viewed as an innocuous way for patients to keep themselves occupied and out of trouble. Such forms of help represented self-treatment; for this reason, next to the use of chiropractors, they were regarded by the ordinary providers of medical care as perhaps worse than no help at all.

People with severe disabilities tend to have chronic medical problems, and consequently have been perceived to need close medical supervision. If anything, they have been overmedicalized. Every problem was thought to require medical supervision, from skin care to bladder problems (even when the medical personnel was bored by such issues). And when it was proven that many tasks, even catheterization, could be self-administered with minimal difficulty, such incidents were dismissed as exceptions. Similarly, when it was shown that relatively untrained people, some even with relatively low I.Q.'s, could become excellent personal care attendants, it was argued that such people needed medical supervision; some argued that without supervision, their service would not be reimbursed by third-party payers.

AMELIORATING FACTORS

With such formidable forces ranged against the severely disabled, how did mutual-aid groups ever succeed? There is no single answer; a number of events pried open the door. For example, World War II had an enormous impact upon Americans' ability to ignore the seamy and unpleasant aspects of life. Once and for all American insulation and isolation were broken. All of us, but particularly those in the armed services, came in contact with different cultures and thus different ways of defining as well as handling problems. In short we saw viable alternatives. Certainly one could argue that the Civil Rights Movement truly got underway here as blacks and whites were forced to come to new definitions of themselves and others. One might have expected this to take place much earlier, aided by the great waves of immigration which inundated our country. However, the immigrants' influence was mitigated both by the vastness of America, which permitted most "natives" to remain isolated from these groups, and by the philosophy of Americanization. Accepted by the immigrants and encouraged by the residents, this philosophy consciously encouraged the newcomers to extinguish all salient aspects of their original heritage (Glazer and Moynihan, 1963).

World War II, however, accomplished even more. The injuries of war created the most massive job of rehabilitation the United States has ever faced, and this made certain kinds of physical handicaps no longer a personal but a national responsibility.

The A-bomb and its more powerful successors provoked deep questioning as to who we were and what our life meant. At least one outcome of this national introspection was a societal commitment in money to the solving of social problems. The National Institutes of Health flourished in the postwar era, and some form of National Health Insurance became increasingly inevitable.

Moreover, the nature of help that people needed was changing. With a host of infectious diseases coming under control, more people were surviving to middle age and beyond. Thus many latent or previously "numerically insignificant" disorders became manifest—arthritis, diabetes, mental illness, heart disease, multiple sclerosis, spinal cord injury, stroke, cancer. Moreover, these disorders were more often disabling than immediately fatal, and for which no "magic bullet," either in prevention or in care, was forthcoming. In truth, they were problems which could require medical management for extended periods of time, some for life.

But there was something more to these disorders. They fundamentally altered the doctor-patient relationship. There was a shift from cure to care. No longer did treatment take place with the doctor doing and the patient receiving. To succeed at all, the patient had to help and, as in psychotherapy, be an active participant. In short, treatment was something in which the patients themselves had a role—a change that both they and their former "caretakers" had to recognize.

Psychiatry's coming of age had a special impact. For it made abundantly clear the importance of behavior in all aspects of disease—from how one gets sick to whether or not one recovers. In a sense it reemphasized the oneness of a person's mind and body—a phenomenon so evident in the almost ever-expanding category of disorders called psychosomatic. Thus, "support" and "relationship" could no longer be the incidentals of medical care; they were at the very core.

Yet many health personnel felt neither trained for nor inclined toward the more recent demands of health care. Even were they willing to undertake such a role, it's not clear that numerically they would ever fill the need. For given the current demand, the shortage of physicians was insurmountable, and society too committed to a line of scientific inquiry and specialization to ever turn back. No matter how many doctors now chose the path of primary care or community medicine, doctors in general continue to be more specialized rather than less. Thus partly by default and partly by delegation, many medical tasks—from history-taking to prescribing drugs, from giving injections to performing certain forms of surgery, from teaching to counseling—ultimately came to be done by people who were not M.D.'s.

The biggest change, however, was not in the delegation of responsibility to less trained personnel, but in the taking over of many therapeutic tasks by people who had "been there." In short, the expertise of patients to help themselves and others began to be recognized.

The slow recognition of such expertise has been at best a struggle. The medical world still too often feels that it alone knows what is in the best interests of the disabled, and the world in general still agrees. Often doctors contend that their years of experience and lack of personal involvement make them see our needs clearer. A personal experience shows how occasionally ludicrous this claim can be:

I entered the workshop of a prosthetist who had been in the business for over fifty years. Noting that I had polio and use a cane to walk, he motioned me to come near.

He: "I wonder if you'd try this cane."

IKZ: "I did."

He: "Well, what do you think?"

IKZ: "It seems solid enough."

He: "Now watch this." He then proceeded to take the cane from me and pushed a little button about three inches from the handle and out popped a twelve-inch blade.

Before I could say another word, he went on: "This one is even handier. Look!" Taking another cane, he also pressed a button and now brandished what might be called a ten-inch iron blackjack. "You know," he went on, "in times like these, crime in the streets and all, things like this self-defense cane should be pretty handy."

IKZ: "Yes," I replied in my best tongue-in-cheek fashion, "particularly if the thief lets me lean on him for support while I dismantle my cane."

I feel that no matter how sophisticated, tolerant, or even understanding the unafflicted become, those with a disability will ultimately have to pursue their own needs by banding together. It is not merely because the general public does not care, but because in a real sense it does not know. For instance, it is not hardly accidental that major changes in the architecture of public buildings have been pushed by paraplegics; reduction of drug maintenance costs by "mended hearts"; extension of medical insurance coverage by ostomates; new speech therapies by the laryngectomies; or a new profession, enterostomal therapy, created and originally staffed by former patients. In any case, public interest is not stirred by large numbers of "problem-bearers" alone. There have always been millions of poor, of blacks, and of consumers, as Michael Harrington has pointed out in *The Other America* (1962). It has always taken something more to stir society to action.

The passage of Section 504 of the 1973 Rehabilitation Act Amendments can be viewed as a shift in the national policies regarding services for disabled persons, a shift from benevolent paternalism toward legal protection of civil rights. Historically, public policy toward disabled persons has been formulated in terms of charity, conceptualized and measured by a medical perspective. Thus the disabled person has been viewed as the passive, if not helpless, recipient of charitable services primarily directed toward provision of medical or custodial care.

The enactment of 504 was brought about largely by the activism of disabled people themselves. A number of sit-ins were necessary before the appropriate regulations were ultimately and officially issued. This political militance, inspired by the successes of the Civil Rights Movement of the 60s, demonstrated that the plight of the disabled is due not just to physical limitation, but to systematic and pervasive discrimination. It also provided a contradiction to the stereotype of the disabled person as powerless.

THE CONTINUING STRUGGLE

While there is strength in numbers, the very act of categorizing and tabulating those of us with disabilities creates a dilemma. By being very specific we may well concretize a need but at the same time distort an important reality. In trying to find strict measures of disability or focusing on severe, particularly "visible" handicaps, we make dichotomous and distinct categories for what are really a series of blurry, continually changing continua. By agreeing that there are twenty million disabled, or thirty-six million, or even half the population in some way affected by disability, we delude ourselves into thinking there is some finite (no matter how large) number of people. In this way, both in the defining and in the measuring, we try to make the reality of disease, disability, and death problematic and in this way make it at least potentially someone else's problem. But it is not and can never be. Any person reading the words on this page may be able-bodied for the moment. But everyone reading them will, at some point, suffer from at least one or more chronic diseases and can be disabled, temporarily or permanently, for a significant portion of his/her life.

Many persist in the denial that they will at some time be disabled, thereby slowing social change. But at least several steps suggest themselves. First of all, we with chronic diseases and disabilities must see to our own interests. We must free ourselves from the "physicality" of our conditions and the dominance of our life by the medical world (Illich 1976). In particular, I refer to the tendency to think of ourselves and be thought of by others in terms of our specific chronic conditions. We are polios, cancers, paras, deaf, blind, lame, amputees, and strokes. Whatever else this does, it blinds us to our common social disenfranchisement. Our forms of loss may be different, but the resulting invalidity is the same (Zola 1982).

Forming organizations around specific diseases may have great advantages in raising research monies, but it has divided our strength and vied one disease group against the other. Not only has this led to an overspecialization of services but to an underdevelopment of our consciousness. It has made us feel so dependent on others (the medical world for treatment, the general public for money) and so personally accountable that we often feel that we have no rights. We—patients all—perhaps the last and potentially the largest of America's disenfranchised, must organize on our own behalf. We must organize across specific disease entities, we must create advocacy, consciousness raising, counseling, and resource groups (Bowe et al. 1978). And wherever and whenever possible, staff and members alike must have a chronic disease and/or physical handicap. I am not claiming that no one else can help or understand, but that, as with women and blacks, we are at a point in history where "having been there" is essential in determining where to go.

Providers must rethink their traditional notions of help and independence. One-way giving keeps the recipient powerless. Caregivers must learn not to act for their clients, but to assist them in acting for themselves. Moreover, the notion of independence must be expanded to include the quality of life that is being lived. It is not always necessary that persons do everything for themselves (e.g. typing every letter) or always do as much as they are capable of doing (e.g. walking long distances or climbing steep sets of stairs) if that effort proves exhausting. The energy lost in these physical exertions cannot be expended elsewhere. The use of a "powered" wheelchair might well diminish the exercise an individual needs, but enormously increase his/her social capabilities and networks. The Independent Living Movement argues that it is more often important for us to have full control over our lives than over our bodies. We will give up doing some things for ourselves if we can determine and control when and how it is done!

The self-help movement is, however, but one part of the struggle. It is a prerequisite for change, but neither the sole nor the sufficient avenue. We must deal as much with social arrangements as with self-conceptions. One, in fact, reinforces the other. Thus the problems of those with a chronic disability should be stated not in terms of the individual defects and incapacities, but in terms of the limitations and obstacles placed in the way of our daily social functioning. What should be asked now is not how much it will cost to make society completely accessible to all with physical difficulties, but why a society has been created and perpetuated which has excluded so many of its members.

There is a growing awareness that this exclusion is not an accidental byproduct of industrial society. There is an ideological compatibility between the rise of capitalism and certain Western religions which have continually justified the hierarchical arrangements of people through "hard work" or "the grace of God." When the notions of religion and law were beginning to lose their power as absolute arbiters of important social values, Darwin, perhaps unwittingly, ushered in the age of biological determinism. One critic of the times realized the social import of his work by exclaiming surprisingly, "Sir, you are preaching scientific Calvinism with biological determinism replacing religious predestination." The fixity of the universe and/or hierarchical relations once attributed to God was now being justified by scientific inevitabilities. In the ensuing hundred years there has been an expansion of the influence of science, and in particular medical science, until it has in some ways replaced religion and law. Where once a social rhetoric made reference to good and evil, legal and illicit, we now think in terms of "healthy" and "sick."

We are undergoing a medicalization of society in which medicine is becoming an agent of social control. And although some have argued that this is a more humane and liberal way to deal with social problems, the notions of health and illness still locate the source of trouble and treatment in individual capacities, not in social arrangements (Zola, 1977b).

Having a portion of our population declared officially unfit serves several social functions, not all of them admirable. It is important to recognize that the health professions offer the fastest growing area of employment in this country; their salaries fall in the highest income brackets; health-related industries are among the most profit-making (Health Policy Adivsory Committee, 1971). Bluntly put, some people are making money off the sufferings of others. In this way both economic and political interests have come to reinforce each another. Until the day that no one benefits economically, socially, or psychologically from someone being beneath them, there will always be categories of exclusion.

CONCLUSIONS

Regardless of whether we join activistic groups, support those that do, or seek in other ways to change the social-political-economic structure of America, we must at very least look into ourselves. For if morality or justice is not a sufficient motivating force, perhaps personal survival will be. All of us must contend with our inevitable vulnerability. Aging may indeed make Independent Living Services necessary for everyone! Not to recognize this can only make us further unprepared for the exigencies of life. For when we grow old, and with today's technology "survive" sick and disabled for increasingly longer periods of time, we will experience a triple sense of powerlessness: first, because of our very conditions, we will indeed be more physically and socially dependent. Second, through our previous denial, we will deprive ourselves of the knowledge and resources to cope. And third, the realization of what we have done to those who "aged" before us will rob us (we will feel) of our own right to protest.

In any case, it is very hard for the aged to demand any redress of their situation—they are left to the largess of others. Is it thus any wonder that study after study reports many of the elderly as feeling that their lives have been worthless? A sour ending to any story cannot help but result in a depreciation of the past as well as the present.

In this light it is especially important to remember what Erik Erikson (1964, p. 133) said about society's continual denigration and isolation of the aged.

> Any span of the [life] cycle lived without vigorous meaning at the beginning, in the middle, or at the end, endangers the sense of life, and the meaning of death in all whose life stages are intertwined.

What we do to the physically handicapped and chronically ill is what we do to ourselves.

20

Structural Constraints in the Doctor-Patient Relationship: The Case of Non-Compliance

When I'm involved with a medical group, and we get down to nitty-gritty issues, the most frequent question I'm asked is, "What can I do about the patient who won't take his medicine?" From a medical perspective this is what compliance is all about—how to get patients to follow a regimen which is "in their best interests." But in this seemingly straightforward task, all our best efforts seem to fail. Nearly 50 percent of patients stop taking their medications long before they are supposed to. Many take the wrong dose at the wrong time. And many more than we realize don't even fill their prescriptions. To paraphrase an advertising slogan, we must be doing something *wrong*.

And so we are. We, the health researchers and providers are doing at least two things which distort our understanding of compliance. We do not sufficiently appreciate what following a medical regimen means to an individual, nor do we fully acknowledge the role that health personnel have in contributing to the very noncompliance we seek to reverse. By examining both of these misconceptions I hope to shed some light on specific facets of the doctor-patient interaction which hinder patient compliance.

Originally appeared as "Structural Constraints in the Doctor-Patient Relationship—The Case of Non-Compliance," in *The Relevance of Social Science for Medicine*, edited by Leon Eisenberg and Arthur Kleinman (Dordrecht, Holland: D. Reidel Publishing, 1981), pp. 241–252.

First, it is necessary to look at several disarming blind spots in regard to patient behavior.

We can start by looking at *when* people see doctors. While some people may go at the first sign of trouble, the far larger number delay and go quite reluctantly. Study after study shows that most people are fearful of seeing a doctor and that it takes a quite complex set of social events to make them go at all (Anderson 1968; Freidson 1961; Suchman 1965a & b; Zola 1973a). Thus, patients cannot be assumed to be a group of willing supplicants, rushing with open arms to seek aid.

Secondly, the importance of the time dimension of most medical problems is too often neglected. Most problems are already chronic by the time a doctor is seen. This probably means that many people have already lived with, and perhaps adjusted to, many aspects of their conditions. It probably also means that they have done a number of things to cope with their problem, some of which have worked and some of which have not. Thus while the doctor may be expected to give some crucial aid, it will not be followed to the exclusion of all other methods. In short, it will rarely, if ever, be the only thing the patient will use.

Thirdly, disease in the modern sense is never a purely personal phenomenon, located in a single individual. It is always a social phenomenon, involving in varying degrees not only family and friends but many aspects of a person's life. Thus, to assume that an individual has the easy ability to make significant life changes without consulting others, is patent nonsense and often makes the medical suggestion appear unrealistic. A specific example will clarify this point. Many years ago my father, whose whole family had a history of heart disease, was diagnosed as having "angina." The doctor who transmitted this information to him was a specialist and recommended most strongly that he change jobs, preferably to one with less physical exertion, perhaps at a desk. My father thanked him dutifully as he left the office. The problem was that my father was a bluecollar worker, a dress-cutter in the garment industry with a less than high school education. He could no more get a desk job than he could climb Mt. Everest. Unfortunately, because he regarded the doctor's basic suggestion as so patently ridiculous, he treated the rest of his quite appropriate medical advice with similar disdain. In other words, he noncomplied.

Finally, it is no longer safe to assume that patients regard the treatment they are asked to undertake as being entirely "for their own good" and "in their best interests." Since the office hours, appointments, and location of visit, are arranged for the doctor's convenience and not the patient's the same may well be seen for the very treatments the patients receive. I refer to all the publicity about unnecessary surgery, the high salaries of medical personnel, the money being made off of Medicare and Medicaid, the profit margins of pharmaceutical companies, the adverse side effects of many drugs. Together they create an unspoken suspicion in many patients' minds as to how much of what they are receiving is really in *their* own interests.

What I am arguing in all these cases is that to "take one's medicine" is in no sense the "natural thing" for patients to do. If anything, a safer working assumption is that most patients regard much of their medical treatment as unwanted, intrusive, disruptive, and the manner in which it is given presumptuous.

In this sense the real work in patient care begins, not ends, when the physician reaches for the prescription pad. The patient has to be made the ally in treatment, not the object of it. As such, the instructions, the form and even dosage of medicines must be integrated into his or her life style. If a four times a day prescription is medically best but socially intolerable, then a one-a-day form should not be second choice, but the best choice. What we need always to understand is the place of the treatment in the everyday life of the patient. Thus, we must seek analogs in people's lives compatible with taking medicine or following a prescribed regimen.

Too much of this is done after the fact—after noncompliance becomes an issue. Then it is often too late. The patient has already been disappointed and is distrustful. The time to start is *before*. But it's hard to change, particularly since health professionals have strong opinions about not letting the patient know too much. In perhaps no other area of human contact has it been so strongly and wrongly assumed that a little knowledge is a dangerous thing.

The strength and self-defeating nature of this attitude was brought home to me at a conference I once attended on Essential Hypertension. This is one of the most prevalent and untreated disorders in our country and one for which there is a wide variety of available drugs. Yet this variety presents problems. It is often necessary that a sequence of medicines and perhaps even dosages must be tried until the most efficacious level is found; then it must be taken for the rest of one's life. Perhaps it is no great surprise that the noncompliance rate in regard to this disorder is extraordinarily high. When I asked my fellow medical panelists if they discussed with their patients the likelihood that the first course of treatment might not work, they answered emphatically, "NO!" They argued that such a statement would discourage their patients and stimulate non-compliance. To me it was hard to conceive that their patients' non-compliance could be any higher than it already was. My contention was that sharing with patients the possible treatment difficulties would not only be good preventitive medicine but an act of caring which would reinforce rather than erode trust. In short, if trust and confidence was not justified the first time the patient gives it, it can hardly be expected to improve the second time it is asked for.

Thus, to make the patient an ally in treatment, we first must know where he or she is coming from; we must regard her or him as an intelligent though anxious adult; and we must look to their available resources.

In regard to available resources, I wish to make an important aside. For socioeconomic, and I would even say political reasons, there has been systematic neglect of an area of research—what people do to and for themselves to prevent, help, and cure a vast amount of physical and psychosocial conditions. The area is called self-treatment and the scanty data that does exist (Dunnell and Cartwright 1972; Zola 1972b) indicates that within any given 36-hour period from 67 to 80 percent of our adult population uses some sort of internal or external medication. The relevance of this data to the study of compliance should hopefully be obvious. For such a high prevalence of self-treatment indicates that the American population as a whole is not averse to using drugs on a regular basis. What it must be averse to are the circumstances and purposes under which *some* drugs *must* be taken.

But as stated in my opening we need not only a better understanding of the recipient of help but also of the giver and their interaction. Too many investigations define noncompliance as almost entirely a patient issue. As such both research and programs emphasize what patient characteristics can be changed (see Becker and Maiman 1975 for general review). Study after study (such as M.S. Davis 1966) notes that physicians overwhelmingly attribute noncompliance to the patient's uncooperative personality or specifically blame the patient's inability to understand physicians' recommendations. In fact, the individual physician seems extraordinarily well-defended against closely examining the problems of noncompliance. Not only do doctors generally underestimate the rates of noncompliance in their practices but they are also inaccurate in identifying noncompliant individuals (Balint et al. 1970; Barsky and Gillum 1974; M.S. Davis 1966). Thus, while almost all clinicians agree that there is a problem, it seems to be someone else's.

The truth is, of course, closer to home. General studies of learning indicate the important role played by the transmitter of information. This role may not even be a conscious one. Several reports have noted that experimenter attitudes have even influenced the results of animal research (Freeman 1967). Surely, if the attitudes of an experimenter can effect the behavior of his rats, it is not too much to expect that the beliefs of prescribing physicians about their patients, their problems and their treatment must similarly influence the actions of those very patients.

My general contention is that there are certain structural barriers in the ordinary treatment situation which specifically impede communication. In short, the doctor-patient consultation, as presently constituted, is ill-suited for learning to take place.

At the most general level, it is important to bear in mind that the doctor-patient encounter is perhaps the most anxiety-laden of all lay-expert consultations. Rarely does someone go for a reaffirmation of a good state. At best, they are told that they are indeed in good health and thus a previous worry should be dismissed (Zola 1972c). More likely they learn that a particular problem is not as serious as they feared. Moreover, given all the untreated medical complaints uncovered by epidemiological surveys, seeking a doctor's help is a relatively infrequent response to symptoms (Zola 1966, 1973a). The visit to a doctor is likely approached with considerable caution. Delay is the statistical norm, fear and anxiety the psychological norms. And while some anxiety has been found to be conducive to learning, the amount in the traditional doctor-patient encounter is surely excessive!

It is also not without significance that recall of the timing, if not the frequency, of doctor visitation is found to be notoriously inaccurate. In the large majority of instances the visit may well have been an experience to be finished as quickly as possible. And the most common way to deal with unpleasant events is to suppress them. In such a situation is it any surprise that a patient is likely to forget much that happened, including their physician's instructions?

But I can be more specific. At present I would contend that in the visiting of a physician, a negative context for answering and asking questions has been created—the result of both a witting and unwitting process of intimidation.

The negative context begins early. It starts with place. I am old enough to remember when the most frequent location of seeing a doctor was in my home. Whatever the sound medical reasons for the shift of almost all visits to hospitals, clinics, or the doctor's office (Gibson and Kramer 1965), it has resulted in a tremendous loss of the patient's power and security at a time when he or she is most vulnerable. The visit is no longer on one's home territory. Everything is now unfamiliar. There are now no social and physical supports, no easy way to relax, no private space to move around in or escape to. Moreover, while most examining rooms are physically closed to other patients and staff, they are often so audibly open that complaints and medical advice are easily overheard (Clute 1963, Stoeckle 1978). And little effort is made in medical settings to change this. If anything, the physical setup emphasizes rather than reduces social distance between patient and the doctor, and heightens the strangeness of the encounter. Thrust amid suffering strangers, one is assaulted by medical signs, equipment, uniforms and sterility. It was quite different when I was a child. My mother would offer the doctor a cup of coffee or tea to make the situation more relaxed. Is there any remotely analogous manner to defuse or make more "familiar" our current visits?

From place we can go to physical position. Whether it be horizontal, or in some awkward placement on one's back or stomach, with legs splayed or cramped, or even in front of a desk, the patient is placed in a series of passive, dependent, and often humiliating positions. These are positions where embarrassment and anger are at war with the desire to take in what the doctor is saying. In this battle learning is clearly the loser.

The standard gathering of essential information also brings in its wake a series of problems (see Waitzkin and Stoeckle 1972 for a general review). It often starts with the taking of the medical history. It's bad enough that I don't know all my family's medical diseases or of what my grandparents, whom I never knew, died, but I begin to feel positively stupid when at the mature age of forty-four I do not know whether as an infant I had the measles or chicken pox. I may do a little better with more recent conditions but the feeling sinks again when it comes to medications I've taken that have given me trouble. "Those little red pills" seems an insufficient answer and the recording physician's dubious look does not help much. It's with difficulty that I recall that prescription drugs have only been labelled within the last fifteen years. By this point in the interview when I am asked questions about the specific timing and location of my varying symptoms, I begin to answer with a specificity born more of desperation than accuracy. Any vagueness I report is responded to as related to my faulty memory than the very reality of the symptoms I am experiencing. The scenario may be different in detail from patient to patient. In short confronted with a situation in which we already feel stupid not only sets a tone for the rest of the encounter but makes it very difficult, if not impossible, to ask the physician simple questions or admit that you do not understand certain things—no matter how much the physician may later encourage one to do so.

Another impediment to communication is the quantity of information to be transmitted in the doctor-patient encounter. Regardless of the potentially upsetting nature of the advice, there is quite simply the problem of *data-overload*. The patient is asked to remember too much, with too few tools, in too short a time. In most other teaching situations, the learner is encouraged to find ways of remembering (like taking notes). But the traditional position of the patient negates this possibility. Giving patients a printed sheet of instructions, as done occasionally in pediatric practice, is not the complete answer, but it is a start.

Next, there is the method of communication. For here is a situation where the physician attempts to distill, in several minutes, the knowledge and experience accumulated in decades. I have spent much of my professional life at medical schools and teaching hospitals but have yet to see much explicit attention given to this problem. As is the case with college teaching, the degree is regarded as sufficient guarantee of the ability to communicate what was learned. But the task is not so simple. In fact, what few self-evident truths there are, are soon forgotten. Experientially, we know that different subject matters, like mathematics in contrast with literature, must be taught and learned in different ways. By analogy, the same is true for a medical regimen, some things can be told, some demonstrated, some only experienced, some written out, some stated a single time, some repeated with variations. This in itself may lead to the further realization that the teaching cannot be done all at once or by the same person.

On a rather mundane level, there is the matter of language which both in tone and content often patronizes and thus further intimidates, and even confuses the patient. First there is the manner of address. Whether it be to bridge the lack of familiarity, physically or socially, or truly to establish authority and keep distance, the use of first names and diminutives seems to have lost its endearing charm. I will admit that it took the women's movement and a certain amount of personal aging to make me realize how awkward it felt to be addressed by a physician ten years my junior as "Irv" while I could only call him by his attached label, "Dr. Smith." But the ultimate ludicrousness was brought home by a colleague during a recent hospitalization. While visiting her I witnessed the following interaction:

Looking down only at the chart and not at the patient in the bed, the
　physician said jocularly, "Well Anne, how are you today?"
"Lousy, Robert, how are you?"
Taken aback, he responded, "My name is Dr. Johnson, I only called
　you Anne to make you feel comfortable."
"Well," my friend responded, "My name is Dr. Greene, I only called
　you Robert to make you feel more comfortable."

While I'm not recommending the above dialogue as a general mode
of response, it did seem ludicrous to have my fellow colleague, herself a Ph.D. and several years older than the M.D., addressed in such a
manner. Few potential patients, however, would be in such control
as to handle the situation as did my colleague. Given that the average
time of doctor-patient interaction is so short (one estimate is that
the average visit is about five minutes with initial visits ranging to
thirty, Waitzkin and Stoeckle 1972) address itself sets a tone. Thus
the use of the diminutive and false familiarity further increases the
already existing gap between the helping provider and the anxious
patient, making the latter feel even more childlike, dependent, and
intimidated.

A second aspect of tone that is worth reexamining is that most
common and important of the doctor's tools—reassurance. That
even this cannot be given without thought was illustrated in a recent
study of pediatric practice (Pessen 1978). Confronted continually by
what are often referred to as "overanxious" mothers, doctors often
responded straightforwardly with, "There, there. You needn't have
worried. Michael is fine." I've begun to realize that the admonition,
"not to worry" is perhaps the most overworked and useless advice in
the English lauguage (Janis 1958). But in pediatric consultation it
had a more dysfunctional effect. It was a truly double-edged sword.
While, on the one hand, it did communicate to the mother that her
child's condition was not medically serious, it also contained an implicit "put down" of the mother's concern. It made her feel foolish
for being bothered by something that turned out to be nothing. As
Pessen revealed, one of the lessons the mother learned was thus a
negative one—to be more cautious in consulting a doctor, lest she
look foolish. The mother, however, did not learn *what* to be cautious
about, but rather in general to think twice about her next visit.

My guess is that in this situation, should the pediatrician try to
correct the mother's perspective, she simply cannot take it in. Already feeling foolish for having bothered the doctor, the mother is
not in a good position to learn anything—the information the pedi-

atrician is trying to transmit just feels like a further scolding. What should have been communicated were *two* separate and distinct messages. First, the physician should state that the child's condition was not medically serious, i.e., nothing to worry about, then the pediatrician should probably tell her that s/he understood and appreciated her concern, i.e., given her newness as a mother and the inarticulateness of infants, a baby's signs and symptoms are naturally puzzling and disturbing. At this time, truly reassured as to both her being a good mother and the lack of medical seriousness of her child's illness, the mother can then take in the pediatrician's instructions about medically "worrisome" signs and symptoms.

My final comment on communications concerns the very words used. The technical jargon confronting a patient might be bad enough, but the major confusion is the different meanings assigned to the same word by doctor and patient. I heard recently of a survey where, of all the patients who were told to take diuretics for fluid retention, over half believed that the drugs helped retain fluid and were, therefore, used to treat nocturia. They altered their use accordingly.

In many instances the process is equally insidious. For when heard by the patients, the dictionary meaning of the instructions is absolutely clear. The confusion sets in only after the consultation, when the patient is at home and must follow the instructions. Let me illustrate:

1. "Take this drug four times a day." Since this means taking it every six hours must I wake up in the middle of the night? What if I forget? Should I take two when I remember?
2. "Keep your leg elevated most of the day." How high is elevated? Is it important that it be above my waist or below? How long is "most"? What about when I sleep?
3. "Take frequent baths." Are they supposed to be hot, cold or warm? Should I soak for a while? Is four times a day frequent? Does it matter when? Should I use some special soap?
4. "Only use this pill if you can't stand the pain." What does "can't stand" mean? How long should I wait? Is it bad to take it? If I do, am I a weak person?
5. "Come back if there are any complications." What is a complication? Must it be unbearable? What if my fingers feel a little numb? Which feelings are related to my problem and which to my treatment? Is it my fault if there are complications?

All of the issues in this paper I have delineated become even more complicated when the health professional is treating a person with chronic disease. When that person is also poor and a woman they are triply cursed (Emerson 1970; Boston Women's Health Book Collective 1976, Cartwright 1964; Kosa and Zola, 1975). Everything becomes more complex—both in the telling and the hearing. Accordingly, the instructions and teaching, like the disorder itself, is a long-term event. Thus, the patient will, in the course of their disorder, inevitably have more questions, more troubles, and more doubts. They must not be made to feel guilty for things that are just starting to bother them now. This should be regarded as the expected and natural course of events and communicated thusly to the patient.

Finally, we come to what the reality of treating a person with a chronic disease means for the provider of care. Particularly for physicians, this is a frustrating task, one for which their training in acute care has left them largely unprepared. Most of the diseases affecting us today cannot be cured, only abated. Death cannot be defeated, only postponed. And these are realities that both doctor and patient must deal with, not deny. Nor will the medical world's previous defense against dealing with their own as well as their patients' frustration be any longer possible. The objectification of the patient as a disease state and the distance this produced will no longer be tolerated. The appendicitis in Room 104 or the rheumatoid arthritis down the hall will not stand for it. There is at long last in this country a consumer health movement. In its wake come many demands: a demystification of expertise, a right to know everything about one's bodies, and a sharing of power in any decision affecting one's life. Thus health personnel are forced to look at their patients as people and in many cases people who are quite different from themselves in gender, in class, race, ethnicity and some of whom they may simply not like. There is no easy answer to these new-found feelings but they are there and must be dealt with.

While I have been detailed in my criticism of the present structure of the doctor-patient relationship, I am by no means pessimistic that I will remain so. As I just mentioned, there is a growing patient movement which will help patients to be more assertive of their rights. It is, however, necessary that the medical world react not merely from a defensive posture. It can and should realize that relinquishing their absolute dominance, while initially a loss, will in the long run give all of us more freedom. (This is a lesson the women's movement is trying to teach men—that their liberation will indeed help men in their own struggles to be free.)

A change in communication patterns between staff and patients can only improve our basic task. There is already research showing that the more information we share the greater the likelihood of patient medical compliance (M.S. Davis 1966; Francis et al. 1969; Williams et al. 1967; Korsch et al. 1968). I believe that this sharing, including the sharing of uncertainty, will also decrease the psychological burden that physicians carry—a burden that I think is reflected in the alarmingly high rates of suicide, emotional breakdown, drug and alcohol addiction among health-care workers. A demystification of the doctor and his power, an opening up of communication, including angry communication between doctors and their patients, may also help stem the growing tide of malpractice suits. Part of the latter is, I believe, a response to dashed expectations. When there is no place to vent dissatisfaction within a system (i.e. the standard doctor-patient consultation) the only recourse is to go outside (i.e. to seek redress in the legal system).

I am essentially arguing for more open communication between the doctor and the patient. As I have delineated in this paper, part of the barrier to such communication lies both in the unjustified assumptions about patient behavior held by the health provider as well as a series of socio-psycho-physical elements which currently structure the ordinary medical consultation. Hopefully, my description of these misconceptions and these barriers has been sufficiently concrete to show how they can be dismantled.

There is, of course, much more that can be done within medical education (and health provider education in general) itself. It starts with an old truism, "Know thyself." I would expand it to say, "Know thyself and you will know your patient." Anything that will help providers be in touch with their own weaknesses as well as strengths, what upsets (as well as what satisfies) them about certain illnesses and certain patients, will contribute to this understanding. If I had to recommend a single psychological dimension with which every health provider should be in touch it would be a sense of vulnerability. A continual awareness of what it is like to be weak, dependent, scared or uncertain will do much to help us understand what it is like to be a patient and ill in Western society. There are psychological exercises in addition to role playing which can sensitize one to this. The use of video-taping is an excellent way in which we can monitor and understand how we affect patients. Continuing clinical seminars on compliance may also provide an important forum for understanding the frustrations of doctors and patients in dealing with this issue. And such seminars or case conferences might well include the recipients of care as well as the providers.

There are many elements of the clinical encounter itself which can and should be changed. While many changes are fairly explicit in my listing of barriers to communication, let me deal with some that may not be. The patient's position within the consultation must be strengthened. Some, as I have mentioned, must take place outside our purview, but others we can at least encourage. We must look more explicitly at the encounter as a learning situation and thus analyze how learning can best take place. At least one suggestion is a more explicit separation in time if not space between the examination and the information that the patients must have to know about their diagnosis, their prognosis, and their care. Where, for whatever reason, there can be no substantial separation, then at least let us give the patient a chance to absorb what s/he has been through— some way of gathering themselves together before we proceed. In a workshop I am currently running, we are teaching patients relaxation exercises so that they can "center" themselves before they receive more information and/or start asking questions.

It may be impossible to shift the place of most medical encounters back to the home, though in long-term care an occasional home-visit will help health providers keep in touch with the reality of their suggestions. What we can do, however, is encourage a trend that is already beginning, what the self-help movement calls the presence of an advocate. To the degree that certain medical conditions as well as regimens involve patients' families and "significant others," we should take this into consideration when we explain the implications of a particular diagnosis and its treatment. Without taking responsibility away from the patient we can encourage and allow the presence of others during all phases of the medical encounter. We have I think "overprivatized" the medical interview to the detriment of all concerned.

Hopefully, I have taken a step in this paper to reverse this process. It is time to reexamine many of the traditional assumptions of what it takes to heal and to help. I am naive enough to believe that knowledge and awareness are powerful tools. While acknowledging the dilemmas in the doctor-patient relationship will not be sufficient to make the problem of noncompliance disappear, it will at least change the context of discussion. The participants, when deciding what is best must be patients as well as doctors. We must remember that giving up power is not the same as abdicating responsibility. There must be less talk of persuasion and more of negotiation. And when we do so, a change in philosophy will be reflected in a change in language. We will no longer speak of "medication compliance" but rather of "therapeutic alliance."

21

"Oh Where, Oh Where
        Has Ethnicity Gone?"

"Oh Where, Oh Where Has Ethnicity Gone?"
conveys in tone, if not in substance, the thrust of this chapter. In
part, I am forced to take a reflective approach in regard to ethnicity
and health care. For despite the dates of my publications, (Zola
1963b,c, 1966, 1972b, 1973a) I have not done an empirical study on
the topic in nearly twenty years. I have, however, paid the price for
my early research for I am continually asked to consult and speak on
the topic. This is a speech or consultation which usually goes quite
well until someone asks either, "What will you do next?" or "What
have you done recently?" The answer to both questions is most often
a slightly regretful, "Nothing." I state this not as a caution but a context. I am both an insider and an outsider on the topic of ethnicity
and health care.

As an outsider it was clearly time to look again at the field. After
reviewing the literature provided by a medline search, I was confronted with the problem of pulling it together. An encyclopedic
article by Chrisman and Kleinman (1980) provided a provocative
take-off point. In the early pages of their paper they asked themselves, "Why study ethnic health beliefs and practices?" Their
answer was interesting.

Originally appeared as "Oh Where, Oh Where Has Ethnicity Gone?" in *Ethnicity and
Aging*, edited by Donald E. Gelfand and Alfred J. Kutzik (New York: Springer,
1979), pp. 66–80.

While health beliefs and practices among all Americans are of interest, those identifiable as belonging to particular ethnic groups are especially significant because they are frequently so closely tied to people's lives that they can provide general insight into the nature of ethnicity in the United States. (p. 454)

People whose ethnic identity is an important part of their daily lives will act in accordance with the traditional beliefs and practices of their ethnic heritage in determining which treatments do and do not make sense. (p. 457)

This link to identity recalled the cautions of Shibutani and Kwan (1965p. VI). They noted that "since ethnic identity lies at the core of the self-conception of so many people, it is not surprising that this subject matter is so explosive and . . . difficult to contemplate dispassionately." As a result they claimed that all too many of the scientific positions on the issue are little more than "political positions." This suggested that one way of understanding "ethnicity and its relation to health services" was *not* to review the literature itself but the ideas behind it—a sociopolitical history of ideas. And so that is what I am offering—a reflective and admittedly speculative interpretation of the development of ethnic and cultural research in the field of health care. My discussion will not focus specifically on the elderly. Since they are major consumers of health care, however, the issues raised herein are certainly applicable to the growing population of elderly from diverse ethnic backgrounds.

THE GROWTH OF ETHNIC RESEARCH

To paraphrase the Virginia Slims cigarette ads, ethnic researchers have "come a long way." My surmise is, however, that in the health care area we have come more slowly, had less impact, and are in for more resistance than in most any other area of applied research. Let me first document the progress.

1. Pick up any textbook on ethnic relations or monograph about an ethnic group written more than a decade ago and you will find barely any mention of health care or illness treatment except to document some exotic custom. Now every year there are dozens of books and hundreds of articles detailing ethnic and cultural factors in health practices and delivery.

2. Where once there was no academic forum for such topics, now there are many international journals, several devoting themselves specifically to cross-cultural and ethnic themes and a professional organization, The Society for Medical Anthropology, which devotes much of its newsletter to reports and conferences on cultural patterning of health practices.

3. In the all-important area of professional practice, references to ethnic and cultural factors have taken a positive turn. Where once such traits were only documented in order to stamp them out, now they are documented so that they can be used to heighten the sensitivity and available resources of health workers. The most common academic rubric is a course entitled medical anthropology. At very least we are likely to find attention to cultural factors part of any course or book on the psychosocial care of patients.

4. Finally, in the public arena, from a period of despairing of such differences to one of merely noting them, we are now in an era of almost celebrating them. From educational to popular television, from the *National Geographic* to *Psychology Today*, the health practices of different ethnic and cultural groups are no longer described for their exotic aspects but their therapeutic ones, not for their distancing functions but for their integrative ones.

Whether or not this shift is a "success" story can be put aside for a minute. What seems worth examination is the social, historical, and even political aspects of this progression.

ETHNIC RESEARCH AND MENTAL HEALTH

As I said in the beginning, research in this area has in general been slow. But *within* the broad area of health care, there has been a discernible difference. For the greatest impact, not only in the study of but also in the delivery of health care, is in the area of mental health. As Kleinman has noted (1977, p. 12), it is a difference which persists even today: "clinically oriented anthropologists . . . have concentrated their investigations on psychiatric problems, while leaving general medical disorders virtually unexamined." Tracing this development may well tell us something.

EARLY RESEARCH EFFORTS

Without calling it the first such study, I would venture a guess that the importance of social and cultural factors in mental health was crystallized in both the scholarly and popular world by the work of Margaret Mead (1928, 1930, 1935). Over fifty years ago she began the first of a long train of cross-cultural investigations. In studying Samoan girls, she claimed that adolescence need not everywhere be a time of turbulence and struggle but in certain cultural circumstances could be a time of calm transition. She continued this questioning of universal myths in the 1930s when she began her New Guinea studies of the Arapesh, the Mundugumor and the Tschambuli. Emphasizing the different value orientations and family structures in these different societies, she noted that to the Arapesh an aggressive person was sick, while to the Mundugumor it was one who was peaceful and considerate and to the Tschambuli a dominant male or gentle female was likely to be thought of a neurotic. In short, with these early investigations there was a growing recognition that what was considered normal in one culture was not necessarily normal in another. But the literature more often referred to faraway places with strange sounding names (Opler 1959). So while there was some recognition that categories of mental health and illness were not as universal as we might like to think, it seemed to have little empirical and theoretical relevance for work in the United States. I do not mean that Americans were unaware of any relationship between culture, ethnicity, and mental functioning but that it was essentially a negative one. On the crassest level, differences in rates of mental illness between different ethnic groups—differences documented since the mid-1800s—were used to demonstrate that "the more foreign" group, whoever they might be at the time—Irish in the mid-1800s, southern and eastern Europeans in the late nineteenth and early twentieth century—were in some ways inferior to the dominant culture. Where the research was more sophisticated it did not focus on the ethnic groups *per se* but rather on the issues of migration and immigration. In the retrospect of some fifty years these studies too had a built-in evaluative component. For while the investigators were often sympathetic to the plight of these immigrants, their explanations for this plight focused on some flaw in these ethnic groups, on variables which affected their ability to cope. Rarely was there any analytic attention, let alone blame, focussed on the receptivity of the host environment. America was, even in the minds of these researchers, "the land of opportunity." That America might take advantage of, use, even destroy such people was left primarily to the writings of the muckrakers (Weinberg and Weinberg, 1961), not the ethnic researchers.

POSTWAR ETHNIC RESEARCH

While World War I only reinforced this phenomenon, World War II had quite a different impact on scientific thinking about ethnicity, mental illness, and their relationship to one another. Though occasionally romanticized in novels about the era, much of the war effort required a forced intermixing and with it a reliance on people of varying backgrounds, religions, even races on one another. Geographically, much of this took place in areas known to the participants previously only through folk tales or movies. And all of these long-term events were symbolically capped by a real one—the possibility of our ultimate destruction through the A-bomb and its successor the H-bomb. A certain American rootlessness became evident. The country immersed itself in a painful bout of cultural introspection.

America suffered a kind of "existential schmerz"—what Allan Wheelis (1958) called "the quest for identity." And it was reflected in an upsurge of all sorts of group-related phenomena, from the human potential movement to religious revivals to ethnic consciousness. This social consciousness was accompanied by a rising political consciousness. One after another civil rights and liberation movements arose. Each demanded more positive attention to their specialness, their uniqueness, their previous exclusion, discrimination, and oppression. And the research of the 50s reflected it. Cultural variables become more prominent than ever but while the researchers (Hollingshead and Redlich, 1958; Srole et al., 1962; Leighton et al. 1963) again documented ethnic differences in mental health rates, they added something else: a documentation of a fairly systematic exclusion of ethnic groups from the services they needed. And sometimes the researchers began, albeit mildly, to criticize the therapeutic models of the providers of services.

CHANGING CONCEPTIONS OF MENTAL ILLNESS

The very thinking about mental illness also changed. Theorists called neo-Freudians—Sullivan, Horney, Fromm, Kardiner—spoke of the social interactional, the social, and the environmental aspects of mental illness. Treatment followed suit and expanded from one-to-one to more social methods, from milieu, group, and family therapy to a consideration of cultural alternatives (Kiev, 1964, 1968). General research paid more attention to differing perceptions of mental illness by both status (Gurin, Veroff, and Feld, 1960; Star 1955, 1957; Woodward 1951) and ethnicity (Opler and Singer 1956, Singer and Opler 1956). In this era social psychiatry as a theoretical discipline and community psychiatry as a practical application were born.

ETHNICITY AND PHYSICAL ILLNESS

In the medical as opposed to the psychiatric world, however, no such dramatic change was evident. Kleinman again echoes this observation (1977, p. 12):

It is curious that applied clinically-based anthropology, which has already contributed substantially to an understanding of the culture-specific categories of ethnic minorities and non-Western populations, had contributed so little an appreciation of the historicity and culture-specific nature of biomedical constructs, or to refurbishing the narrowly conceived and notoriously inadequate medical model.

This is no accidental phenomenon. Simply put, there was much greater resistance to admitting the importance of culture in regard to physical disease than mental disorder. There was much more politically at stake. And this showed itself in both macro-societal explanations and micro-professional concerns.

As with rates of mental disorder, there had long been a documenting of cultural and ethnic differences in regard to phsycial illness. The early data focused on acute infectious diseases and their concomitants: tuberculosis, pneumonia, influenza, scarlet fever, measles, diarrhea. It is again in the explanations that the unverbalized value positions of the investigators were revealed. While the words *working conditions, living arrangements,* and *poverty* dotted the findings, the major attention and ultimately the blame was directly placed on the individuals themselves:

their wish to live in crowded cramped quarters led to the spread of infections;

their eating incorrect and often ethnic foods led to nutritional difficulties;

their washing insufficiently and poor hygiene led to unsanitary conditions;

their bizarre customs of dress got them caught in machines or made them either over- or underdressed in what were once called sweatshops.

While thus recognizing ethnic and cultural differences in rates of illness as well as in health care itself, America's ideological, political, and economic system blamed the ethnics and their culture for their own physical ills. In other words, the physical disorders which each person suffered were the result in some way of individual ills and faults not societal ones. And there was an ideological out—social mobility—the notion that anyone in America could get out of the mire of poverty and their cultural background by simply trying harder and assimilating.

PHYSICAL ILLNESS IN THE 1970S

I must stress the political implications of this by jumping to the mid-1970s. Today we are confronted not by marked differences in the acute infectious diseases but in the chronic diseases. Pneumonia, influenza, tuberculosis are replaced by lung cancer, heart disease, obesity, and stroke. But the political consequences of our explanatory models are still the same. Today the newest "buzz word" is *lifestyle behavior,* a term which easily incorporates ethnic health practices. The elements to my hearing are the same as several generations ago. Again the lip service exists. Most speakers and writers on the health care of Americans acknowledge that America is a very materialistic, achievement-oriented, indeed stressful society. And yet beneath these apparent negatives lurks the feeling that it can be overcome if we the public only lived right. So now the people who are "sicker" are criticized for not knowing how to relax, thereby exacerbating their hypertension; for eating greasy and fast foods, which contribute to their obesity and circulatory troubles; for smoking too much, which leads to lung cancer and heart attacks; for relying too heavily on alcohol and drugs, which leads to all manner of addictions.

Once more it is the individual who is indicted. Once more it seems easier to point a finger at the individual behavior and practices that correlate with specific diseases rather than to ask what it is about American society economically, socially, or politically which makes us unrelaxed, eat unnutritiously, smoke, drink, and use drugs prodigiously, and what political and economic interests might be served by our so doing (Navarro, 1976; Waitzkin and Waterman, 1974).

My point is a simple one. As long as we view disease as an individual problem we will seek individual solutions. It is no wonder that we are the last of the large industrial nations to provide any kind of national health insurance or any kind of national health care. How could it be otherwise? For if we conceive of getting ill as an individual problem and responsibility, then preventing and treating the illness is similarly an individual problem. Based on such assumptions, good health care is a privilege of those who can pay for it, not a right of all. And providers who give services to the poor do it out from a sense of charity for some, not of equality for all.

THE ACCEPTANCE OF ETHNIC RESEARCH IN MENTAL AND PHYSICAL HEALTH

The playing out of this scenario is perhaps best seen in further contrasting the political threats of cultural research in the mental and physical health areas. While incorporating social causes into thinking about the etiology of mental illness did imply a criticism of the American way of life, it was less threatening to its basic fabric. The societal forces that affected our mental health often seemed more ephemeral and indirect. To say that America was inhospitable, materialistic, achievement-oriented—in short stressful—for segments of our population seemed a long way from saying it was inherently destructive. Societal forces in regard to physical illness seemed to imply a more causal and direct relationship. A look at history may clarify this point. Mental illness is claimed (Rosen, 1968) to have always existed with its form changing from country to country, from era to era. Not so with many of the physical diseases that plague us today. While some forms of heart disease, stroke, and arthritis are found in many ancient civilizations, many others, like the varying cancers, lung and circulatory problems, and the vast number of occupational diseases, are not. Our industrial society has created them. If the blame is to be placed anywhere it is as much to be placed at the heart of what we often call industrial progress than in the hearts and minds of our industrial workers. To look closely or to accept this relationship between society and disease might mean that we would have to do something about it—elimate the causes and provide for treatment.

In this light it is not surprising that the recognition of ethnic and cultural forces in relation to physical disease has a shorter and more tortured history than that of mental disorder. There are no comprehensive reviews of ethnicity and physical illness as there are of ethnicity and mental disease (Giordano, 1973; Giordano and Giordano, 1977), no famous impactful surveys (Gurin, Veroff, and Feld 1960; Leighton et al., 1963; Srole et al., 1962), no treatises integrating cultural factors into theoretical models (Kiev, 1972; Opler, 1967; Leighton, 1959; Spiegel and Papajohn, 1975), no centers of cross-cultural research (as McGill University and University of Washington are for mental illness). The same political drama that we noted at the societal level of explanation is thus played out when we look at the micro-professional level. This should, of course, be no surprise, since recent thinkers are finally beginning to debunk the myth that scientific and medical thinking is independent of social and political events (Kuhn, 1964; Foucault, 1965; Ackerknecht, 1967).

Again the contrast between mental and physical illness is helpful. The most well-known critic of psychiatry is Thomas Szasz. And yet his series of books, *The Myth of Mental Illness* (1961) or *The Manufacture of Madness* (1970), wherein he questions and chides his fellow workers, somehow do not threaten the basic enterprise of psychiatry or psychotherapy. Not so I would contend with the critics of physical medicine. Though occasionally divided into camps, the criticisms of both groups go deep to the basic service that medicine offers. One group—Navarro's *Medicine Under Capitalism* (1976) and Waitzkin and Waterman's *The Exploitation of Illness in a Capitalist Society* (1974)—criticize the basic priorities, organization, and delivery of health care. But the most well-known and caustic critic, Ivan Illich, writes books entitled *Medical Nemesis* (1975) and *Disabling Professions* (1977), in which he indicts medicine for its role in maintaining, if not causing, the very illnesses it is supposed to treat.

So too the data of ethnic medical research reflects a potentially more critical perspective. For it emphasizes not merely differing perceptions of physiological phenomena but different physiological states which the people consider worthy of attention, not merely complementary methods of dealing with disorder but often alternative or conflicting ones (Newell 1975). Kleinman, Eisenberg, and Good, reflecting on cultural research (1978, p. 251) stated it well when they noted:

> Modern physicians diagnose and treat diseases (abnormalities in the structure and function of body organs and systems) whereas patients suffer illnesses (experience of disvalued changes in states of being and in social function).

In short, the true impact of ethnic research confronts the provider with changing not merely his language but his priorities. It calls into question the basis of medicine, the very boundaries of its territory.

This then is my rendering of the history of ethnic and cultural research into the delivery of health services. It is slow in coming because it has been and is threatening to established interests. If we somewhat arbitrarily divide the work into mental and physical aspects, there is a differential path, precisely along dimensions of threat.

PROBLEMS AND PITFALLS OF ETHNIC RESEARCH

Although this trail of progress has been convoluted, one can argue that the implications of ethnic research are being gradually accepted. And so they are, but I would further contend that the success carries with it certain problems, and it is to these dangers I wish to devote my final paragraphs.

CONCEPTUAL PROBLEMS

The first is the one-sided way we continue to use the concepts of culture and ethnicity. In light of the resistance to thinking of illness as anything but a biological entity, the need to emphasize that it is much more is understandable. But it is not merely the illness and hence its recipient which need to be regarded as multifaceted but also the service and its provider. The latter is simply no longer, if it ever truly was, a technical task, expertly and actively given to a passive and grateful taker.

Let me illustrate how logically absurd the one-sided approach is. In recent years, there has been some documentation that the attitudes and beliefs of an experimenter have an influence on the results of their animal experiments. Surely if the background and beliefs of an experimenter can effect the behavior of his rats, is it too much to expect that the backgrounds and beliefs of a practitioner will similarly affect not only how and what she/he transmits but how and what is received? Yet we never seem to tire of denying this. We see endless books and papers on the doctor-patient relationship, but they deal overwhelmingly with the patient, not the doctor, and little with the dyadic nature of the relationship. Being more specific, they deal with the patient's feelings about the doctor, but rarely if ever vice versa. Analytically speaking, they deal with transference and not countertransference. (The few that deal with both are interestingly enough in psychiatry, and the most provocative of these deal with cultural contacts [Spiegel 1959, 1976].) In the medical world this literature itself is virtually nonexistent.

ETHNICITY AND COMPLIANCE

The medical area of compliance illustrates all the dilemmas of which I am writing (Zola, 1977a). The culture that *is* examined is still only the patients' and still the negative side—how the individual's culture gets in the way of his/her obeying or complying with the doctor's orders. It is claimed that patients will not take a drug or follow a regimen for a long period of time, and yet there is research that indicates that people are quite willing to self-medicate on a regular basis. In fact, from studies I've analyzed I would estimate that between 67 and 80 percent of adult Americans self-treat and medicate themselves in any given 36-hour-long period. It is claimed that many cultural forces weigh against the integration of health practices into one's daily life. In fact, the study of popular and folk medicine claims the opposite—it is this integration that lies at the heart of many ethnic health practices. Thus, perhaps the culture that is getting in the way of integrating certain medical recommendations is not that of the recipients of care but that of the providers. For the sake of argument I would say that for every study or technique we create to understand the culture and ethnicity of the recipient of help we must match it with one of the provider and to the interaction of the two worlds. In the sociomedical world, we too easily feel that someone else, the recipient of care, is the one with a culture, not the provider.

It is probably not an accident that I learned this insight from a person who made his early reputation in ethnic research—Everett C. Hughes (1943). Yet he was also the guiding spirit behind the now classic *Boys in White* (Becker et al. 1961), which documented the overwhelming socialization of students into the medical world, the development of a changing ideology where idealism gradually died in the service of other needs, the evolution and persistence of a medical culture, reflective of their gender, class, and ethnicity, which subsequently colored all of their future service orientation. The lesson we need to remind ourselves of is an old and ancient truism: to know others we must first know ourselves.

But the ignoring of culture of the provider on the micro-level is not my only concern. Again we must return to the macro-level. For medicine itself is part and parcel of a cultural system and thereby embodies, albeit implicitly, unwittingly, and unconsciously certain social values and political and economic beliefs (Kleinman, 1973; Navarro, 1976; Waitzkin and Waterman, 1974) which, if not fully understood, may undermine human dignity, reinforce certain negative social roles, and become a major instrument of social control (Zola, 1972a). Let me dwell a final moment on each of these three dangers.

ETHNIC RESEARCH AND STEREOTYPES

In the pressure to be practical we may be seduced into stereotyping. From the very first time that my research appeared I was asked to write manuals on the handling of American ethnic groups. Although the overt intent was to help the health providers in their work, I always feared my efforts would do just the opposite. I felt I was being asked to construct a social reality that paralleled the biological one. Today we realize that even biological realities do not remain the same over time. Not only the general environment but the varying treatments we use alter that reality. Thus, society is not only continually creating new diseases but constantly altering the forms of the old ones (Dubos 1961). Thus too with social reality (Berger and Luckman, 1966). Pure ethnics, in fact, rarely exist in American culture. Being an Italian, even a southern Italian, was not the same at the turn of the century as it is now. And its subjective experience and persistence varied not only through time but also through space—whether you lived in Palermo, Sicily, or the North End of Boston or in Mobile, Alabama. It depended on who you married and lived near, what education you attained, your social mobility, and your degree of exposure to the "American way."

My original research point was (Zola 1963a,b,c, 1966, 1973a), and is, that everyone has a cultural heritage which is part and parcel of an individual's health practices. The practical answer is not to learn in detail the infinite varieties of culture but to be aware of these varieties and how they *might* affect one's health practices (Kleinman, Eisenberg, and Good 1978 offer an exceptionally useful model in this regard). Thus, I am totally opposed to training anyone in the details of a particular ethnic group, for this will ultimately squeeze people into unreal categories, and reify their culture as we have rigidified diagnoses. What I favor is making practitioners sensitive to the patient's heritage, their own heritage, and to what happens when different heritages come together.

ETHNICITY AND PROFESSIONAL CONTROL

I am wary of giving anyone the tools to make them more powerful in interaction over someone else. The language of medical compliance is not a socially irrelevant one. It uses the words *comply, obey,* and *orders.* Thus, it reinforces in the society certain hierarchical relations to which I am politically opposed, and blocks awareness to other therapeutic alternatives of which I am in favor. The women's movement has, for example, recently pointed out that the sick role and the labeling of many of their physical issues as sickness has to a very large extent been a way of keeping them in their place (Boston Women's Health Book Collective, 1976). This has given power to the battle cry that anatomy is *not* destiny. On the therapeutic level, I feel the patient should have much more say as well as a role in anything that has to do with his health and illness, his living and dying. I worry that success in dealing with, or more cynically put, manipulating the patient to do what the health provider feels is in the patient's best interest, raises important moral questions.

ETHNICITY AND MEDICALIZING

And finally I am concerned with an evergrowing "medicalizing of daily life," a medicalizing fostered by a certain kind of chemical and surgical success in which the real problems of survival in modern society are trivialized and reduced to treatable medical symptoms, with social problems too often reduced to individual pathologies, all treated symptomatically, with little regard for the larger moral and political consequences (Zola, 1977b). For example, despite the increasing recognition of the so-called stress-related diseases, all efforts to reduce this stress are not on the social level but the individual one. One is instructed on all sides how to deal with these socially induced tensions, from the soothing effects of chemical tranquilizers to the relaxing effects of meditation, from the techniques of mind control to the techniques of centering—each method in the end is an individual one. I do not question the success of these therapies. In a sense I fear them. For with each successful so-called coping method the original source problem, be it social, economic, political, becomes further removed from vision. They are not only ignored, they are perpetuated.

CONCLUSION

I can do litle better than end where I began, with the cautionary words of Shibutani and Kwan (1965, p. 19):

There is a moral responsibility of scientists for the use made of their work. The successful development of more adequate knowledge will not automatically solve social problems. Knowledge is a source of power for it facilitates control—a person who understands how something works can manipulate some of the conditions so that the course of events can be redirected to his benefit. But knowledge is ethically neutral. In itself it is neither good nor bad, and it can be used in many ways. Although it is generally used to implement the values accepted in a society, in our pluralistic world men are not always agreed on what ought to be done. Generalizations about inter-ethnic contacts might be used to facilitate exploitation as well as to further the welfare of mankind. Colonial governments may use the generalizations to devise more effective techniques of suppression, just as social reformers may use them to implement their values. Precisely because of the possibilities of exploitation the problems of the development of knowledge cannot be separated from the considerations of political power and moral standards.

Part Six

The Medicalizing
of Society

22 *The Political "Coming-Out" of I.K.Z.*

All my work is rooted deeply in the events of my life. Though I did not write specifically about medicine as an institution of social control until 1971, that was merely the year when my thoughts became public. In much of my earlier work on delinquency, ageing, gambling, "unmotivated clients," I had raised the question of how people get labelled deviant, and as early as 1963 ("Problems of Communication . . .") I had documented one particular instance of the arbitrary use of diagnostic labels by medical practitioners. By the mid 1960s I was delivering talks called varyingly "What's in a Name" and "The Trouble with Labels," but it was not till 1968, in a graduate course, that I coined the term "medicalization." It took three more years, however, (after being prompted by Egon Bittner in a seminar) for me to describe, but not analyze, examples of this "medicalization of everyday life" and its implications for social control. For my part I thought I was doing little new, merely extending the work of C. Wright Mills' work (1942) "On the Ideology of Social Pathologists" and the societal reaction school of deviance (most evident in the writings of Becker [1963, 1964] Erikson [1963, 1966] and Kitsuse [1962]). Moreover, at least three prominent sociologists—Parsons (1951a), Goffman (1961) and Freidson (1970a)— had spoken articulately of the "moral dimensions of medicine," and one critic, Dr. Thomas Szasz, had lambasted the moral pretensions of psychiatry (1961).

And yet as I read and was influenced by all these writings, I still experienced a gnawing discomfort. As an activist in the 1960s from the Civil Rights Movement to Vietnam protests, I had become increasingly wary of the institutions of modern society. Like many consistent liberals, I had faith in the basic institutions and felt that only some reform was necessary. However, as the Vietnam disaster deepened and the gains of the Civil Rights Movement paled, I began to harbor serious doubts. The Women's Movement, in particular the early newsprint predecessor (Boston Women's Health Collective 1970) of the book *Our Bodies, Ourselves*, made me realize that some of our institutions were more inherently flawed than I realized. For years I had attempted to articulate the cases of the powerless (the poor, the weak, the elderly, the patients, the handicapped); now I felt drawn to analyze the powerful. In the late 1950s I came to perceive that "physical illness," because of its perceived objectivity and measurability, was an ideal subject with which to demonstrate the effect of social and cultural factors. Now I realized that by studying an institution that was generally considered value-neutral and above political considerations, I would be saying something about the social and political roots of all institutions.

My writings on this subject, however, also mark a stylistic shift. I was disturbed that the political implications of Parsons', Goffman's, and Freidson's work on medicine had caused so little concern, even among sociological audiences. I was even more perturbed about the greater public acceptance of Szasz's work. I felt that Szasz, though essentially correct in his criticisms of psychiatry, was far off base in his analysis—psychiatry by no means had distorted the social mandate of medicine but was instead in the vanguard of its promulgation. The point had to be made stronger, the sociopolitical dangers more explicit. After a deep breath I decided to venture forth.

The opportunity came easily enough when Steve Miller asked me to collaborate with him on an article on medicine in the twentieth century. "The Erosion of Medicine from Within" (1973), though my opening shot, proved "a dud." It was probably accurate in its analysis of challenges (other occupations, paraprofessionals and the self-help movement) to the structure of medicine, but I soon realized that I had not allowed myself enough room to expound my thesis. Several other opportunities soon presented themselves. Though three are essentially book reviews, their very titles reveal that I took the opportunity to do more than criticize a particular book. The first paper, "Whither Medicine" (1970b), took on three critics of medicine—Magraw (1966), Rutstein (1967), and Lasagna (1968)—and tried to show that their analyses of the psychiatric, computer, and humanistic "revolutions" in medicine did not go far enough. The second review, "On the Problems of Professing" (1973b), articulated why Freidson's book, *Profession of Medicine* (1970a), lacked real political impact. The two other forays were more focussed. "On the Marriage of Medicine and Machine" (1972f) looked critically at a supposedly major medical innovation—the use of computers in automatic multiphasic testing; "The Fix We Are In" (1975b) examined the path down which the new medical specialty of genetics is taking us. I knew I was on the right track, for these four brief notes stirred more controversy and response than almost anything else I had written. Not only did I receive many requests for offprints (an unusual phenomenon for a book review) but even requests for reprinting.

Thus my writing about medicalization parallels that on other topics. First I speak broadly of the implications of my perspective and only later detail the case and the data on which it is based. I first made my case public in the fall of 1971, thanks to an invitation from the Medical Sociology Section of the British Sociological Society to deliver an address at their annual meeting. Realizing that this paper was in itself a condensed version of what I had to say, I shortly thereafter accepted the offer of the Netherlands Institute of Preventive Medicine to deliver a series of six public lectures on the same topic. These I delivered in the spring of 1972, a version of which was eventually published first as a limited edition in English and then as a book in Dutch (1973c). Since 1971 I have written at least ten separate papers on varying aspects of "medicalization," but the basics were laid down during that 1971-72 period.

The three papers I include here offer the most complete statements of my thesis of medicalization. The first, "Medicine As an Institution of Social Control" (chapter 23) lays out the theoretical and historical basis for the current medicalization of society. The second, "In the Name of Health and Illness" (chapter 24) details the political consequences of this phenomenon. And the third, "Individual Choice and Health Policy" (chapter 25) outlines one particularly insidious outcome of this process. The first two papers are altered from their original published form. I edited out some overlap and also made some additions (their original presentation was oral and thus I had limitations of space). And so to "Medicine As an Institution of Social Control" I have added its original historical introduction and to "In the Name of Health and Illness" I have elaborated the examples and analytic dimensions.

Reediting this work gives me the opportunity to correct one error. I do not mean to suggest that the paper possess no others—merely that this particular error is one which I want very much to acknowledge. In the first major publication in this series ("Medicine as an Institution of Social Control"), I included a line in the introduction which I have since regretted. It goes as follows: "If we search for the why of this phenomenon (i.e. medicalization) we will instead see that it is rooted in our increasingly complex technological and bureaucratic system—a system which has led us down the path of reluctant reliance on the expert." As the only place in the paper where I even allude to causal explanations, this statement has been taken by some as my explanation for the main reason for the process. Nothing could be further from the truth—the statement was glib, I apologize for it. In later expansions of my thesis I argue, as do many others (Ehrenreich and Ehrenreich 1975, Ehrenreich and English 1979, Ehrenreich 1978, Navarro 1976, Waitzkin 1978, Waitzkin and Waterman 1974), that the roots lie deep in our sociopolitical system. I am sure I have not gone far enough. On the other hand, I am very grateful that others, such as Peter Conrad (1979, 1980) and Robert Crawford (1977, 1979, 1980), are extending the analysis of medicalization further.

23

*Medicine As an Institution
of Social Control*

The theme of this essay is that medicine is be-
coming a major institution of social control, nudging aside, if not
incorporating, the more traditional institutions of religion and law.
It is becoming the new repository of truth, the place where absolute
and often final judgments are made by supposedly morally neutral
and objective experts. And these judgments are made, not in the
name of virtue or legitimacy, but in the name of health. Moreover,
this is not occurring through the political power physicians hold or
can influence, but is largely an insidious and often undramatic
phenomenon accomplished by "medicalizing" much of daily living,
by making medicine and the labels "healthy" and "ill" *relevant* to an
ever-increasing part of human existence.

Although many have noted aspects of this process, they have confined their concern to the field of psychiatry (Leifer 1969; Szasz
1961). But psychiatry has by no means distorted the mandate of
medicine, as these critics claim. Quite the contrary, its pace is perhaps faster than that of other medical specialties, it is moving in the
same direction as the entire profession. Nor is this extension into
society the result of any professional "imperialism," for this leads us

Originally appeared as "Medicine as an Institution of Social Control," *Sociological
Review* 20 (1972): 487-504.

to think of the causes in terms of misguided human efforts or motives. Instead, the causes are rooted in our increasingly complex technological and bureaucratic system—a system which has led us down the path of reluctant reliance on the expert (Toffler 1970; Slater 1970).

Frankly, what is presented in the following pages is not a definitive argument, but rather a case in progress. As such it draws heavily on observations made in the United States, though similar murmurings have long been echoed elsewhere (Wooton 1959).

A SPECULATIVE HISTORY

Concern with medical influence is not new. Over a hundred years ago Goethe feared that the modern world might turn into one giant medical institution. Philip Rieff (1961) updated this concern when he noted that "the hospital is succeeding the church and the parliament as the archetypal institution of Western culture." This shift, one that is far from complete, has spanned centuries. To understand this phenomenon we must be aware of two rather important characteristics of professions: the territorial nature of specialties and their tendency to generalize their expertise beyond technical matters. Everett Hughes stated these characteristics rather concisely (Freidson 1970a, p. 204).

> Not merely do the practitioners, by virtue of gaining admission to the charmed circle of colleagues, individually exercise the license to do things others do not, but collectively they presume to tell society that is good and right for the individual and for society at large in some aspect of life. Indeed, they set the very terms in which people may think about this aspect of life.

How a professional gains the exclusive right and license to manage its work has been documented very well by others (Freidson 1970a,b). For now I wish to dwell on the second aspect—what Bittner (1968) has stated as a profession's desire to extend its limits beyond its traditionally assumed competence. It is here that we enter our brief examination of religion, law, and medicine.

The Christian ministry as the prototype of all professions is as good a place as any to start. Ever since Christianity achieved its European dominance in the early Middle Ages, its ministry wrestled with the conflicts between its limited and diffuse functions. The former involved the specific administration of the means of grace to individuals, while the latter involved the functions of prophecy—the direct application of the message of the gospel to the structure of the community. It is in the conveyance and elaboration of this "message" that the Christian ministry wove itself deeply into communal life. Thus, well into the Reformation one could claim that all communities were in a real sense religious ones, all leaders religiously committed, and the meaning and values of all relationships derived from a religious framework.

But during the seventeenth and eighteenth centuries the influence of religious teachings on community life faded. In England, some date this to the 1640s, the Age of Cromwell, when the common law was becoming the law of the land. Though it is perhaps impossible to pinpoint a single cause, the culmination may be seen in what Hobsbaum (1962) called the dual revolution—the Industrial Revolution, itself not a single event but a series of events spanning centuries, as well as the French Revolution and its successors. As the Industrial Revolution drastically altered the relationship within and between communities, families and people, a new basis to explain as well as define (and perhaps to control) these relationships was sought. The old order faded and a new codifier was needed. The seeding had been going on for a long time. Tracts were being written about the nature of man based on a less transcendental framework. They embodied the concept of the social contract. Their terms were legalistic and their espousers, Hobbes, Rousseau, Mills, Locke, were of varying persuasions. The American and French constitutions perhaps enthroned the tools and transformation of this thinking. They spoke of human affairs without religious reference, instead using secular terms such as justice, right, duty, franchise, liberty, contract. And as once it had been in religious teaching, so now the search for the meaning and understanding of human life was sought in the law. In America it was a sentiment well expressed in the colloquialism "There ought to be a law." And this law was a more earthbound taskmaster. Where once we sought truth in delineating the wisdom of God, now we sought answers in deciphering the nature of man. And when we found such truth we reified it, at least in rhetoric, declaring "that no man was above the law."

Religion concentrated more on matters of the inner life, leaving the secular sphere to law. And law flourished with little challenge for over a century. But two world wars including "a war to end all wars" led to the questioning of such untoward confidence. And two legal events ironically chimed its death knell—a set of trials in Nuremburg and Jerusalem where men unsuccessfully invoked obedience to law and authority as their defence against charges of genocide. In addition, despite the laws the poor in the United States (at least) still seemed poorer, the minorities still exploited, the consumer cheated, until the idea of law itself began to be questioned. The symbol of justice as blindfolded was being replaced by one with its eyes slightly open and with its hand slightly extended. In America, a relatively new concept emerged, one almost "unthinkable" a couple of decades previously, the concept of a "bad law." An old tactic caught fire again—civil disobedience, and with it debates arose as to the circumstances under which it was just to violate the law. Again the interpretative system of values was beginning to crumble.

There is another way of stating this historical situation. Bittner (1968, p. 427) has said it most eloquently:

> The ultimate ground of Christian influence, its charisma, was *The Truth* . . . [This does not mean] that what was preached was true or not true but merely that it was with reference to its truth-value that the claims of Christian influence were asserted. In an equally fundamental sense, the idea of *authority* was the basis of the influence of jurisprudence . . . Obviously it cannot be said that Christianity did not claim authority; nor can it be maintained that the law neglected questions of truth. However, what in the former was the authority of truth became in the latter the truth of authority. The crisis of the ministry and of jurisprudence consists precisely in the fact that the former could not sustain its truth claims and that the latter was failing in its authority claims.

But again there was another group of codifiers waiting in the wings—new purveyors of both truth and authority. Medical science was there to fill the vacuum.

WHY MEDICAL SCIENCE

There is a reason why the growing influence of medical science is reflected more clearly in the United States than elsewhere.

Perhaps it is necessary to begin with a truism: that modern medicine has never succeeded nor been accepted in any country merely because it is better in some way than the existing method—not even if it can be shown to significantly reduce mortality or disability (Paul 1955). Thus we can more easily understand the acceptance of medical science in the United States by noting how well it suited at least three central values which have been dominant almost since the creation of that nation (Parsons 1958). The first of these can be labelled activism—a continual emphasis on mastering the environment, the struggle of man over nature instead of the effort to adjust or submit to it. In the United States there was no river that could not be dammed, no space that could not be bridged and ultimately no disease that could not be conquered. The idea of conquest is an appropriate one; the United States waged successive "wars" against polio, measles and now against heart disease, stroke, cancer. The second of these values might be called worldliness, which consists of a general preference for practical secular pursuits over more aesthetic, mystical, or theoretical ones. This phenomenon was no doubt aided by the absence of any state or institutionalized religion. As a result, medical science faced no formidable institutionalized opponent, as it did in other countries. Finally, there is the American value on instrumentalism—an emphasis on doing—on doing something, almost anything, when confronted with a problem. "Doing nothing in a difficult situation," interestingly enough, was an item diagnostic of neuroticism on a popular American psychological test. Sometimes the emphasis on movement became so great that speed itself was emphasized—often for no logical reason. Where else but in America could a selling point of a TV-set be that it turns on thirty seconds faster than its nearest competitor?

A second reason medicine's ascendency is the maturity of its technology. Again there is no single pivotal event.

After the revolution in bacteriology and the Flexner report in the United States, medicine wedded itself not only to science but became the great incorporator of knowledge. Thus, long before it claimed to be the truth, it began to garner to its bosom any form of knowledge (admittedly some more grudgingly than others) that might be relevant to its ends. From biology to physics to economics to psychology to engineering to philosophy to ethics, all found a place in the medical curriculum. And once in, no piece of knowledge seemed ever to be dropped, and so the scope of medical training continued to expand and lengthen. Although this may be the source of much consternation to curriculum committees, it did give medicine the claim of being involved in more aspects of life than any other discipline or institution; it placed medicine in a central position to be a codifier of the meaning of life in the twentieth century.

Medicine also wedded itself to an important "geist" of the times— the new wave of "humanism." For while medicine was still concerned with the more traditional issues of authority and truth, it brought to preeminence something else—the notion of service, the idea of helping others directly.

Other events were happening on the social level—the standard of living, eating, and housing were on the rise, and as a result mortality was in decline (Dubos 1961). At very least this gave medicine another kind of relevance vis-à-vis religion. It may seem reaching, but it does not strike me as inconsistent that religion and notions of the hereafter are especially relevant when "the here" is lousy and short. But when "the here" increases dramatically, when more people live to fifty, sixty or seventy and suffer from diseases they never dreamed of, such as cancer, heart disease, and stroke, then this life and its most concrete embodiment, the human body, becomes of greater interest and concern.

Now let us turn to the broad ideological fit between the promises of modern medicine and the needs of certain segments of modern society. Again a long view is necessary.

It is probably safe to say that the wave of legalism introduced by the American and French constitutions brought with it some settling as well as unsettling notions. For in addition to other ways of defining man's life, its meaning, his relationship to others, it used some rather heady concepts, such as individual liberty, freedom, and perhaps most difficult, equality. The words sounded good but "surely" they were not meant to be practiced. "Surely" some people were "more equal" than others. So theories began to appear in many fields explaining some of the "given" inequalities of man. Among the more popular—all done up in the wrappings of scientific measurements and figures—was the phrenology movement and a text which went through several editions, count de Gobineau's *The Inequality of the Races*. Almost all were relatively short-lived. One theory, however, achieved success not only as an accepted scientific work, but as a guide for social action—a theory which in relatively short time reached what Bertrand Russell called the "cult of common usage." This was the concept of evolution, the work of Charles Darwin. It had enormous appeal. For though the idea of evolution was not new, the process by which he postulated it taking place was: a competition, the survival of the fittest. Social Darwinists like Herbert Spencer extended the theory. What was applicable to flora and fauna was seen also to be relevant for man. Whatever else this implied, it seemed to be an easy step to say that what is here today is here because it is in some way better. This was applied not only to civilizations but ultimately to man vis-à-vis other men. Hence the people who at this point in time were on top were there because in some way they deserved to be. Though we often tend to think of Darwin's theory as antireligious, even an attack on established society, it is apparent that some perceived its long-range implications right away. Upon hearing the postulates at a scientific congress, one attender is reported to have said, "Sir, you are preaching scientific Calvinism with biological determinism replacing religious predestination."

Instead of a fixity of the universe, of hierarchical relations promulgated by God, we now had a universe fixed by scientific laws. As judged by the political, social, and legal implementations of such theorizing, people seemed willing to act upon these assumptions, though they might not acknowledge them directly. For example, it would be my contention that the concept of progress in science, and later in medical science, was of a particular kind. Medical science became the ultimate articulator and conveyor of the message of Darwin and Spencer. This was a social message more comforting (to many) than some of the competing views, such as those of Saint-Simon or Marx and Engels, and certainly a more comforting social approach than offered by the abortive revolutions of 1848. So, too, medical science began to define both progress and health in new terms. Health itself became not merely the means to some larger end but the end in itself, no longer one of the essential pillars of the good life, but the very definition of what is the good life. Its full articulation was seen in the 1948 World Health Organization declaration that health was "a state of complete physical, mental, and social being and not merely the absence of disease and infirmity." Its codifiers carried not the Bible or Blackstone but the Merck Manual. Robes remained but changed in color from red and black to white.

THE MYTH OF ACCOUNTABILITY

Even if we acknowledge such a growing medical involvement, it is easy to regard it as primarily a "good" one—involving the steady destigmatization of many human and social problems. Thus Barbara Wooton (1959, p. 206) was able to conclude:

> Without question . . . in the contemporary attitude toward antisocial behaviour, psychiatry and humanitarianism have marched hand in hand. Just because it is so much in keeping with the mental atmosphere of a scientifically-minded age, the medical treatment of social deviants has been a most powerful, perhaps even the most powerful, reinforcement of humanitarian impulses; for today the prestige of humane proposals is immensely enhanced if these are expressed in the idiom of medical science.

The assumption is thus readily made that such medical involvement in social problems leads to their removal from religious and legal scrutiny and thus from moral and punitive consequences. In turn the problems are placed under medical and scientific scrutiny and thus in objective and therapeutic circumstances.

The fact that we cling to such a hope is at least partly due to two cultural-historical blindspots—one regarding our notion of punishment and the other our notion of moral responsibility. Regarding the first, if there is one insight into human behaviour that the twentieth century should have firmly implanted, it is that punishment cannot be seen in merely physical terms, nor only from the perspective of the giver. Granted that capital offences are on the decrease, that whipping and torture are less common practices in criminal proceedings in Western democracies, as is the use of chains and other physical restraints for mental patients, yet our ability if not willingness to inflict human anguish on one another does not seem similarly on the wane. The most effective forms of brainwashing deny any physical contact and the concept of relativism tells much about the psychological costs of even relative deprivation of tangible and intangible wants. Thus, when an individual because of his "disease" and its treatment is forbidden to have intercourse with fellow human beings, is confined until cured, is forced to undergo certain medical procedures for his own good, perhaps deprived forever of the right to have sexual relations and/or produce children, *then* it is difficult for that patient *not* to view what is happening to him as punishment. This does not mean that medicine is the latest form of twentieth century torture, but merely that pain and suffering take many forms, and that the removal of a despicable inhumane procedure by current standards does not necessarily mean that its replacement will be all that beneficial. In part, the satisfaction in seeing the chains cast off by Pinel may have allowed us for far too long to neglect examining with what they had been replaced.

It is the second issue, that of responsibility, which requires more elaboration, for it is argued here that the medical model has had its greatest impact in the lifting of moral condemnation from the individual. Some sceptics note that while the individual is no longer condemned, his disease still *is*; they do not go far enough. Most analysts have tried to make a distinction between illness and crime on the issue of personal responsibility. The criminal is thought to be responsible and therefore accountable (or punishable) for his act, while the sick person is not. While the distinction does exist, it seems to be more quantitative than qualitative, with moral judgments but a pinprick below the surface. For instance, while it is probably true that individuals are no longer directly condemned for being sick, it does seem that much of this condemnation is merely displaced. Though his immoral character is not demonstrated in his having a disease, it becomes evident in what he does about it. Without seeming ludicrous, if one listed the traits of people who break appointments, fail to follow treatment regimen, or even delay in seeking medical aid, one finds a long list of "personal flaws." Such people seem to be ever ignorant of the consequences of certain diseases, inaccurate as to symptomatology, unable to plan ahead or find time, burdened with shame, guilt, neurotic tendencies, haunted with traumatic medical experiences—or else members of some lower status minority group: religious, ethnic, racial or socio-economic. In short, they appear to be a sorely troubled if not disreputable group of people.

The argument need not rest at this level of analysis, for it is not clear that the issues of morality and individual responsibility have been fully banished from the etiological scene itself. At the same time as the label "illness" is being used to attribute "diminished responsibility" to a whole host of phenomena, the issue of "personal responsibility" seems to be reemerging within medicine itself. Regardless of the truth and insights of the concepts of stress and the perspective of psychosomatics, whatever else they do, they bring man, *not* bacteria to the center of the stage and lead thereby to a reexamination of the individual's role in his own demise, disability and even recovery.

The case, however, need not be confined to professional concepts and their degree of acceptance, for we can look at the beliefs of the man in the street. As most surveys have reported, when an individual is asked what caused his diabetes, heart disease, upper respiratory infection, etc., we may be comforted by the scientific terminology if not the accuracy of his answers. Yet if we follow this questioning with the probe: "Why did you get X now?" or "Of all the people in your community, family etc. who were exposed to X, why did you get it?" then the rational scientific veneer is pierced and the concern with personal and moral responsibility emerges quite strikingly. Indeed the issue "Why me?" becomes of great concern and is generally expressed in quite moral terms of what they did wrong. It is possible to argue that here we are seeing a residue and that it will surely be different in the new generation. A recent experiment I conducted should cast some doubt on this. I asked a class of forty undergraduates, mostly aged seventeen, eighteen and nineteen, to recall the last time they were sick, disabled, or hurt and then to record how they did or would have communicated this experience to a child under the age of five. The purpose of the assignment had nothing to do with the issue of responsibility and it is worth noting that there was no difference in the nature of the response between those who had or had not actually encountered children during their "illness." The responses speak for themselves.

The opening words of the sick, injured person to the query of the child were:

"I feel bad"
"I feel bad all over"
"I have a bad leg"
"I have a bad eye"
"I have a bad stomach ache"
"I have a bad pain"
"I have a bad cold"
The reply of the child was inevitable:
"What did you do wrong?"
The "ill person" in no case corrected the child's perspective but
rather joined it at that level.
On bacteria
"There are good germs and bad germs and sometimes the bad
germs . . ."
On catching a cold
"Well you know sometimes when your mother says, 'Wrap up or
be careful or you'll catch a cold,' well I . . . "
On an eye sore
"When you use certain kinds of things (mascara) near your eye
you must be very careful and I was not . . . "
On a leg injury
"You've always got to watch where you're going and I . . . "
Finally to the treatment phase:
On how drugs work
"You take this medicine and it attacks the bad parts . . . "
On how wounds are healed
"Within our body there are good forces and bad ones and when
there is an injury, all the good ones . . . "
On pus
"That's the way the body gets rid of all its bad things . . . "
On general recovery
"If you are good and do all the things the doctor and your mother
tell you, you will get better."

In short, on nearly every level, from getting sick to recovering, a
moral battle raged. This seems more than the mere anthropomorphiz-
ing of a phenomenon to communicate it more simply to children.
Frankly it seems hard to believe that the English language is so poor
that a *moral* rhetoric is needed to describe a supposedly amoral phenomenon—illness.

In short, despite hopes to the contrary, the rhetoric of illness by
itself seems to provide no absolution from individual responsibility,
accountability and moral judgment.

THE MEDICALIZING OF SOCIETY

The involvement of medicine in the manage-
ment of society is not new. It did not appear full-blown one day in the
mid-twentieth century. As Sigerist (1943) has aptly claimed, medicine

was never only a social science but an occupation whose very practice was inextricably interwoven into society. This interdependence is perhaps best seen in two branches of medicine which have had a built-in social emphasis from the very start: psychiatry (Foucault 1965; Szasz 1961) and public health–preventive medicine (Rosen 1958, 1963). Public health was always committed to changing social aspects of life, from sanitation and housing to working conditions, and often used the arm of the state (through laws and legal power) to gain its ends (quarantines, vaccinations). Psychiatry's involvement in society is a bit more difficult to trace, but one notes the almost universal reference to one of its early pioneers, a physician named Johan Weyer. Weyer's and thus psychiatry's involvement in social problems stemmed from his objection to burning witches; he maintained that they were not possessed by the devil, but rather bedeviled by their problems. Namely, they were insane. From its early concern with the issue of insanity as a defense in criminal proceedings, psychiatry has come to dominate the rehabilitation of society's "legal" deviants. Psychiatry, like public health, has also used the legal powers of the state in the accomplishment of its goals (the cure of the patient) through the legal proceedings of involuntary commitment and its concommitant removal of certain rights and privileges.

This is not to say, however, that the rest of medicine has been "socially" uninvolved. For a rereading of history makes it seem a matter of degree. Medicine has long had both a *de jure* and a *de facto* relation to institutions of social control. The *de jure* relationship is seen in the idea of reportable diseases wherein if certain phenomena occur in his practice the physician is required to report them to the appropriate authorities. Although this seems straightforward and appropriate where highly contagious diseases are concerned, it is less so when the possible spread of infection is not the primary issue, e.g. gunshot wounds, attempted suicide, drug use, and what is now called child abuse. The *de facto* relation to social control can be argued through a brief look at the disruptions of the last two or three American Medical Association conventions. For there the American Medical Association—and really all ancillary health professions—were accused of practicing social control (the term used by the accusers was genocide) through (1) *whom* they have traditionally treated with *what*—giving *better* treatment to more favored clientele, and (2) *what* they have treated—a more subtle form of discrimination, in that limited resources requires focussing on some diseases while others are neglected. Here the accusation was that medicine has focussed on the diseases of the rich and the established—cancer, heart disease, stroke, and ignored the diseases of the poor, such as malnutrition and high infant mortality.

Although other historical examples could be cited, the full exercise and expansion of medicine's influence has awaited the mid-twentieth century. Only now is the process of "medicalization" upon us—a phenomenon which Freidson (1970a, p. 251) has operationalized most succinctly: "The medical profession has first claim to jurisdiction over the label of illness and *anything* to which it may be attached, irrespective of its capacity to deal with it effectively."

For illustrative purposes this "attaching" process may be categorized in four concrete ways:

1. Through the expansion into any area deemed relevant to the good practice of medicine.
2. Through the retention of absolute control over certain technical procedures.
3. Through the retention of near absolute access to certain "taboo" areas.
4. Through the expansion of what in medicine is deemed relevant to the good practice of life.

1. THROUGH THE EXPANSION INTO ANY AREA DEEMED RELEVANT TO THE GOOD PRACTICE OF MEDICINE

The change of medicine's commitment from a specific etiological model of disease to a multicausal one and the greater acceptance of the concepts of comprehensive medicine, psychosomatics, etc., have enormously expanded that which is or can be relevant to the understanding, treatment and even prevention of disease. Thus it is no longer necessary for the patient merely to divulge the symptoms of his body, but also the symptoms of daily living, his habits and his worries. Part of this is greatly facilitated by the computer, for what might be too embarrassing, or take too long, or be inefficient in a face-to-face encounter can now be asked and analyzed impersonally by the machine, and moreover be done before the patient ever sees the physician. With the advent of the computer a certain guarantee of privacy is necessarily lost, for while many physicians might have probed similar issues, the data was stored in the mind of the doctor and only rarely in the medical record. The computer, on the other hand, has a retrievable, transmittable and almost inexhaustible memory.

It is not merely, however, the nature of the data needed to make more accurate diagnoses and treatments, but the perspective which accompanies it—a perspective which pushes the physician far beyond his office and the exercise of technical skills. To rehabilitate or at least alleviate many of the ravages of chronic disease, it has become increasingly necessary to intervene to change permanently the habits of a patient's lifetime—be it of working, sleeping, playing or eating. In prevention the "extension into life" becomes even deeper, since the very idea of primary prevention means getting there *before* the disease process starts. The physician must not only seek out his clientele but once found must often convince them that they must do something *now* and perhaps at a time when the potential patient feels well or not especially troubled. If this in itself does not get the prevention-oriented physician involved in the workings of society, then the nature of "effective" mechanisms for intervention surely does, as illustrated by the statement of a physician trying to deal with health problems in the ghetto (Norman 1969, p. 1271): "Any effort to improve the health of ghetto residents cannot be separated from equal and simultaneous efforts to remove the multiple social, political and economic restraints currently imposed on inner city residents."

Certain forms of social intervention and control emerge even when medicine comes to grips with some of its more traditional problems, such as heart disease and cancer. An increasing number of physicians feel that a change in diet may be the most effective deterrent to a number of cardio-vascular complications. They are, however, so perplexed as to how to get the general population to follow their recommendations that a leading article in a national magazine (*Time Magazine* January 10, 1969) was entitled "To Save The Heart: Diet by Decree?" It is obvious that there is an increasing pressure for more explicit sanctions against the tobacco companies and against heavy smokers. What would be the consequences if even stronger evidence links age at parity, frequency of sexual intercourse, or the lack of male circumcision to the incidence of cervical cancer?

2. THROUGH THE RETENTION OF ABSOLUTE CONTROL OVER CERTAIN TECHNICAL PROCEDURES

In particular this refers to skills which in certain jurisdictions are the very operational and legal definition of the practice of medicine—the right to do surgery and prescribe drugs.

Both of these take medicine far beyond concern with ordinary organic disease.

In surgery this is seen in several different subspecialties. The plastic surgeon has at least participated in, if not helped perpetuate, certain aesthetic standards. What once was a practice confined to restoration has now expanded beyond the correction of certain traumatic or even congenital deformities to the creation of new physical properties, from size of nose to size of breast, as well as dealing with certain phenomena—wrinkles, sagging, etc.—formerly associated with the "natural" process of ageing. Alterations in sexual and reproductive functioning have long been a medical concern. Yet today the frequency of hysterectomies seems less correlated with the presence of organic disease than one might think. (What avenues the very possibility of sex change will open is anyone's guess.) Transplantations, despite their still relative infrequency, have had a tremendous effect on our very notions of death and dying. And at the other end of life's continuum, since abortion is still essentially a surgical procedure, it is to the physician-surgeon that society is turning (and the physician-surgeon accepting) for criteria and guidelines.

In the exclusive right to prescribe and thus pronounce on and regulate drugs, the power of the physician is even more awesome. Forgetting for the moment our obsession with youth's illegal use of drugs, any observer can see, judging by sales alone, that the greatest increase in drug use over the last ten years has not been in the realm of treating organic disease, but in treating a large number of psychosocial states. Thus we have drugs for nearly every mood: to help us sleep or keep us awake; to enhance our appetite or decrease it; to tone down our energy level or to increase it; to relieve our depression or stimulate our interest. Recently the newspapers and more popular magazines, including some medical and scientific ones, have carried articles about drugs which may be effective peace pills or anti-aggression tablets, enhance our memory, our perception, our intelligence, and our vision (spiritually or otherwise). This led to the easy prediction:

> We will see new drugs, more targeted, more specific and more potent than anything we have . . . And many of these would be for people we would call healthy.

This statement incidentally was made not by a visionary science fiction writer but by a former commissioner of the United States Food and Drug Administration (Goddard 1966, p. 33).

3. THROUGH THE RETENTION OF NEAR ABSOLUTE ACCESS TO CERTAIN "TABOO" AREAS

These "taboo" areas refer to medicine's almost exclusive licence to examine and treat the most personal of individual possessions—the inner workings of our bodies and minds. My contention is that if anything can be shown to affect the workings of the body and to a lesser extent the mind, then it can be labelled an "illness" itself or jurisdictionally "a medical problem." In a sheer statistical sense the import of this is especially great if we look at only four such problems—ageing, drug addiction, alcoholism, and pregnancy. The first and last were once regarded as normal natural processes and the middle two as human foibles and weaknesses. Now this has changed and to some extent medical specialties have emerged to meet these new needs. This expands medicine's involvement not only through more years of human life, but it opens the possibility of medicine's services to millions if not billions of people. In the United States, at least, the implication of declaring alcoholism a disease (the possible import of a pending Supreme Court decision as well as laws currently being introduced into several state legislature) would reduce arrests in many jurisdictions by ten to fifty percent and transfer such offenders when "discovered" directly to a medical facility. It is pregnancy, however, which produces the most illuminating illustration. It was barely seventy years ago in the United States that virtually all births and the concomitants of birth occurred outside the hospital as well as outside medical supervision. I do not frankly have a documentary history, but as this medical claim was solidified, so too was medicine's claim to a whole host of related processes: not only to birth but to prenatal, postnatal, and pediatric care; not only to conception but to infertility; not only to the process of reproduction but to the process and problems of sexual activity itself; not only when life begins (in the issue of abortion) but whether it should be allowed to begin at all (e.g. in genetic counselling). The labelling of pregnancy as a disease has had still further implications in the political and social role of women and their right to control their own bodies. What has happened in this arena becomes even of greater concern when we talk about ageing.

While some of us take drugs, and a few more of us drink, and half of us have the possibility of having babies, all of us age. The tone is set by Ilya Metchnikoff (1969, pp. 283-284), a pioneer in anti-ageing research:

> It is doubtless an error to consider ageing a physiological phenome-
> non. It can be considered normal because everyone ages, but only to
> the extent that one might consider normal the pains of childbirth
> that an anaesthetic might relieve; on the contrary, ageing is a *chronic
> sickness* for which it is much more difficult to find a remedy.

Already this disease model has surfaced in the specter of heroic
measures to save a life at all costs. Will it soon redefine and unwittingly make even worse what it is to be old in a society of youth?

Medicine has already responded, not only in the creation of new
specialties called geriatrics and gerontology, but more "extensively"
in the new interest in death and dying. No one dies anymore of old
age or natural causes. Now one dies of some disease or disorder.
Medicine has helped prolong not only the process of living but also
the process of dying. The sum total is that people no longer die at
home but in hospitals, no longer among their familiars, but among
strangers, no longer quickly but over a long period of time. Perhaps
because of the decreasing viability of religion they no longer turn
primarily to the priest and minister for solace, comfort, and even
reflections on the meaning of life—but to the doctor.

Partly through this foothold in the "taboo" areas and partly
through the simple reduction of other resources, the physician is increasingly becoming the choice for help for many with personal and
social problems. Thus a recent British study reported that within a
five-year period there had been a notable increase (from twenty-five
to forty-one percent) in the proportion of the population willing to
consult the physician with a personal problem (Dunnell and Cartwright 1972).

4. THROUGH THE EXPANSION OF WHAT IN MEDICINE IS DEEMED RELEVANT TO THE GOOD PRACTICE OF LIFE

Though in some ways this is the most powerful
of all "medicalization" processes, the point can be made simply.
Here we refer to the use of medical rhetoric and evidence in the arguments to advance any cause. For what Wooton attributed to
psychiatry is no less true of medicine. To paraphrase her, today the
prestige of *any* proposal is immensely enhanced, if not justified,
when it is expressed in the idiom of medical science. To say that
many who use such labels are not professionals only begs the issue,
for the public is only taking its cues from professionals who increasingly have been extending their expertise into the social sphere or
have called for such an extension (Alinsky 1967; Wedge 1961). In

politics one hears of the healthy or unhealthy economy or state. More particularly, the physical and mental health of American presidential candidates has been an issue in the last four elections and a recent book claims to link faulty political decisions with faulty health (Etang 1970). For years we knew that the environment was unattractive, polluted, noisy and in certain ways dying, but now we learn that its death may be related to our own demise. To end with a rather mundane if depressing example, there has always been a constant battle between school authorities and their charges on the basis of dress and such habits as smoking, but recently the issue was happily resolved for a local school administration when they declared that such restrictions were necessary for reasons of health.

To some extent this expansion into the direct handling of life's problems is conscious. Two examples, one on an international level and one on a national, aptly illustrate this process. In the January 1972 issue of the *American Journal of Public Health* (p. 73), Dr. Lee M. Howard, Director of the Office of Health, Technical Assistance Bureau of the Agency for International Development wrote about the relevance of health and medicine to international development. I can do no better than quote him directly:

> The former official seal of the American Public Health Association depicts the figure of a woman kneeling, hands outstretched, beneath a tree. Upon the seal, these words are inscribed, "And the leaves of the tree were for the healing of nations." Whatever the intended symbolism, the seal suggests a relevance between public health and the healing of nations. Does the symbolism imply a fragile hope or a real possibility? A dream or a dilemma?
>
> If we define the health of nations in the broad WHO terms of physical and social well-being, and if we take a simultaneous look at the state of the world's well-being as reported in the daily newspapers, one might ask the extent to which the focus and impact of traditional international health activities actually serve to improve the well-being of nations, much less heal them.
>
> In the 98 years since the APHA was founded, has the Middle East become a healthier place to live? Have the prospects for social well-being in Southeast Asia improved or decreased? In America, have traditional health efforts been relevant to the growing social unrest in many segments of our nation?
>
> If the leaves of the public health tree are indeed to be used for the healing of nations, what is that we are trying to heal? What is that the nations of the earth are seeking?

Several pages later (Howard 1972, p. 76) he elaborates the relationship between health and modernization:

> The concept of health is subject to as much confusion as the

concept of disease. Health is not a term synonymous with death control. It is the state of man's adjustment to his environment—a measure of man's fulfillment, not of his survival. As a development activity, health is that sector of the modernization process which assists man himself to make a maximum physical and psychological adjustment to his internal and external environment consistent with available resources. This view coincides with the World Health Organization definition of health as a state of "physical, mental and social well-being and not merely the absence of disease or infirmity." This positive view of well-being, in a very real sense, is the ultimate objective of modernization. It refers to the quality of man himself. The well-being of mankind is what development is all about.

The healing of nations, considering the aspirations and dreams of the developing world, requires a multidisciplinary approach far beyond the current limitations we place upon our own traditional health role. The healing of nations cannot be less than a social process which corrects a whole range of adverse social factors which perpetuate or accentuate maladjustment to man's environment—his poverty, food shortages, poor education, rapid population growth, insecurity, and, not least, his attitudes towards his neighbors and the world in which he lives.

It does not follow that modification in population quantity alone will automatically lead to improved population quality. The production of a ton of grain by itself is no guarantee of the improved well-being of the man that produced the grain.

The health of man or of nations is a concept which requires recognition that well-being depends upon attention to all the key social, political and economic variables that affect the lives of men.

The second example, although national in origin, is no less expansive in mandate. In his 1971 Presidential address to the British School Health Service Group, Dr. P. Henderson (1971) issued a clarion call to his fellow school health workers to get involved in the following "health problems":

Poverty and slum or new slum housing;
Behavior and emotional difficulties;
Maladjustment;
Juvenile delinquency;
Drug taking;
Suicide;
Children in care;
Venereal diseases;
Teenage illegitimate pregnancies;
Abortion.

In addition to these which he singles out for special attention, he adds the more traditional problems of children with visual, hearing, physical handicaps, those with speech and language difficulties, the epileptics, the diabetics, the asthmatics, the dyslexics, the emotionally, the educationally and intellectually retarded. One wonders who or what is left out?

CONCLUSION

The list of daily activities to which health can be related is ever growing and with the current operating perspective of medicine it seems infinitely expandable. The reasons are manifold. It is not merely that medicine has extended its jurisdiction to cover new problems, or that doctors are professionally committed to finding disease, nor even that society keeps creating disease. For if none of these obtained today we would still find medicine exerting an enormous influence on society. The most powerful empirical stimulus for this is the realization of how much everyone has or believes he has something organically wrong with him, or put more positively, how much can be done to make one feel, look or function better.

The rates of "clinical entities" found on surveys or by periodic health examinations range from fifty to eighty percent of the population studied. We used to rationalize that this high level of prevalence did not, however, translate itself into action since not only are rates of medical utilization not astonishingly high but they also have not gone up appreciably. Some recent studies, however, indicate that we may have been looking in the wrong place for this medical action. It has been noted in the United States and the United Kingdom that within a given twenty-four to thirty-six hour period, from fifty to eighty percent of the adult population have taken one or more "medical" drugs (Dunnel and Cartwright 1972).

The belief in the omnipresence of disorder is further enhanced by a reading of the scientific, pharmacological and medical literature, for there one finds a growing litany of indictments of "unhealthy" life activities. From sex to food, from aspirins to clothes, from driving your car to riding the surf, it seems that under certain conditions, or in combination with certain other substances or activities or if done too much or too little, virtually anything can lead to medical problems.

These facts take on particular importance not only when health becomes a paramount value in society, but when the control of diagnosis and treatment has been restricted to a certain group. For this means that that group, perhaps unwittingly, is in a position to exercise great control and influence about what we should and should not do to attain that "paramount value."

It is in this potentiality for action wherein lies the greatest danger.

For the labels health and illness are remarkable "depoliticizers" of an issue. By locating the source and the treatment of problems in an individual, other levels of intervention are effectively closed. By the very acceptance of a specific behaviour as an "illness" and the definition of illness as an undesirable state, the issue becomes not whether to deal with a particular problem, but *how* and *when*. Thus the debate over homosexuality, drugs or abortion becomes focused on the degree of sickness attached to the phenomenon in question or the extent of the health risk involved. And the more principled, more perplexing, and even moral issue, of *what* freedom an individual should have over his or her own body is shunted aside.

As stated in the very beginning, this "medicalizing of society" is as much a result of medicine's potential as it is of society's wish for medicine to use that potential. Why then has the focus been more on the medical potential than on the social desire? In part it is a function of space, but also of political expediency. For the time rapidly may be approaching when recourse to the populace's wishes may be impossible. Let me illustrate this with the statements of two medical scientists who, if they read this essay, would probably dismiss all my fears as groundless. The first was commenting on the ethical, moral, and legal procedures of the sex change operation (Russell 1968, p. 536):

> Physicians generally consider it unethical to destroy or alter tissue except in the presence of disease or deformity. The interference with a person's natural procreative function entails definite moral tenets, by which not only physicians but also the general public are influenced. The administration of physical harm as treatment for mental or behavioral problems—as corporal punishment, lobotomy of unmanageable psychotics and sterilization of criminals—is abhorrent in our society.

Here he states, as almost an absolute condition of human nature, something which is at best a recent phenomenon. He seems to forget that there were laws promulgating just such procedures through much of the twentieth century, that within the past few years at least one Californian jurist ordered the sterilization of an unwed mother as a condition of probation, and that such procedures were done by Nazi scientists and physicians as part of a series of medical experiments. More recently, there is the misguided patriotism of the cancer researchers under contract to the United States Department of Defence who allowed their dying patients to be exposed to massive doses of radiation to analyze the psychological and physical results of simulated nuclear fall-out. True, the experiments were stopped, but not until they had been going on for *eleven* years.

The second statement is by Francis Crick (1971) at a conference on the implications of certain genetic findings: "Some of the wild genetic proposals will never be adopted because the people will simply not stand for them." Note his emphasis: on the people not the scientist. In order, however, for the people to be concerned, to act and to protest, they must first be aware of what is going on. Yet in the very privatized nature of medical practice, plus the continued emphasis that certain expert judgments must be free from public scrutiny, there are certain processes which will prevent the public from ever knowing what has taken place and thus from doing something about it. Let me cite two examples. Recently, in a European country, I overheard the following conversation in a kidney dialysis unit. The chief was being questioned about whether or not there were self-help groups among his patients. "No," he almost shouted, "that is the last thing we want. Already the patients are sharing too much knowledge while they sit in the waiting room, thus making our task increasingly difficult. We are working now on a procedure to prevent them from ever meeting with one another."

The second example removes certain information even further from public view. The issue of fluoridation in the U.S. has been for many years a hot political one. It was in the political arena because, in order to fluoridate local water supplies, the decision in many jurisdictions had to be put to a popular referendum. And when it was, it was often defeated. A solution was found and a series of state laws were passed to make fluoridation a public health decision and to be treated, as all other public health decisions, by the medical officers best qualified to decide questions of such a technical, scientific and medical nature.

A few years ago, based on current knowledge, a physician constructed a composite picture of an individual with a low risk of developing atherosclerosis or coronary-artery disease (Meyers 1968, pp. 215–216). He would be:

> an effeminate municipal worker or embalmer completely lacking in physical or mental alertness and without drive, ambition, or competitive spirit; who has never attempted to meet a deadline of any kind; a man with poor appetite, subsisting on fruits and vegetables laced with corn and whale oil, detesting tobacco, spurning ownership of radio, television, or motorcar, with full head of hair but scrawny and unathletic appearance, yet constantly straining his puny muscles by exercise. Low in income, blood pressure, blood sugar, uric acid and cholesterol, he has been taking nicotinic acid, pyridoxine, and long term anti-coagulant therapy ever since his prophylactic castration.

Thus I fear with Freidson (1970a, p. 354):

A profession and a society which are so concerned with physical and functional wellbeing as to sacrifice civil liberty and moral integrity must inevitably press for a "scientific" environment similar to that provided laying hens on progressive chicken farms—hens who produce eggs industriously and have no disease or other cares.

Nor does it really matter that if, instead of the above depressing picture, we were guaranteed six more inches in height, thirty more years of life, or drugs to expand our potentialities and potencies; we should still be able to ask: what do six more inches matter, in what kind of environment will the thirty additional years be spent, or who will decide what potentialities and potencies will be expanded and what curbed?

I must confess that given the road down which expertise has taken us, I am willing to live with some of the frustrations and even mistakes that will follow when the authority for decisions becomes shared with those whose lives and activities are involved. For I am convinced that patients have as much to teach their doctors as do students their professors and children their parents.

24

In the Name of Health and Illness

INTRODUCTION

Several years ago, a popular American satirist, himself a physical scientist, wrote a song dedicated to our rocket experts (Lehrer 1965):

> Once they are up who cares where they come
> down:
> "That's not my department," says Werner
> von Braun.

It is a statement with implications far beyond rocketry. For all too long anything "not my department" provided a shield for scientists in general and medical scientists in particular—a defense against the uses to which their techniques and discoveries *might* be used. Moreover, the statement that we *must* do something because we *can* do it is, as Dubos (1968a) claimed . . . tantamount to an intellectual abdication. As a result he calls for science to exercise value judgments, to set priorities. While I agree that new priorities have to be set, my concern is not that medical science should finally exercise values, but that for a long time it has been making value judgments in the

Originally appeared as "In the Name of Health and Illness: On Some Socio-Political Consequences of Medical Influence," *Social Science and Medicine* 9 (1975): 83–87.

name of health and illness. And unless we become aware of this and explicate the nature of these judgments no corrective is really possible.

Freidson (1970a, p. 346) sets the terms for our initial discussion:

> Medicine is not merely neutral. . . . As applied work it is either deliberately amoral—which is to say, guided by someone else's morality—or it is actively moral by its selective intervention.

There are thus two categories of examples I will present—first, medicine used and perhaps abused; second, medicine that seeks to be moral, that takes sides based either on implicit assumptions of the profession or on values in the background of its practitioners.

THE NEUTRALITY OF MEANS IN THE SERVICE OF A MORAL END

The business of medicine is the diagnosis and treatment of illness—in itself a noble and hopefully neutral task. And yet can medicine achieve either nobility and neutrality under the circumstances in which it is practiced? This conflict is sharpest in that most troublesome of situations—the pursuit of national goals in a time of war. That medical personnel should do their best to save lives and treat the wounded—the civil population on both sides—is fairly clear, but after this the road gets murky.

Clarity begins to fade with the recruitment of combatants. There has long been a debate, for example, over whether alcoholism is a disease. In a move welcomed by many, the United States Army took a forward step on March 8, 1971 (*International Herald Tribune*). On that day the Pentagon announced that alcoholism was now a treatable disease. Dr. Richard S. Wilbur, Assistant Secretary of Defense for Health and Environment, announced the new rehabilitation program and stated that "Until now we took a punitive approach toward treatment including denial of promotion, loss of security classification and expulsion from the service." Later on the release noted that "Under the Pentagon's new policy an alcoholic is not to be considered physically unfit for military service on the basis of his alcoholism provided the individual undergoes treatment and makes progress." But at this time, during the most unpopular war the United States had yet waged, when psychiatric impairment, including alcoholism, was one of the most common methods of disqualification and discharge, can such a decision have been devoid of political connotations? One can only wonder what other conditions might under certain circumstances be recognized as "treatable" diseases and thus *not* qualify for military discharge.

The moral dilemmas thicken during actual combat. The study of medicine in wartime often reveals that physicians were in the position of choosing between the goals of rehabilitation and the "war effort." All too often practitioners noted that they might be sacrificing the long-term health of their patients to the short-term goal of the army commander. During the Vietnam era there was a *cause célèbre* of a physician who felt he was being asked to step over the line—the case of Dr. Howard Levy who was courtmartialed and imprisoned because he refused to train Green Berets in first aid and other medical treatments. He claimed that such training had primarily a political aim—to gain the help of the local population in tracking down Viet Cong.

Finally there are medicine's direct contributions to "winning" wars, including social-psychiatric help in undermining a population's will to fight, the interrogation of prisoners, or biomedical efforts in bacteriological warfare. In the fall of 1971, a particularly uncomfortable instance of the mixing of national goals and medical research came to light. A group of cancer researchers, under contract to the United States Department of Defense, allowed their dying patients to be exposed to massive doses of radiation in order to analyze the psychological and physical results of simulated nuclear fall-out. This was no short-term delusion. By the time the experiments were halted they had been pursued for *eleven* years.

It is perhaps appropriate to end this discussion on the "neutrality of means" with two seeming innocuous and technical medical procedures—Automatic Multiphasic Testing and periodic health examinations. The first, Automatic Multiphasic Testing, has been a method hailed as an aid to the doctor if not a replacement for him. While it has been mainly publicized as a more efficient way of bringing conditions to the forefront for better treatment, a major use has been for quite a different purpose. At least three large institutions have used Multiphasic Testing as a method of "deselection"—the armed services to weed out the physically and mentally unfit, insurance companies to reject "uninsurables" and large industrial firms to isolate "high risks." At a conference I once asked representatives of these same institutions what responsibility they assumed toward those they rejected. They calmly and universally stated none—neither to provide them aid nor put them in touch with any source of aid. The second procedure, periodic health examinations, has also been hailed for its preventive benefits. Yet here too the data derived from such check-ups has served other purposes. One such use is its control of business executives—"If you do not lose weight, take care of your ulcer, etc." Another is in its increasing relevance in retirement policies. I have seen contracts of older professors that eliminated "age," which is thought to be a discriminatory criterion, and substituted "health," which is apparently thought to be fair and objective. But what disease or condition is detrimental to being a professor and who decides?

Thus there is no guarantee that merely doing the job of "healing" frees one from examining the context within which it is carried out. Indeed, the very context of that job may alter the morality of a seemingly neutral act.

THE "MORAL" INTERVENTIONS OF MEDICINE

There is an aura of objectivity and respectability which surrounds not only medicine but its pronouncements. Since the opinions of medicine weigh heavily on public issues, it is important to describe some of the situations in which it actively takes sides.

The issue of drug safety should seem straightforward, but both words in that phrase display some interesting flexibility—namely, what is a drug and what is safe? During Prohibition, alcohol was regarded as a drug and often prescribed as a medicine. Yet in recent years, when the issue of dangerous substances and drugs has come up for discussion in medical circles, alcohol has been officially excluded from the debate. Another more uncomfortable matter of definition was heard before the United Nations Commission on Biological and Chemical weapons in 1969. The commission solicited medical testimony in the attempt to classify bacteriological toxins as chemicals, thus exempting them from a possible ban on biological weapons (*Health Pac Bulletin* 1971). As for safety, many have applauded the AMA's judicious position in declaring the need for much more extensive, longitudinal research on marihuana and its unwillingness to back legalization until more data is in. This applause might be muted if the public read the 1970 Food and Drug Administration "Blue Ribbon" Committee Report on the safety, quality, and efficacy of *all* medical drugs commercially and legally on the market since 1938 (Drug Efficacy Study 1969). Though appalled at the lack and quality of evidence of any sort, few recommendations were made for the withdrawal of drugs from the market. Moreover, there are no cases of anyone dying from an overdose or of extensive adverse side effects from marihuana use, but the literature on adverse effects of a whole host of "medical drugs" on the market today is legion.

Although there are other sociopolitical causes which medicine has consciously supported, it is the controversial issues surrounding the "production" of life which have given full vent to the physician's personal views, all too often in the guise of objective, scientific data.

There has, of course, long been experimentation with varying forms of birth control. Today, however, it is only medicine which has the exclusive right to dispense these methods, particularly for women. Nor is the medical procedure equally available to all. The better educated, higher socioeconomic classes have no difficulty acquiring whatever data they need; not so the less privileged. To be sure, in many cases the clientele do not directly ask for birth control information. On the other hand, the physician advises on a large range of preventive measures which he thinks important *without* the patient asking; why not this one? I am not necessarily recommending that he advise the patient to use contraception, but he can at least inform them of availability. Moreover, while dispensing birth control information the physician often functions in a moral capacity. Personal experience as well as the literature of female liberation are replete with cases of young single women being lectured, chastized, ridiculed, embarrassed and even refused help or a referral when they approached a physician for "the pill," an IUD, or a diaphragm.

With a monopoly on knowledge about birthing, it is not surprising that medicine has extended its educational activities into related activities, such as sex and sex counseling. Although still a sensitive topic in many parts of the world, one place where it seems possible to talk about sex is the doctor's consulting room. Yet I cannot think of a subject on which the physician is more willing yet less equipped to expound. Why do I think medicine is ill prepared on this subject? First of all, the physician learns about the body as a machine, with an overwhelming emphasis on pathology. His training hardly prepares him to deal with the complexities of love, diverse sexual strivings, and the ever-changing relations between man and woman—and not at all with homosexual relations. The physician's inadequacies are evident in what medical students are taught (Hordern 1971, p. 44):

> It is hardly surprising that the longstanding disinclination of the medical profession to involve itself in problems of sexuality and contraception was carried over into the teaching curricula of British medical schools, even though the recent unprecedented accumulation of knowledge in these areas could and should have been imparted to

medical students. Thus the results of a survey of 1,167 undergraduates with more than 20 months of clinical experience showed that whilst all but 3 per cent had had teaching in infertility, only between one-fifth and three-fifths had had teaching on normal psychosexual development, marital adjustment, and sexual difficulties, and less than three-fifths felt that their knowledge was adequate in any of these fields. One student commented, "The only teaching we have here on sex, marital adjustment, etc., is one lecture on the mating habits of cats," whilst another remarked, "It is ridiculous that the study of venereal disease is compulsory when the study of sexual relations is ignored."

This probably compares favorably with what is available in the United States, where sexual relations are still largely regarded as not worth teaching since they only involve "doing what comes naturally." Yet if there is one lesson that Freud and Kinsey taught us, it is that what is natural has considerable variation in time, space, and frequency. Kinsey documented that what some people think is unnatural occurs with uncommon frequency. Moreover, as Masters and Johnson have so painstakingly and dully documented, sexual relations are less natural for many of us than many of the rest of us would like to believe. Female liberation has also shown that what is claimed to be natural for men is not necessarily so for women, and that a male medical bias has for years totally distorted if not oppressed aspects of female sexuality. Despite such ignorance, the medical and allied professions do not seem loath to give advice—though what they base their information on might make one shudder. For we probably have childhood experience conditioned by social class and religious factors reified into clinical knowledge.

The physician's values come even more clearly into play with the subject of abortion. Hern (1971, p. 7) himself a physician-gynecologist, offers a perceptive analysis of the "clinical perspective" as a male-dominated view of where women should be:

> The use of the term, "normal pregnancy" in obstetrical practice, then, is the extension of the broader cultural influence into the professional setting. The term is useful, in a specialized sense, to distinguish pregnancies which are routine. Unfortunately, its continued use by physicians is carried back to the non-professional context and reinforces the folk idea that pregnancy is more "normal" than the non-pregnant state. Its use within the medical profession results in certain awkward dilemmas, particularly when the pregnancy is unwanted.
> This reaches to the core of our current difficulties and controversy about abortion, since pregnancy has traditionally been defined in Western culture as "normal," and the desire to terminate the pregnancy therefore, as "pathological." It follows that every woman who

wants an abortion must need to have her head examined, and that is exactly what has happened. Liberalized abortion laws in several states have resulted in a situation in which psychiatric consultation is mandatory for women seeking a legal hospital abortion; and hospital boards and the medical community still maintain this ritual in some places where there are no legal reasons for its maintenance.

Moreover, testimony from the 1969 English Abortion Act hearings reveals that many "scientific physicians" were quite explicit in their not-so-scientific views about women who seek abortions. Included were such perceptive and objective observations about "unwanted pregnancy" as the following (Hordern 1971):

- it encourages promiscuity by rewarding certain missteps.
- mothers are always filled with joy at a child's birth and thus the physician must "support the woman through her pregnancy until her courage returned."
- the chastisement of such women "whose only objection to their pregnancy is on grounds of inconvenience."

Because of the "conscience clause" in the British law (physicians cannot be forced to perform an operation against their personal views) and general opposition elsewhere, there is also functionally a class bias against lower socioeconomic women getting an abortion. Although theoretically available in many places, it takes money. Where time is of the essence, the "conscience clause" has still another "delaying" implication, for it allows physicians to seek other opinions. Although this may seem reasonable on the surface, it actually represents a curiosity. In general, patients informed of the necessity of an operation are also pushed to comply immediately, but not in the case of an abortion. Here, where it *is* "medically" true that even a short delay changes the condition of the woman as well as the nature of the operation necessary, she has no power to force a more rapid decision. The physician, ironically enough, is the one who is safeguarded, who is given the opportunity if not encouraged to think it over, not rush into it, etc. Clearly it is doctor-father who is thought to know best about such sensitive issues.

To my thinking the most dangerous instance where personal views march forth in the guise of medical wisdom is seen in the new role of genetic counseling. For with the increased ability to detect inheritable and congenital disorders and predispositions, "whether life should be allowed to begin at all" can only become an increasing controversial issue. The play of values in such a medical matter was seen at a conference to discuss "what to do when there is a documented probability of the offspring of certain unions being damaged." There a position was taken that it was not necessary to pass laws or bar marriages that might produce such offsprings. Recognizing the power and influence of medicine and the doctor, one participant argued (Eisenberg 1966, p. 57):

> There is no reason why sensible people could not be dissuaded from marrying if they know· that one out of four of their children is likely to inherit a disease.

This statement contains certain value assumptions about marriage that may be popular, but are not necessarily shared by all. Thus in addition to presenting the argument against marriage, it would seem that doctors should—if they were to engage in the issue at all—present at the same time some other alternatives. Let me suggest several possibilities:

1. Some "parents" could be willing to live with the risk that out of 4 children, 3 may turn out fine.
2. Depending on the diagnostic procedures available they could take the risk, and if indications were negative, abort.
3. If this risk were too great but the desire to bear children was there, and depending on the type of problem, artificial insemination might be a possibility.
4. Barring all these and not willing to take any risk, they could adopt children.
5. Finally, there is the option of being married without having any children.

To abdicate to physicians the major power in decision-making over such matters allows them the full exercise of their personal values and morality. Though there are objective considerations (e.g. in that attendant "medical" risks are different stages of abortion) in these issues, there is *no* medical or scientific answer as to when life begins or should be ended, how it should be lived or who should live it. These are ultimately sociopolitical questions, no matter how much we might like them to be otherwise.

THE GENERALIZING AND DISCREDITING FUNCTIONS

Kenneth Burke (1959, p. 4) once stated:

Call a man a villain and you have the choice of either attacking or avenging. Call him mistaken and you invite yourself to attempt to set him aright.

I would add, "Call him sick or crazy and all his behavior becomes dismissable." Because a man has been labelled ill, all his activity and beliefs, past, present, and future becomes related to, and explainable in terms of his illness. Once this occurs we can then deny the validity of anything which he might say, do, or stand for.

The generalizing implications of such labelling is further seen when it is applied to a discussion of a controversial social issue. Today the best weapon is to label the other side as mentally ill (being "physically ill" does not lag far behind). In such a situation the separate evaluations of badness and madness and wrongness become unnecessarily and unfortunately intertwined. A very old joke illustrates this principle:

> A man is changing a flat tire outside a mental hospital when the bolts from his wheel roll down a nearby sewer. Distraught, he is confronted by a patient watching him who suggests, "Why don't you take one bolt off each of the other wheels, and place it on the spare?" Surprised when it works, the driver says, "How come you of all people would think of that?" Replies the patient, "I may be crazy, but I'm not stupid."

This anecdote demonstrates the flaw in thinking that a person who is mad is *therefore* stupid or incapable of being insightful about anything. Today, however, if something is felt to be bad, the most effective discreditation is to label it mad, for if mad, then it is "naturally" wrong. In fact, if madness can be demonstrated, then it may be unnecessary to argue the other steps, particularly its wrongness. The sound advice of Thomas Hobbes (1651, p. 26) applies as much today as three hundred years ago when he wrote:

> Seeing then that truth consists in the right ordering of names in our affirmations, a man that seeks precise truth has need to remember what every name he uses stands for; and to place it accordingly; or else he will find himself entangled in words as a bird in lime twigs; the more he struggles the more belimed.

There are, of course, many places where considerations of illness are relevant to the debate over social issues, but their importance as a key datum or cornerstone in the argument has been vastly overplayed.

Furthermore, such considerations can be utilized by both sides in any argument, to the subsequent confusion of the major issue. Two examples illustrate this. For years there have been attempts to discredit, by reference to their emotional instability, those who have either defected to the Communist world or been extremely critical of our own (Almond 1954). On the other hand, the words and criticisms of Communist defectors are readily accepted as little short of the revealed truth. As a report in the *New York Times* demonstrated (February 25, 1968, E13) it was only a matter of time before the Soviet Union responded in kind:

> Recently there has been a great deal of slander in the Western Press against several of our writers whose works played into the hands of our enemies. The campaign by the Western Press in defense of (Valery) Tarsis (author of *Ward 7*) ceased only when he went to the West where it became evident that he was not in his right mind.
>
> At the moment (Aleksandr) Solzhenitsyn (author of *One Day in the Life of Ivan Denisovitch*) occupies an important place in the propaganda of capitalistic governments. He is also a psychologically unbalanced person, a schizophrenic. Formerly he was a prisoner and justly or unjustly was subsequently subjected to repressions. Now he takes his revenge against the government through his literary works. The only topic he is able to write about is life in a concentration camp. This topic has become an obsession with him. . . .

Closer to home there has been a similar turnabout with reference to the involuntary segregation of Blacks. In many discussions, a key datum was the presumed negative effect of segregation on the mental health of the Black. In other words, segregation was argued to be wrong because it impaired Black psyches. A prominent psychoanalyst, however, has argued that given the long history of Black-White relations in the South, the Black in his subservient, defeated role has become essential to the precarious mental health of the "poor White" Southerner. With clever adversaries, mental health-illness considerations may thus only confuse the basic moral or social issue. Thus, there is no necessary and incontrovertible association between being right and being sane or being wrong and being crazy, no matter how much we would like to think so.*

---

*While we contend that the *general* use of "medical labels" to discredit is a product of our times, apparently its possibilities were recognized well over a hundred years ago. Thus the *Athenaeum* of 23 March 1850 carried the following commentary on the "1848 democrats":

> In Berlin, a curious subject for a thesis has been found by a student in medicine, the son of M. Groddeck, the deputy, seeking his degree. M. Groddeck has discovered a new form of epidemic, whose virus has of late circulated throughout the continental nations with a rapidity contrasting strongly with the solemn and stately march of cholera. Its development, indeed, has been all but simultaneous in the great European Capitals, but we know not that it has before occurred to anyone to treat it medically. M. Groddeck's thesis publicly maintained is entitled "De morbo democratico, nova insaniae Forma" (On the democratic disease, a new form of insanity). The Faculty of Medicine, with the usual dislike of Faculties of Medicine to new discoveries, refused admission, it appears to this dissertation, but the Senate of the Uni-

THE GO-NO-FURTHER
FUNCTION

Still other issues emerge when we look for the source of "social ills" in individual problems. Any emphasis on the latter inevitably locates the source of trouble as well as the place of treatment primarily in individuals and makes the etiology of the trouble asocial and impersonal, like a virulent bacteria or a hormonal imbalance.

A rather typical example of this process occurred at a conference I attended on the care of the elderly. A social worker presented the following case:

> This 81 year old man claimed that he was being systematically robbed of all his possessions—money, clothes, mementos, everything. And when everything was gone, he would die. His murderer, however, would never be caught because there would be no evidence that he [the elderly man] had ever lived.

The entire discussion following this case presentation focussed on the mental difficulties and impediments of ageing and the therapies available to deal with them. There is little doubt that this man was by current psychiatric standards clinically paranoid, but was the reality of his growing old (and perhaps ageing itself)—the feeling of loss, neglect, abandonment—any less true? We were so caught up in the psychiatric perspective that no one at the conference, including myself, seemed capable of seeing this issue; nor were we capable of discussing any other social, economic or political aspect of ageing. Too often we forget that what we can do about a particular "trouble" depends on what we are willing to look at. Every phenomenon, be it a physical disease or a social problem, has an almost unlimited set of levels of analysis. There are probably as many levels as there are disciplines willing or able to dissect a phenomenon (religious, economic, social, psychological, biochemical, cellular, and more recently, nutitional). And each plane of analysis represents a possible place for intervention.

Sometimes the focussing on individual problems not only indirectly affects public policy (as in programs for the aged based on "findings" from the conference mentioned above) but has a more direct impact. The words of an administrator reflecting upon the poor and disadvantaged (Kruse 1957, p. 109):

---

versity reversed their decision. Reported in the *American Journal of Insanity*. 1851. 8:195.

> The next push in public welfare should be the development of a high
> quality of professional program dealing with the problems of social
> and emotional adjustment to economic dependency.

Economic dependency is assumed. The social and emotional problems resulting from it are the target for change. Such a view could
put a sealer on the basic problem of economic dependency by ignoring its causes and treating only its consequences. Most cynically put,
it could mean being satisfied with having millions of unemployed
and then exploring how we can make these people less of a problem.

What becomes operative in all such examples is a "go-no-further
effect," which is largely due to that aspect of the medical model
which locates the source of trouble as well as the treatment primarily
in individuals. While this may have a pragmatic basis in the handling
of a specific organic ailment when a social problem is located primarily in the individual or his immediate circle, it blinds us to larger
and discomfiting truths. Slater (1970, p. 15) talks about this as the
"Toilet Assumption":

> Our ideas about institutionalizing the aged, psychotic, retarded and
> infirm are based on a pattern of thought that we might call the Toilet
> Assumption—the notion that unwanted matter, unwanted difficulties,
> unwanted complexities, and obstacles will disappear if they are
> removed from our immediate field of vision. . . . Our approach to
> social problems is to decrease their visibility: out of sight, out of
> mind . . . The result of our social efforts has been to remove the
> underlying problems of our society farther and farther from daily
> experience and daily consciousness, and hence to decrease in the
> mass of the population, the knowledge, skill, resources, and motiva-
> tion necessary to deal with them.

The specifying of any problem as an individual disease means that by
definition it is not a social problem. If anyone is to blame it is
individuals—usually the carriers of the problem—certainly not the
rest of us, or society at large. It is far less overwhelming to blame the
concentration camps and genocide or World War II upon the
madness of a few men (Gilbert 1950) than upon the banal complicity
of millions (Arendt 1963; Davidowicz 1976; Morse 1968). For individuals are theoretically manageable units. What a Pandora's box
would be opened if senility, drug addiction, alcoholism, poverty, the
need for abortions, etc., were considered indicative of something
wrong in the basic structure of the society at large rather than (or as
well as) in the basic structure of a relatively small collection of
individual psyches.

THE MORAL NEUTRALITY OF THE
MEDICAL MODEL

There are many reasons why the medical model has been widely used to understand, diagnose, and treat "society's ills." Not the least of these reasons is the assumed moral neutrality of such a mode. Herein, however, lies the greatest potentiality for abrogating and obfuscating moral issues. Illness, in the medical perspective, assumes something painful and undesirable, and thereby something that can and should be eliminated. It is because of the latter element that great caution must be exercised in the equating of social problems or unpleasant social phenomena with illness. Narcotic use and homosexuality provide two recent examples of this process. Both are behaviors considered by many to be morally reprehensible. In many parts of the world to engage in either is a criminal offense. This situation is changing. Such behavior is less often regarded as crime and more as a sign of illness, if not *ipso facto* illness itself (Ford and Beach 1951; Schur 1965). While this may be more humanitarian and therapeutic, it provides no answer to the underlying ethical and moral issues. Thus the fact there are significant medical, psychological, and even physiological differences between homosexuals and non-homosexuals, and between narcotic users and nonusers is no demonstration that homosexuality and narcotic addiction are primarily medicopsychological problems. Nor is the fact that homosexuals or narcotic users can be treated or changed any argument that they *should* be forced to change. Yet we continually find these assumptions in the medical model. Popular articles have even begun to use such reasoning as an argument against homosexuality. At least one, citing evidence on "improvement" of homosexuals through psychotherapy, concluded that homosexuals therefore have no excuse for not undergoing treatment. Within this framework, such questions as the homosexual's or addict's wish for change, his satisfaction with the situation, and his right to dispose of his body in his own way if he does not harm others, will not even be asked. A social illness, like an individual one, is by definition to be eliminated, *regardless* of the wish of the individual.

The word "regardless" is a key element. In the process of labelling a social problem an illness, there is a power imbalance of tremendous import. For illness is only to be diagnosed and treated by certain specified licensed and mandated officials—primarily M.D.'s. In such a situation the potential patient has little right to appeal the label/diagnosis. In fact when a patient does object to what is being done for him, the social rhetoric once again may obscure the issue:

since he is sick, he does not really know what is good for him. The treater-diagnosticians, of course, think *they* know, since there is nothing "in it" for them, the experts who made the diagnosis. Their very expertise, being socially legitimated, makes this judgment seem morally neutral. The greatest deception lies in such reasoning. Even granting that diagnosticians and their tools may be morally neutral (which I seriously doubt), society's decision that a particular social problem is relevant to their province is not without moral consequences. Establishing the "problem's" relevance as the key dimension for action helps prevent the moral issue from being squarely faced, or even from being raised. If a specific behavior is defined as an illness and illness is (as we know) undesirable, the issue becomes not whether to deal with a particular problem, but how and when. Thus the debate over homosexuality, drugs, abortion, hyperactive children, antisocial behavior, becomes focussed on the degree of sickness attached to the phenomenon in question (and its carriers) and the extent of the "health" risk. And the more perplexing, moral issue of the control an individual should exercise over his/her body is shunted aside.

CONCLUSION

Thus ends my analysis of the perils of the wholesale transfer of the medical model to our workaday world. Basically my contention is that the increasing use of illness as a lever in the understanding of social problems represents no dramatic shift from a moral to an objectively neutral view, but merely to an alternative strategy. The dean of a Catholic university, commenting on the revival of witchery on college campuses, saw it in exactly those terms (*New York Times Magazine* June 1, 1969):

> We've really become progressive around here. A couple of hundred years ago we would have burned them. Twenty-five years ago I would have expelled them. Now we simply send them all to psychiatrists.

Thus, the shift in the handling of such social problems is primarily in the hands of those who undertake the change (psychiatrists and other medical specialists) and where the change takes place (in the individual's psyche and body). The problem being scrutinized and the person being changed is no less immoral for all the medical rhetoric. It or he is still a "problem," though the rhetoric may convince us that he and not society is responsible, and he not society should be changed. Even the moral imperatives remain; if such a problem-person can be medically-treated-changed, it-he *should* be.

But in addition to the basic depoliticizing effect of the labels "health and illness," there is also an exclusionary one. That the Women's Movement is making its most important inroads in the delivery of medical services is no accident. In a powerful movie called *Taking Our Bodies Back* and an extraordinary book, *Our Bodies, Ourselves* (Boston Women's Health Book Collective 1976), women not only decry what power they have given up, but also how biological and supposed health differences have been used to exclude them from many aspects of life. I fear that this phenomenon of "anatomy being destiny" will become even more widespread. Where once one was excluded from jobs because of race, ethnicity, gender, and age, now one will become ineligible for promotion, inappropriate for work, pushed to early retirement—all on the basis of one's physical status or health. If you do not think ours is already an exclusionary society, look at the architectural barriers we have created to exclude full access and participation of our citizens from schools, restaurants, theaters, public buildings, court houses, and even private dwellings. Look at the social barriers wherein a cult of youthful beauty makes us repelled by the old or by people in any way deformed. Look at the communication barriers that prevent us from talking comfortably with those who are blind and deaf, gazing directly at someone who is facially disfigured, and listening for long to anyone with a speech defect.

The reasons for all this go deep. As long as the deliverers of service are markedly different in gender, economic class, and race from those to whom they offer services, as long as accessibility to medical care is a privilege rather than a right, as long as the highest income groups are health-care professionals, as long as the most profit-making enterprises include the pharmaceutical and insurance industries, society is left with the uncomfortable phenomenon of a portion of its population living, and living well, off the sufferings of others and to some extent having a vested interest in the continuing existence of such problems.

A web of political, economic, and even social psychological forces support this system, and only with awareness can the dismantling begin. It is for all these reasons that I am convinced that the health area has become the battleground of today's identity crisis—what is or will become of the self. It is the battleground not because there are visible threats and oppressors, but because they are almost invisible—not because the perspective, tools, and practitioners of medicine and the other helping professions are inherently evil, but because they are not. It is frightening because there are elements here of the banality of evil so uncomfortably written about by Hannah Arendt (1963). But here the danger is greater, for not only is the process masked as technical and scientific, but as one done for our own good. In short, the road to a healthist society may well be paved with supposedly good intentions.

25

Individual Choice and Health Policy: A Sociopolitical Scenario for the 1980s

INTRODUCTION

Trying to forecast the future is always a dangerous enterprise. In fact, going public with one's predictions may alter the very situation you are trying to understand. In this instance, no such concern bothers me. Indeed, I hope that by pointing out certain tendencies in the formulation of health policies, the situation I fear will never come to pass.

THE PERCEIVED ECONOMIC CONTEXT

For nearly two decades we have been warned about the ever-increasing costs and questionable benefits of medical care. In the mid 1960s Brian Abel-Smith analyzed the health expenditures in twenty-nine widely scattered countries and concluded that there was *no* limit to personal health expenditures. He found that developed countries transferred an additional 1 to 2 percent of their Gross National Product to health services every ten years and that the total expenditure bore little relationship to any demonstrated health need (Abel-Smith 1967). The data in our own country is quite similar. In the fifteen years since the passage of Medicare and Medicaid, our annual medical budget has quadrupled and now exceeds $200 billion. Nationally, spending for health care, which consumed

6.2 percent of the 1965 GNP, accounted for 9.1 percent of the 1978 GNP (Altman 1980). The Health Care Financing Administration projects that if all health care costs continue to rise at the present rate, by 1990 medical expenditures will represent 11.5 percent of the American GNP (Health Care Financing Administration 1979). Some critics feel this may be a conservative estimate.

Such economic concerns are escalated when others ask what we are getting for all this money. There seems to be little relationship between investment and the need for services, even among countries at a similar stage of development. Brian Abel-Smith went so far as to say that the distribution of resources between the various components of health services was inversely related to their effectiveness (Abel-Smith 1974). Even more disturbing, the McKinlays conclude that what has long been found for mortality data—namely, little relation between decreased mortality and health expenditure—is also true when they studied a number of selected diseases. So again we find little relation between the overall provision of services and the rates of morbidity (McKinlay and McKinlay 1977, 1980). In fact, according to one analysis, during the years 1966–76 while the American population grew by 10 percent, the number of people with a disability increased by 37 percent (Colvez and Blanchet 1981). While such data question the good of such services, more recent critics, such as Illich (1975), are questioning the possible harm. No matter. Health services, health costs, and health expenditures continue to rise.

I will leave the basic causes of this spiral to others (Krause 1977, Navarro 1976). For my present purposes I wish only to note that the general direction is perceived as upward and climbing. A former deputy assistant secretary of HEW, Stuart Altman (1980 p. 14), summed up current efforts at containment:

> Methods of controlling the costs and use of medical care include regulating (planning) new construction and development of services, establishing limits on hospital reimbursement, and experimenting with new reimbursement methods. Some analysts argue that marketplace forces should be permitted to control the supply and provision of medical services, since economic laws would force equilibrium between price and demand thereby rendering government regulation unnecessary. But the structural factors in the health care system make this, at best, a very long-term solution. What is even more likely is that in the short run, the political and health care system will not let the market operate, and spending for health services will continue to rise far faster than other sectors of the economy.
>
> Since the erosion of market forces in the health system is not likely

to be revised, policy options in medical care inevitably include regulating the health sector.

I essentially agree with his conclusion, namely that given that policy makers see these costs as excessive and uncontrollable by market factors, regulation is inevitable. But where? My observations of the public and professional debates is that regulation will not occur in the general provision of medical and hospital services. Nor will it occur in high technology medicine where bigger and more complex is still perceived as better, if not best. And while there is a continual debate about cutting nonessential medical services— those perceived as cosmetic (dermatology, dentistry) or support services (counseling, social work, physiotherapy) or simply non-traditional (chiropractic, acupuncture)—I feel these are only skirmishes, not the major battle. My sociopolitical sense tells me that the major cuts will take place where the political constituency is weakest. By weakest I mean where protest is least likely to take place, probably because of a combination of weak coalitions, fragmented popular support and disinterest of the major providers (e.g. monetarily, professionally, vocationally [careerwise] or scientifically.) I believe such preconditions are most likely to exist in an area of service involving a chronic disease or disability. The specifics of this process can be seen through a series of scenarios.

THE PSYCHOSOCIAL SCENARIO

We are in the midst of an ideological backlash. I neither know nor care whether one labels it "conservative," "moderate," or a "return to basic values." There is a reaction against explanations involving large-scale forces and a growing frustration in being unable to do anything about them. It is an almost desperate turning inward toward areas where we have some control. Like any deep-seated trend, its predecessors—at least in hindsight—lurked on the horizon of social theorizing over twenty years ago. In 1959 Thomas Szasz wrote his first paper on "The Myth of Mental Illness." And while we may have paid more attention to his critiques of psychiatry, hand in hand with his efforts at demystification came a theory of personal conduct which emphasized individual responsibility (Szasz 1961). Other theorists followed suit and in the general area of social problems, the old debate between free will and determinism took on new currency (Matza 1969). Warning notes about the policy implications of such an approach were sounded—William Ryan's treatise on *Blaming the Victim*, written in the late 1960's, was the earliest—but they were largely ignored. The trend has continued unabated until it has finally burst full-blown in the field of medicine and public health. Here the emphasis on individual responsibility has reemerged in the reconditioned concept of "life-style behavior." Its most articulate exponents—such as the authors in John Knowles' now famous *Doing Better and Feeling Worse* (1977)—do recognize the importance of large-scale social and political phenomena in the production of mortality and morbidity. But when "push comes to shove" the social causes are generally recognized as outside the province of medicine. Medicine, it is argued, must turn to what it can do, not what it cannot. Medicine's strength, it is contended, comes in dealing with small-scale individual behavior, not large-scale social forces.

My inference from all this is straightforward—that in the 1980s this "life-style" focus will increasingly be translated into social policy.

THE LEGAL SCENARIO

In 1976 the case of *General Electric* v. *Gilbert* came before the Supreme Court of the United States. It was played up in the media as purely a feminist issue, so its other significance may have been lost. The essential question was whether excluding health insurance disability benefits related to pregnancy constituted a discrimination against women (D.A. Lewis 1976). By a 6 to 3 margin the Supreme Court decided that such an exclusion did not. One of their arguments was especially interesting. The justices said that pregnancy was a voluntary act.

In late June of 1980 the Lutheran Church was similarly engaged in a debate about health insurance coverage. They were bewailing the high cost of their group rates and sought a way to reduce it. A factor contributing to the high premium of many plans often revolved around the coverage of pre-existing conditions. The Lutheran Board of Pensions came up with a rather unusual answer. They recommended the exclusion of adopted children with pre-existing handicaps from the health benefit plans. Their rationale was that adopted children were chosen (*Daily Camera* June 21, 1980, p. 9).

A recent session of the Massachusetts legislature illustrated yet another extension of the concept of voluntarism into health policy. Citing the high costs to the American public of diseases where smoking was associated, a bill was introduced to tax smokers (*Boston Daily Globe* February 27, 1979).

There are some observations I draw from these seemingly isolated examples. First, the issue under debate comes to public view cloaked in economic concerns. Secondly, in each instance, the factor which excluded one party from the services under consideration was that the act leading to the condition, if not the condition itself, was perceived to be voluntary—i.e., under the individual's control. More crassly put, the individual could have avoided it if he or she had wanted to. My third observation is that the definition of "voluntary," far from being based on scientific data, is instead based on sociopolitical considerations. In recent memory the American Psychiatric Association declared by vote that homosexuality was no longer *ipso facto* a disease but a matter of individual preference (Conrad and Schneider 1980). The shift goes both ways. During the Vietnam war, perhaps the most unpopular conflict in which we have ever engaged, alcoholism was declared a treatable disease and thus no longer a reason for either medical deferment or medical discharge (*International Herald Tribune* March 8, 1971). In the Supreme Court Decision mentioned above, Justice Brennan in his dissent somewhat acidly noted that "other than for childbirth disability General Electric had never construed its plan as eliminating *all* so-called 'voluntary' disabilities including sports injuries, attempted suicides, venereal disease, disabilities incurred in the commission of a crime or during a fight, and elective cosmetic surgery" (*General Electric* v. *Gilbert et al.* 1976).

The key element in this line of thinking is the issue of individual responsibility couched in the notion of voluntarism. For the Supreme Court the act of conception was voluntary. For the Lutheran Synod, on the other hand, the act of conception was in God's hands but the act of adoption was not. Though voluntarism is a growing issue in the determination of health policy, what constitutes voluntary behavior clearly depends on who is doing the judging and what is deemed at stake.

THE OPERATIONALIZATION SCENARIO

In foreseeing where such a confluence of economic and political concerns might lead, I wish to disclaim any originality. Two novelists alerted me to these problems. The first, Anthony Burgess, wrote about the costs of overpopulation in a book called *The Wanting Seed* (1976). I thought he argued convincingly that the most efficient method was to take conception out of the hands of the individual and place it in some regulatory body. The end result in his novel was that people needed permission to reproduce. Nobel Laureate William Shockley (1972a) came to a similar conclusion and in another 1972 article (Shockley 1972b) he outlines five steps to a population control plan. It begins by first convincing people that population limitation is desirable and necessary for survival. The Census Bureau then calculates the number of children each woman may have (2.2 if one-third of one percent increase is permitted each year). The Public Health Department then sterilizes every girl as she enters puberty by a subcutaneous injection of a contraceptive capsule which provides a slow seepage of contraceptive hormones until it is removed. When the girl marries, she is issued 22 deci-child certificates. Her doctor will remove the contraceptive capsule on payment of ten certificates, and replace it after a baby is born. After two babies, the couple may either sell their remaining two certificates (through the Stock Exchange), or try to buy eight more on the open market and have a third child. Those who do not have children have 22 certificates to sell.

I stored all this away in my mind until I read *The Bladerunner* by Alan Nourse (1974). Nourse also postulated a time when the national economy was going bankrupt because of ever-increasing demands for health services. One of the protagonists in his story, Dr. John Long, explains the datum which enabled the government to break the spiral:

> Throughout most of history diabetes had been a relatively uncommon affliction that was uniformly fatal for lack of any effective treatment. As a disease strongly influenced by heredity, the fatal nature of diabetes served as a powerful limitation on its spread. Death often occurred during childhood, and even in adulthood, the development of a pregnancy so greatly accelerated the destructive nature of the disease that few children were born of diabetic mothers. For centuries the disease, cause unknown, had remained stable and uncommon, a tragedy for those few who developed symptoms, but with very few of them passing the disease tendency on to their children.
> The discovery of insulin in the early 1920's changed all that. For the first time, diabetes could be treated, and more and more victims survived long enough to have diabetes-prone children (Nourse 1974, pp. 79–80)

To this point we could well have been reading a public health text. But in "1993" a leading scientist named Rupert Heinz estimated

> that as many as 40 percent of the nation's entire population carried at least one part of the complex genetic linkage for diabetes, up from 37 percent just ten years earlier. Looking into the future, Heinz predicted that, as a result of medical intervention in detecting and treating diabetes, as much as 85 percent of the population would be carrying some diabetic factors within another forty years and that some 40 percent would be actively diabetic. His message was simple and to the point: keep treating diabetes the way it had been treated

for three quarters of a century and everybody would be diabetic or diabetes-prone by the late part of the next century." (Nourse 1974, p. 80)

A eugenics control program was created to curb the transmission of genetically linked diseases, but it faltered; the scientists concluded

> that a eugenics program alone would not be enough to turn the tide. Even with compulsory sterilization of all victims of diabetes, schizophrenia and a dozen other hereditary-connected diseases and the compulsory euthanasia of all identifiably defective babies, the destructive spiral would continue as long as widespread medical intervention continued. Only if *all* individuals who wished to have medical treatment were first sterilized was there hope that the spiral could be broken. (Nourse 1974, p. 81)

The scientists felt that there were many bugs in this system, but unfortunately the economic crises proved overwhelming and severe restrictions on the use of medical services were introduced.

My conclusions are a little different. In contemporary America the economic crisis is not so great, the political power of an aging population is not so strong, and the available technology is not so crude. And yet I think the projections of both authors may largely come true. It is merely that the pace will be slower, the first limitation on service more restricted, and the process more insidious.

THE HEALTH POLICY SCENARIO

There are, of course, many health care areas in which human beings can be held responsible for the consequences of their actions. Yet I feel they will be most systematically held responsible in the area of reporduction. Though there has been a long-term increase in the medicalization of childbirth (Arms 1975; Boston Women's Health Book Collective 1983; Ehrenreich and English 1979; Oakley 1980; Wertz and Wertz 1977), my conclusion may seem ironic at a time when "the right to life" movement seems so popular. And yet the cessation of a life (by whatever sociopolitical definition currently in fashion) seems a quite different act of control than a decision not to have a child. The medical world itself is far more divided on any intervention that they perceive has to do with ending life (e.g. in abortion, euthanasia) than on acts perceived to deal with the starting (e.g. genetics) or continuing of life (e.g. "heroic" measures, "life support" systems, transplants).

Medical scientists were concerned with the physiological nature of the populations that modern civilization was producing long before economic crisis was an issue. Rene Dubos (1968a, p. 110) concluded:

The potential ability of mankind to survive the threats arising from new technologies and new ways of life constitutes but a limited aspect of the problem of adaptation. Many seemingly fully adaptive biological and social changes desirable today will have to be paid for in the future at a cruel price in terms of human values. A threatening consequence of medical and technological progress is the accumulation in our communities of hereditary defectives, people who today survive into reproductive age and in the past would have died without progeny. Modern ways of life are thus interfering with natural elimination of undesirable genes and are probably creating some measure of genetic hazard. Eventually this wide-spread impairment of genetic quality will express itself in overt disease or at least in reduced vitality.

I would argue that such a concern can only escalate when population growth for whatever reason becomes more controlled. For then what will inevitably follow is the attempt to improve the quality of those who are produced. Dubos (1968a, pp. 139–40) delineates the process:

Family planning, however, is likely to create new biological problems which are little if at all understood. Once infant mortality has been reduced to levels as low as those prevailing in prosperous countries, an average of three children per family is far too high for population control. Surprising as it may be, this family size results in a doubling of the populaltion within a very few decades. The population can be stabilized only if the average number of children born per couple does not exceed 2.3. Such low birth rates would leave little room for the operation of the selective forces that have maintained the genetic characteristics of the human race in the past. The fear that genetic self-correction may no longer operate is creating a renewal of scientific and popular interest in the problems of eugenics. Some geneticists claim that man can avoid genetic deterioration only if that approximate 20 percent of the population who are heavily laden with genetic defects can either fail to live until maturity or fail to reproduce.

The scientific data linking genetic factors to disease is impressive and ever growing. In the same year that Nourse's novel was published, a report on the Subcommittee on Science and Astronautics of the United States House of Representatives (Science Policy Research Division 1974) indicated that the list of recognized genetic disorders caused by a single gene now includes nearly 2,000 and is growing at the rate of 75 to a 100 newly identified disorders each year. By 1980, the same subcommittee (Science Policy Research Division 1980) raised the list to 2,500 (in mid-1981 *Newsweek* [May 18, 1981] thought it might hover near 3,000) and the rate of increase to 100 newly identified disorders each year. Disorders caused by multiple genes or chromosomal defects, such as Down's syndrome (mongolism) are not included, so the number is even larger. The list also does not include conditions suspected of a genetic component nor the still largely unknown mutagenic effect of exposure to various environmental factors. From such data it is not especially surprising that a November 1974 article in the *Journal of the American Medical Association* which the above report cited gave the conservative estimate, based on existing studies, of chromosome defects occurring in one of every two hundred *live* births (cited in Science Policy Research Division 1974, p. 3). By 1981 *Newsweek* (May 18, 1981) reported that of 3 million babies born in the United States each year, 2 to 3 percent have a major genetic defect or congenital disease.

The impact of this on medical care and costs can be stated quite graphically. As many as 12 million Americans suffer from a disease or disability caused, in whole or in part, by genetic factors (National Institute of General Medical Sciences 1975). Thus it has been estimated that persons with genetic diseases occupy as many as 25 percent of the hospital beds in this country (Grant 1978).

To many, society's response is inevitable. Genetic screening would be the critical factor in reducing the incidence of such conditions (Soskies 1980), and individuals carrying the genes would "be prevented from reproducing" (Grant 1978).

A conference over fifteen years ago, anticipating such data, was convened to decide what to do when there was a documented possibility of offspring being "damaged." The conference determined that it was unnecessary to institute laws to bar such marriages (though there was ample legal precedent for such a move; there have been state laws prohibiting marriages between "mental defectives" and between epileptics). Instead the members felt that doctors themselves should simply warn and thus persuade prospective parents against the consequences of certain unions (Eisenberg 1966). Dubos (1968a, p. 139) agreed with the necessity but was wary as to how easy it would be:

> No one disagrees with eliminating the gross physical and mental defects which afflict the human race, although even this limited approach poses problems of judgement and of execution far more complex than usually realized.

And in recent years he has been proven right. There has been considerable debate among genetic counselors and physicians generally as to how much they should involve themselves in a potential parent's decision (Etzioni 1973). I fear, however, that procedures exist, both scientifically and legally, so that the medical world can "safely" abdicate a direct responsibility in this decision-making process.

Building on the techniques developed in automatic multiphasic testing and computer technology, society is capable of instituting large-scale programs of genetic screening. In the last few years, hearings have been held and bills introduced in the state of California. Varying versions of this bill have recommended voluntary screening and the availability of specialized techniques for high risk populations—e.g. amniocentesis for women over the age of thirty-five. One version of the bill went so far as to recommend this procedure for all women. With a spate of law suits in process against physicians who did not advise prospective parents that they risked producing a "defective" child, the pressure for such universal testing has increased (Shaw 1977). Already many industries have instituted large-scale genetic screening programs (Severo 1980). And on what, according to some scientists, are quite arbitrary levels and standards, they have initiated certain "remedies," including sanctioning the sterilization of potential mothers, transfer of employees from one setting to another, and outright exclusion of certain other groups (e.g. sickle-cell carriers from admission to the Air Force Academy).

Most screening programs start out as voluntary at least theoretically. No one has to participate. But if one does not, one may be declared ineligible for inclusion in the company's health plan and thus ineligible for employment. So, too, I predict that barring an even greater fiscal crisis, when such programs are introduced on a state or federal level, initially they will also be voluntary. On the other hand, with the extension of health insurance, there will be a claimed need for more base line data, and thus such testing may become more automatic and less voluntary. For this, too, there is ample precedent. There is the mandatory PKU at all births, the mandatory three vaccinations for entering school-age children, the mandatory chest X-ray and TB tests for many industry and university employees, and the mandatory Wasserman test before issuance of a marriage license.

While the genetic screening tests may become mandatory, I believe that for a long time society will stress voluntarism or individual choice in what one does about it. Presented with information, the individual will be free to decide whether to marry or to bear children. But consequences will follow from the individual decision. The individuals, or really their offspring, will pay for that decision. Insurance policies may well add exclusionary clauses when the individual(s) choose to have children in the face of medical evidence (i.e. based on some actuarial but arbitrary level of probability). It is even possible that various tax penalties as suggested by the Boston physician mentioned earlier may ensue (*Boston Globe* February 27, 1979).

A SUMMING UP

A cynical interpretation of science's continual need to control was stated a quarter of a century ago by C. S. Lewis (1947). He warned that man's power over Nature is really the power of some men over other men, with Nature as their instrument. And after Elhul's (1981) critique of our technological society, one realizes that such testing and instrumentalism frequently takes on a life of their own. Thus within the last decade many critics (Ehrenreich and English 1979; Ehrenreich 1978; Illich 1975) including myself (Zola 1972a, 1975a, 1977b) have called attention to the phenomenon of medicalization—a process whereby more and more of everyday life has come under medical dominion, influence and supervision. Its early impact was perceived as a humane one (Fox 1977; Wooton 1959). Many people and problems which were once "punished" are now "treated" (Conrad and Schneider 1980). But the outcome is never automatic. Medicalization does not guarantee that either the problem or the society will be better off because of this intervention.

Perhaps the greatest sociopolitical danger is when "a social ill" becomes transformed into a "personal problem" (Mills 1959). It is just such a phenomenon which I have described in this paper. Medical costs are escalating—some claim they may soon bankrupt our society. So what are we to do about it? We do not ask, as does Krause (1982), what role the state or society inself plays in the production of disease and disability (Navarro 1976; Waitzkin and Waterman 1974). Since illness and medicine are still felt to be individual matters, it is on this level that our society seeks answers. It is far easier to find ways in which individuals are at fault (Crawford 1977, 1979), for we perceive we can control problems of this sort. So it is with the field of genetics and its applied arm, genetic counseling. Beneath all its marvelous discoveries is a rhetoric with great appeal: it offers the hope of controlling some part of one's individual destiny (Cooke 1977; *Newsweek* October 16, 1978; August 20, 1979; May 18, 1981). Thus it becomes relatively easy to ignore or play down the social factors which may produce these "genetic problems" and instead focus on individual capacities, solutions, and choices (Severo 1980). But the "choice" or "freedom" involved many prove quite illusory, as Petchesky (1980, p. 674) has argued in regard to reproductive freedom:

the critical issue . . . is not so much the content of women's choice, or even the "right to choose," as it is the social and material conditions under which choices are made. The "right to choose" means very little when women are powerless . . . women make their own reproductive choices, but they do not make them just as they please; they do not make them under conditions which they themselves create but under social conditions and constraints which they, as mere individuals, are powerless to change.

That's exactly what I fear. Bombarded on all sides by realistic concerns (the escalation of costs) and objective evidence (genetics) and techniques (genetic counseling), the basic value issue at stake will be obfuscated. The freedom to choose will be illusory. Someone will already have set the limits of choice (cuts in medical and social benefits but not in defense spending), the dimensions of choice (if you do this then you will have an X probability of a defective child) and the outcomes of choice (you will have to endure the following social, political, legal, and economic costs).

So ends my scenario. It is, of course, quite possible that the details of my projected future may never come to pass. Nevertheless, I think we need be wary of a situation which is exacerbated (though it began long before) by the economic and political philosophy of the current federal administration. I see a pattern in a series of seemingly disparate events. Building on existing scientific and economic data, I see an ideological interpretation taking hold. Specifically, I see a "blaming the victim" philosophy made into a false scientific truth, institutionalized into a national health policy, and imposed on an impotent segment of the population.

Part Seven

A Postscript

26

Looking Back . . .
and Ahead

As I look over my sociomedical work, I see how trapped I have been between my liberal and radical leanings. In the 1950s I was a part of the humanist-critical group of medical sociologists that sought to reform medicine. I saw that physicians did not sufficiently listen to their patients, so I gave them voice. I felt that physicians needed to incorporate a social science perspective in their education, so I sought out every opportunity to write in *their* journals and teach in *their* courses. I believed that the structure of their research and practice needed to be humanized, so I accepted every chance to review *their* investigations or advise in the reorganization of *their* services. When a new movement in medicine—primary care and family medicine—found itself under attack, I lent them support, helped them create curricula, lectured their residents.

And yet each of these involvements (even when successful) has brought with it a set of dilemmas. All too often I felt I was engaged in the wrong battle in the wrong place. Although I thought my colleagues in primary care and family medicine were right in their fight for survival against other medical specialties, at some point I realized it was really a battle over turf. Yet they were so engaged in their struggle that they failed to see that the medical needs of the populace could never be solved by more physicians on the "frontiers of care," but rather by a conscious redistribution of services and redelegation of responsibilities not only to less highly trained personnel but to the people themselves.

One of the more sobering experiences I had in this regard seems worth recalling. From 1970 to 1973, I was a consultant to the Program for Ambulatory Care Service, a joint project of the Harvard Medical School at the Beth Israel Hospital and the staff of the Massachusetts Institute of Technology's Lincoln Laboratory (Zola 1970a). With the possible exception of my work with Edith Lenneberg at the Stoma Rehabilitation Clinic of the New England Deaconess Hospital, no consulting experience was to draw on so many different parts of my work and my life. No other colleagues were to immerse me so suddenly in a new body of knowledge (engineering and computer technology). No group of physicians seemed so committed to changing the world, or at least their corner of it as at the Beth Israel Hospital.

The details of the original project are unimportant. Suffice it to say that when I joined the team, they were in the process of creating protocols which would assist in the diagnosis and treatment of a wide range of physical conditions. At the outset the protocol was flashed on a TV screen in front of which the patients sat with a keyboard on which they could type in their responses. But the patients were found to be resistant and an aid was added to help them deal with the complexities of the console. Finally the console was eliminated and the protocol was eventually administered directly by the "aide."

It was at this time that I wrote my first extensive consultant's report. I was excited about the potentialities of this aide and was clearly optimistic when I wrote (Zola 1970a, pp. 2-3):

> It is the premise of this paper, and indeed of the project of which it is a part, that, with the systematic aid of computer technology and the cooperation of existing medical and nursing personnel, a new cadre of ancillary medical personnel could be trained to become the major therapeutic figure in the day to day chronic disease management.

Only much later was I to discover that the following criticism of "the field in general" would come to apply to the project itself (Zola 1970a, p. 2):

> Admirable and needed as they are, the attempts to upgrade existing professionals (from medical corpsmen to public health nurses) have primarily emphasized the technical side and the preliminary stages of medical care. Thus at best they free doctors to see *more* patients but do little to cope with the area where *needs* are expanding most rapidly—chronic disease management.

As it turned out, the project got stuck on the technical level. We were able to show that with the use of a protocol these aides were able to make clinical conclusions comparable to those of a physician. But I was never able to convince the staff to extend aides' duties to include issues of instruction, management, and psychosocial support. I do not know why my vision of the project never influenced its later development (Sherman and Komaroff 1974). Perhaps it was because I was not a physician. Perhaps it was because I did not stay around long enough. Perhaps as a naive academic I was content with winning a local battle (gaining nonprofessionals the right to do some of the work of physicians) and did not realize the greater war of which it was a part. I am certainly not pleased with how it has turned out.

A new cadre of health personnel has been created. But instead of using the lowest level of personnel available, many of the protocols are used by highly trained nurses. Instead of being the disseminators of information and support, they have become the purveyors of new technologies and tests. Instead of becoming the potential allies of the patients, they have become the trusted "handmaidens" of the doctors. Instead of being the base for a new group of mobile and independent practitioners, they have become still another group of "dependent professionals." And instead of being "chronic disease managers," they have become "physician extenders."

These dilemmas are crystallized in the term "physician's extender." It conveys the image of a gross medical appendage—a Rube Goldberg invention. In function, it implies only an extension of the physician's work—no new alternative to the care so greatly needed in chronic disease. In responsibilities, it tells the patient that any thing of importance is to be left to the doctor. And in potentiality, it says to the holder that he/she is in a job with limited mobility and possibility for growth.

When I wrote the first draft of this chapter, I was summering in a progressive city in the Southwest. It was 1980, and I found that history was repeating itself. On the local scene home birthing was vigorously opposed; midwives were recently prevented from joining a local OB-GYN staff; and "physician extenders" were not being allowed to practice in one of the local hospitals. The argument against all of these "practices," particularly the latter, was that they would lower the quality of care. As I read the newspaper accounts, it seemed evident that the people using that term did not even know the meaning of it. If anything, it is this resistance to sharing their territory which reduces the quality of the care they so piously claim to preserve. But aside from being an outsider, I did not join the battle on behalf of the "physician extenders." As presently constituted, it was the wrong battle fought by the wrong people for the wrong reasons at the wrong time.

My dilemma—which battles to fight, and when—persists. Recently I have realized that all my attempts to "humanize" medical care have had some unanticipated side effects. In "Oh Where, Oh Where Has Ethnicity Gone?" I articulated this issue. Every time I succeed in giving the physician tools to better understand the psychological, social, and political situation of patients, I find myself contributing to the very medicalization of everyday life of which I am so wary (Crawford 1980; Illich et al. 1977).

It is perhaps because of this awareness that I have consistently refused (though tempted) to join any health professional faculty on a permanent basis. Remaining anchored in a college of liberal arts has not only helped preserve my sanity but also helped salve my conscience. For I felt that here at least I was able to educate not only future generations of health personnel *before* their professional socialization took hold, but also large numbers of consumers and patients. Indeed, the creation of a daily health calendar (chapter 15) and the self-medication survey (chapter 16) were eyeopeners for many students. As one woman stated, it was akin to the first time she had done a pelvic self-examination. It revealed parts of herself that had long been hidden. But over the years even teaching combined with my more critical writings has not been enough. Finally, building on my civil rights and Vietnam war protest experience, I joined with others in 1971 to form a mental health collective, Greenhouse Inc. The collective was ideologically committed to sharing power between therapist and client, to giving the client the tools to change his/her own life. With the experience gained here, I sought an even more focussed effort in the mid 1970s. I began to work with an "oppressed" group which I had only recently acknowledged that I belonged to—people with disabilities (Zola 1981a, 1982a,b,c, 1983a).

Realizing that people needed not only the tools "to get their shit together" but also a forum in which to practice what was learned, I began meeting with several other professionals who also had disabilities (Zola 1983a). We were influenced in our planning by two insights from the Women's Movement (perhaps best exemplified in the work of the Boston's Women's Health Book Collective, 1976): first, that at this point in history, and for certain issues, you had to have *been there* to help someone else; second, that a movement without a political direction would eventually drift and be coopted. In 1978 we incorporated as the Boston Self Help Center—a counseling, advocacy, resource, and educational organization run by people with chronic diseases and disabilities (Zola 1983a).

In the foreword to this volume, I hoped that putting together this book would let me see not only where I have been, but where I am going. Some things have indeed become clearer. Ever since my polio and accident I have been aware of the fragile nature of human existence, aware that my time on this earth could be cut short at any moment. This has already affected me in ways that I cannot yet disentangle. But a few things are clear. One is that I like to marshall my energy. I don't like to waste time. This does not mean that I am impatient, but rather that I like to make my efforts count for something. Nor do I like to do things because I have to, although I have no aversion to "dirty work." I can spend hours patiently licking stamps, making phone calls, or alphabetizing references. I only need to be convinced that the activity is really needed or that I can do it "better" than anyone else available. Another way of putting this is that I like to be needed, and it is not hard to see how this is related to my disability. For far too long, people like myself have been thought "unable," "unworthy," or "invalid" (Goffman 1963; Zola 1981a, 1982a,b, 1983a). Thus "being needed" is a way to reclaim one's worthiness, one's selfhood. This was evident in my earliest work, where I wrote not only about people with whom I could identify because of some common disenfranchisement, but whom I could also "help" by giving them voice.

Another work-related outcome of this issue is that I like to work at more than one thing at a time. Like the people I wrote about in "Observations on Gambling . . . " (Zola 1963a), a variety of projects allows me to hedge my bets. It diffuses the possibility of failure and allows me more opportunities in which to feel and be worthy. Because I am a good judge of time and commitments, I am rarely overwhelmed. For someone like me, who because of the polio, the accident, and its residuals, feels that so much of my life has been out of my control or under someone else's (i.e., because of the medical or physical dependency), this range of interest gives me more control over my life.

Although I have many irons in the fire at a time, I am tenacious. If I care about an idea I will not easily give it up (Good examples are found in "Getting Involved as Well as Concerned" [chapter 18], which deals with my long-term consulting, and in my work on medicalization). This also means that if I think a paper is good, and I receive at least some support, then I will keep sending it out no matter how many rejection slips I receive. Several papers in this volume share that history, as does one of my most recent books, *Missing Pieces—A Chronicle of Living With a Disability* (Zola 1982a). *Missing Pieces* had thirty-five fullscale rejections before finding a home with Temple University Press.

Although I see with some clarity where I have been, and why, my future is harder to predict. My twenties gave little hint what I would be working on in my thirties, which in turn provided no clear guidelines for my forties. So here I am in my late forties trying to peer into the next decade. My intellectual autobiography gives some clue what lies ahead. By the late 1960s my life ceased to be, or at least feel, so compartmentalized. It is likely that the integration of all my parts will not only continue but be more explicit. For instance, my personal, professional and political lives have become even more intertwined. Many times throughout this book I have mentioned the influence of the Boston Women's Health Book Collective. Over the years I have visited their center, critiqued their papers, worked with some as colleagues and others as students. It should come as no surprise (though again I didn't predict it) that in October of 1981 I married one of their members—Judy Norsigian

It is safe to assume that my future work and writing will be even more political, personal and public. The political aspect seems evident in my outside activities, as well as in my most recent and current writings. On the desk in front of me I have drafts of three papers— on sociocultural disincentives to rehabilitation (Zola 1983b), on the sociopolitical implications of genetic screening (Zola 1983c), and on the apolitical nature of medical sociology. To me, they are a personal announcement that the cutting edge of health-care analysis and action may well lie in issues related to gender and to disability. Both are areas where the role of biology and society intersect. Both are areas where academic interest has been spurred by the activism of the laity—be it the Women's Self Help Movement (Ruzek 1979) or the Independent Living Movement (Crewe and Zola 1983).

The more personal nature of my work is represented by at least two papers in this volume: "Structural Constraints . . . " and "When Getting into the Field . . ." Both in style and content I explicitly drew on my own life experience to make more general points. Yet these are but a beginning, as is clear from several recent pieces which draw heavily on a short time I spent living in Het Dorp, a Dutch village especially designed for the physically handicapped (Zola 1979b, 1981, 1982a,b., 1983b). From this experience, my counseling, my research, and my own life, I am writing about what it is like to have a disability in a society that shuns and avoids facing disabilities. Thus my writings, research, and academic involvements have also become increasingly focussed in the field of rehabilitation and disability.

Finally, I am no longer content to write for and reach only professional audiences. By keeping my writing relatively free of jargon and by publishing in a wide variety of professional journals, I tried to make my work more accessible. In the early 60s I ventured outside academia, and as head of a local civil rights group edited a weekly column for several suburban newspapers. It was called "Liberty's Ledger" and included reviews, critiques and updates on legislation and events of concern to the Civil Rights Movement (I returned to journalism with renewed personal and political relevance in the 1980s when I became the restaurant reviewer and cultural critic-at-large of *Together*, a statewide newsletter to organizations of and serving the disabled community). By the late 60s I was ready to bring this kind of writing experience into my academic work, but did not know how. Once more my personal background provided the link. As I explained in the essay introducing this collection, my social, ethnic, and economic background helped me understand the phenomenon of gambling. Two opportunities related to gambling came my way, and I grabbed them. The first was a request to review Marvin Scott's *The Racing Game* (1968a). My opening sentence began: "Heads apart three glistening thoroughbreds thunder toward the finishing line..." The horses were off and running, and so was I. A few months later opportunity knocked again. This time it was a call from the Canadian Broadcasting Company. They felt that my article "Observations on Gambling in a Lower Class Setting" (Zola 1963a) had great potentiality as a dramatized documentary. I felt flattered and gave them permission to do whatever they thought necessary. What they thought necessary was that I write the script. Ironically enough, if they had given me a year in which to complete it, I would have thought it too overwhelming a task and would have refused. As it was, they said I had only six weeks. In my personal philosophy of limited time and various commitments, this seemed a worthwhile investment; within a few weeks I produced a useable script (Zola 1968b). And so the door to a new world opened a crack.

To be honest, it has taken considerable effort to open it wide. My own training and background, detailed especially in "The Continuing Odyssey ..." (chapter 1) and "When Getting into the Field Means Getting Into Oneself" (chapter 17), led to considerable resistance. And though my subsequent papers in the 70s evince a looser, more open style, it was no easy step to the writing of *Missing Pieces* (Zola 1982a). At least part of the reason for the delay in publication (the experience in which *Missing Pieces* was based took place in 1972, but the book was not published until 1982) was my initial reluctance to share anything so personal as dealing with my own disability, as well as doubts whether anyone would care. One way this reluctance showed itself was in my writing the first version as an ethnography of the Village. Only after many drafts was I able finally "to surrender" (Wolff 1976) to the experience and write it in the format it needed— a first-person narrative. When this draft was completed in the late 1970s, I knew I was onto something.

I soon realized that there were many aspects of my personal as well as sociological life that could lend themselves to this format. And so in 1978 I began to turn some of these experiences into short stories. Since so much of my sociology is biographically influenced, it is logical that my biographical writing is sociologically influenced. Drawing on what I have known and seen, I am writing about social issues— about growing old, going crazy, being black, having a handicap, and being a man in relationships. So far only a few pieces have seen the light of day. One is a collection of stories written with my children (Zola, Zola, and Zola 1978). A second, "And The Children Shall Lead Us" (Zola 1979d), is the story of how my daughter explained to others what my physical disability was all about. A third is my most ambitious attempt. It is an anthology titled *Ordinary Lives: Voices of Disability and Disease* (Zola 1982c), and includes stories and poems by authors as varied as Alexander Solzhenitsyn and Adrienne Rich, as well as three stories of my own. Over the years I have written nearly thirty such stories, some of which are reaching the public in an unexpected manner. When I first wrote them, I needed a way of testing their impact. Instead of circulating them as I do drafts of papers, I decided to gather some audiences together and "tell them stories." What started out as a short excursion has now become a major activity. Now several times a year I find myself "performing" before very diverse audiences—from conventions to classes, from clubs to fundraising dinners. Aside from the pleasure the activity gives me, like the stories themselves, I have the chance to reach people who would not ordinarily read one of my articles or listen to any of my lectures.

I have come full circle. As Phil Slater observed, I'm spending my time in integration. And I follow my grandparents' advice: I never throw an experience away.

References

Abel-Smith, B. 1967. An International Study of Health Expenditures and Its Relevance for Health Planning. *Public Health Papers*, No. 32. Geneva: World Health Organization.

———. 1974. Value for Money in Health Services. *Social Security Bulletin* 37: 17-28.

Ackerknecht, E. H. 1942a. Problems of Primitive Medicine. *Bulletin of the History of Medicine* 11: 503-521.

———. 1942b. Primitive Medicine and Culture Pattern. *Bulletin of the History of Medicine* 12: 545-574.

———. 1947. The Role of Medical History in Medical Education. *Bulletin of the History of Medicine* 21: 135-145.

———. 1946. Natural Diseases and Rational Treatment in Primitive Medicine. *Bulletin of the History of Medicine* 19: 457-497.

———. 1947. The Role of Medical History in Medical Education. *Bulletin of the History of Medicine* 21: 135-145.

Adorno, T. W., Frenkel-Brunswik, E., Levinson, D. J., and Sanford, R. N. 1950. *The Authoritarian Personality*. New York: Harper.

Aitken-Swan, J., and Patterson, R. 1955. The Cancer Patient: Delay in Seeking Advice. *British Medical Journal* 1: 623-627.

Alinsky, S. 1967. The Poor and the Powerful. In *Poverty and Mental Health*, Psychiatric Research Report No. 21 of the American Psychiatric Association.

Allan, F. N., and Kaufman, M. 1948. Nervous Factors in General Practices. *Journal of the American Medical Association* 138: 1135-1138.

Allport, G. W. 1960. Scientific Models and Human Morals. In *Personality and Social Encounter*. Chapter 4. Boston: Beacon Press.

Almond, G. 1954. *The Appeals of Communism*. Princeton, New Jersey: Princeton University Press.

Alpert, J., Kosa, J., and Haggerty, R. J. 1967. A Month of Illness and Health Care Among Low-Income Families. *Public Health Report* 82: 705–713.

Altman, S. 1980. The Federal Government and Health Cost Containment: The Politics of a Non-Policy. *The Brandeis Quarterly* 1: 14–15.

Anderson, R. 1968. Behavioral Model of Families' Use of Health Services. Chicago: Center for Health Administration Studies Research, Series No. 25.

Apple, D. 1960. How Laymen Define Illness. *Journal of Health and Human Behavior* 1: 219–225.

Arendt, H. 1963. *Eichman in Jerusalem—A Report on the Banality of Evil*. New York: Viking Press.

Arensberg, C., and Kimball, S. T. 1948. *Family and Community in Ireland*. Cambridge: Harvard University Press.

Arms, S. 1975. *Immaculate Deception: A New Look at Women and Childbirth in America*. Boston: Houghton-Mifflin.

Back, K. W., Coker, R. E. Jr., Donnelly, T. G., and Phillips, B. S. 1958. Public Health as a Career of Medicine: Secondary Choice Within a Profession. *American Sociological Review* 23: 533–541.

Backett, E. M., Heady, J. A., and Evans, J. C. 1954. Studies of a General Practice, Doctor's Job in an Urban Area. *British Medical Journal* 1: 109–115.

Badgley, R. F., and Hetherington, R. W. 1961. Medical Care in Wheatville. *Canadian Journal of Public Health* 52: 512–517.

Baizerman, M., and Ellison, D. L. 1971. A Social Role Analysis of Senility. *The Gerontologist* 2: 163–170.

Bakan, D. 1969. *Disease, Pain and Sacrifice*. Chicago: University of Chicago Press.

Bakwin, H. 1945. Pseudodoxia Pediatrica. *New England Journal of Medicine* 232: 691–697.

Balint, M. 1957. *The Doctor, His Patient, and the Illness*. New York: International Universities Press.

———. 1961. The Pyramid and the Psychotherapeutic Relationship. *Lancet* 2: 1051–1054.

Balint, M., Hunt, J., Joyce, D., Marinker, M., and Woodcock, J. 1970. *Treatment or Diagnosis—A Study of Repeat Prescriptions in General Practice*. London: Tavistock Publications.

Barber, B. 1963. Some Problems in the Sociology of the Professions. *Daedalus* 92: 669–688.

Baric, L. 1969. Recognition of the 'At-risk' Role. *International Journal of Health Education* 12: 2–12.

Barrabee, P., and von Mering, O. 1953. Ethnic Variations in Mental Stress in Families with Psychotic Children. *Social Problems* 1: 48–53.

Barsky, A., and Gillum, R. 1974. The Diagnosis and Management of Patient

Non-Compliance. *Journal of the American Medical Association* 228: 1563–1567.

Bartlett, H. M. 1940. The Meaning of Illness to the Patient. In *Some Aspects of Social Casework in a Medical Setting*. Chapter 3. Chicago: G. Danta.

Barzini, L. 1965. *The Italians*. New York: Bantam.

Becker, H. S. 1963. *Outsiders*. Glencoe, Illinois: The Free Press.

————., ed. 1964. *The Other Side—Perspectives on Deviance*. Glencoe, Illinois: The Free Press.

Becker, H. S., Geer, B., Hughes, E. C., and Strauss, A. 1961. *Boys in White: Student Culture in Medical School*. Chicago: University of Chicago Press.

Becker, M. H., and Maiman, L. A. 1975. Sociobehavioral Determinants of Compliance with Health and Medical Care Recommendation. *Medical Care* 13: 10–24.

Behavioral Science and Medical Education, Report of a Conference. May 14–16, 1969. Boiling Springs, Pennsylvania. Bethesda, Maryland: National Institute on Child Health and Human Development.

Bender, M. 1964. Chiropractic, Osteopathy and Medicine: Patterns of Conflict in Three Health Professions. Senior Honors Thesis, Brandeis University.

Bender, M. 1965. Pathways to Chiropractice Utilization, Health Research and Training Program. New York: Columbia University School of Public Health and Administrative Medicine.

Benne, K. D., and Bennis, W. 1959. Role Confusion and Conflict in Nursing. *American Journal of Nursing* 59: 196–198.

Berger, P. L., and Luckman, T. 1966. *The Social Construction of Reality*. Garden City, New York: Doubleday.

Bertrand, A. L., and Storla, C. A., Jr. 1955. *Lay Knowledge and Opinion about Heart Disease*. New Orleans: Louisiana Heart Association.

Bittner, E. 1968. The Structure of Psychiatric Influence. *Mental Hygiene* 52: 423–430.

Blackwell, B. 1963. The Literature of Delay in Seeking Medical Care for Chronic Illness. Health Education Monographs, No. 16.

Blum, R. H. 1960. *The Management of the Doctor-Patient Relationship*. New York: McGraw-Hill.

Bodkin, N. J., Glaze, R. B., Gomez, G., Howlett, M. J., and Leigh, D. 1953. The General Practitioner and Psychiatrist, A Study in Cooperation. *British Medical Journal* 2: 723–725.

Boston Globe. February 27, 1979. Boston, Massachusetts. "MD Urges Health Tax," p. 21.

Boston Women's Health Book Collective. 1976. *Our Bodies, Ourselves*. rev. ed. New York: Simon and Schuster.

————. 1983. *Our Bodies, Ourselves*. rev. ed. New York: Simon and Schuster.

Boston Women's Health Collective. 1970. *Women and Their Bodies—A Course*. Boston: New England Free Press.

Bott, E. 1957. *Family and Social Network*. London: Tavistock Publications.

Bowe, F., Jacobi, J. E., and Wiseman, L. D. 1978. *Coalition Building*. Washington, D.C.: American Coalition of Citizens with Disabilities, Inc.

Bowen, E. S. 1964. *Return to Laughter*. Garden City: Anchor Books.

Bremer, J. 1951. A Social Psychiatric Investigation of a Small Community in Northern Norway. *Acta Psychiatrica Scandinavica* 62: 1–166.

Brodman, K., Erdmann, A. J., Longe, I., Gershenson, C. P., and Wolff, H. G. 1952. The Cornell Medical Index Health Questionnaire. IV. The Recognition of Emotional Disturbances in a General Hospital. *Journal of Clinical Psychology* 8: 289–293.

Brodman, K., Erdmann, A. J., Longe, I., Wolf, H. G., and Broadbent, T. H. 1951. The Cornell Medical Index Health Questionnaire, II. As a Diagnostic Instrument. *Journal of the American Medical Association* 140: 152–157.

Brotherston, J. H., and Chave, S. P. 1957. Incidence of Neurosis on a New Housing Estate. *British Journal of Preventive Social Medicine* 11: 196–202.

Brotherston, J. H., Chave, S. P., Cledwyn-Davies, A., Hunter, A. S., Lindsay, D. A., Scott, A., Thompson C. B., and Trimmer, E. J. 1956. General Practice on a New Housing Estate. *British Journal of Preventive Social Medicine* 10: 200–207.

Brown, A. C., and Fry, J. 1962. The Cornell Medical Index Health Questionnaire on the Identification of Neurotic Patients in General Practice. *Journal of Psychosomatic Research* 6: 185–190.

Bruch, H. 1957. *The Importance of Overweight*. New York: W. W. Norton.

Bucher, R. 1962. Pathology—A Study of Social Movements Within a Profession. *Social Problems* 10: 40–51.

Bucher, R., and Strauss, A. 1961. Professions in Process. *American Journal of Sociology* 66: 325–334.

Buck, R. W. 1930. Mental Hygiene in the General Clinics. *Bulletin of the Massachusetts Society of Mental Hygiene* 9:

Budd, M., Reiffen, B., Rodman, M., and Sherman, H. 1969. *A Program For An Ambulatory Care Service*. Massachusetts: MIT Lincoln Laboratory DOR-541.

Budd, M., Reiffen, B., and Sherman, H. 1970. *Manual for Development of Chronic Disease Management Protocols*. Massachusetts: MIT Lincoln Laboratory and Beth Israel Hospital DS-9516.

Burgess, A. 1976. *The Wanting Seed*. New York: W. W. Norton.

Burke, K. 1959. *Attitudes Toward History*. rev. ed. California: Hermes.

Butterfield, W. J. H. 1968. *Priorities in Medicine*. The Nuffield Provincial Hospital Trust.

Cabot, R. C. 1907. Suggestions for Reorganization of Hospital Out-Patient Departments with Special Reference to Improvement of Treatment. *Maryland Medical Journal* 50: 81.

Caplan, G. 1954. The Mental Hygiene Role of the Nurse in Maternal and Child Care. *Nursing Outlook* 2: 14–19.

Cargill, D. 1967. Self-Treatment as an Alternative to Rationing of Medical Care. *Lancet* 1: 1377–1378.

Carter, B. L. 1965. Non-Physiological Dimensions of Health and Illness. Waltham, Massachusetts: Brandeis University.

Cartwright, A. 1964. *Human Relations and Hospital Care.* London: Routledge and Kegan Paul.

———. 1969. Study of Medicines. Medical Care Research Unit. Bethnal Green, London: Institute of Community Studies.

Cassee, E. T. 1970. Deviant Illness Behavior: Patients of Mesmerists. *Social Science and Medicine* 3: 389-396.

Chapman, H. O. 1953. Neurosis in General Practice. *Medical Journal of Australia* 2: 407-415.

Chapman, W. P., and Jones, C. M. 1944. Variations in Cutaneous and Visceral Pain Sensitivity in Normal Subjects. *Journal of Clinical Investigation* 23: 81-91.

Chrisman, N. J., and Kleinman, A. 1980. Health Beliefs and Practices Among American Ethnic Groups. In *Harvard Encyclopedia of American Ethnic Groups*, edited by S. Thernstrom. Cambridge: Belknap Press.

Churchill, E. D. 1961. Medical Wants and Needs in Mature and Developing Nations. *Medical Times* 89: 1169-1176.

Clark, M. 1958. *Health in the Mexican-American Culture.* Berkeley: University of California Press.

Clarke, M. 1969. *Trouble with Feet.* Occasional Papers on Social Administration, No. 29. London: G. Bell and Sons, Ltd.

Clausen, J. A., and Radke Yarrow, M. 1955. The Impact of Mental Illness on the Family. *Journal of Social Issues* 11.

Clute, K. F. 1963. *The General Practitioner—A Study of Medical Education and Practice in Ontario and Nova Scotia.* Toronto: University of Toronto Press.

Cobb, S. 1963. Epidemiology of Rheumatoid Arthritis. *Academy of Medicine of New Jersey* 9: 52-60.

Coleman, J., Katz, E., and Menzel, H. 1966. *Medical Innovation: A Diffusion Study.* Indianapolis: Bobbs-Merrill.

Coleman, J. V. 1962. Mental Health, Patient Care and Medical Practice. *Integration of Mental Health Concepts with the Human Relations Professions*, Proceedings of a Lecture Series Sponsored by the Bank Street College of Education as a Memorial to Ruth Kotinsky. pp. 30-42.

College of General Practitioners. 1958. Psychological Medicine in General Practice. *British Medical Journal* 2:585-590.

Colvez, A., and Blanchet, M. 1981. Disability in the U.S. Population 1966-1976—Analysis of Reported Cases. *American Journal of Public Health* 71: 464-471.

Commission on Chronic Illness. 1957. *Chronic Illness in a Large City.* Cambridge: Harvard University Press.

Conrad, P. 1979. Types of Medical Social Control. *Sociology of Health and Illness* 1: 1-11.

Conrad, P., and Schneider, J. W. 1980. *Deviance and Medicalization: From Badness to Sickness.* St. Louis: C. V. Mosby.

Cooke, R. 1977. *Improving On Nature: The Brave New World of Genetic Engineering.* New York: Quandrangle/The New York Times Book Co.

Corwin, R. G., and Taves, M. J. 1963. Nursing and Other Health Professions. In *The Handbook of Medical Sociology*, edited by H. E. Freeman, S. Levine and L. G. Reeder. Englewood Cliffs, New Jersey: Prentice-Hall.

Coser, L. A. 1951. Some Aspects of Soviet Family Policy. *American Journal of Sociology* 56: 424–437.

———, ed. 1963. *Sociology Through Literature*. Englewood Cliffs, New Jersey: Prentice-Hall.

———. 1965. *Men of Ideas*. New York: The Free Press of Glencoe.

Crawford, J. C. C. 1954. A Study of Two Years' Work in Northern Ireland General Practice. *British Journal of Preventive Social Medicine* 8: 81–90.

Crawford R. 1977. You Are Dangerous to Your Health: The Ideology of Politics of Victim Blaming. *International Journal of Health Services* 7: 663–680.

———.1979. Individual Responsibility and Health Politics. In *Health Care in America: Essays in Social History*, edited by S. Reverby and O. Rosner. Philadelphia: Temple University Press.

———. 1980. Healthism and the Medicalization of Everyday Life. *International Journal of Health Services* 10: 365–388.

Cremerius, J., Ehlhardt, S., Hose, W., Oetze, M., and Seitz, W. 1954. Psychosomatics in the Framework of a Medical Polyclinic. *Münchener Medizinische Worchenschrift* 96: 185–187.

Crewe, N., and Zola, I. K., eds. 1983. *Independent Living in America*. San Francisco: Jossey-Bass.

Crick, F. April 19, 1971. Reported in *Time*. 97: 33–52 Man into Superman—The Promise and Peril of the New Genetics.

Crombie, D. L. 1957. The Prevalence of Psychiatric Illness in General Practice. *College of General Practice Journal Research Newsletter* 4: 218.

Crombie, D. L., and Cross, K. W. 1954. Use of a General Practitioner's Time. *British Journal of Preventive Social Medicine* 10: 141–144.

Croog, S. H. 1961. Ethnic Origins and Responses to Health Questionnaires. *Human Organization* 20: 65–69.

Culpan, R. H., Davis, B. M., and Oppenheim, A. N. 1960. Incidence of Psychiatric Illness Among Hospital Out-Patients, and Application of the Cornell Medical Index. *British Medical Journal* 1: 855–857.

Cumming, E., and Cumming, J. 1957. *Closed Ranks: An Experiment in Mental Health Education*. Cambridge: Harvard University Press.

Cunningham, C. 1970. Thai Injection Doctors. *Social Science and Medicine* 4: 1–24.

Curtius, F., and Adam, R. 1949. Concerning Psychogenic and Functional Illness in Internal Medicine (Frequency Conditions for Origin, Diagnosis and Treatment). *Deutsches Archiv Fuer Klinische Medizin* 196: 170.

Daily Camera of Boulder Colorado, June 21, 1980.

Davidowicz, L. S. 1976. *The War Against the Jews 1933–1945*. New York: Bantam.

Davis, F. 1963. *Passage Through Crisis*. Indianapolis: Bobbs-Merrill.

———, ed. 1966. *The Nursing Profession: Five Sociological Essays*. New York: Wiley.

Davis, M. S. 1966. Variations in Patients' Compliance with Doctors' Orders. *Journal of Medical Education* 41: 1937-1948.

Davis, M. S., and Eichhorn, R. 1963. Compliance with Medical Regimens. *Journal of Health and Human Behavior* 4: 240-249.

Derow, H. A. 1958. The Nephrotic Syndrome. *New England Journal of Medicine* 258: 124-129.

de Tocqueville, A. 1961. *Democracy in America*. Heffner, R. D., ed. New York: New American Library.

Devereux, G. 1956. Normal and Abnormal: The Key Problem of Psychiatric Anthropology. In *Some Uses of Anthropology: Theoretical and Applied*, edited by J. B. Gaeagrande and T. Galdwin. Brooklyn, New York: Theo Gaus.

DiCicco, L., and Apple, D. 1960. Health Needs and Opinions of Older Adults. In *Sociological Studies of Health and Sickness*, edited by D. Apple. New York: McGraw-Hill.

Dowling, H. F. 1963. How Do Practicing Physicians Use New Drugs? *Journal of the American Medical Association* 185: 233-236.

Dowling, H. F., and Shakow, D. 1952. Time Spent by Internists on Adult Health Education and Preventive Medicine. *Journal of the American Medical Association* 149: 628-631.

Downes, J., and Simon, K. 1954. Characteristics of Psychoneurotic Patients and Their Family as Revealed in a General Morbidity Study. *Millbank Memorial Fund Quarterly* 32: 42-64.

Drug Efficacy Study—Final Report to the Commissioner of Food and Drugs. 1969. Food and Drug Administration. Medical National Research Council. Washington, D.C.: National Academy of Science.

Dubos, R. 1961. *Mirage of Health*. Garden City, New York: Anchor.

———. 1965. *Man Adapting*. New Haven: Yale University Press.

———. 1968a. *Man, Medicine and Environment*. London: Pall Mall.

———. 1968b. *So Human an Animal*. New York: Scribner.

Duhl, L., ed. 1969. *The Urban Condition*. New York: Simon and Schuster.

Dunnell, K., and Cartwright, A. 1972. *Medicine Takers, Prescribers, and Hoarders*. London: Routledge and Kegan Paul.

Eaton, J., and Weil, R. J. 1955. *Culture and Mental Disorders*. Glencoe, Illinois: The Free Press.

Efron, D., ed. 1967. *Ethnopharmacologic Search for Psychoactive Drugs*. Proceedings of a Symposium held in San Francisco, California, January 28-30, 1967. Washington, D.C.: G. P. O., P. H. S. Publication No. 1645.

Ehrenreich, B., and Ehrenreich, J. 1975. Medicine and Social Control. In *Welfare in America: Controlling the Dangerous Classes*, edited by B. Mandell. Englewood Cliffs, New Jersey: Prentice-Hall.

Ehrenreich, B., and English, D. 1979. *For Her Own Good*. Garden City, New York: Anchor Books.

Ehrenreich, J., ed. 1978. *The Cultural Crisis of Modern Medicine*. New York: Monthly Review Press.

Eisenberg, L. 1966. Genetics and the Survival of the Unfit. *Harper's Magazine* 232: 53-58.

Elinson, J. 1963. Methods of Sociomedical Research. In *Handbook of Medical Sociology*, edited by H. E. Freeman, S. Levine and Leo G. Reeder. Englewood Cliffs, New Jersey: Prentice-Hall.

Elling, R. H. 1976. Political Influences on the Methods of Cross-National Sociomedical Research. In *Methods of Cross-National Sociomedical Research*, edited by M. Pflanz and E. Schach. Stuttgart, West Germany: Thieme.

———. 1978. To Strike a Balance. In *Medical Sociologists at Work*, edited by Ray H. Elling and Magdalena Sokolowska. New Brunswick, New Jersey: Transaction Books.

Elling, R. H., and Sokolowska, M. 1978. *Medical Sociologists at Work*. New Brunswick, New Jersey: Transaction Books.

Ellul, J. 1981. *The Technological Systems*. Translated by Joachim Neugrosch. New York: Continuum Publishing.

Emerson, J. P. 1970. Behavior in Private Places: Definitions of Reality in Gynecological Examinations. In *Recent Sociology*, edited by J. P. Dreitzel. London: MacMillan Company.

Erikson, E. H. 1964. *Insight and Responsibility*. New York: W. W. Norton.

Erikson, K. 1962. Notes on the Sociology of Deviance. *Social Problems* 9: 307-314.

———. 1966. *Wayward Puritans—A Study in the Sociology of Deviance*. New York: John Wiley and Sons.

Etang. H. L. 1970. *The Pathology of Leadership*. New York: Hawthorne Books.

Etzioni, A. 1973. *Genetic Fix*. New York: Macmillan.

Fantl, B., and Schiro, J. 1959. Cultural Variables in the Behavior Patterns and Symptom Formation of 15 Irish and 15 Italian Female Schizophrenics. *International Journal of Social Psychiatry* 4: 245-253.

Feldman, J. J. 1960. The Household Interview Survey as a Technique for the collection of Morbidity Data. *Journal of Chronic Diseases* 11: 535-537.

Field M. 1957. *Doctor and Patient in Soviet Russia*. Cambridge, Massachusetts: Harvard University Press.

Finlay, B., Gillison, K., Hart, D., Mason R. W. T., Mond, N. C., Page, L., and O'Neill, D. 1954. Stress and Distress in General Practice. *Practitioner* 172: 183-196.

Ford, C., and Beach F. 1951. *Patterns of Sexual Behavior*. New York: Ace Books.

Foucault, M. 1965. *Madness and Civilization: A History of Insanity in the Age of Reason*. New York: Pantheon.

Fox, R. 1977. The Medicalization and Demedicalization of American Society. *Daedalus* 106: 9-22.

Fox, T. F. 1960. The Personal Doctor and his Relation to the Hospital. *Lancet* 1: 743-760.

Francis, F., Korsch, B. M., and Morris, M.J. 1969. Gaps in Doctor-Patient Communication: Patients' Response to Medical Advice. *New England Journal of Medicine* 280: 535-540.

Fraser, R. 1947. *Incidence of Neurosis Among Factory Workers*. Medical Research Council Industrial Health Board, Rep. No. 90. H.M.S.O. London.

Freeman, N. 1967. *The Social Nature of Psychological Research*. New York: Basic Books.

Freidson, E. 1959. Specialties Without Roots: The Utilization of New Services. *Human Organization* 18: 112–116.

———. 1960. Client Control and Medical Practice. *American Journal of Sociology* 65: 374–382.

———. 1961. *Patients' Views of Medical Practice*. New York: Russell Sage.

———. 1961–62. The Sociology of Medicine: A Trend Report and Bibliography. *Current Sociology* 10–11: 123–192.

———. 1970a. *Profession of Medicine*. New York: Dodd-Mead.

———. 1970b. *Professional Dominance*. New York: Atherton.

Fried, M. 1973. *The World of the Urban Working Class*. Cambridge: Harvard University Press.

Friedan, B. 1963. *The Feminine Mystique*. New York: Dell.

Fry, J. 1952. A Year of General Practice, a Study of Morbidity. *British Medical Journal* 2: 249–252.

———. 1954. The Psychoneurotic in General Practice. *Medical World* 80: 657–666.

———. 1957. Five Years of General Practice, a Study in Simple Epidemiology. *British Medical Journal* 2: 1453–1457.

Galdston, I., ed. 1956. Salerno and the Atom. In *Medicine in a Changing Society*. New York: International Universities Press.

———. 1958. The Birth and Death of Specialties. *Journal of the American Medical Association* 167: 2056–2057.

———. 1959. The Natural History of Specialism in Medicine. *Journal of the American Medical Association* 170: 294–297.

Gans, H. J. 1962. *The Urban Villagers*. New York: Free Press.

Garland, L. H. 1959. Studies on the Accuracy of Diagnostic Procedures. *American Journal of Roentgenology, Radium Therapy and Nuclear Medicine* 82: 25–38.

General Electric Company v. Gilbert et al., 429 U.S. 125 (1976).

Gibson, C. D., and Kramer B. M. 1965. "Site of Care in Medical Practice." *Medical Care.* 3: 14–17.

Gilbert, G. M. 1950. *The Psychology of Dictatorship*. New York: Ronald.

Gilliam, S. 1961. *The Study of the Patterns of People Seeking Medical Care*. Research in progress. Medical and Health Research Association of New York City.

Giordano, J. 1973. *Ethnicity and Mental Health*. New York: Institute on Pluralism and Group Identity.

Giordano, J., and Giordano, G. P. 1977. *The Ethno-Cultural Factor in Mental Health. A Literature Review and Bibliography*. New York: Institute on Pluralism and Group Identity.

Glazer, N., and Moynihan, D. P. 1963. *Beyond the Melting Pot*. Cambridge: MIT Press.

Goddard, J. L. August 7, 1966. Quoted in the *Boston Globe*. "FDA Problem-Learning, Happiness Drug Goal" p. 33.

Goffman, E. 1961. The Medical Model and Mental Hospitalization. In *Asylums*. New York: Anchor.

———. 1963. *Stigma—Notes on the Management of Spoiled Identity*. Englewood

Cliffs, New Jersey: Prentice-Hall.

Goldzieher, J. W. 1969. Quoted in McGrady, P. *Youth Doctors*. New York: Ace. p. 311.

Goode, W. J. 1960. Encroachment, Charlatanism, and the Emerging Profession; Psychology, Sociology and Medicine. *American Sociological Review* 25: 902-914.

Gordon, G. 1966. *Role Theory and Illness*. New Haven: College and University Press.

Gordon, R. E., and Gordon, K. K. 1958. Psychiatric Problems of a Rapidly Growing Suburb. *Archives of Neurology and Psychiatry* 79: 543-548.

Gordon, R. E., Gordon, K. K., and Gunther, M. 1962 *The Split-Level Trap*. New York: Dell.

Goslings, W. R. O., Valkenburg, H. A., Boots, A. W., and Lorier, J. C. 1963. Attack Rates of Streptococcal Pharyngitis, Rheumatic Fever and Glomeralonephritis in the General Population. I. A Controlled Pilot Study of Streptococcal Pharyngitis in One Village. *New England Journal of Medicine* 268: 687-694.

Goulston, K., and Cooke, A. R. 1968. Alcohol, Aspirin, and Gastro-intestinal Bleeding. *British Medical Journal* 4: 664-665.

Graham, S. 1956. Ethnic Background and Illness in a Pennsylvania County. *Social Problems* 4: 76-81.

Grant, M. 1978. Genetic Control and the Law. *Medical Trial Technique Quarterly* 24: 306-327.

Grobin, W. 1958. Personal Experience in the Practice of Internal Medicine. *Canadian Medical Association Journal* 79: 259-265.

Gruenberg, E. M. 1963. A Review of Mental Health in the Metropolis; the Midtown Manhattan Study. *Millbank Memorial Fund Quarterly* 41: 77-94.

Gurin, G., Veroff, J., and Feld, S. 1960. *Americans View Their Mental Health*. New York: Basic Books.

Habenstein, R. W., and Christ, E. A. 1963. *Professionalizer, Traditionalizer, and Utilizer*. 2nd ed. Columbia, Missouri: University of Missouri Press.

Hamman, L. 1939. Relationship of Psychiatry to Internal Medicine. *Mental Hygiene* 23: 177-189.

Hammond, P. E., ed. 1964. *Sociologists at Work*. New York: Basic Books.

Handlin, O. 1959a. *Boston's Immigrants*. Cambridge, Massachusetts: Harvard University Press.

Handlin, O., ed. 1959b. *Immigration as a Factor in American History*. Englewood Cliffs, New Jersey: Prentice-Hall.

Hanlon, J. J. 1960. *Principles of Public Health Administration*. St. Louis: Mosby. Esp. 21-35, 673-686.

Hardy, T. D., Wolff, H. G., and Goodell, H. 1952. *Pain Sensations and Reactions*. Baltimore: Williams and Wilkins.

Hare, A. P. 1967. *Handbook of Small Group Research*. New York: Free Press of Glencoe.

Harley, G. W. 1941. *Native African Medicine*. Cambridge, Massachusetts: Harvard University Press.

Harrington, M. 1962. *The Other America: Poverty in the United States*. New York: MacMillan.

Hartwell, E. A. 1967. Cultural Assimilation, Social Mobility, and Persistence of Cognitive Style. Unpublished Ph.D. dissertation. Brandeis University.

Hassinger, E. W. and McNamara, R. L. 1958. Relationships of the Public to Physicians in a Rural Setting. *Agricultural Experiment Station Research Bulletin* No. 653 Columbia, Missouri: University of Missouri Press.

———. 1959. Family Health Practices Among Open-Country People in South Missouri County. *Agricultural Experiment Station Research Bulletin* No. 699 Columbia, Missouri: University of Missouri Press.

———. 1960. The Families, Their Physicians, Their Health Behavior in a Northeast Missouri County. *Agricultural Experiment Station Research Bulletin* No. 754 Columbia, Missouri: University of Missouri Press.

Health Care Financing Administration. 1979. *Health Care Financing Review*. Winter issue.

Health Policy Advisory Committee., ed. 1971. *American Health Empire: Power, Profits, Politics*. New York: Random House.

Heiman, M. 1959. Separation From a Love Object as an Etiological Factor in Functional Uterine Bleeding. *Journal of the Mount Sinai Hospital* 26: 56-62.

Henderson, P. 1971. Some Continuing Health Problems of School Children and Young People and Their Implications for a Child and Youth Health Service. *Public Health London* 85: 58-66.

Hern, W. M. 1971. Is Pregnancy Really Normal? *Family Planning Perspectives* 3: 5-10.

Hinkle, L. E., Jr., Redmont, R., Plummer, N., and Wolff, H. G. 1960. An Examination of the Relation Between Symptoms, Disability, and Serious Illness in Two Homogeneous Groups of Men and Women. *American Journal of Public Health* 50: 1327-1336.

Hinkle, L. E., Jr., and Wolff, H. G. 1958. Ecologic Investigations of the Relationship Between Illness, Life Experiences and the Social Environment. *Annals of Internal Medicine* 49: 1373-1388.

Hobbes, T. 1950. *Leviathan*. New York: Dutton.

Hobsbaum, E. J. 1962. *The Age of Revolution—Europe 1789–1848*. London: Weidenfeld and Nicolson.

Hochbaum, G. 1958. *Public Participation in Medical Screening Programs*. Public Health Services Publication No. 572. Washington, D.C.: G.P.O.

Hodgkin, K. 1970. The General Practitioner and Industrial Absenteeism. *Proceedings of the Royal Society of Medicine* 63: 1131-1195.

Hollingshead, A. B., and Redlich, F. C. 1958. *Social Class and Mental Illness*. New York: Wiley and Sons.

Hopkins, P. 1955. The General Practitioner and the Psychosomatic Approach. In *Modern Trends in Psychosomatic Medicine*, edited by D. O'Neill. New York: D. Hoeber.

———. 1956. Psychotherapy in General Practice. *Lancet* 2: 455-457

———. 1960. Psychiatry in General Medicine. *Postgraduate Medical Journal*

36: 323–330.

Horder, J., and Horder, E. 1954. Illness in General Practice. *Practitioner* 173: 177–187.

Hordern, A. 1971. *Legal Abortion: The English Experience*. Oxford, England: Pergamon.

Howard, L. M. 1972. Three Key Dilemmas in International Health. *American Journal of Public Health* 62: 73–78.

Hughes, C. C. 1968. Ethnomedicine. *International Encyclopedia of the Social Sciences*. Section I. New York: MacMillan.

Hughes, E. C. 1943. *French Canada in Transition*. Chicago: University of Chicago Press.

———. 1958. *Men and Their Work*. New York: Free Press.

———. 1961. *Students' Culture and Perspectives*. Lawrence, Kansas: University of Kansas School of Law.

———. 1963. Professions. *Daedalus* 92: 655–668.

Hughes, E. C., Hughes, H. M., and Deutscher, I. 1958. *Twenty Thousand Nurses Tell Their Story*. Philadelphia: Lippincott.

Huntley, R. R. 1963. Family Practice—An Impending Crisis. Epidemiology of Family Practice. *Journal of the American Medical Association* 185: 175–178.

Illich, I. 1975. *Medical Nemesis: The Expropriation of Health*. London: Calder and Boyars.

Illich, I., Zola, I. K., McKnight, J., Caplan, J., and Shaiken, H. 1977. *Disabling Professions*. London: Marion Boyars.

International Herald Tribune. March 8, 1971. Paris, France.

Janis, I. 1958. *Psychological Stress—Psychoanalytic and Behavioral Studies of Surgical Patients*. New York: Wiley and Sons.

Jansen, M. G. 1954. An Approach to Neurosis in General Practice. *Medical Journal of Australia* 2: 422–428.

Jefferys, M., Brotherston, J. H. F., and Cartwright, A. 1960. Consumption of Medicines on a Working-Class Housing Estate. *British Journal of Preventive Social Medicine* 14: 64–76.

Johnson, A. S. 1956. Changing Patterns of Medical Practice. *New England Journal of Medicine* 254: 648–651.

Jones, H. B. 1960. The Relation of Human Health to Age, Place and Time. In *Handbook of Aging and the Individual*, edited by J. E. Birren. Chicago: University of Chicago Press.

Kadushin, C. 1958. Individual Decisions to Undertake Psychotherapy. *Advancement of Science Quarterly* 3: 379–411.

———. 1966. The Friends and Supporters of Psychotherapy: On Social Circles in Urban Life. *American Sociological Review* 31: 786–802.

———. 1969. *Why People Go to Psychiatrists*. New York: Atherton Press.

Kahn, R. L., and Cannell, C. F. 1957. *The Dynamics of Interviewing*. New York: Wiley and Sons.

Kahn, R. L., Pollack, M., and Fink, M. 1959. Socio-psychologic Aspects of Psychiatric Treatment in a Voluntary Mental Hospital. *A.M.A. Archives of General Psychiatry* 1: 565–574.

Kasl, S. V., and Cobb, S. 1964. Some Psychosocial Factors Associated with Illness Behavior and Selected Illnesses. *Journal of Chronic Diseases* 17: 325-345.

————. 1966. Health Behavior, Illness Behavior, and Sick Role Behavior. *Archives of Environmental Health* 12: 246-266, 531-541.

Katz, A. H., and Bender, E. I. 1976. Self Help Groups in Western Society, History and Prospects. *Journal of Applied Behavioral Science* 12: 265-282.

Kaufman, M. R., and Bernstein, S. 1957. Psychiatric Evaluation of Problem Patient; Study of a Thousand Cases From a Consultation Service. *Journal of the American Medical Association* 163: 108-111.

Kegeles, S. S. 1963. Why People Seek Dental Care. *Journal of Health and Human Behavior* 4: 166-173.

Kellner, R. 1963. *Family Ill Health*. London: Tavistock Publications.

Kessel, N., and Shepherd, M. 1965. The Health and Attitudes of People Who Seldom Consult a Doctor. *Medical Care* 3: 6-10.

Kessel, W. I. N. 1960. Psychiatric Morbidity in a London General Practice. *British Journal of Preventive Social Medicine* 14: 16-22.

Kiev, A. ed. 1964. *Magic, Faith, and Healing*. New York: Free Press of Glencoe.

————. 1968. *Curanderismo: Mexican-American Folk Psychiatry*. New York: Free Press of Glencoe.

————. 1972. *Transcultural Psychiatry*. New York: Free Press of Glencoe.

Kinsey, A. C., Pomeroy, W. B., and Martin, C. C. 1953. *Sexual Behavior in the Human Male*. Philadelphia: W. B. Saunders.

Kitsuse, J. 1962. Societal Reaction to Deviance: Problems of Theory and Method. *Social Problems* 9: 247-256.

Kleinman, A. 1973. Toward a Comparative Study of Medical Systems. *Science, Medicine, and Man* 1: 55-65.

————. 1977. Lessons from a Clinical Approach to Medical Anthropological Research. *Medical Anthropology Newsletter* 8: 11-15.

Kleinman, A., Eisenberg, L., and Good, B. 1978. Culture, Illness and Care: Clinical Lessons from Anthropological and Cross-cultural Research. *Annals of Internal Medicine* 88: 251-258.

Kluckhohn, F. R. 1958. Dominant and Variant Value Orientations. In *Personality in Nature, Society and Culture*, edited by C. Kluckhohn, H. A. Murray and D. M. Schneider. New York: Alfred Knopf.

Knapp, D. A. 1968. Self-Medication and Community Health. College of Pharmacy. Ohio State University. Columbus, Ohio.

Knapp, D. A., Knapp, D. E., and Engle, J. F. 1966. The Public, the Pharmacist, and Self-Medication. *Journal of American Pharmaceutical Association* 6: 460-462.

Knowles, J., ed. 1977. *Doing Better and Feeling Worse: Health in the United States*. New York: W. W. Norton.

Koos, E. 1954. *The Health of Regionsville*. New York: Columbia University Press.

————. 1955. Metropolis—What City People Think of Their Medical Services. *American Journal of Public Health* 45: 1551-1557.

Korsch, B. M., Gozzi, E. K., and Francis, V. 1969. Gaps in Doctor Patient Communication: Doctor-Patient Interaction and Patient Satisfaction. *Pediatrics* 42: 855-871.

Kosa, J., Alpert, J., and Haggerty, R. J. 1967. On the Reliability of Family Health Information. *Social Science and Medicine* 1: 165-181.

Kosa, J., Alpert, J., Pickering, R., and Haggerty, R. J. 1965. Crisis and Family Life: A Re-Examination of Concepts. *The Wisconsin Sociologist* 4: 11-19.

Kosa, J., Antonovsky, A., and Zola, I. K., eds. 1969. *Poverty and Health—A Sociological Analysis*. Cambridge, Massachusetts: Harvard University Press.

Kosa, J. and Zola, I. K. ed. 1975. *Poverty and Health: A Sociological Analysis*. Cambridge, Massachusetts: Harvard University Press.

Kozol, J. 1967. *Death at an Early Age: The Destruction of the Health and Minds of Negro Children in the Boston Public Schools*. New York: Houghton-Mifflin.

Krause, E. 1977. *Power and Illness*. New York: Elsevier.

————. 1982. Social Crises and the Future of the Disabled. In *Disabled People As Second-Class Citizens*, edited by M. Eisenberg. New York: Springer.

Krietman, N., Sainsbury, P., Morrissey, J., Towers, J., and Scrivener, J. 1961. The Reliability of Psychiatric Assessment: An Analysis. *Journal of Mental Science* 107: 876-886.

Kruse, A. 1957. Implications for Voluntary Agencies. *The Social Welfare Forum*. National Conference on Social Welfare. New York: Columbia University Press.

Kuhn, T. 1964. *The Structure of Scientific Revolutions*. Chicago: University of Chicago Press.

Kutner, B., and Gordon, G. 1961. Seeking Aid for Cancer. *Journal of Health and Human Behavior* 2: 171-178.

Kutner, B., Makover, H. B., and Oppenheim, A. 1958. Delay in the Diagnosis and Treatment of Cancer. *Journal of Chronic Diseases* 7: 95-120.

Lambert, C., and Freeman, H. E. 1967. *The Clinic Habit*. New Haven, Connecticut: College and University Press.

Lasagna, L. 1968. *Life, Death and the Doctor*. New York: Alfred Knopf.

Lea Associates. 1960. *Study of General Practice. National Disease and Therapeutic Index*. Flourtown, Pennsylvania.

Leach, J. E., and Robbins, G. F. 1947. Delay in the Diagnosis of Cancer. *Journal of the American Medical Association* 135: 5-8.

Lee, J. A. H. 1964. Prescribing and Other Aspects of General Practice in the Towns. *Proceedings of the Royal Society of Medicine* 57: 1041.

Lee, J. A. H., Draper, P. A., and Weatherall, M. 1965. Primary Medical Care: Prescribing in Three English Towns. *Millbank Memorial Fund Quarterly* 43: 285-290.

Lehrer, T. 1965 Wernher Von Braun. *That Was the Year That Was—1965*. Reprise- 6179.

Leifer, R. 1969. *In the Name of Mental Health: The Social Functions of Psychiatry*. New York: Science House.

Leighton, A. H. 1959. *My Name is Legion—Foundations for a Theory of Man in Relation to Culture*. New York: Basic Books.

Leighton, D. C., Harding, J. S., Macklin, D. B., MacMillan, A. M., and Leighton, A. H. 1963. *The Character of Danger.* New York: Basic Books.

Lemert, E. M. 1951. *Social Pathology.* New York: McGraw-Hill.

Lemkau, P., Tietze, C., and Cooper, M. 1943. A Survey of Statistical Studies on the Prevalence and Incidence of Mental Disorder in Sample Populations. *Public Health Reports.* 58: 1909-1927.

LeShan, L. 1959. Psychological States as Factors in the Development of Malignant Disease: A Critical Review. *Journal of the National Cancer Institute* 22: 1-18.

Levy, H. 1978. The Military Medicinemen. In *The Cultural Crisis of Modern Medicine*, edited by J. Ehrenreich. New York: Monthly Review Press.

Lewis, A. 1953. Health as a Social Concept. *British Journal of Sociology* 4: 109-124.

Lewis, C. S. 1947. *The Abolition of Man.* New York: Macmillan.

Lewis, D. A. 1976. Insuring Women's Health. *Social Policy* 7: 19-25.

Lewis, K. K. 1959. Role of Depression in the Production of Illness in Pernicious Anemia. *Psychosomatic Medicine* 21: 23-27.

Lichtner, S., and Pflanz, M. 1971. Appendectomy in the Federal Republic of Germany: Epidemiology and Medical Care Patterns. *Medical Care* 9: 311-330.

Lindemann, E. 1956. The Meaning of Crisis in Individual and Family Living. *Teachers College Record* 57: 310-315.

———. 1979. *Beyond Grief: Studies in Crisis Intervention.* New York: Jason Aronson.

Linn, E. L. 1961. Tolerance of Deviant Behavior-Agents, Timing and Events Leading to Mental Hospitalization. *Human Organization* 20: 92-98.

Livni, S. 1948. Reflections on the Psychosomatic Approach. *South African Medical Journal* 22: 56-63.

Logan, W. P. D. 1953. *General Practitioner's Records, An Analysis of Clinical Records of Eight Practices During the Period April 1951 to March 1952.* London: H.M.S.O.

———. 1954. Morbidity Statistics From General Practice. *Practitioner* 173: 188-194.

Logan, W. P. D. and Cushion, A. A. 1958. *Morbidity Statistics from General Practice.* Vol. 1 No. 14 Studies of Medical and Population Subjects, London: H.M.S.O.

McCord, W., McCord, J., and Zola, I. K. 1959. *Origins of Crime: A New Evaluation of the Cambridge-Somerville Youth Study.* New York: Columbia University Press.

McGrady, P. M., Jr. 1969. *The Youth Doctors.* New York: Ace Publications.

McGregor, R. M. 1950. The Work of a Family Doctor. *Edinburgh Medical Journal* 57: 433-453.

McKinlay, J. B. 1972. Some Approaches and Problems in the Study of the Use of Health Services: An Overview. *Journal of Health and Social Behavior* 13: 115-152.

———. 1981. A Case for Refocusing Upstream: The Political Economy of Illness. In *The Sociology of Health and Illness*, edited by P. Conrad and R.

Kern. New York: St. Martin's Press.

McKinlay, J. B., and McKinlay, S. M. 1977. The Questionable Contribution of Medical Measures to the Decline of Mortality in the United States in the Twentieth Century. *Millbank Memorial Fund Quarterly/Health and Society* 55: 405-528.

———. 1980. A Refutation of the Thesis the Health of the Nation is Improving. Unpublished manuscript.

Magraw, R. M. 1959. Psychosomatic Medicine and the Diagnostic Process. *Postgraduate Medicine* 25: 639-645.

———. 1966. *Ferment in Medicine—A Study of the Essence of Medical Practice and of its New Dilemmas.* New York: Saunders.

Magraw, R. M., and Dulit, E. P. 1958. The Patient's Presenting Complaint—Signpost or Goal? *University of Minnesota Medical Bulletin* 29: 329-340.

Mair, L. 1969. *Witchcraft*. London: World University Library.

Mannucio, M., Friedman, S. M., and Kaufman, M. R. 1961. Survey of Patients Who Have Been Attending Non-Psychiatric Outpatient Department Services for Ten Years or Longer. *Journal of the Mount Sinai Hospital* 28: 32-52.

Marmor, S. 1958. The Psychodynamics of Realistic Worry. In *Psychoanalysis and Social Sciences*, edited by W. Muensterberger and S. Axelrod. Vol. 5 New York: International University Press.

Martin, J. P. 1957. *Social Aspects of Prescribing*. London: Heinemann.

Matza, D. 1969. *Becoming Deviant*. Englewood Cliffs, New Jersey: Prentice Hall.

Mauksch, H. O. 1966. The Organizational Context of Nursing Practice. In *The Nursing Profession*, edited by F. Davis. New York: Wiley and Sons.

Mead, M. 1928. *Coming of Age in Samoa*. New York: Morrow.

———. 1930. *Growing Up in New Guinea*. New York: Morrow.

———. 1935. *Sexual Temperament in Three Societies*. New York: Morrow.

———. 1949. *Male and Female*. New York: Morrow.

———. 1950. *Sex and Temperament in Three Primitive Societies*. New York: Mentor.

———. 1972. *Blackberry Winter*. New York: Morrow.

Meador, C. K. 1965. The Art and Science of Non-Disease. *New England Journal of Medicine* 272: 92-95.

Mechanic, D. 1959. Illness and Social Disability: Some Problems in Analysis. *Pacific Sociological Review* 2: 37-41.

———. 1962. The Concept of Illness Behavior. *Journal of Chronic Diseases* 15:189-194.

———. 1964. The Influence of Mothers on Their Children's Health Attitudes and Behavior. *Pediatrics* 33: 444-453.

———. 1966. The Sociology of Medicine: Viewpoints and Perspectives. *Journal of Health and Human Behavior* 7: 237-248.

———. 1968. *Medical Sociology*. New York: Free Press.

Mechanic, D., and Volkart, E. H. 1960. Illness Behavior and Medical Diagnosis. *Journal of Health and Human Behavior* 1: 86-94.

————. 1961. Stress, Illness Behavior and the Sick Role. *American Sociological Review* 26: 51–58.

Meigs, J. W. 1961. Occupational Medicine. *New England Journal of Medicine* 264: 861–867.

Melzack, R. 1961. The Perception of Pain. *Scientific American* 204: 41–49.

Merton, R. K., Reader, G., and Kendall, Pa. eds. 1957. *The Student Physician*. Cambridge, Massachusetts: Harvard University Press.

Mestitz, P. 1957. A Series of 1817 Patients Seen in a Casualty Department. *British Medical Journal* 2: 1108–1109.

Metchnikoff, I. 1969. Quoted in McGrady, P. *The Youth Doctors*. New York: Ace Publications.

Mills, C. W. 1942. The Professional Ideology of Social Pathologists. *American Journal of Sociology* 49: 165–180.

————. 1959. *The Sociological Imagination*. New York: Oxford University Press.

Mills, D. 1964. *Study of Chiropractors, Osteopaths and Naturopaths in Canada*. Canada: Royal Commission on Health Services.

Mintz, M. 1967. *By Prescription Only*. Boston: Beacon Press.

Mishler, E. G., and Waxler, N. E. 1963. Decision Processes in Psychiatric Hospitalization. *American Sociological Review* 28: 576–87.

Moersch, F. P. 1932. Psychiatry in Medicine. *American Journal of Psychiatry* 11: 831–843.

Monks, J. P., and Heath, C. W. 1954. A Classification of Academic, Social and Personal Problems for Use in a College Health Department. *Student Medicine* 2: 44–62.

Morris, J. B. 1967. *Uses of Epidemiology*. 2nd ed. Edinburgh: E&S Livingstone.

Morse, A. D. 1968. *While Six Million Died—A Chronicle of American Apathy*. New York: Ace Publications.

Moser, R. H. 1964. *Diseases of Medical Progress*. Springfield, Illinois: C. C. Thomas.

Murphree, A. 1965. Folk Medicine in Florida: Remedies Using Plants. *The Florida Anthropologist* 18: 175–185.

Murphy, F. J., Shirley, M. M., and Witmer, H. L. 1946. The Incidence of Hidden Deliquency. *American Journal of Orthopsychiatry* 16: 686–696.

Myers, G. S. 1968. Quoted in Lasagna, L., *Life, Death and the Doctor*. New York: Alfred Knopf.

Myrdal, G. 1944. *An American Dilemma—The Negro Problem and Modern Democracy*. New York: Harper & Brothers.

National Institute of General Medical Sciences. National Institutes of Health. 1975. What Are the Facts about Genetic Disease? Washington, D.C.: HEW Pub. NIH 75–370.

Navarro, V. 1976. *Medicine Under Capitalism* New York: Prodist.

New York Times. February 25, 1968. Another Opinion. P. E13.

New York Times Magazine. June 1, 1969. There's a New-Time Religion on Campus. pp. 14–28.

Newell, K. W., ed. 1975. *Health by the People*. Geneva: World Health Organization.

Newsweek. October 16, 1978. Our Selfish Genes. pp. 118–123.

———. August 20, 1979. The Secrets of the Cell. pp. 48–54.

———. May 18, 1981. The New Gene Doctors. pp. 120–124.

Norman, J. C. 1969. Medicine in the Ghetto. *New England Journal of Medicine* 281: 1271–1275.

Notman, R. 1956–1957. Demographic Patterns of Hospital Use as a Basis for Estimating Needs and Utilization. Unpublished report. Boston State Hospital.

Nourse, A. 1974. *The Bladerunner*. New York: Ballantine Books.

Nunnally, J. C. 1961. *Popular Conceptions of Mental Health*. New York: Holt, Rinehart & Winston.

Oakley, A. 1974a. *Housewife*. London: Allen Lane.

———. 1974b. *The Sociology of Housework*. London: Martin Robertson.

———. 1979. *Becoming a Mother*. New York: Schocken Books.

———. 1980. *Women Confined: Towards a Sociology of Childbirth*. New York: Schocken Books.

Office of Health Economics. 1968. *Without Prescription—A Study of the Role of Self-Medication*, No. 27. London: Office of Health Economics.

Office of Home Economics. 1971. *Off Sick*. Lutton, England: White Crescent Press.

Olin, H. S., and Hackett, T. P. 1964. The Denial of Chest Pain in 32 Patients with Acute Myocardial Infarction. *Journal of the American Medical Association* 190: 977–981.

O'Neill, D. 1959. Therapy of Stress Disorders: Its Scope and Limits. *Lancet* 2: 301–303.

Opler, M. K., ed. 1959. *Culture and Mental Health*. New York: Macmillan.

———. 1967. *Culture and Social Psychiatry*. New York: Atherton Press.

———., and Singer, J. L. 1956. Ethnic Differences in Behavior and Psychopathology: Italian and Irish. *International Journal of Social Psychiatry* 2: 11–22.

Orzack, L. H. 1961. Issues Underlying Role Dilemmas in Professionals. In *Emotional Factors in Public Health Nursing*, edited by A. B. Abromavits. Madison, Wisconsin: University of Wisconsin Press.

Pack, G. T., and Gallo, J. S. 1938. The Culpability for Delay in the Treatment of Cancer. *American Journal of Cancer* 33: 443–461.

Parsons, A. 1960. Family Dynamics in Southern Italian Schizophrenics. *Archives of General Psychiatry* 3: 507–518.

———. 1961. Patriarchal and Matriarchal Authority in the Neapolitan Slum. *Psychiatry* 24: 109–121.

Parsons, T. 1951a. Social Structure and Dynamic Process: The Case of Modern Medical Practice. *The Social System*. Chapter 10. Glencoe, Illinois: The Free Press.

———. 1951b. *The Social System*. Glencoe, Illinois: The Free Press.

———. 1951c. Illness and the Role of the Physician, A Sociological Perspective. *American Journal of Orthopsychiatry* 21: 452–460.

————. 1954. *Essays in Sociological Theory*. Glencoe, Illinois: The Free Press.

————. 1958. Definition of Health and Illness in the Light of American Values and Social Structure. In E. G. Jaco ed., *Patients, Physicians and Illness*. Glencoe, Illinois: Free Press.

Parsons, T., Bales, R. F., and Shils, E. A. 1953. *Working Papers in the Theory of Action*. Glencoe, Illinois: The Free Press.

Paul, B., ed. 1955. *Health, Culture and Community*. New York: Russell Sage.

Paulett, J. D. 1956. Neurotic Ill Health, a Study of General Practice. *Lancet* 2: 37-38.

Pearse, I. H., and Crocker, L. H. 1938. *Biologists in Search of Material*. Interim Report of the Work of the Pioneer Health Center. Peckham, London: Faber and Faber.

————. 1949. *The Peckham Experiment*. London: George Allen and Unwin, Ltd.

Pearson, R. S. B. 1938. Psychoneurosis in Hospital Practice. *Lancet* 1: 451-456.

Pemberton, J. 1949. Illness in General Practice. *British Medical Journal* 1: 306-308.

Perth, E. R. 1957. Psychosomatic Problems in General Practice. *College of General Practice Research Newsletter* 4: 295.

Pessen, B. 1978. Learning to be a Mother: The Influence of the Medical Profession. Ph.D. dissertation, Brandeis University.

Petchesky, R. P. 1980. Reproductive Freedom: Beyond 'A Woman's Right to Choose.' *Signs: Journal of Women in Culture and Society* 5: 661-685.

Peterson, O., Barsamian, J. and Eden, M. 1966. A Study of Diagnostic Performance: A Preliminary Report. *Journal of Medical Education* 41: 797-803.

Pitts, J. 1968. Social Control: The Concept. In *International Encyclopedia of Social Sciences*, Vol. 14, edited by D. Sills. New York: Macmillan.

Plougher, J. C. E. 1955. Neurosis in General Practice. *British Medical Journal* 2: 409-410.

The Pocket University. 12 vols. 1934. Garden City, New York: Doubleday, Doran & Company. First published under the title *Master Classics*, 1920.

Powers, E., and Witmer, H. 1951. *An Experiment in the Prevention of Delinquency*. New York: Columbia University Press.

Pratt, L., Seligman, A., and Reader, G. 1957. Physicians' Views on the Level of Medical Information Among Patients. *American Journal of Public Health* 47: 1277-1283.

Priest, W. M. 1962. A Thousand Out-Patients. *Lancet* 2: 1043-1047.

Primrose, E. J. R. 1962. Psychological Illness. In *A Community Study*. Springfield: C. C. Thomas.

Raper, A. B. 1958. The Incidence of Peptic Ulceration in Some African Tribal Groups. *Transactions of the Royal Society of Tropical Medicine and Hygiene* 152: 535-546.

Ratner, H. 1962. Medicine. An interview by Donald McDonald with H. Ratner, M.D. From the series on the American Character, sponsored by the Center of the Study of Democratic Institutions' Fund for Republicans.

Ravitz, M. J. 1957. Occupational Values and Occupational Selection. *Nursing Research* 6: 25-40.

Reader, G. G., Pratt, L., and Mudd, M. C. 1957. What Patients Expect from Their Doctor. *Modern Hospital* 89: 88-94.

Reidenberg, M. M., and Lowenthal, D. T. 1968. Adverse Drug Reactions. *New England Journal of Medicine* 279: 678-679.

Reissman, L., and Rohrer, J. H. 1957. *Changes and Dilemma in the Nursing Profession*. New York: Putnam.

Rennie, T. A. C., Srole, L., Opler, M. K., and Langner, T. S. 1957. Urban Life and Mental Health. *American Journal of Psychiatry* 113: 831-836.

Reynolds, G. P. 1930. The Etiology of Psychoneurosis Encountered in the Practice of Internal Medicine. *New England Journal of Medicine* 203: 312-316.

Rieff, P. 1961. *Freud: The Mind of the Moralist*. Garden City, New York: Doubleday.

Robbins, G. F., Conte, A. J., Leach, J. E., and MacDonald, M. C. 1950. Delay in Diagnosis and Treatment of Cancer. *Journal of the American Medical Association* 143: 346-349.

Roberts, B. H., and Norton, N. M. 1952. The Prevalence of Psychiatric Illness in a Medical Out-Patient Clinic. *New England Journal of Medicine* 245: 82-86.

Robinson, H. A., Finesinger, T. E., and Bierman, J. C. 1956. Psychiatric Considerations in the Adjustment of Patients with Poliomyelitis. *New England Journal of Medicine* 254: 975-980.

Romano, J. 1961. Basic Contributions to Medicine by Research in Psychiatry. *Journal of the American Medical Association* 178: 1147-1150.

Rome, H. P. 1962. Automation Techniques in Personality Assessment, the Problem and Procedure. *Journal of the American Medical Association* 182: 1069-1072.

Roney, J. G., and Nall, M. L. 1966. The Folk-Professional Boundary in the Use of Medications. Presented at Health Education Session, 94th Annual Meeting, American Public Health Association.

Roper, E., and Associates. 1950. *People's Attitudes Concerning Mental Health*. New York: Private Publications.

Rosen, G. 1944. *The Specialization of Medicine with Particular Reference to Ophthalmology*. New York: Froeben.

———. 1958. *A History of Public Health*. New York: MD Publications.

———. 1963. The Evolution of Social Medicine. In *Handbook of Medical Sociology*, edited by H. E. Freeman, S. Levine and L. G. Reeder. Englewood Cliffs, New Jersey: Prentice- Hall.

———. 1967. People, Disease and Emotion: Some Newer Problems for Research in Medical History. *Bulletin of the History of Medicine* 41: 9-10.

———. 1968. *Madness in Society*. Chicago: University of Chicago Press.

Rosenfeld, L. S., Katz, J., and Donabedian, A. 1957. *Medical Care Needs and Services in the Boston Metropolitan Area*. Boston: Medical Care Evaluation Studies, Health, Hospitals, and Medical Care Division, United Community Services of Metropolitan Boston.

Rosenstock, I. 1966. Why People Use Health Services. *Millbank Memorial Fund Quarterly* 44: 94-127.

Roth, H., and Caron, H. S. 1968. Patients' Cooperation with a Medical Regimen: Difficulties in Identifying the Non-Cooperator. *Journal of the American Medical Association* 203: 922-926.

Roth, H., Caron, H. S., Ort, R. D., Berger, D. G., Merrill, R. S., Albee, G. W., and Streeter, G. A. 1962. Patients' Beliefs about Peptic Ulcer and its Treatment. *Annals of Internal Medicine* 56: 72-80.

Rushing, W. A. 1966. The Hospital Nurse as Mother Surrogate and Bedside Psychologist. *Mental Hygiene* 50: 71-80.

Russell, D. H. 1968. The Sex-Conversion Controversy. *New England Journal of Medicine* 279: 535-536.

Rutstein, D. D. 1967. *The Coming Revolution in Medicine*. Cambridge: MIT Press.

Ruzek, S. B. 1979. *The Women's Health Movement: Feminist Alternatives to Medical Control*. New York: Praeger.

Ryan, W. 1970. *Blaming the Victim*. New York: Pantheon.

Ryle, A. J. 1960. The Neurosis in a General Practice Population. *College of General Practioners Journal* 3: 313.

Sainsbury, P. 1960. Psychosomatic Disorders and Neurosis in Out-Patients Attending a General Hospital. *Journal of Psychosomatic Research* 4: 261-273.

Saunders, L. 1954a. The Changing Role of Nurses. *American Journal of Nursing* 54: 1094-1098.

———. 1954b. *Cultural Differences and Medical Care*. New York: Russell Sage.

Schacter, S., and Singer, J. 1962. Cognitive, Social, and Physiological Determinants of Emotional State. *Psychological Review* 69: 379-387.

Scheff, T. 1964. Preferred Errors in Diagnosis. *Medical Care.* 2: 166-172.

———. 1966. *Becoming Mentally Ill*. Chicago: Aldine.

Schenthal, J.E. 1960. Multiphasic Screening of the Well Patient. *Journal of the American Medical Association* 172: 51-64.

Schmale, A. J. 1958. Relationship of Separation and Depression to Disease. I. A Report on a Hospitalized Medical Population. *Psychosomatic Medicine* 20: 259-277.

Schmideberg, M. 1961. Social Factors Affecting Diagnostic Concepts. *International Journal of Social Psychiatry* 7: 222-230.

Schulman, S. 1958. Basic Functional Roles in Nursing: Mother Surrogate and Healer. In *Patients, Physicians and Illness*, edited by E. G. Jaco. Glencoe, Illinois: The Free Press.

Schur, E. 1965. *Crimes Without Victims*. Englewood Cliffs, New Jersey: Prentice-Hall.

Schwartz, C. G. 1957. Perspectives on Deviance—Wives' Definitions of Their Husbands' Mental Illness. *Psychiatry* 20: 275-291.

Schwartz, J., and Baum, G. L. 1957. The History of Histoplasmosis. *New England Journal of Medicine* 256: 253-258.

Science Policy Research Division. Congressional Research Service. Library of Congress. 1974. *Genetic Engineering—Evolution of Technological Issue*. Supplemental Report 1 prepared for The Subcommittee on Science and

Astronautics, U.S. House of Representatives. Ninety-Third Congress. Washington, D.C.: G.P.O.

———. Congressional Research Service. Library of Congress. 1980. *Genetic Engineering, Human Genetics, and Cell Biology—Evolution of Technological Issues—Biotechnology.* Supplemental Report 3 prepared for The Subcommittee on Science, Research, and Technology of the Committee on Science and Technology, U.S. House of Representatives, Ninety-Sixth Congress. Washington, D.C.: G.P.O.

Scott, R., Anderson, J. A. D., and Cartwright, A. 1960. Just What the Doctor Ordered: An Analysis of Treatment in a General Practice. *British Medical Journal* 2: 293–299.

Seeley, J. R. 1963. Social Science? Some Probative Problems. In *Sociology on Trial,* edited by M. Stein and A. Vidich. Englewood Cliffs, New Jersey: Prentice-Hall.

Seidenstein, H. R. 1957. A Suburban General Practice. *New York State Journal of Medicine* 57: 2827–2836.

Selye, H. 1956. *The Stress of Life.* New York: McGraw-Hill.

Severo, R. February 3–6, 1980. The Genetic Barrier: Job Benefit or Job Bias. 4 articles in the *New York Times.*

Shaw, M. W. 1977. Genetically Defective Children: Emerging Legal Considerations. *American Journal of Law and Medicine* 3: 333–340.

Shepherd, M., Fisher, M., Stein, L., and Kessel, W. N. N. 1959. Psychiatric Morbidity in an Urban Group Practice. *Proceedings of the Royal Society of Medicine* 52: 269–274.

Sherman, H. E., and Komaroff, A. L. 1974. *Ambulatory Care Project, Progress Report 11A, 1969–1974.* Massachusetts: MIT Lincoln Laboratory and Beth Israel Hospital.

Shibutani, T., and Kwan, K. M. 1965. *Ethnic Stratification.* New York: Macmillan.

Shockley, W. 1972a. Dysgenics, Geneticity, Raceology: A Challenge to the Intellectual Responsibility of Educators. *Phi Delta Kappan* 1: 297–307.

———. 1972b. Dysgenics—A Social Problem, Reality Evaded by the Illusion of Infinite Plasticity of Human Intelligence. *Phi Delta Kappan* 1: 291–295.

Shryock, R. H. 1959. *The History of Nursing.* Philadelphia: Saunders.

Siegel, G. S. 1963. *Periodic Health Examinations—Abstracts from the Literature.* Public Health Service Publication, No. 1010. Washington, D.C.: G.P.O.

Siegel, S. 1956. *Non-Parametric Statistics for the Behavioral Sciences.* New York: McGraw-Hill.

Sigerist, H. 1943. *Civilization and Disease.* New York: Cornell University Press.

Silver, G. A. 1958. Beyond General Practice: The Health Team. *Yale Journal of Biology and Medicine* 3: 29–39.

Singer, J. L., and Opler, M. K. 1956. Contrasting Patterns of Fantasy and Motility in Irish and Italian Schizophrenics. *Journal of Abnormal and Social Psychology* 53: 42–47.

Slater, P. 1970. *The Pursuit of Loneliness*. Boston: Beacon Press.

———. 1977. *Footholds—Understanding the Shifting Sexual and Family Tensions in our Culture*. Boston: Beacon Press.

Smith, H. L., and Hightower, N. C. 1948. Incidence of Functional Disease (Neurosis) Among Patients of Various Occupations. *Occupational Medicine* 5: 182–185.

Soskies, C. W. February 1980. Genetic Screening: Some of the Issues. Reprinted from *Health Law Project Library Bulletin* (January 1980) in *Second Opinion*, The Coalition for the Medical Rights of Women.

Spiegel, J. P. 1959. Some Cultural Aspects of Transference and Countertransference. In *Science and Psychoanalysis: Individual and Family Dynamics*, edited by J. Masserman. Vol. 2. New York: Grune and Stratton.

———. 1964. Conflicting Formal and Informal Roles in Newly Acculturated Families. In *Disorders of Communication*, Vol. 42, Research Publications, Association for Research in Nervous and Mental Disease.

———. 1976. Some Cultural Aspects of Transference and Countertransference and Countertransference Revisited. *Journal of the American Academy of Psychoanalysis* 4: 447–467.

Spiegel, J., and Bell, N. W. 1959. The Family of the Psychiatric Patient. In *American Handbook of Psychiatry*, edited by S. Arieti. Vol. 1 New York: Basic Books.

Spiegel, J. P., and Papajohn, J. 1975. *Transition in Families: A Modern Approach for Resolving Cultural and Generational Conflicts*. San Francisco: Jossey-Bass.

Srole, L., Langer, T. S., Michael, S. T., Opler, M. K., and Rennie, T. A. C. 1962. *Mental Health in the Metropolis*. New York: McGraw-Hill.

Stanton, A. H. and Schwartz, M. S. 1954. *The Mental Hospital*. New York: Basic Books.

Star, S. 1955. The Public's Ideas About Mental Illness. Paper presented at the Annual Meeting of the National Association for Mental Health, Indianapolis.

———. 1957. The Place of Psychiatry in Popular Thinking. Paper presented at the Annual Meeting of the American Association for Public Opinion Research, Washington, D.C.

Stein, L. 1960. Morbidity in a London General Practice. Social and Demographic Data. *British Journal of Preventive Social Medicine* 14: 9–15.

Stoeckle, J. 1978. *Encounters of Patients and Doctors—A Book of Readings with Commentary*. Unpublished manuscript.

Stoeckle, J. D., and Davidson, G. E. 1962a. Use of 'Crises' as Orientation for the Study of Patients in a Medical Clinic. *Journal of Medical Education* 37: 604–613.

———. 1962b. Bodily Complaints and the Other Symptoms of a Depressive Reaction, Its Diagnosis and Significance in a Medical Clinic. *Journal of the American Medical Association* 180: 134–139.

———. 1963. Communicating Aggrieved Feelings in Initial Visits to a Medical Clinic. *Journal of Health and Human Behavior* 4: 199–206.

Stoeckle, J. D., Noonan, B., Farrisey, R. M., and Sweatt, A. 1963. Medical

Nursing for the Chronically Ill. *American Journal of Nursing* 63: 87–89.

Stoeckle, J. D., and Zola, I. K. 1964a. After Everyone Can Pay for Medical Care—Some Perspectives on Future Treatment and Practice. *Medical Care* 2: 36–41.

———. 1964b. Views, Problems, and Potentialities of the Clinic. *Medicine* 43: 413–422.

Stoeckle, J. D., Zola, I. K., and Davidson, G. E. 1963. On Going to See the Doctor: The Contributions of the Patient to the Decision to Seek Medical Aid, A Selective Review. *Journal of Chronic Diseases* 16: 975–989.

———. 1964. The Quantity and Significance of Psychological Distress in Medical Patients—Some Preliminary Observations about the Decision to Seek Medical Aid. *Journal of Chronic Diseases* 17: 959–970.

Suchman, E. A. 1964. Sociomedical Variations Among Ethnic Groups. *American Journal of Sociology* 70: 319–331.

———. 1965a. Social Patterns of Illness and Medical Care. *Journal of Health and Human Behavior* 6: 2–16.

———. 1965b. Stages of Illness and Medical Care. *Journal of Health and Human Behavior* 6: 114–128.

Szasz, T. S. 1959. The Myth of Mental Illness. *American Psychologist* 15: 113–118.

———. 1961. *The Myth of Mental Illness*. New York: Hoeber-Harper.

———. 1970. *The Manufacture of Madness*. New York: Harper and Row.

Taubenhaus, L. J. 1955. A Study of One Rural Practice, 1953. *General Practice* 12: 97–102.

Taylor, S. 1954. The Medical Background of General Practice. *Good General Practice* Chapter 14. London: Oxford University Press.

Thompson, D. S., Haber, R. W., and Gerson, S. 1968. A Study of Medications Kept on Hand by College Students. *Journal of the American College Health Association* 16: 386–387.

Time. January 10, 1969. To Save the Heart—Diet by Decree. p. 42.

Tipler, H. B. 1948. Extent of Neurosis. *British Medical Journal* 1: 570–571.

Titchener, J. L., Zwerling, I., Gottschalk, L., Levine, M., Culbertson, W., Cohen, S., and Silver, H. 1956. Problem of Delay in Seeking Surgical Care. *Journal of the American Medical Association* 160: 1187–1193.

Toffler, A. 1970. *Future Shock*. New York: Random House.

Tonge, W. L., Cammock, D. W., Winchester, J. S., and Winchester, E. N. M. 1961. Prevalence of Neurosis in Women. *British Journal of Preventive Social Medicine* 15: 177–179.

Tyler, S. H. 1950. On the Nature of Private Practice and the Need for Psychotherapy. *American Practitioner* 1: 1303–1308.

United States National Health Survey. 1958. *Preliminary Report on Volume of Physicians' Visits, United States, July-Sept. 1957*. Washington, D.C.: Public Health Service.

U.S. Department of Health, Education and Welfare. 1961. *Health, Education and Welfare Trends*. Washington, D.C.: U.S. Government Printing Office.

Valkenburg, H. A., Goslings, W. R. O., Botts, A. W., de Moor, C. E., and

Lorrier, J. C. 1963. Attack Rate of Streptococcal Pharyngitis, Rheumatic Fever, and Glomerulonephritis in the General Population. II. The Epidemiology of Streptococcal Pharyngitis in One Village During a Two-Year Period. *New England Journal of Medicine* 268: 694-701.

Wade, L., Thorpe, J., Elias, T., and Bock, G. 1962. Are Periodic Health Examinations Worthwhile? *Annals of Internal Medicine* 56: 81-93.

Wadsworth, M. E. J., Butterfield, W. J. H., and Blaney, R. 1971. *Health and Sickness—The Choice of Treatment*. London: Tavistock Publications.

Waitzkin, H. 1978. Regressive Policy Implications of the 'Medicalization' and 'Self-Care' Concepts: The New Reductionism in Health Care Research. In *Sante Medecine et Sociologie*. Paris: Centre Nationale de la Recherche Scientifique.

Waitzkin, H., and Stoeckle, J. C. 1972. Communication of Information about Illness. In *Advances in Psychosomatic Medicine*, edited by Z. Lipowski. Vol. 8. Basel: Karger.

Waitzkin, H., and Waterman, B. 1974. *The Exploitation of Illness in Capitalist Society*. Indianapolis: Bobbs-Merrill.

Wald, F. S., and Leonard, R. C. 1964. Toward Development of Nursing Practice Theory. *Nursing Research* 13: 309-313.

Wallace, A. F. C. 1959. Cultural Determinants of Response to Hallucinatory Experience. *Archives of General Psychiatry* 1: 58-69.

Warren, J. V., and Walter, J. 1954. Symptoms and Disease Induced by the Physician. *General Practitioner* 9: 77-84.

Washburn, F. A. 1939. The Out-patient Department and Emergency Ward. In *The Massachusetts General Hospital*. Boston: Houghton Mifflin.

Watts, C. A. H. 1962. Psychiatric Disorders. In *Morbidity Statistics from General Practice*, Chapter 3. Studies on Medical and Population Subjects, No. 14. The Research Committee of the Council of General Practitioners. London: H.M.S.O.

Watts, C. A. H., and Watts, B. M. 1952. *Psychiatry in General Practice*. London: Churchill.

Wedge, B. 1961. Psychiatry and International Affairs. *Science* 157: 281-285.

Weeks, H. S., Davis, M., and Freeman, H. 1958. Apathy of Families Toward Medical Care. In *Patients, Physicians and Illness*, edited by E. G. Jaco. Glencoe, Illinois: The Free Press.

Weinberg, A., and Weinberg, L. eds. 1961. *The Muckrakers*. New York: Simon and Schuster.

Wertz, R. W., and Wertz, D. C. 1977. *Lying-In: A History of Childbirth in America*. New York: Free Press.

Wheeler, S. in collaboration with Bonacich, E., Cramer, R., and Zola, I. K. 1968. Edited by S. Wheeler. *Controlling Delinquents*. New York: Wiley and Sons.

Wheelis, A. 1958. *The Quest for Identity*. New York: W. W. Norton.

Whipple, H., ed. 1969. Home Medication and Public Welfare. *Annals of the New York Academy of Sciences* 120: 807-1024.

Whitby, J. 1943. Neurosis in a London General Practice During the Second and Third Years of War. *Proceedings of the Royal Society of Medicine* 36: 123-128.

White, K., Anjelkovic, D., Pearson, R. J. C., Mabry, J., Ross, A., and Sagan, O. K. 1967. International Comparisons of Medical Care Utilization. *New England Journal of Medicine* 277: 516-522.

White, K., Williams, F. T., and Greenberg, B. G. 1961. The Ecology of Medical Care. *New England Journal of Medicine* 265: 885-892.

White, T. H. 1978. *In Search of History: A Personal Adventure.* New York: Harper-Row.

Wilensky, H. L. 1964. The Professionalization of Everyone? *American Journal of Sociology* 70: 137-158.

Williams, R. M. Jr., and Goldsen, R. K. 1960. *Selection or Rejection of Nursing as a Career.* New York: Cornell University Press.

Williams, T. F., Marten, P. A., Hogan, M. D., Watkins, J. D., and Ellis, E. V. 1967. The Clinical Picture of Diabetes Control Studied in Four Settings. *American Journal of Public Health* 57: 441-451.

Williams, T. F., White, K. L., Andrews, L. P., Diamond, E., Greenberg, B. G., Hamrick, A. A., and Hunter, E. A. 1960. Patient Referral to University Clinic. Patterns in Rural State. *American Journal of Public Health* 50: 1493-1507.

Williamson, J., Stok, I. H., Gray, S., Fisher, M., Smith, A., McGhee, A., and Stephenson, E. 1964. Old People At Home—Their Unreported Needs. *Lancet* 23: 1117-1120.

Wolff, H. 1953. *Stress and Disease.* Springfield: C. C. Thomas.

Wolff, K. H. 1976. *Surrender and Catch: Experience and Inquiry Today* Boston Studies in the Philosophy of Science, vol. 51. Dordrecht and Boston: D. Reidel.

Wolford, H. 1966. The Nurse of the Future. *Nursing Outlook* 14: 41-42.

Woodward, J. L. 1951. Changing Ideas on Mental Illness and Its Treatment. *American Sociological Review* 16: 443-454.

Wooton, B. 1959. *Social Science and Social Pathology.* London: Allen and Unwin.

Yedidia, M. 1981. *Delivering Primary Health Care—Nurse Practitioners at Work.* Boston: Auburn House.

Yudkin, S. 1961. Six Children with Coughs, The Second Diagnosis. *Lancet* 2: 561-563.

Zborowski, M. 1952. Cultural Components in Response to Pain. *Journal of Social Issues* 8: 16-30.

Ziegler, L. H. 1931. Mental Hygiene and Its Relationship to the Medical Profession. *Journal of the American Medical Association* 97: 1119-1122.

Zinsser, H. 1935. *Rats, Lice and History.* Boston: Little and Brown.

Zola, A. B., Zola, W. K., and Zola, I. K. 1978. *Episodes and Stories.* A Collection privately published.

Zola, I. K. 1962a. Feelings About Age Among Older People. *Journal of Gerontology* 17: 65-69.

———. 1962b. Sociocultural Factors in the Seeking of Medical Aid. Unpublished Ph.D. dissertation, Harvard University.

————. 1963a. Observations of Gambling in a Lower-Class Setting. *Social Problems* 10: 353–361.

————. 1963b. Socio-Cultural Factors in the Seeking of Medical Aid—A Progress Report. *Transcultural Psychiatric Research* 14: 62–65.

————. 1963c. Problems of Communication, Diagnosis and Patient Care: The Interplay of Patient, Physician and Clinic Organization. *Journal of Medical Education* 38: 829–838.

————. 1964. Illness Behavior of the Working Class: Implications and Recommendations. In *Blue-Collar World*, edited by A. Shostak and W. Gomberg. Englewood Cliffs, New Jersey: Prentice-Hall.

————. 1965. Motivation—A Social Scientist's Perspective on the Problem of Unmotivated Clients. *Education for Social Work with Unmotivated Clients— Proceedings of an Institute*. Brandeis University Papers in Social Welfare.

————. 1966. Culture and Symptoms—An Analysis of Patients Presenting Complaints. *American Sociological Review* 31: 615–630.

————. 1968a. A review of Marvin Scott's *The Racing Game. American Sociological Review* 33: 641–642.

————. 1968b. How to Win While Losing—Some Observations on Off-Track Betting. Radio script written and narrated by I. K. Zola for the Canadian Broadcasting Company.

————. 1970a. The Uses of Aides in a Management Program for Chronic Disease. Project Report ACP-13. Massachusetts: Lincoln Laboratory and the Beth Israel Hospital.

————. 1970b. Whither Medicine—Three Views. *Social Science and Medicine* 4: 687–690.

————. 1970c. *How Sick is Sick: Working Notes and Reflections on the Cross-Cultural Study of Illness*. Technical report written for the Division of Epidemiology and Communications Sciences. Geneva: World Health Organization.

————. 1971a. Helping—Does It Matter: The Problems and Prospects of Mutual Aid Groups, Part I. *Cleveland Ostomy News* 2: 5–12.

————. 1971b. Helping—Does It Matter: The Problems and Prospects of Mutual Aid Groups, Part II. *Cleveland Ostomy News* 2: 5–11.

————. 1972a. Medicine as an Institution of Social Control. *Sociological Review* 20: 487–504.

————. 1972b. The Concept of Trouble and Sources of Medical Assistance. *Social Science and Medicine* 6: 673–679.

————. 1972c. Studying the Decision to See a Doctor: Review, Critique, Corrective. In *Advances in Psychomatic Medicine*, edited by Z. Lipowski. Vol. 8. Basel: Karger.

————. 1972d. The Problems and Prospects of Mutual Aid Groups. *Rehabilitation Psychology* 19: 180–183.

————. 1972e. *Issues and Suggestions in the Study of Health and Illness Behavior—* A Consultant's Report. Netherlands Institute for Preventive Medicine, Leiden, Netherlands.

————. 1972f. The Marriage of Medicine and Machine—Critique of the Subcommittee Report on Human Factors Guidelines. In *Provisional Guide-*

lines for Automated Multiphasic Health Testing and Services, Vol. 3. Proceedings of the Invitational Conference on AMHTS. DHEW Publications No. HSM 72-3011.

———. 1973a. Pathways to the Doctor—From Person to Patient. *Social Science and Medicine* 7: 677–689.

———. 1973b. On the Problems of Professing. *Social Science and Medicine* 7: 80–82.

———. 1973c. *de medische macht: de invloed van de gezondheidszong op de maatschappij*. Translated by M. Vellema. Amsterdam: Boom Meppel.

———. 1975a. In the Name of Health and Illness: On Some Socio-Political Consequences of Medical Influence. *Social Science and Medicine* 9: 83–87.

———. 1975b. The Fix We Are In . . . *Social Science and Medicine* 9: 559–661.

———. 1976. The Social and Psychological Context of Non-Compliance. In *Proceedings of the Interprofessional Conference on Compliance with Medical Regimes by the Hypertensive Patient*. The University of Mississippi, Bureau of Pharmaceutical Services.

———. 1977a. Taking Your Medicine—A Problem for Doctor or Patient. In Medication Compliance—A Behavioral Management Approach, edited by I. Barofsky. Thorofare, New Jersey: Charles B. Slack.

———. 1977b. Healthism and Disabling Medicalization. In I. Illich, I. K. Zola, J. McKnight, J. Caplan, H. Shaiken, *Disabling Professions*. London Marion Boyars.

———. 1979a. When Getting Into the Field Means Getting Into Oneself. *New England Sociologist* 1: 21–30.

———. 1979b. A Story Difficult to Hear and Tell. *The Exceptional Parent* 9: D3–D8.

———. 1979c. Helping One Another: A Speculative History of the Self Help Movement. *Archives of Physical Medicine and Rehabilitation* 60: 452–456.

———. 1979d. And the Children Shall Lead Us. *Disabled USA* 3: 6–7.

———. 1979e. Oh Where, Oh Where Has Ethnicity Gone? In *Ethnicity and Aging*, edited by D. E. Gelfand and A. J. Kutzik. New York: Springer Publishing Company.

———. 1981a. Communication Barriers Between "The Able-Bodied" and "The Handicapped." *Archives of Physical Medicine and Rehabilitation* 62: 356–359.

———. 1981b. Structural Constraints in the Doctor- Patient Relationship: The Case of Non-Compliance. In *The Relevance of Social Science for Medicine*, edited by L. Eisenberg and A. Kleinman. Dordrecht, Holland: Reidel Publishing Company.

———. 1982a. *Missing Pieces: A Chronicle of Living with a Disability*. Philadelphia: Temple University Press.

———. 1982b. Denial of Emotional Needs to People with Handicaps. *Archives of Physical Medicine and Rehabilitation* 63: 63–67.

———., ed. 1982c. *Ordinary Lives: Voices of Disability and Disease*. Watertown, Massachusetts: Applewood Books.

———. 1983a. The Evolution of the Boston Self Help Center. Working Paper No. 3. In *Working Paper Series on Independent Living*, edited by G. Clark. RT-29. Lawrence, Kansas: University of Kansas.

———. 1983b. Disincentives to Independent Living. Working Paper No. 1 In G. Clark ed. *Working Paper Series on Independent Living*, (RT-29). Lawrence, Kansas: University of Kansas.

———. 1983c. Individual Choice and Health Policy—A Sociopolitical Scenario for the 1980's. In I. K. Zola, *Sociomedical Inquiries: Recollections, Reflections, and Reconsiderations* Philadelphia: Temple University Press.

Zola, I. K., and Croog, S. 1968. Work Perceptions and Their Implications for Professional Identity. *Social Science and Medicine* 2: 15-28.

Zola, I. K., and Miller, S. J. 1973. The Erosion of Medicine From Within. In *The professions and Their Prospects*, edited by E. Freidson. California: Sage.

Index